PENSIONS, INFLATION AND GROWTH

Pensions, Inflation and Growth

A Comparative Study of the Elderly in the Welfare State

Edited by

Thomas Wilson

HEINEMANN EDUCATIONAL BOOKS
LONDON

Heinemann Educational Books Ltd
LONDON EDINBURGH MELBOURNE TORONTO
AUCKLAND JOHANNESBURG SINGAPORE
IBADAN NAIROBI HONG KONG LUSAKA NEW DELHI

ISBN 0 435 82967 X

© T. Wilson 1974
First published 1974

(c

Published by
Heinemann Educational Books Ltd
48 Charles Street, London WIX 8AH

Printed in Great Britain by
Cox & Wyman Ltd,
London, Fakenham and Reading

Preface

Much concern is frequently expressed about the position of the elderly in societies that are both affluent and inflationary. How has that concern found practical expression in the various pension schemes and other forms of assistance adopted in different countries? What meanings may be given to 'the poverty level'? In what ways are the elderly protected against poverty and with what degree of success? How much stress should be placed on the replacement of previous incomes? How may pensions be financed? How can the elderly be protected against inflation and given a share in economic growth?

This book begins with an analysis of issues such as these and discusses the role of both official and private schemes. An attempt is thus made to set the framework for the detailed studies of six European countries which follow but current issues in Britain and the USA are also reviewed. There follow six studies of policies for the elderly in Western Germany, the Netherlands, Sweden, France, Italy and Belgium. Attention is not confined to pensions and means-tested benefits but includes some account of other ways of helping the elderly; in particular, assistance with housing and medical care. In these chapters we have sought, as far as possible, not merely to describe current legislation but to show how the various schemes have evolved, to assess their operation in the early seventies, and to comment on probable future developments.

Although there is no common EEC policy on pensions, membership of the Community has naturally stimulated interest in comparative studies. Moreover the relevance of such comparisons is not confined to those who are members of the EEC but extends to other countries as well. This point is recognized in the last

chapter where the main facts are summarized and some conclusions drawn. This chapter includes a review of some of the more
important developments in the treatment of the elderly in the UK
and the USA.

This research was supported for two years (October 1969–
September 1971) by a grant from the Social Science Research
Council. Research into European pension schemes was then continued for another year on contract for the Department of Health
and Social Security and reports on a number of countries were in
due course submitted to this Ministry.

Mr. Roger J. Lawson of the Department of Sociology and
Social Administration at the University of Southampton was a
senior member of the research team during the first two years of
its work and was engaged in particular on a study of the whole
range of welfare services in Western Germany. We are particularly indebted to him. We must also acknowledge our indebtedness to Mr. G. R. Denton (University of Reading) and Mr. M. C.
MacLennan (formerly University of Glasgow; now with the
EEC) for much general advice on European affairs. We must also
refer to the research done by Mrs. Cindy Stevens on social aid in
France and jointly sponsored by Professor M. Rein of MIT and
ourselves. Her work on this subject was published in 1973 by
G. Bell & Sons, London: Occasional Papers on Social Administration, No. 50.

We have received much help and guidance from members of
Government departments, pension organizations and other organizations and would mention in particular the following.

In Britain: the Department of Health and Social Security, the
Government Actuary's Department, the Treasury, the Inland
Revenue and the Central Statistical Office; managers of certain
pension funds.

In Germany: Bundesministerium für Arbeit und Sozialordnung, Familieministerium, Verband Deutscher Rentenversicher-
ungstrager and Bundesversicherungsanstalt.

In the Netherlands: Ministerie van Sociale Zaken, Ministerie
van Cultuur, Recreatie, en Maatschappelijk Werk, Sociaal-
Economisch Raad, and Nederlands Federatie voor Bejaardenbeleid; Dr G. O. J. van Tets, Unilever N.V.

In Sweden: the Ministry of Health and Social Affairs, the
National Social Insurance and Health and Welfare Boards, the Em-

ployers' Federation (SAF), the Trade Unions Organizations (LO), the Union of Salaried Employees (TCO), the Association of Municipalities, the staff of the Swedish Institute in Stockholm. We are grateful to Dr. Ako Elmer of the University of Lund for having read an earlier version of the Swedish chapter and having put us right on so many points. We are also very grateful to Mrs Kerstin Lindholm of the Stockholm Socialhögskola.

In Italy: Professor Lafranconi and Dr Grossetti of INPS (Istituto Nazionale per la Previdenza Sociale), Dr. Umberto del Canuto and Dr Veniera Ajmone Marsan of IRI, the British Embassy in Rome, Dr Ballanti and Dr Costantini of the Federazione Nazionale Pensionati, Dr Corsini of the Istituto per gli Studi di Servizio Sociale, the Comitato Italiano di Servizio Sociale, Mr Barone of 'La Stampa', Professor Giugni at the Ministry of Labour and Social Security and Dr de Sanctis of CENSIS.

In France: Commissariat du Plan (Section des Affaires Sociales), Ministère de la Santé Publique et de la Sécurité Sociale, ARRCO, Madame Questiaux (President, Intergroupe personnes âgées), Confédération Générale du Travail, Confédération Nationale du Patronat Français.

In Belgium: Ministère de la Prévoyance Sociale, Monsieur Louis Davin (Banque de Bruxelles).

In the USA: the Department of Health, Education and Welfare.

We also had discussions with members of the EEC, the ILO and the International Social Security Association.

We are grateful to the Centre for Environmental Studies who kindly arranged a small conference on pensions in April 1972 which allowed us to present some preliminary findings for comment and debate.

We are deeply indebted to those responsible for the secretarial work: Miss C. MacSwan, Mrs T. Campbell, Mrs M. Christie and Miss C. Kerr of the University of Glasgow.

Finally we must acknowledge our indebtedness to a large number of individuals in the different countries with which we were concerned who are not covered by the references above but who in various ways assisted our work.

None of those who assisted us are responsible for any of the views expressed or errors committed.

University of Glasgow   T.W.

Contents

PART I

CHAPTER ONE

Issues and Responses in Europe and the USA

I—INTRODUCTION

Whether viewed as benefit or cost, official pensions and other forms of assistance for the elderly must be placed among the most important forms of public expenditure. The cost is admittedly heavy. In some countries it is the largest item in social expenditure and a substantial part of total budgetary outlay.[1] As a proportion of gross national product, official expenditure on the elderly has risen instead of declining, although growing affluence should make private provision easier to achieve. Moreover, on present plans, this rise can be expected to continue in many countries. That is one side of the social account book. On the other side of the account is the social benefit which is thus provided. There will be little disagreement about this social benefit when the object of the public expenditure is to protect the elderly from destitution. Although the hope has sometimes been expressed that as countries grow richer the need for such protection will diminish, it is unlikely to disappear completely. Even in countries as rich as the USA or West Germany, it is generally conceded that the elderly cannot

---

[1] The statistics in support of some of these and other statements in this chapter will be found in Part III of this volume, or in the chapters on the individual countries. In the present chapter the statistics have been kept to a minimum because their use, especially when international comparisons are attempted, would involve much explanation and qualification which would be premature and inadequate at this stage.

simply be left to rely on resources accumulated by themselves during their working lives. For there will always be some who have been victims of ill-fortune or accident, some who have been too ignorant about how to invest their savings, some who, for one reason or another, have had incomes during their working lives that were too low to leave them with adequate margins that could have been set aside for the future. With varying degrees of explicitness, public policy in different countries is based on the assumption that no one should be allowed to fall into complete destitution in old age, not even in those cases where a stern mentor in an earlier generation might have objected that such poverty could be regarded as the penalty of improvidence in earlier life. This principle may be generally accepted but the fact remains that poverty among the old has been by no means abolished. The need for still higher expenditure would, therefore, seem to follow from the acceptance of the principle that poverty in old age is something that all developed countries should seek to prevent. This may indeed be the case but the position is, of course, more complicated than such a simple inference would imply. *First* there is the question of what one means by 'poverty' which will occupy our attention in the next section. *Secondly*, expenditure on the old is by no means confined to protection against destitution, and official pensions are provided *as of right* to elderly people many of whom may have incomes from other sources which would be sufficient to protect them from destitution. These official pensions may be *flat-rate*, as in Britain[1] and the Netherlands, or *graduated* with the further objective of replacing some appropriate proportion of previous incomes, as in the USA and most European countries. Naturally the *replacement* of previous income will often serve to prevent destitution, but the pursuit of the two objectives will not always coincide by any means. When previous incomes have been very low, then even a high replacement ratio will not prevent poverty; when these incomes have been high, part of the pensions received may lift those who receive them well above any official poverty level. Thus both current expenditure on the old and

---

[1] This statement is not strictly true of the official British pensions which include a small graduated element. The new scheme established by the Social Security Act of 1973 is however flat-rate. See p. 19, below. For an earlier review of pensions in Britain, see *The Complete Guide to Pensions and Superannuation*, G. D. Gilling-Smith, Pelican, 1967.

whatever increases may be anticipated in future are by no means solely designed in order to cope with poverty. Attention must therefore be paid not only to total expenditure but to the manner in which this expenditure is allocated between different objectives. These matters, together with the merits and limitations of selectivity in the giving of assistance, will be of central concern throughout this chapter and throughout the book as a whole. The inference which can properly be drawn from these facts is that the *objectives* of pensions policy need to be clearly examined and the *alternatives* carefully assessed. In attempting to carry out this task, a comparative study of the experiences of a number of different countries should be illuminating; for different paths have been followed and common problems have often been tackled in different ways. If foreign experience may afford valuable guidance to countries such as the USA or Australia, a comparative study is still more directly relevant to Britain as a new member of the European Economic Community. Moreover, as it has happened, Britain's entry into Europe coincided with the launching of a new plan of her own which can usefully be compared with the policies of other member countries.

An attempt will be made in the present chapter to indicate the nature of at least the more important issues. Naturally any such discussion of pensions policy raises certain basic questions both of public finance and of social administration and touches upon some fundamental issues about the proper delineation of the spheres for public responsibility and for private initiative. Some of the main questions will thus be posed and the reader will be reminded of the manner in which the issues have been faced in the UK and the USA. We shall then turn, in Part II of this volume, to our next concern which is to describe the evolution and discuss the future prospects of pensions policy in the Federal Republic of Germany,[1] the Netherlands, France, Belgium, Italy and Sweden. After these more detailed essays by different authors we shall return, in Part III, to a further consideration of the main issues that emerge in formulating and implementing appropriate policies. These issues will be analysed with reference to the experience of the six European countries whose systems have just been described in Part II and also with particular reference to Britain and the USA.

---

[1] Abbreviated hereafter to 'Germany'.

Although we shall be largely concerned with official pensions
and other forms of general cash assistance, attention will be paid in
the following chapters to other benefits as well—in particular,
assistance with the costs of housing and medical care. Moreover
attention must be paid to the provisions made for widows and for
the disabled, mainly because these are of such obvious importance
in their own right and also for the secondary reason that disability
pensions are sometimes (as in Italy) a partial substitute for old age
pensions. We must also take account of the fact that pensions may
partially replace unemployment benefit if the age of retirement
continues to decline. Nor can our scope be confined to governmental measures, for private occupational pensions are an important part of the income of the elderly in a number of countries.
In Britain and the Netherlands, in particular, it is official policy to
rely upon these occupational pensions as a means of supplementing
the official flat-rate pensions and thus of providing second-tier
pensions graduated according to previous income. But occupational
pensions are also important in other countries as well and it is
necessary to assess the case for such schemes and to investigate the
problems that may arise. In doing so it will become clear that the
distinction between the wholly official and the purely private is less
sharp than is sometimes supposed; but important differences often
remain which not only affect the beneficiaries but may have
implications for the national economies in particular through
possible effects on the supply of savings. More generally, both
payroll taxes and contributions based on payrolls to private
schemes may not only have far-reaching economic effects but may
also affect quite markedly the choice between alternatives which
the individual citizen can be expected to make.

II—POVERTY AND MEANS TESTS

Such words as 'destitution' and 'poverty' have been used so far
without any attempt to define their meaning. To do so is not easy.
It is best to recognize at the outset that such terms have no clear
and unambiguous meaning but necessarily involve subjective
judgements which are neither unchanging nor unanimously held.
What would mean 'poverty' to a rich family would be luxury to
one long enured to lower standards and the objective of avoiding

'poverty' may thus be held to coincide, at least up to a point, with that of providing for the replacement of a substantial proportion of income in old age. But to adopt this approach and leave the matter there would be to concede that there are an indefinite number of poverty lines reflecting any previous inequality of income. Clearly this is not what people have in mind when they speak of 'destitution'! Various attempts have been made in Britain and elsewhere to break out from subjectivity by estimating the expenditure required to obtain enough food for adequate nutrition, to pay for housing and to obtain clothing and a few little luxuries, all on a modest scale. Unfortunately it is not really possible to establish an objective, scientific measurement of the income below which a family of a given size will be 'in poverty'. This is so even if attention is confined to a short period of time in any one country or, indeed, in any one district of one country. It is a little easier to establish the minimum expenditure on food that would be required for adequate nutrition than it is to establish minimum requirements for housing, clothes and other items of expenditure.[1] Even in the case of food, however, a single unequivocal estimate cannot be made. Then there is the further complication of 'secondary poverty' which results from the fact that poor families may not spend the incomes available to them in ways which would be regarded as 'appropriate' by scientific investigators. Should secondary poverty be ignored? Or should some allowance for it be included in determining a poverty line and, if so, how much? Without labouring the point any further, one can conclude that subjective judgements are involved and several different poverty lines may therefore be proposed. It follows that the proportion of the population deemed to be 'in poverty' at any given time and place will vary with the standard chosen. There is no single answer.

Although several poverty levels may thus be estimated, it does not follow that these statistical exercises are uninformative. There may indeed be no objective scientific basis for making a definitive choice between them, but the alternative measurements are not,

---

[1] For a discussion of some of these difficulties see, for example: *The Concept of Poverty*, edited by Peter Townsend (Heinemann, London, 1970). In an essay in this volume, Martin Rein reviews some of the attempts to establish food requirements and then gross up the figure thus obtained by applying the appropriate Engels coefficient. Clearly such estimates will be a mixture of the normative and the empirical.

for that reason, to be regarded as merely arbitrary. Thus it may be thought interesting to take more than one bench-mark and then estimate the changes in the proportion of families that fall below each of these bench-marks over a period of years. Even this approach, however, encounters objections. Not only will there be difficulties in finding an appropriate price index if the period of years is a very lengthy one, but account must be taken of the effect of a rising average standard of living on what most people would understand by 'poverty'—ill-defined and subjective though that notion may be. What would have seemed a tolerable standard of living in 1900 would not be so regarded today in any developed country. What would be felt to be bitter hardship by most Americans would be affluence to most of the inhabitants of Africa or India. The unemployed in Britain in the nineteen-thirties were certainly thought to be poor although they may have been better off, in terms of goods and services, than the average Russian wage-earner. And so on. Clearly the concept of poverty has a relative aspect which is of crucial importance to an understanding of the problem.

This relative aspect of the concept of poverty can be pushed so far that the measurement of poverty becomes closely identified with the measurement of inequality. 'Poverty' can then be measured by the proportion of a year's national income going to the poorest x per cent of a nation's families. It is true that this will not give a single estimate, for it is still necessary to place a value on x—5 per cent, 10 per cent or whatever. But, for any given value, comparisons can be made over time and, of course, further refinements should be introduced by attempting to take account of other benefits as well as cash income. Although there will still be a number of measurements of poverty, and of changes in poverty, all these measurements will be relative. Calculations of this kind are clearly informative and of great social importance. One must object, however, that it would be a confusing use of language to suggest that such estimates can be described as adequate measurements of all that is commonly conveyed to people's minds by the use of the word 'poverty'.

Suppose, for example, that we apply this relative concept internationally. Country A is underdeveloped with a level of income a head that is only 10 per cent that of country B. Admittedly international statistical comparisons of this kind are somewhat dangerous but let us accept at least the broad conclusion that A is a much poorer country. Then, over a decade, income a head doubles in country A and other social indicators (such as literacy and infantile mortality) also record marked improvements. Suppose, however, that the gap between the two countries is as big as ever. Would it, in these circumstances, be a proper use of language to say that A was just as 'poor' at the end of the decade as at the beginning? The answer must surely be in the negative. Country A has clearly made progress and is less poor than before in *one* generally accepted sense of the term. We must recognize that this is so however much we may regret the fact that the gap between country A and country B is as big as ever.

Thus confusion is bound to follow if the word 'poverty' is used as though it had a single generally accepted meaning. It should indeed go without saying that the relative positions of different income groups within a society has an important bearing on what should be understood by 'poverty'. Relative social deprivation is part of the problem. To ignore this fact would be wrong. It would also be wrong to claim that poverty should be simply identified with inequality and measured only by some index of inequality. Thus it is not without meaning to take a bench-mark, such as the US 'poverty line' of 1962,[1] and then to observe that the number of families falling below this poverty line has declined substantially in subsequent years. Of course we may wish to repeat the calculation with some different bench-marks and we should certainly be careful to avoid the suggestion that any one of them affords an objective, scientific measurement of 'poverty'. But changes relatively to such bench-marks over a limited number of years remain illuminating, provided the limitations are recognized. If, however, poverty is simply identified with inequality, then it may be inferred that neither the growth of output nor the welfare state have made much impact on 'poverty' in any country where the

[1] See the Annual Report of the Council of Economic Advisers, published with the *Economic Report of the President 1964*, Government Printing Office, 1964. The relevant section is reprinted in *Wealth, Income and Inequality*, edited by A. B. Atkinson, Penguin Books, 1973. See also, *Government Action Against Poverty* by Joseph A. Kershaw, Brookings Institution, 1970. See subsequent *Economic Reports of the President* and the *Social Security Bulletin* of the Department of Health, Education and Welfare, Washington, for changes in the number of families below this 'poverty line'.

relative share of those with lower incomes has not increased. To argue thus would be to confuse the issue. Many people would interpret such statements to mean that the standard of living of the poorer families, as measured by the goods and services available to them, had not improved. In this latter sense, 'poverty' may well have been reduced and, if so, it is necessary to record this fact without implying for a moment that relative social deprivation is not also important. For poverty is not a one-dimensional problem and it would be unhelpful to treat it as such.[1]

Progress, as measured by reasonable bench-marks held constant over a period, can thus be observed and this is of real interest and meaning. There remains, however, the task of determining the minima to be applied at any time in practical policy. One of the most striking features of welfare policy since the war has been the fact that these minimum standards in so many countries have been altered very much more frequently than appears to have been anticipated when welfare systems were being reconstructed after the Second World War.

When the poverty line itself is frequently raised, the position is radically altered. This, of course, is what has happened in Britain, where the 'official poverty line'—as measured by the scale on which means-tested assistance is provided—has been raised repeatedly

---

[1] Paretian welfare economics, in its traditional form, leaves the relativist approach out of account and the debate has centred around the problems that arise when there are both gainers and losers. Suppose, however, that all are better off in period 2 than in period 1, in the sense that *all* have more goods (with leisure included as a good) than they could have had in period 1. It would then be inferred not only that 'social welfare' had increased but that the poor were 'better off'—even if inequality had not diminished. For the satisfaction of one individual is not assumed to be directly affected by what he sees others are getting. There is, that is to say, no resentment at 'relative deprivation'; or, for those who prefer a different emotive term, there is no 'jealousy'. Nor is there any 'middle-class conscience'. For a discussion of some modifications of this theory, see *The Economics of Social Policy* by A. J. Culyer (Martin Robertson, 1973), chapter 4.

In John Rawls' exposition of 'justice as fairness' the burden of proof is placed squarely on those who defend inequality, although it is not suggested that no such defence can be successfully made. According to his 'difference principle', inequality may raise the level of efficiency and may thus be justified if, as a consequence, the poorest members of society are better off. This view is clearly opposed to the relativist position mentioned above according to which 'poverty' will not be reduced unless the *relative* position of the poor has been improved. (See *A Theory of Justice* by John Rawls, Oxford University Press, 1973, p. 75f.)

and, in 1972, was nearly twice as high in real terms as it had been in 1948 when the new social welfare scheme was launched. Naturally it is far more difficult to abolish 'poverty', even in an affluent society, when the poverty line itself is rising and may even be made to rise as fast on trend as average incomes from work, as again has happened in Britain. Plenty of scope has thus been provided for misunderstanding and even misrepresentation. To say that there has therefore been much confusion about the persistance of 'poverty' is not, of course, to say that such increases in minimum standards are socially undesirable. On the contrary, it may be held that such standards ought to be relative and should therefore alter as other incomes do. But it is one thing to say so explicitly and quite a different matter to use language in such a way as to imply that neither rising output nor the welfare state has done much to raise the standard of living of those with low incomes. Poverty, as measured by Beveridge's standard, has been much reduced in Britain today, although economic growth has been slow by international standards.[1]

In some countries, the social security minima are frankly relative but are thought to provide bench-marks even if these are somewhat arbitrary ones. Thus the measure is sometimes the minimum wage or some fraction of it, but this only pushes the question back to those who determine the minimum wage. Alternatively, the minimum benefit may be some fraction of the average wage or of the median. Apart from their use in the assessment of the position in each country viewed in isolation, such relative measures can be helpful up to a point in international comparisons—or could be at least in principle even if the statistics are sometimes lacking or imperfectly comparable in practice. Direct international comparisons of poverty levels (or, for that matter, of average or other incomes) involve the translation of estimates from one currency to another and this poses familiar difficulties. Not only may the current exchange rates fail to reflect purchasing-power parities even in those cases where patterns of expenditure are very similar, but these patterns may vary so much as to give rise to problems of weighting for which there is no unequivocal solution.[2] When

---

[1] *Social Insurance and Allied Services*, Cmd. 6404, HMSO, 1942.

[2] That these difficulties were not quantitatively trivial was shown by Milton Gilbert and associates in *Comparative National Products and Price Levels*, OEED, 1958

differences between countries expressed in terms of a common unit are very large, some broad presumption may be established, but that is about as far as one can go.

If a poverty level has been fixed, at least for the time being, what means can be adopted to prevent people from falling below it? 'From each according to his ability, to each according to his needs'. Presumably the application of the Marxian slogan could best be achieved by a widespread use of means tests in order to determine needs and have them met. Admittedly the Marxian slogan was meant to refer to full Communism when scarcity would be abolished and every desire could be fully met. That has scarcely been a relevant model so far—nor is it one that is ever likely to become relevant especially if the pressure of population on limited resources gives rise to even a fraction of the difficulty which the 'doomsters' predict. It does not follow, however, that the Marxian principle of allocation has no practical relevance at all to conditions of scarcity. One can envisage a welfare state based firmly on means tests with the costs met from general public revenue. This would imply a high degree of selectivity and would be a way of meeting basic needs at minimum cost. This, in very broad terms, is the Australian model. But it is not a model that has been generally adopted. It is true that in the European countries whose arrangements are described in Part II, means-tested assistance plays an important part and this is also true of the USA and Britain. But, of course, pensions are also paid as of right without means tests. One of our tasks throughout this study must therefore be to compare these two approaches and to discuss their respective merits and disadvantages. We must ask why the two methods have continued to exist side by side and consider whether it is probable that the one will to an increasing extent supercede the other.

In Britain there has long been a school of thought which is strongly opposed to selective assistance based on means tests. For means tests are unpopular and the acceptance of supplementary benefit is still felt by many people to involve a stigma. Is the same attitude to be found in Europe? The chapters on the six countries in Part II throw some light on this question. In part the outcome may be affected by the position at which the poverty level is set. In part it will depend upon the kind of inquisition that is entailed and the tone of voice in which it is carried out. Memories of the inter-war years colour attitudes in Britain even in the nineteen-seventies, although vast improvements have long since been made. Is this equally true elsewhere? The administrative arrangements for applying means tests are also important. The responsibility of making cash payments rests with the central Government in Britain, but this is not so in some other countries such as the USA, West Germany or the Netherlands. It is then necessary to ask whether there are local differences in 'poverty levels', and whether such differences can be justified. It is also necessary to inquire whether local administration is likely to be more resented or less resented than central. Sometimes the means tests are built into the central Government's pension plan itself, as in France, Belgium and Italy, and it is conceivable that this may affect the acceptability of the method.

III—BENEFITS AND SOCIAL INSURANCE

Means-tested assistance when financed from general revenue may be regarded as a straightforward transfer payment designed to prevent destitution. But, as we have seen, the welfare state extends far beyond this. For welfare arrangements have also been devised with the objective of embodying a different principle, that of 'social insurance', which implies that people should receive certain benefits as of right without any investigation of their needs and their means. This was the core of the Beveridge philosophy, although social insurance is, of course, much older than the Beveridge Report, whose philosophy is: 'Let people contribute to a social insurance fund on an agreed basis and derive benefits from it on an agreed scale in specified circumstances.' Payments are not then made on the basis of any inquisition into personal circumstances but rather when people fall into certain categories—the aged, the unemployed, the sick and so on—partly with the intention that a sense of personal dignity and responsibility will thus be preserved and the suggestion of public charity removed. This approach has made a strong appeal in the past and continues to do so. In the words of a Labour Government's White Paper: 'People do not want to be *given* rights to pensions and benefits; they want to *earn* them by their contributions.'[1]

---

[1] *National Superannuation and Social Security*, Cmnd. 3883. HMSO, January 1969, p. 12. (The Crossman plan.)

The social insurance principle has, however, been severely criticized of late.[1] It has been pointed out that the analogy with private insurance is misleading, for people may not really have paid on an actuarial basis for what they are getting. There is sometimes an Exchequer contribution, but even when this is not the case—as in many European pension schemes—the individual's benefits cannot be related to his own contributions as in an insurance policy. To begin with, contributions are not, as a rule, paid into an accumulating fund from which the benefits will be derived. It is now exceedingly rare in official schemes for benefits to be based on funding in this way even when, for one reason or another, some funds have been accumulated. Current benefits are rather met mainly, or wholly, from current receipts on the 'pay-as-you-go' principle. These benefits have often differed, and even differed substantially, from what could have been obtained by the investment of the contributions in a pension fund or an insurance policy.[2] Part of the explanation is sometimes to be found in the fact that official social insurance schemes have been so used as to bring about a redistribution of income.

(1)   This redistribution may be vertical in the sense that those with low incomes who have paid small contributions may receive benefits that are larger relatively to contributions than do those with high incomes.

(2)   There may be some redistribution between generations. This, in turn, may take two forms. (a) When a new pension scheme has been introduced, or the pensions provided under an existing one substantially increased, some retired people with an incomplete record of contributions under the new arrangements have been given larger benefits than would be sanctioned by the normal rules. This is what is described as 'blanketing-in'. Or (b) the pensions paid may be raised to

---

[1] Cf., for example, *Social Security, Perspectives for Reform* by J. A. Pechman, H. J. Aaron and M. K. Taussig, Brookings Institution, Washington DC, 1968.

[2] Cf., for example, the analysis of US pensions in the essays submitted by Colin D. Campbell and John A. Brittain to the Joint Economic Committee of Congress and published in *Old Age Income Assurance*, Part III, US Printing Office, Washington, 1967. See also Alan Prest's criticism of the plan proposed by Crossman for Britain: 'Some Redistributional Aspects of the National Superannuation Fund', *Three Banks Review*, June 1970. We shall return to this issue towards the end of this chapter and, more fully, in Part III and in the Mathematical Appendix.

some target level, at the cost of higher current contributions, to such an extent that the implicit 'rate of return' even on a full record of contributions is well above what could have been earned on the capital market. (This second test encounters some difficulties of interpretation as we shall see in Chapter 8, p. 390.)

There is another and, in a sense, a still more fundamental complication. Official pensions are financed mainly, sometimes entirely, by taxes on payrolls. The taxes are often described as 'contributions' which helps to strengthen the apparent analogy with insurance. The crucial question then is where the incidence of the payroll taxes may be deemed to rest. The employer's tax (or contribution) may be largely passed on in the form of higher prices and thus becomes an indirect tax. This may clearly have serious implications for the insurance analogy, for attempts to relate benefits to contributions assumes implicitly that the contributions are really paid by those responsible for them in the first instance.

There can be no doubt that the term 'social insurance' is a thoroughly confusing one. Clear thinking would be helped if the term could now be decently interred and forgotten; but it would be foolish to suppose that this is likely to happen and we must resign ourselves to coping as best we can with the ambiguities that arise from its continued use. Apart from abandoning the label the critics are not always clear, still less unanimous, about the changes of substance they would wish to see. It would, indeed, be possible to argue that the Australian model is the right one for providing assistance to the old with benefits provided subject to a means test, and financed from general taxation. As we have observed, past experience scarcely suggests that such an alternative is likely to be popular in Europe or North America;[1] but it is necessary to recognize that there is a growing interest in conditional assistance provided in a different way through the mechanism of a negative income tax.[2] The state, it may be urged, should not be responsible

---

[1] There have, of course, been proposals in Australia for departing from this system and coming more into line with the practice of other countries. See, for example, 'National Superannuation, Means Tests and Contributions' by R. I. Downing in *The Australian Economy*, ed. by H. W. Arndt and A. H. Bower, Cheshire, Melbourne, 1972.

[2] See below, p. 376, where it will be seen that a negative income tax does not really provide as easy alternative as may sometimes be supposed.

for doing more than this. In particular it should not attempt to provide graduated pensions that vary in amount with the previous incomes of the beneficiaries.

This is one side of the argument, but there is another. Or rather there are several others. To begin with it may be held that the Beveridge philosophy contained some important elements of truth which must still be respected even if much of the humbug about social insurance is recognized for what it is. In particular many people seem to want pensions (and other social security benefits) which they receive as of right, without means tests. Such pensions could, of course, be financed from general taxation[1] and the abandonment of means testing need not in itself commit a country to the collecting of contributions specifically designed for social security. It may, however, be the case that the suggestion of public charity will be more adequately dispelled if there is some form of social security tax. For people will then feel that they, or their employers, have paid for what they are getting. Even if, in the event, they get more than the accumulated value of these contributions, the fact that the schemes are at least in part contributory may be of some psychological importance. This psychological aspect may have a bearing on the attitude of the public to the burden of taxation. If part of the taxes they pay is hypothecated, they may be willing to pay more. If part is not recognized to be a tax at all, but regarded more benignly as a social insurance contribution, then taxpayers may be still more willing to carry a heavy total burden—although this is not, perhaps, a point that could be securely defended on grounds of social ethics. There are also some institutional considerations which cannot be ignored especially in a comparative study. For special social security schemes, with their separate revenues and obligations, may leave people in some countries with a greater sense of security than they would have if all benefits were to come from a country's general budget for all forms of public expenditure.[2] They may prefer not to be at the mercy of

---

[1] The basic pension is financed in this way in Denmark and Luxembourg.

[2] Professor James M. Buchanan would abolish the payroll-tax but require people to buy 'bonds' up to some prescribed limit in order to ensure that minimum standards in old age would be provided for. The proceeds of the bonds would be used to pay current pensions; and the scheme would not therefore be funded. The term 'bonds' is misleading. 'Certificates of credit' might be better and would indicate clearly that their purpose was to protect pensioners from the danger of subsequent changes in policy under pay-as-you-go arrangements. The

annual budgets. More generally they may like certain accepted rules and principles which will inform them about the nature of their rights and the scale on which future expectations can reasonably be based. Admittedly it is sometimes held that the whole procedure could be simplified by regarding all social benefits as simply transfers to be provided at appropriate rates after an appropriate assessment of social priorities and financed from general revenues. But it might be rash to take it for granted that in practical terms an arrangement of this kind would work more smoothly and simply.

It should now be possible to reach a general conclusion about 'social insurance'. Clearly these schemes are not, in any strict sense, insurance schemes at all. As we observed above, there are two reasons for saying this: first, the schemes are not funded, or are only partially so; second, there is no prescribed relationship between contributions and benefits. The last point can be clearly seen when graduated contributions are paid in return for flat-rate benefits but, even when the benefits are also graduated, there is really no 'insurance link' between the benefits and the contributions. The fact remains that an attachment to the insurance myth causes confused thinking on some issues and affects practical decisions. To accept all this does not mean that there is no case for hypothecated taxes (or contributions) and no case for separating pensions and other social benefits from general Exchequer expenditure. That is a different matter and it is important to make the distinction.

If it is assumed, for the moment, that hypothecated social security taxation is accepted in principle, it is still necessary to consider the *form this tax should take*. In Britain the basic taxes are flat payments—so much in cash each week—from both employees and employers.[1] This raises at once the question of *incidence*. As we have observed the employers' contribution is likely to be treated like another addition to the cost of labour and passed on in

---

rate of return would not be specified but would be either the rate on long-term US Treasury bonds or the rate of growth of total money gross national product, whichever was higher. See 'Social Insurance in a Growing Economy: A Proposal for Radical Reform', *National Tax Journal*, December 1968. For some critical comments, see the note by A. R. Prest in the same journal for December 1969.

[1] In Britain these payments go into the general social security scheme, not to a special pensions scheme. There is also a fixed state contribution from general revenue of 15 per cent.

higher prices. Part at least of the employees' contribution may conceivably be passed on if money wages are pushed up—especially
when contributions are increased. But part may remain as a
regressive flat-rate income tax which falls on the individuals
concerned. This regressive method of finance has been regarded
as one of the unsatisfactory features of the Beveridge scheme. It is
true that, if the contributions are a larger fraction of low incomes
than of high ones, the same holds for the flat-rate benefits. But to
accept this defence would imply the abandonment of any idea of
vertical redistribution.[1] In the Netherlands the employees pay the
whole of the tax but do so on a scale proportionate to their incomes
(up to a maximum). Thus the Dutch method of financing is, in
effect, a proportional income tax and, although there are still some
uncertainties about incidence,[2] there is a presumption that the
incidence is not shifted as much in a scheme where there is no tax
nominally paid by the employers. In Britain the total contributions
have also, in effect, been proportional since 1961 when a supplementary scheme was introduced with graduated payments and
graduated contributions within a specified income band in addition
to the basic flat-rate contributions. The sums paid out on graduated pensions have been small so far and the receipts from the
contributions have been used to pay a high proportion of the
costs of the basic pensions. This supplementary graduated system
is to be phased out and the new scheme, to be implemented in
1975, will be based explicitly on what has been the implicit
arrangement: flat-rate pensions financed by graduated contributions together with an Exchequer contribution of about 15 per cent.[3]
Thus the Dutch and British models are similar in principle.
Account must, however, be taken of private occupational pensions
as well and this we shall attempt to do later.

Although the principle of the hypothecated tax is to remain in
both countries, both have departed from the insurance principle
not only in that their schemes are unfunded but also in that proportional levies are to be used to finance flat-rate benefits. Thus

---

[1] See, for example, 'Inequality and Social Security' by A. B. Atkinson in
Labour and Inequality, Fabian Society, 1972, p. 18.

[2] See Ch. 3, p. 122, for a discussion of how this question of incidence comes
into collective bargaining in the Netherlands.

[3] See *Strategy for Pensions*, Cmnd. 4755, Sept. 1971; *Social Security Act
1973*; *Explanatory Memorandum on the Social Security Bill 1972*, Cmnd. 5142,
1972.

there is to be some vertical redistribution of income from higher to lower incomes. The pension plan put forward by Mr Crossman when the Labour Party was in power also provided for graduated contributions but the benefits were to be graduated as well. It is true that the graduation of the benefits was to be carried out in two parts so that their increase would be less for higher incomes than for lower ones and some vertical redistribution was thus to have been achieved.[1] But the Conservative Government's pension plan provides greater scope in principle for vertical redistribution, although the outcome in practice will partly depend upon the particular level chosen for pensions each year. (Keith Joseph plan.)

Flat-rate pensions might be fixed at the 'official' poverty level for means-tested assistance or might be above or below that level. This is, of course, one of the burning issues in Britain. Official pensions are below the official poverty level defined as the supplementary benefit in cash plus the average cost of housing met by the state. As a consequence about 30 per cent of pensioners are said to be 'in poverty'. It is often strongly urged that this continuing poverty is a scandal which should be ended. That there is indeed much hardship and misery which can and should be removed is clearly true. But it is also necessary to observe that we have here an example of the danger to which we have referred of getting caught up in the ambiguity of the language. This can be illustrated by considering one of the ways in which the gap could be closed. Both pensions and the supplementary benefit level are raised every year and it would be possible to raise the former by more than the latter until the difference was eliminated. Everyone would then have a basic benefit received as of right which was no longer below the poverty line. No one would then be 'in poverty' but, out of any given sum of expenditure on the old, a larger proportion would go to those who would be seen to be in less need if means tests were still to be applied. 'Poverty' would have been abolished but the poor would be worse off! The other way of closing the gap would be to raise the official pensions gradually to the supplementary benefit level without reducing the rate of growth of the latter. How precisely this would be done has not always been clear, for the increases in supplementary benefits are not predetermined by

---

[1] The element of redistribution in the Government Plan was estimated by A. B. Atkinson in 'National Superannuation: Redistribution and Value of Money', *Bulletin of the Oxford Institute of Statistics*, April 1970.

some explicit formula: perhaps the previous trend could be
extrapolated, or the previous relationship to the rate of growth of
wages could be maintained. The basic unconditional benefit could
then be raised by whatever extra amount was required to close the
gap. The cost would be large: about £700 million in 1971 if the
gap had been closed in one act. The question which has then to be
asked is whether this money could not be better spent on some
different social purpose or for that matter, on providing more
generous means-tested assistance for the aged poor themselves.
Unfortunately the debate in Britain is often carried on with too
little regard for the ambiguity of such terms as 'poverty'. Two
points can, however, be made at this stage. The first is that graduated contributions have made it easier to raise the level of the
flat-rate pension without either imposing an intolerable burden on
the lower-income contributors or requiring larger assistance from
general taxation. The second point is that some people do not take
up the means-tested assistance to which they are entitled. Although
there may be large numbers who would be in poverty without this
assistance, its availability ought ideally to ensure that no one is left
in such poverty. This, as we know, does not happen. It was the
establishment of the fact that it does not happen, first by independent research and then by official enquiry, which caused so
much justifiable concern in the sixties and stimulated the search
for new policies.[1] Unfortunately more recent information is
fragmentary and a new investigation is required. It is believed
that take-up has been much improved but hard evidence is lacking.

The problems just discussed in the British context are also
encountered in some of the other countries with which we shall be
concerned. In the Netherlands, as in Britain, the flat-rate pension
stands below the poverty level. What difficulties are then encountered and what means are employed in dealing with them? In the
other European countries, as in the USA, pensions are graduated

---

[1] About 850,000 (12 per cent) who might have qualified did not apply; about
300,000 (over 4 per cent) were well below the level set for means-tested assistance.
See *Financial and other Circumstances of Retirement Pensioners* (HMSO, 1960).
See also *The Aged in the Welfare State* by Peter Townsend and Dorothy Wedder-
burn, Bell, 1965; *The Economic Circumstances of Old People* by Dorothy Cole
and J. E. G. Utting, Caldicote Press, 1962. *The Poor and the Poorest* by Brian
Abel-Smith and Peter Townsend, Bell, 1965; *Poverty in Britain and the Reform
of Social Security* by A. B. Atkinson, Cambridge University Press, 1970; *Labour
and Inequality*, ed. by Peter Townsend and Nicolas Bosanquet, Fabian Society,
1972; *Family Poverty*, ed. by David Bull, Gerald Duckworth, 1972.

but one of the questions which must then be considered is the relationship between the minima in these official pension schemes and the poverty levels. It will be found that means tests continue to play an important part, just as it will be found that poverty, as judged by any reasonable standards, remains a problem. There is the further complication that in some of the European countries—notably France and Italy—there is a diversity of schemes. There are sometimes large groups of elderly people who have no claims to the main graduated pensions or claims to only partial pensions. Their lot can often be a sorry one and the adequacy of the means used for easing it must be assessed. In Germany those formerly self-employed were incompletely covered before 1973. Moreover pensions are not only graduated in Germany but there has been no minimum. A person may therefore receive a very low pension and be obliged to turn to the Länder for means-tested assistance. What is remarkable is that this problem is of such small quantitative importance in Germany with only about 3 per cent of the elderly 'in poverty' in this sense of the term. Naturally, the official arrangements and the circumstances for which they are designed vary from country to country, but it is a fair generalization that a quite high proportion of those in need are women.

One of the problems in dealing with poverty by providing cash payments at some flat rate, with or without means test, is that the money required to meet minimum needs may vary a good deal. Obviously there may be differences in the cost of living between different parts of the country and these should be reflected in different benefits. There are, however, more troublesome causes of variation, in particular the need for medical treatment and differences in housing costs. In Britain the procedure for dealing with these issues is to provide a free health service on the one hand and to meet directly the varying costs of housing. This implies differences between one family and another in the assistance provided in kind (mainly medical services) and differences in the value of the assistance provided by the Supplementary Benefit Commission in meeting the rents and rates. We shall find that a variety of different methods have been adopted in our six European countries in order to deal with these same problems.

Meanwhile we may again note in passing the ambiguity surrounding the word 'poverty'. If 'poverty' is measured by the number below some level, or levels, at which means-tested assistance is provided, the index of poverty has been identified with an index of the extent to which the welfare arrangements are selective. There is a further difficulty. Are the 'poor' only those entitled to general cash assistance subject to means tests? Or are they those subject to means tests for any one of a number of specific purposes? This distinction greatly affects international comparisons. Only a very small percentage of pensioners in Sweden receive general means-tested assistance but about half receive assistance with housing. It must then be recalled that in Britain much the greater part of the means-tested assistance given to old people is, in effect, to meet the cost of housing. Must we then extend the scope of the definition and say that anyone is 'poor' who receives *any* form of means-tested assistance? To widen the definition to this extent would be to create new confusion. For example it would then be necessary to say that any family in Britain receiving more than the basic minimum grant for a university student must be classed as poor! There are a large number of means-tested grants and presumably it would be silly to include all of them without regard to their importance or their purpose. This, however, leaves open the question of how many should be brought in.

IV—GRADUATED BENEFITS

Income replacement is obviously accorded more emphasis in schemes which provide for official pensions to be graduated rather than flat rate. Graduated schemes are by no means new, but have been more widely adopted and extended in scope since World War II. It is now the flat-rate official pension, after the Dutch and British models, that is the exception—although this in itself need not be taken as condemnation! How has this movement in favour of graduated pensions come about? What are the principles on which these pensions are based? Value judgements are clearly involved, and differences of opinion are likely to persist. But there is also a question of fact that has to be considered. Is there reason to believe that the social choice in favour of graduated pensions has been properly made in the sense that—whatever the value judgements—the facts of the situation have been sufficiently understood? There is, as we shall see, reason to suspect that this condition has not been satisfied.

We have already assumed that few people nowadays would dispute the case for assistance designed to protect the old from destitution. This requires, at the very least, means-tested assistance, which will lift recipients to some tolerable minimum level of income. Many people would go beyond this and support flat-rate pensions received as of right by all who are citizens. Even if some of the recipients have income from other sources and do not need such pensions to protect them from poverty, this need may be sufficiently widespread for a general scheme to be justified on grounds of convenience. But graduated pensions imply a still further departure from the criterion of need and it would be natural to suppose that such pensions would have provoked more debate and disagreement than appears to have been the case in the countries with which we are concerned. Of course it is true that the incomes people will wish to have in retirement will depend in part upon the standards to which they have grown accustomed during their working lives. If payments from the state were the only source of income of elderly people, then a flat-rate pension set at a level which provided a tolerable standard of living for those who were formerly low-paid workers would entail some hardship for the more highly paid. The desire for graduation in retirement *incomes* is not in doubt, but this graduation could be provided from other sources of income apart from benefits received from the state. What is in doubt, then, is the case for using the compulsory powers of the state to provide these graduated margins in excess of some tolerable official minimum. There are some who would hold that the state has in fact done all it should attempt to do when it has established a decent floor to incomes. The rest is for personal choice and personal initiative. This view may indeed be dismissed as old-fashioned individualism; but perhaps it may be viewed in a different light if we change the language and ask whether in a 'permissive' society a person should not be free to choose whether to spend more during his active years even at the price of accepting only a low minimum income in his retirement. Why should he not be left to decide for himself? Or, from an entirely different point of view, it may be objected that the state has no business to help to perpetuate in retirement something of the inequality of working years.

'In my opinion', says Professor Meade, 'Governments would be well advised to concentrate on measures which will ensure

incomes to everyone at the basic minimum standard and to leave
supplementation above this to private savings without any special
governmental assistance or tax privileges.'[1] Indeed, one might
expect graduated pensions to be attacked on one flank by indivi-
dualists and on the other by socialists. Admittedly such objections
can easily assume an exaggerated form when presented in general
terms without reference to quantities. The scope for debate is
restricted by the graduated schemes themselves with their maxima
and minima which limit the range in the size of benefits. These
limits may lie between, say, one-half average wages and one-and-a-
half times average wages and, when this is so, the question of
principle raised above will clearly carry less practical force. For it
is not then so much a question of perpetuating in retirement the
full range of any inequality between the really rich and the really
poor as of allowing pensions to reflect at least partially the differentials between the more highly paid workers and those at the bottom
of the scale. (This, of course, is one of the reasons why some trade
unions support graduated benefits.) There are, however, cases
where the range of inequality in pensions is much greater than that
suggested by the figures above, for example, in Italy.

The use of compulsion in order to graduate pension schemes
may over-ride personal preferences. One would expect different
people to have different views about the desired pattern of expenditure over a life-time. Some may wish to keep down their current
consumption for the sake of greater comfort in old age; others may
prefer to spend more now. The question is why the state should
force people to follow one pattern of behaviour rather than
another. It is sometimes argued that the justification lies in the
irreversibility of decisions over time. In one's old age, one may
regret the extravagance of youth, but it is then too late. Why this
reasoning should be thought to justify compulsion is not clear.
For this implies that the ordinary citizen is not to be treated as a
responsible adult but must have this decision made for him by a
state which knows best. Thus the 'bias' in the one direction may be
resented by a man who would prefer to spend more in his active
years even at the cost of greater frugality when he is old. After all,
the argument about irreversibility can cut both ways, and is sadly

---

[1] 'Poverty in the Welfare State', *Oxford Economic Papers*, Nov. 1972. See also
Pensions in a Free Society by Arthur Seldon, Institute of Economic Affairs
1957.

echoed in the old complaint: 'Si la jeunesse savait, si la vieillesse pouvait.'

Let us suppose that the contemporary debate about permissiveness were to be extended beyond such well- worn topics as obscenity and sexuality so as to include that with which we are here concerned: freedom of choice in making provision for old age. How far is this freedom already available? What are the restrictions placed upon it and what would be the cost, in terms of some sacrifice of other objectives, of permitting greater permissiveness? Of course it is not implied that such a policy would be pushed to such extremes as to involve the abandonment of the principle which appears to be generally accepted: that the state should provide whatever assistance may be needed to prevent poverty. This assistance would still be there and the active population would still be taxed in order to pay for it. What is at issue is not at all the abandonment of the minimum but the case for permitting greater freedom of choice with regard to benefits beyond this minimum. A reference to the Italian arrangements, described in detail in Part II, may be the best way of throwing the matter into focus. For the Italian scheme, mentioned above, when mature, will provide for the replacement of three-quarters of the average income earned in the few years before retirement with no upper limit placed on the income to which this will apply. Naturally the charges levied through the payroll tax are geared accordingly. Can this measure of compulsion be justified? Or even the less extreme measure of compulsion practised in some of the countries with which we shall be concerned?

Freedom of choice would mean that anyone could, if he wished, opt out of the official arrangements. We may envisage three alternatives: first, to belong to a graduated pension scheme run by the state; second, to belong to some private occupational scheme; third, to belong to no scheme of this kind but to accept personal responsibility for one's income in retirement—above the minimum provided on a flat-rate basis by the state. Professor Meade would provide only the third alternative, but we shall suppose all three to be available. Would many employees in fact choose the third? It seems unlikely if those who did so were to be excused payment only of the employee's part of the payroll tax. A tax adjustment would also be necessary. That is to say the person opting out should not only be allowed to retain the employee's contribution he would have had to make but this amount should be treated as tax-free income.[1] The third alternative would, however, remain a poor one unless those opting out were given a further allowance, also tax-free, which would correspond to the employers' payroll contribution.[2] Suppose the combined payroll taxes required to provide a man with a graduated pension in excess of a prescribed poverty level came to 5 per cent. Those opting out would have a tax-free supplement above this amount added to their salaries. Alternatively the tax privilege could be removed from the pension schemes and the supplement to those opting out could then also be taxable.

Even if individuals were to be given a choice, and one devised as fairly as possible, some might still prefer to belong to a state scheme because they positively desired the discipline of paternalism and mistrusted their own judgement or strength of will. Some might turn away from the personal option because of their ignorance about the best way of investing whatever savings they choose to make. The second alternative, membership of a private occupational scheme, would, of course, meet this need. (There are, however, other important differences between official and private occupational schemes and these will occupy our attention shortly.)

Clearly these three possibilities have their respective advantages and drawbacks, but the case for providing the option of remaining outside any graduated scheme does not require the assumption that an overwhelming majority would choose to adopt it. It is the opportunity to exercise freedom of choice with which we are concerned, even if only a minority should choose to exercise it.

It must be said at once that this whole debate is not really relevant in considering the basic flat-rate pension in Britain. For there would still be a compulsory minimum and this minimum could not, with any decency, be placed below that set by the British pension. The point is of rather more relevance to occupational pensions in Britain which will be backed up to prescribed limits by legal compulsion. But the whole matter is—to my mind at least—much less important in Britain than are some others such as the

---

[1] This exemption from tax should *not* be conditional upon this sum being saved if the objective is to provide greater scope for freedom of choice.

[2] Where there is also an Exchequer contribution, there should be a further corresponding concession to those who opt out.

problem of poverty. It is, however, an important issue in a number
of other countries, notably France and Italy, with high graduated
pensions, at least as targets.

On more general grounds, the debate deserves attention because
it focuses attention on the proper aims for pensions policy, and on
the role of the state and the responsibility of the individual. We
have already mentioned the possibility of conflict in official policies
between the objectives of income replacement and the prevention
of poverty. This latter objective may indeed suffer to some extent
if attention is mainly concentrated on the replacement of unequal
incomes by unequal pensions after retirement. The Germans, for
their part, have placed great stress in principle on the preservation
of status and the propriety of regarding a wage or salary as one
that continues into retirement. They have also, however, a fairly
low upper limit beyond which the state does not use its powers of
compulsion to provide graduated pensions. This is the 'principle
of subsidiarity' which will be discussed in the next chapter.

Why have graduated schemes, sometimes providing for the replacement of a high proportion of incomes that are well above the
average, been popular with Governments and electorates in various
countries? Why have trade unions sometimes pressed for such
schemes? There may be several answers but the principal one is
surely to be found in the method of financing these schemes, in
particular in the importance of the employers' contributions.

The contributions of the employees themselves presumably give
rise to less distortion than those of the employers. The incidence
of the former may indeed be shifted a bit in favour of higher wages
and consequently higher prices. But it is probably right to assume
that the main incidence is that of a proportional income tax
without personal or other allowances but, in most cases, with
minima and maxima. The employers' contributions are a different
matter. This charge may sometimes be passed back in the form of
lower wages than would otherwise have been paid. The hypothetical level of wages involved in any such comparison is hard to
establish and quantification is likely to be largely guesswork. If,
however, workers believe that this tax is partly passed back—as
they appear to do in Sweden, for example—then to this extent the
cost of the social benefits will not be concealed. The greater part of
the levy may be shifted forward, in most countries in the form of
higher prices. The incidence of this levy is to this extent that of a

general indirect tax which happens to have its amount determined by a link with payrolls. Here we come back to the question posed above. In giving political support for compulsory graduated pensions, do people understand the nature of the options? Probably they do in the case of the employees' contributions or, for that matter, the contributions of the self-employed. These are recognized to be part of the cost of providing the welfare benefits, and when the cost seems high, there are grumbles. Thus one brings to mind the frequently quoted observation of the French trade unionist, not indeed about pensions but about family allowances: 'We are getting paid less and less for our work, and more and more for being Father Rabbit.'[1]

The truth of the situation is probably a lot less apparent in the case of the employers' contributions. It seems likely, however, that many people believe these contributions to fall on the employers and do not appreciate that the public in general is paying higher prices as a consequence of this tax. This admittedly is only a speculation about attitudes and it might be contradicted by opinion polls held in the different countries. If, however, it is the case that the incidence of this part of the payroll tax is very imperfectly understood, then the pressure for larger and larger benefits becomes more explicable. It is natural enough for an Italian worker to support pensions which will replace about three-quarters of pre-retirement income if the employer is thought to be meeting most of the cost.

This shifting of incidence has brought the payroll tax under heavy criticism, in particular in the USA.[2] More generally, the whole principle of social insurance is often challenged. Thus it is pointed out that social benefits are transfer payments which can be met, in real terms, only from current production. The only question for social decision is then how much should be directed to the old, the unemployed, the sick, and so on. All the calculations of contributions and benefits, all the devising of formulae, all the labour of official actuaries—all this is humbug and a waste of time. That there is indeed much humbug in social insurance systems is undeniable and much distortion of choice by the imperfect under-

[1] See *Comparative Labour Movements*, ed. by N. Galenson, Prentice Hall, 1952, p. 362.

[2] See, for example, the work by Pechman, Aaron and Taussig mentioned on p. 14, above. See, in particular, *The Payroll Tax for Social Security* by John A. Brittain, Brooking Institution, 1972.

standing of who pays the cost. But the practical inferences need to be drawn with care. We have already discussed the various approaches and have accepted as facts, first, that people wish to receive certain benefits as of right and, second, that hypothecated taxes have certain advantages. We must now recognize that, if hypothecated taxes were to be abolished altogether, graduated benefits would have to go as well. For it is hard to believe that there would be political support for the provision from general taxation of benefits that varied in amount with the previous incomes of the beneficiaries. Of course other taxes can be hypothecated as well as payroll taxes, but for the purpose in hand the tax paid should clearly be related to the incomes of members of the scheme. If some such relationship cannot be achieved, then this is a strong case against graduation. The kind of payroll tax usually applied does not pass the test at all adequately. It may be, however, that the payroll tax could be reformed or part of a general income tax substituted for it with the proceeds hypothecated. To take one example, even the employee's part of the US social security tax has been denounced because there is no lower cut-off point. Thus quite poor people are required to pay a proportional income tax which imposes a heavy burden upon them. But this particular fault could be removed. More far-reaching changes may, however, be needed and may be hard to achieve. There is indeed a case for abolishing the employers' contributions altogether and shifting the burden to the employees in their role as future beneficiaries. An obvious difficulty would be to ensure that prices had in fact been thus lowered and to convince the employees that they were paying no more in total, in view of these lower prices.

In the preceding paragraphs the question of graduation has been viewed from the point of view of the individual as contributor and beneficiary. The matter may, one must admit, be viewed differently by employers and by the state itself. Occupational pensions have been a way of attracting and retaining staff and these are usually related in some way to earnings except in the case of manual workers who often receive flat payments. The usefulness of such pensions as rewards for loyalty which could be lost on a change of job will be much reduced if proper arrangements are made by the Government for the preservation of rights. The fact remains that a good scheme may attract good employees, like a good level of current pay, and a graduated scheme will give employees an incentive to raise their incomes in order not only to gain during working life but to carry some gain over into retirement. Similar considerations presumably influence the state as employer and might even make Government turn a favourable eye on graduation in industry. It is interesting in this connection to note that the incentive effects of graduated pensions have received some weight in the Russian system. 'We are told repeatedly', says Bernice Madison, 'that the economic principle of socialism—"to each according to his work"—must continue to be reflected in the social-security system: the size of pensions must depend directly on previous earnings which, in turn, are determined by the quantity and quality of the work performed by each individual worker.'[1]

These possibilities need not be pursued further at this stage but it is appropriate to add a word about the various pension formulae for income replacement described in detail in the second part and summarized in the third. The extreme iconoclasts are inclined to dismiss all such formulae as nonsense and to repeat the old claim that pensions are simply transfers from current production to be provided from general taxation on whatever basis 'society' regards as appropriate. But what is 'society' and how does it decide? How is the proper basis for transfers to be identified? It is surely clear that 'society', in choosing the 'appropriate basis' for the payments to be made, would in effect be confronting issues broadly similar to those already encountered in formulating, operating and occasionally modifying the pension schemes in force in various countries. To dismiss all this as unnecessary mystification would betray a failure to understand the nature of the problem. To urge the need for some reforms is a different matter.

V—INCOME REPLACEMENT

How do pension levels in Britain and the USA respectively compare with those in the six European countries with which we are

---

[1] 'Soviet Income Maintenance Policy for the 1970s', *Journal of Social Policy*, Cambridge University Press, April 1973. She goes on to suggest that welfare may receive a little more emphasis in the future. The distinction between the socialist principle to which she refers and the principle appropriate to full Communism (p. 12, above) should be noted. It must also be recorded that there is a minimum in the Russian graduated pension.

concerned? This is a question to be taken up in Part III after the pension schemes of these countries have been scrutinized in turn. The view is frequently expressed that British pensions are low by the 'European' standard and will not be raised to that standard by the British legislation of 1973. In fact there is no 'European' standard but rather a wide variety of different arrangements in different countries. Even within a particular country, there is often diversity in the provision made for the needs of the old. Even the 'general schemes' are not usually so general as to be universal. 'Special schemes' often exist for particular industries and particular groups in the occupational structure and the position may be further complicated by complementary pensions of one kind or another. We have dismissed the view that pension schemes could be regarded as 'simple transfers', but this is not to deny that some of the schemes in operation are still encrusted with unnecessary complications for historical reasons. While these complications need not be traced in wearisome detail, it is necessary to remember that they are there.

International comparisons are made more difficult by this complexity but by no means impossible. Various points on the income scale may be chosen and the relative position of the pensioner estimated with sufficient generality for the comparison to be informative. Thus one may estimate the proportion of average manual earnings which will be replaced by a pension in different countries. On this basis it becomes clear that British pensions are indeed low by comparison with those in the six European countries. By extending the calculation it can also be shown that the comparison is increasingly more favourable to Britain as one turns attention to the replacement of incomes from work that were increasingly below average earnings. This conclusion follows naturally from the flat-rate basis of the British pension. The same is true of the Dutch flat-rate pension although the general level of income replacement is higher in the Netherlands than in the UK at all levels. The calculation in the succeeding chapters is first carried out in terms of gross income, which is the usual procedure. We have felt it desirable, however, to extend the calculation in order to cover pensions as a percentage of income net of direct taxes. The results are set out in Part III, where it will be seen that Britain's replacement ratio is then somewhat improved but remains low. To say this is not necessarily to imply that our position on the league table was something to be ashamed of. A low record for income replacement but a successful record in assisting the poor is one that we might feel we could defend—if we were quite satisfied that that was our record.

A misleading impression would be conveyed if the existing position in the UK and Holland were compared simply with the targets for income replacement in the European countries. For there are old people in some of these countries with incomplete pension claims under general or special schemes or with no claims at all except to low 'social pensions' subject to means tests. There is also reason to suspect that in some cases the incomes reported for taxation to which pensions will ultimately relate have been less than the incomes actually received.

VI—INFLATION AND GROWTH

When pension levels or poverty levels have been fixed at whatever positions seem appropriate, these positions must be held in face of changes in the value of money. In principle, the pensioner should be protected against inflation. In practice, he is often said to be one of the principal victims. Is this in fact the case? What does the evidence show?

In the succeeding chapters a good deal of attention will be devoted to this issue. It will be seen that the retired person with an official pension has been much better protected against inflation than is often alleged. This is clearly the case in Britain, where pensions have gone up over the years by substantially more than prices with the result that, by 1972, the real value of pensions was nearly twice as high as in 1948 when the new social insurance scheme, inspired by the Beveridge Report, was brought into operation. In the six European countries pensions have also risen in real terms over the trend, and this is also true of the USA.[1]

In the short run the situation is different and pensions may be eroded by inflation between the periodic pension reviews. The techniques employed for making these adjustments vary from country to country. In some cases there are threshold formulae by which pensions will be adjusted upwards whenever prices (or wages) rise by more than a specified amount. In other cases the

---

[1] See charts on p. 405–414.

reviews take place at specified intervals and pensions are then adjusted in line with prices (or wages) sometimes by means of an averaging formula (as in Germany and in France). For those retired people who have low incomes, the lag between adjustments may create problems when prices are rising rapidly. Moreover their sense of security will obviously be greater if they know in advance that changes will be made at specific times or when some specified threshold has been passed.

In Britain pensions used to be reviewed at irregular intervals. Then the reviews were held every two years but this changed to annual reviews under the pressure of inflation. British pensioners have been assured that their pensions will be raised once a year at least by the amount needed to offset rising prices. That is to say, pensions are now raised as frequently as most incomes from work. Whether even annual changes would be frequent enough might be doubtful if prices were to continue to rise at the pace reached in 1972. Perhaps adjustments twice a year might appear to be necessary, as in the Netherlands. Or some threshold formula might have to be devised. It is certainly of great interest to look at the European arrangements and consider the speed and sensitivity of the devices employed. It is also necessary to keep in mind the fact that rapid adjustments in a time of inflation add to the inflation itself. Thus the effect on general economic policy has to be taken into account although there might be support for the value judgement that the old have a particularly high claim to protection.

The USA is clearly the laggard among the countries with which we are primarily concerned. There has been no automatic adjustment, and the increases in pensions have come irregularly. From the beginning of 1975, there will be an official mechanism for raising pensions when prices increase. Thus uncertainty will be reduced. It is only fair to add that in the past US pensions have gone up by substantially more than was required to protect the pensioners from inflation.

In investigating the arrangements for linking pensions to prices or wages as the case may be, it is necessary to distinguish between the linking (or dynamizing) of *pension rights* and the linking (or dynamizing) of *pensions in payment*. The first point arises when the right to a pension is based on income received over a period of years, perhaps over a whole life-time at work. A convenient

example is to be found in the conditions set down for the
recognition of occupational schemes in the pension plan which
became law in Britain in 1973. (Although the reference in
this example is to private schemes, the same reasoning can
be applied to public ones.) One of the several possible tests
which a scheme has to pass in order to be recognized is that a
pension should be provided equivalent to 1 per cent of earnings
each year as assessed for tax. If a man worked forty years and
if his income remained unchanged over his life-time, then he
would, of course, get 40 per cent of his final year's pay as his
pension—a very decent pension to have in addition to the basic
state pension. But the assumption of constant earnings is crucial. If
his earnings have risen, partly with inflation and partly in real
terms, then his pension may be a far smaller proportion of his final
earnings. The 'dynamizing' of pension rights is designed to cope
with this kind of problem. Thus the figures for yearly income
might be scaled up year by year and expressed in the price level of
the final year of work, or of the first year in retirement. Or the
adjustment might be made by using a wage index rather than a
price index. These adjusted figures might not then be required to
yield a pension equivalent to 1 per cent a year; that coefficient
could be adjusted as might seem appropriate. But the real value
of future pensions would no longer be left as uncertain as in the case
where previous earnings are not adjusted. Some of the European
schemes are designed to provide this kind of protection. To introduce another bit of jargon, pension rights are 'revalorized'.

These adjustments will affect the pension first received after
retirement and further arrangements are needed for the adjustment
of pensions in payment. There will presumably be general agreement that pensioners should be protected against inflation and
differences of opinion will relate only to the speed and the manner
in which adjustments are made. A different proposition has,
however, been put forward. This is that the pensioner should be
given a share in the real growth of the economy.

What does this mean? If it means that pensions should rise in
sympathy with gross national product or with total expenditure on
consumption, this condition has often been satisfied and more
than satisfied. Or it may mean that the average pension should rise
in real terms in line with average output a head, or average consumption a head, or average wages. Which is it to be?

In a number of countries, pensions are linked to the wage level and move upwards in sympathy with it. In Britain there is no official formula designed to bring such adjustments about and no general undertaking that changes on this scale will be made. In practice, however, this is what has occurred.[1] Thus the British pensioner has not only been protected against inflation over the years but has been given his share in growth, though accelerating inflation has created problems. This is *not* to imply that pensions are therefore high enough, still less too high. For what we are concerned with here are simply relative rates of growth. Even a roughly proportionate rate of growth leaves the UK pension for the average wage-earner at a lower level relatively to average earnings than our other European countries or the USA regard as appropriate, at least in principle.

VII—OCCUPATIONAL SCHEMES AND FUNDING

The term 'occupational pension' is ambiguous. In Britain and America one may be inclined to think of these as private complementary arrangements for making payments in addition to basic public pensions. But a different pattern has emerged in some countries. To begin with we must distinguish between the occupational pensions of former public servants and those of people formerly in private industry. The pensions paid by the state to its former employees are sometimes a substitute for the general official pension instead of being paid in addition to it. There may also be official schemes for groups of employees in private industry which are separate from the general pension. In Italy there are quite a number of such arrangements and separate schemes for railway workers and miners are not uncommon elsewhere. Thus there are what are called 'special schemes' for both public and private employees, which are on the 'first-tier'. When

---

[1] See Chart 1 on p. 405, below. It is true that pensions have not quite kept pace with hourly earnings and the latter may be taken to be the more appropriate index because shorter hours of work can be regarded as a form of higher real income. But pensions have fallen less behind weekly earnings. Moreover it is on weekly earnings that the social security contribution is levied. In international comparisons, indices of hourly earnings have often to be used for reasons of statistical comparability.

occupational schemes are private, they form a 'second-tier' and are included in the category of 'complementary' or 'supplementary' pensions.

The provisions made by the state for its own employees are usually on a fairly generous scale and account for a substantial proportion of total expenditure on the elderly.[1] These official occupational schemes are on a pay-as-you-go basis—like official general schemes. These pensions are backed by the power of the state to raise money by compulsion. Private occupational schemes have not this backing and security must be sought in some other way. What this often means is that the private schemes are funded and this in turn raises the question whether funded schemes can perform as well as schemes based on pay-as-you-go.

The merits and weaknesses of funded schemes are of immediate and direct concern to people in Britain and the Netherlands. For, as we have already recorded, both countries are to rely upon private occupational schemes which will be mainly funded, for their second-tier pensions. In Britain there will be an official alternative in the form of the Reserve Scheme but this too will be funded—indeed more strictly so than many private schemes. In the USA, West Germany, Sweden and Belgium there are official graduated schemes on a pay-as-you-go basis but occupational pensions are also, of course, important. In Italy private occupational schemes have a very minor role and in France, where such schemes have a very important role, the basis is the pay-as-you-go principle, not funding.

Private occupational pensions might simply be paid out from the current revenue of each firm concerned. The snag is, of course, that with pay-as-you-go in each firm, no sufficiently reliable guarantee can be provided for payments some of which may be far in the future. A step towards slightly greater security for the pensioner is provided when pension claims are at least recorded as a liability in the firm's balance sheet. This procedure is followed in a number of our countries, notably in West Germany, the USA and Sweden. The advantages from the firm's point of view is that contributions for pensions can be a source for providing funds for direct investment in the firm itself. The disadvantage is that pensions are still at hazard for the firm may not do well and may

---

[1] See Part II for schemes in the individual countries.

even close down. It may be possible, as in Sweden, to insure against this risk.[1] An alternative which has usually been adopted by Britain, the USA and the Netherlands among our eight countries is to create a special pension fund outside the firm with an independent life of its own which will hold securities or property with an appropriate spreading of risk.

The pension may then depend simply upon the contributions made and upon the rate of return achieved. Its amount will not be fixed beforehand either in absolute amount or as a fraction of salary. This is the 'cash purchase' method. It has declined in popularity over the years but the British Government clearly has something of the sort in mind for the official Reserve Scheme. What is more customary nowadays is to provide pensions which are a fraction of final income or of income over a number of years or a whole lifetime.

Private occupational schemes which grow up naturally are likely to vary in several respects. It is, in fact, this variety which has been regarded as their principal merit. Instead of having a uniform, centrally imposed set of arrangements, let various alternatives emerge and let collective bargaining affect a man's position in retirement as well as during his working life. This was the view put forward some years ago by Professor Michael Fogarty.[2] In fact some state intervention is to be expected and, if sufficiently restricted, need not deprive these schemes of the merits claimed for them. In the first place, some official regulation and supervision may simply serve to make the schemes more sufficiently secure. Secondly, further action may be needed to ensure that pension rights are not lost on a change of job. The Swedes and the Dutch have turned their attention to this problem and the British Government is pledged to do so under the Social Security Act of 1973. But a big step towards state control is taken when, as in Britain in the future, people will be *required* to belong to a recognized occupational scheme or to the official Reserve Scheme. Still further interference with private action is entailed when minimum standards are prescribed for contributions or benefits as a condition for the official recognition of schemes.

It may then be asked whether it is really worth while to have thousands of different schemes. Whatever the answer in the

---

[1] For an account of these special Swedish arrangements, see p. 179–80, below.
[2] *The Undergoverned and the Overgoverned*, Chapman, 1962.

hypothetical case of a country starting from scratch, the fact remains that these schemes are there and, if reasonably well managed, there may seem to be a case for leaving them alone provided certain conditions are satisfied. If, moreover, the Government wants complementary pensions to be funded, then an official takeover would imply a quite gargantuan official pension fund with all sorts of implications for the capital market. But, it may be asked, is it right in any case to lay such stress on funding as has been done in Britain? From the point of view of the pensioner, will a funded scheme be as satisfactory? Will funded schemes afford adequate protection against inflation? Will pensions derived from accumulated funds reflect the real growth of the economy as official pay-as-you-go pensions have come to do in a number of countries? If the latter have more to offer the pensioner on balance, what offsetting advantages, if any, can be claimed for funded schemes from a national point of view?

These questions will be encountered again in the chapters on the individual countries in Part II and will be further discussed on a comparative basis in Part III. It is, however, helpful to set out the alternative assumptions in a more rigorous manner and this I have sought to do in the Mathematical Appendix. Meanwhile this introductory discussion can usefully be carried forward a little further by noting that the case for funding would be weakened if the insecurity of pay-as-you-go pensions derived from a single firm could be removed. This could be largely achieved if firms formed some large co-operative institutions for the purpose of handling their pensions. Each firm would then pay the current contributions for pensions into an appropriate co-operative which in turn would become responsible for paying the pensions. No fund need be accumulated, apart from a small reserve, but the pensioners would be protected by the spreading of risks against the danger that any particular firm would be unable to meet its obligations. This, as we shall see, is broadly what has been done in France. Why, it may be asked, should Britain not follow a similar course? Pensions organized in this way are well protected against inflation and no problem of vesting or transferability arises.[1] There is a further point. 'Blanketing-in' becomes easy. That is to say

---

[1] When a worker leaves one job for another his claim to a pension from his former employer may be protected by his right being 'vested'. Or he might have his credit transferred to the pension fund of his new employer.

pensions can be given quickly or increased quickly without a long waiting period for the accumulation of funds.

It is the common experience in a number of countries that the cover provided by private occupational pensions is very uneven. Generally speaking a high proportion of the white collar workers have acquired such claims but among the blue collar workers the position is different. Many of the latter have no claims, or very small ones. It would be possible for a Government to take the line that this unevenness was not its concern. As we have seen, its responsibility might be said to stop at providing a tolerable minimum as a protection against poverty and the rest might be left to spontaneous private arrangements. It is a different matter when an official decision has been taken to make second-tier occupational pensions compulsory. It can then be a source of embarrassment that many workers have no claims to such pensions or only trivial ones. For, on a strictly funded basis, forty years or more will be needed to earn a full pension. Thus the official Reserve Scheme is not expected to pay full pensions until the year AD 2019. Private occupational pensions may well do better because less closely wedded to the cash-purchase principle. Whether a firm sets up a scheme of its own or asks an insurance company or mutual society to do so for it, the arrangements made are likely to be more flexible than those apparently contemplated for the official Reserve Scheme. Thus the older workers may receive pensions larger than could strictly be justified on the basis of accumulated contributions, i.e. on the cash-purchase principle. It may be objected that, if the sum to be spent on pensions is given, then this generosity towards the older worker may be at the expense of the younger worker. In reply it might be argued that the older workers should not be penalized on retirement because the pension arrangements had not been made at an earlier stage. In any case, it is, perhaps, misleading to suppose that the sum made available for pensions is given for more may be provided in order to benefit the older workers. Such flexibility is important. The fact remains that there is likely to be a substantial lag before it can be said that the great majority of blue collar workers have occupational pensions of a substantial size.

A pay-as-you-go arrangement would obviously permit a great speeding up. It may be asked whether such an expansion of the outlay on pensions would not place a heavy additional burden on

c

contributors or on the general taxpayer. For if the accumulated fund is insufficient, where will the extra money come from? The answer is, of course, that contributions could remain unchanged but could be passed on immediately to pensioners instead of being accumulated in a fund. Some of these pensioners would get pensions that were substantially larger than could be 'justified' by contributions made on their behalf. They could, therefore, be said to be receiving a bonus—or an inter-generational transfer. But at whose expense? The current contributors have been assumed to be paying no more. The difference is that no fund will be accumulating to their credit. (Or rather no further increases in existing funds would be made from new contributions.) But they, in due course, would expect to be looked after in their retirement on a pay-as-you-go basis by a new working generation.

This is what Professor Paul Samuelson called the 'Social Security Paradox'. To quote from a well-known passage: 'Let mankind enter into a Hobbes–Rousseau social contract in which the young are assured of their retirement subsistence if they will today support the aged, such support to be guaranteed by a draft on the yet-unborn.'[1] Or, as Dr Onorato Castellino has put it: 'Perhaps we might say that the burden is imposed on to the last generation, the one which comes of age when the pension scheme is abolished or the end of the centuries comes.'[2]

So far, of course, only one side of the case has been presented. There are two main points to be made on the other side.

First, there is the question of security. Whereas it is possible to protect the pensioner against the risk that his firm will go bankrupt, the pay-as-you-go basis leaves him dependent upon the willingness of people in the working generation to contribute.[3] There may indeed be no real danger of a complete repudiation of responsibility, but the flow of contributions might be raised only at a disappointing rate—perhaps by less than enough to provide the linkage of pensions to wages that is sometimes claimed as the great merit of unfunded schemes. The danger is perhaps greater when

---

[1] 'An Exact Consumption-Loan Model of Interest with or without the Social Contrivance of Money', *Journal of Political Economy*, Dec. 1958, pp. 479–80.

[2] *Public Finance*, 1971, p. 465n. See also pp. 59–60 and 266 below.

[3] This danger has been stressed by Professor James Buchanan even with regard to the official pay-as-you-go pension in the USA. 'Social Insurance in a Growing Economy: a Proposal for Radical Reform', *National Tax Journal*, 1968. See the footnote to page 16, above.

pensioners are directly dependent upon payments from the general exchequer and are therefore at the mercy of annual budgetary requirements. Even then benefits may not be cut but may not rise much in real terms. The danger is probably less with autonomous pay-as-you-go schemes as in France; but there, too, demographic developments are imposing strains.

One must add at once that the alternative funding basis also entails risks. Admittedly the risk in current money terms can be eliminated, or largely so, by investment in fixed interest securities, but the return in real terms would then—to say the least of it—be gravely at risk. Investment in equities and property provides a hedge against inflation and some promise of a growing real return with the growth of the economy; but it need scarcely be said that uncertainty remains especially when the cash-purchase basis is stressed as in the official Reserve Scheme. Thus both funded and unfunded arrangements involve their respective dangers that have to be assessed in the light of particular circumstances. It may be reasonable, however, to guess that the risk entailed in pay-as-you-go arrangements will be less because official powers of compulsion can be extended to contribution rates. This may be reassuring for the pensioner, if not for the contributor.

The second argument in favour of funding is a different one. It is the claim that saving can thus be increased and ought to be so increased. The first step in deploying this argument is to challenge the view that pensions are merely transfers to be provided over any period from current production. For the level of production is not something that is given and fixed but may be affected by the flow of savings and investment and thus by the manner in which pensions are financed. In so far as these pensions are derived from funds invested in industry or property, the pensions correspond to a productive contribution, according to the usual conventions, and should not be regarded in the same light as social security transfers. The Samuelson argument presented above is now seen as only a special case; for Samuelson was explicitly excluding capital accumulation. When this special assumption is removed, his conclusion must also be changed.

Here we are becoming involved in far-reaching issues. As a first step, it is at least possible to acquire some sense of perspective by looking at the statistics for the finance of investment. The next question may appear at first sight more difficult. What would be the net effect on savings of reducing the flow into funded pension schemes? Would there be an offsetting rise in other forms of personal saving? The answer is not in fact so difficult after all for there is no reason to suppose that people will be paying less as pension contributions. Thus the personal propensity to save may be unchanged. It is rather that the proceeds will be differently employed. Instead of being accumulated in a fund these payments will be passed on at once to people who will spend them. A net decline in saving is therefore to be expected unless some other form of offsetting action can be taken by Government. If there is some fall in the funds available for investment the national output may be at a lower level thereafter with implications for future pensioners as for the rest of the population. Here, of course, we are involved in growth theory and the clouds begin to gather. We are also liable to become involved in attempts to explain differences in rates of growth or levels of real output in different countries. To take specific examples, how has France fared in finding the resources for investment with complementary pensions on an unfunded basis? What other institutional differences are relevant? How do such institutional differences affect not only real output but the possibility of having successful funded schemes? Both the USA and the UK with their highly developed stock exchanges are clearly better placed in this respect than some of the European countries. These are large and complex issues. It goes without saying that they are not issues which can be treated at all adequately in the present volume. It should also go without saying that such matters must be kept in mind even if their implications cannot be adequately explored in these pages. For these wider issues have naturally affected Governments in choosing between different possible schemes and should clearly be brought into the reckoning if any final assessment of alternatives is being made.

PART II

CHAPTER TWO

The Federal Republic of Germany

I—INTRODUCTION

The German statutory pension system is generous in the benefits it provides and, comparatively speaking, it is straightforward both in organization and in the social objectives it is meant to serve. There are two schemes of dominating importance, those for blue-collar workers and white-collar workers respectively. These schemes are indeed so similar in their arrangements and so integrated in their operation as to constitute almost a single scheme. Although these two schemes are not completely comprehensive, the self-employed and public employees still being covered in other ways, it remains true that Germany has nothing like the number of special first-tier schemes to be found in, say, France or Italy.[1] In this respect Germany is more similar to the Netherlands, Britain or Sweden. This is so at the basic level or the 'first tier'. At the second tier, there are no official complementary schemes. The state is responsible for the basic graduated pensions and any responsibility for providing more than this rests with the private pension schemes.

In many countries, official pensions are designed with two

---

[1] Table 2.1 indicates the over-riding importance of the two main schemes in terms of expenditure. The importance of the special pension scheme for public servants can also be clearly seen. This group is entirely exempt from membership of one of the social insurance schemes.

objectives in mind: first, the provision of a basic minimum as a safeguard against poverty and, second, the replacement of some tolerable proportion of income during retirement. Some compromise then results. In Germany the position is more clear-cut. The stated objective is to replace about 60 per cent of income after a standard working life of forty years up to a maximum of about twice the individual's average gross pre-retirement earnings. It is hoped that statutory pensions will be supplemented by private schemes.[1] Thus these pensions should allow a person to maintain his status in old age and to enjoy an income which is not too drastically below what he has had in his earlier years subject to this ceiling. Pensions are related to contributions (actual or otherwise accredited). It will be appreciated, therefore, that although the official pension schemes are unfunded, the insurance principle is otherwise rather firmly applied: there is no minimum pension,[2] no allowance for dependent spouses and no restriction on the earnings of pensioners.

The apparent simplicity of the German arrangements may, however, raise questions which are not so simple. Thus the absence of any minimum in the pensions scale may seem to imply a somewhat ruthless disregard of the other traditional objective of pension schemes: the provision of enough assistance to prevent serious hardship. The Germans, themselves, in discussing their pension schemes, sometimes speak in a manner which seems to confirm this apparently callous approach. 'Poverty does not interest us in Germany,' said one of those interviewed. But what does this mean? It may mean that poverty—as somehow defined—is successfully averted by the existing arrangements and is not, therefore, a problem. The numbers receiving means-tested assistance is simply identified in some countries with the numbers 'in poverty'. It might be expected that a substantial proportion of old people in Germany would be in poverty, in this sense of the term, for there is no minimum in the statutory scheme, and those in need must seek minimum assistance subject to means tests from the state governments. In fact, however, only about 3 per cent of

---

[1] The target is that a total of 75 per cent of previous gross income should be replaced by pension provisions, either statutory, occupational, or private.

[2] There was no minimum pension in the two general statutory schemes until 1973. Since then a minimum pension has been payable in certain very restricted circumstances. This is discussed in full in Section IV.

the old have to fall back on help of this kind—or choose to do so. Special means-tested assistance to war victims affords a partial explanation. In part the explanation also lies in the fact that the basic pensions are not only designed to replace a substantial proportion of income but pensions on a fairly generous scale have been provided for those elderly people who had retired too soon after the establishment of the schemes to have a full record of contributions. That is to say, additional contributions have, in effect, been credited to them. The pay-as-you-go technique has thus been used to permit 'blanketing-in'. All these points may help to explain the situation with regard to poverty. As always, of course, it must be borne in mind that 'poverty' is an ambiguous concept. Is it to be interpreted in relative or absolute terms? Is it moreover to be resented as a social grievance or viewed as evidence of personal failure which some may seek to conceal even at the cost of forgoing assistance? There may be national differences to take into account.

At the other end of the scale are those whose incomes exceed the maximum of the basic general scheme. For them income replacement will be on a more modest scale. One might expect substantial supplements to be provided by private pension schemes. These are not, indeed, negligible, but, as we shall see, they have not expanded as much in size or developed as fully in sophistication as might have been expected.

The official pensions in Germany are adjusted every year in line with a lagged three-year average of wages. This is another generous feature of the arrangements. It is also, as will be seen, a feature which is giving cause for some anxiety in view of demographic developments.

So far we have been concerned with pensions but these are, of course, only part of the story. Thus in Section V, we look at other areas of policy such as the special attempts in Germany to encourage personal saving, the provision of housing allowances, the assistance with medical costs and the other general social services. Germany's experience in some of these other areas—especially, perhaps, the encouragement of thrift and the manner of assistance with housing—may be of interest and value to other countries. Although the record in most of these fields does not seem to be open to heavy criticism there are naturally some deficiencies. The provision of community services for the elderly and the provision of geriatric facilities in hospitals or residential homes leaves much to be desired. This area has tended to remain in the shadow while income-maintenance provisions have stolen the limelight. There are, however, signs that this is changing and that these services will soon be developed more fully as has already been done with regard to official pensions.

II—INCOME PROVISIONS FOR THE ELDERLY

(a) *Statutory pension insurance: the general schemes*

Any review of pensions in Germany must of necessity devote the bulk of attention to statutory pensions which form the first tier of provisions and also constitute the main source of income for the vast majority of the elderly. Statutory pensions have, however, not always been of such importance. For much of their history they have provided essentially a minimum income which had to be supplemented by income from other sources. The turning point came in 1957 with the major pension reform which forms the basis of current provisions.[1]

The historical background may be briefly recorded. Pension insurance in Germany has a long history, dating back to Bismarck's social reforms at the end of the nineteenth century. This first scheme was designed to protect the worker against abject poverty and had strong paternalistic undertones. Bismarck's prime aim was to increase the dependence of the working classes on the state and thus forestall socialist tendencies.[2]

This pension scheme provided a basic minimum pension payable to all insured plus a supplement related to the amount of contributions paid to the scheme. Membership of the scheme was confined to employees. In accordance with his paternalistic doctrine, Bismarck had intended that the scheme should be financed by general taxation, but he was defeated by his Government on this issue and the scheme was instead financed on a funded basis

---

[1] In the course of writing this chapter, we have benefited greatly from discussions with Roger J. Lawson, formerly a senior member of the research team at Glasgow.

[2] For a full discussion of the origins of social insurance in Germany, see Gaston V. Rimlinger, *Welfare Policy and Industrialization in Europe, America and Russia*, Wiley, New York, 1971.

by the contributions of employers and employees. The administration of the scheme was in the hands of corporate pension institutes whose executive bodies were formed by elected representatives of those concerned in the insurance scheme; that is, employers and employees. The pension insurance scheme in this form showed remarkable stability and survived with few changes until the end of World War II. Even after the drastic inflation of 1923/4, when the pension funds were virtually wiped out, the use of a system of revalorization made it possible to rebuild the scheme along its original lines. The first change of note was the setting up of a separate pension insurance scheme for white collar workers in 1911, to function alongside that for manual workers. Secondly, in 1934, with the advent of National Socialism, the self-administration structure was abolished and replaced by so-called 'leadership from above' in accordance with the principles of the National Socialist movement. The benefit structure, however, remained unchanged. Benefits continued on the whole to be small, and had generally to be supplemented from some other source. This stability was, however, destroyed during and after World War II, and change became vital if pension insurance provisions were to remain in existence at all.

The immediate post-war period, between 1945 and 1957, can be viewed as a period of transition. Emergency regulations were in force. During the occupation the occupying powers sought to rebuild the pension insurance scheme but records had been destroyed or were incomplete, and thousands of pension claims remained unprocessed. To make matters worse, experienced personnel was lacking to deal with these administrative problems because of dismissals by the Nazi authorities on the ground of race or political creed. There was some discussion at the time of a reform of pension arrangements by the occupying powers, but this was never carried out. On the one hand there were difficulties in co-ordinating the activities in the four zones. On the other hand, even more urgent problems required attention, such as the influx of refugees, the housing crisis, and the reconstruction of the economy in general. For the time being, therefore, pre-war pension insurance provisions were retained (except in the Soviet zone).[1]

---

[1] See 'Social Insurance in Post-War Germany' by Max Bloch in *International Labour Review*, September 1948, pp. 306–44.

Circumstances were such, however, that a reform could not be delayed indefinitely. That it was not implemented without considerable delay, even after the setting up of the Federal Republic in 1949, was merely indicative of the complexity of the current issues and of the recognized need for a major reform. One factor was, of course, the post-war inflation and ensuing currency reform of 1948, when the mark was revalued at only one fifteenth of its nominal value. As far as the elderly were concerned this had serious implications. It will be remembered that the statutory pension had been designed only to supplement other forms of income. Many of the elderly had, however, lost their private sources of income in the war; those who had managed to hold on to their savings then found them destroyed by the currency collapse. The majority were, therefore, dependent solely on the state for support, but inflation had seriously affected the pension insurance schemes. A large part of the pension fund reserves were wiped out by the post-war inflation.[1] Admittedly the fund could have been revalorized, as happened in the 1920s, but the alternative solution chosen was to finance pensions from current contributions levied on employers and employees and to an increasing extent from subsidies from the central authorities. When, for example, attempts were made in 1949 and 1951 to improve the income position of the old by raising benefit levels, the additional cost was almost entirely met from general taxation.

The finance in this way of insurance provisions through general taxation was quite foreign to the German concept of social security. A clear distinction had traditionally been maintained between contributory pension insurance and the non-contributory assistance scheme. The post-war developments blurred this basic distinction and created a situation which was unacceptable to the status-conscious Germans. Many of the elderly population (as well as other groups) had to supplement whatever pension benefit they might receive by not only public assistance allowances, but also help from charitable organizations, families and friends. The position was unsatisfactory and could only be tolerated as an interim measure until a long-term solution to the problems of pension insurance provision could be found. This long-term solution, the 1957 pension insurance reform, entailed a complete

---

[1] Only a very small part of the pension funds had been invested in equities; the Nazi Government had required the fund to be invested in government securities.

break away from the schemes of the past and the introduction of what was claimed to be a 'new concept in pension insurance'.[1]

The mood of the time was one of distrust among the general public as well as the occupying powers of any form of central power. 'People now had only one urgent desire: to be rid of every sort of tutelage, to see state regulation dismantled, to recover the freedom to exert individual energies. In short, the nation craved a more liberal economic order.'[2]

This craving for a more liberal economic order found its expression in the writings of a group of so-called neo-liberal economists at the University of Freiburg (one of the most prominent being Ludwig Erhard), who advocated an economic order based on free competition—a market economy. This group conceded, however, that state intervention would be permissible if it were 'market-conforming'; if, in other words, it were limited to situations where it was necessary to promote or simulate market conditions which would otherwise not exist. This concept was taken one step further by Professor Müller-Armack, who suggested that intervention would be justified in cases where the free working of market forces would have socially undesirable consequences. The aim of his economic doctrine, which became known as the *Social Market Economy* and was adopted by the Federal Republic, was not economic freedom alone, but 'a combination of freedom and justice'.[3] In so far as social and economic policy are inter-related, the projected pension reform had to be compatible with general economic thinking. Thus these economic principles were, as we shall see, of considerable importance in determining the nature of the pension insurance reform which was to follow.

It is true that some of the general features of the previous pension insurance scheme relating to coverage and administration were retained in 1957 if these were in accordance with the new doctrine. Thus coverage continued to be organized on an occupational basis. The two main schemes, referred to in this study as the

---

[1] 'Pension Reform in the Federal Republic of Germany' by Professor Dr Kurt Jantz, *International Labour Review*, 1961, p. 136. Dr Jantz was closely involved in the pension reforms as Ministerialdirektor at the Ministry of Labour and Social Affairs.

[2] Cf. *The German Economy 1870 to the Present* by Gustav Stolper, Weidenfeld and Nicolson, 1967, p. 204.

[3] Cf. *Die Wirtschafts-und Sozialordnung* by H. Lampert, Günter Olzog Verlag, München, 1966, p. 56.

'general' schemes, were for manual workers and white collar employees. Although benefits granted by the two schemes were identical, conditions relating to compulsory membership differed. Whereas all manual workers were under an insurance obligation, this applied only to those white collar workers whose incomes were below a certain affiliation limit.[1] Above this limit voluntary membership was possible, but only on certain conditions.

This exclusion from compulsory membership of higher paid white collar workers was in accordance with the principle known as 'subsidiarity'. In the sphere of social provisions the social market economists believed that the individual should be allowed wherever possible to make his own provisions for old age (and other contingencies). It seemed feasible that those white collar workers excluded from compulsory coverage would be able to do so.[2] Only in circumstances where the individual was likely to be unable to make his own provisions or where certain conditions existed in which this would be difficult should the state intervene. The principle of subsidiarity is, in other words, that the will of the state is subsidiary to that of the individual.

It is interesting that this principle of subsidiarity, if wholeheartedly adopted, should have meant that state intervention, although undoubtedly necessary in the post-war period, should have ceased as soon as the individual was in a position to make his own personal provision for old age. This has, however, not happened. An opposing tendency—not confined to Germany—has become apparent for social provisions to be maintained once they have been introduced. The schemes have survived and have indeed grown although circumstances have changed.

A third scheme for employed persons existed in the mining employees' scheme, and there were small separate schemes for independent farmers and independent artisans. These last two groups formed the exception to the general principle adopted in the reform that the self-employed, in view of the subsidiarity principle, should not be subject to compulsory membership of a statutory pension insurance scheme since it was generally felt that

---

[1] In both schemes there is no insurance obligation for persons in temporary low paid jobs, students, those undergoing retraining or persons receiving free keep in lieu of payment. All public employees are also exempt since they have their own special scheme.

[2] When the affiliation limit was set in 1957 it excluded in fact only about 5 per cent of white collar employees.

they were in a position to make personal provision. The self-employed farmers and artisans, as well as the miners, were, however, subject to special economic pressures (as we will see in the following section), and considered therefore to be in need of special pension insurance coverage. We shall return later to look at the schemes for these special groups, but in the meantime attention will be devoted to the two general pension insurance schemes for manual and white collar workers.

The occupational basis of pension provision is reflected also in the administrative structure of the schemes, a second feature retained from the Bismarckian period. The administration of pension insurance continued to be in the hands of the self-governing autonomous pension institutes which were re-established in 1951–52 after being abolished during the Nazi regime. These institutes, of which there are twenty for the manual workers' scheme and one centralized institute for the white collar workers' scheme, are formed by elected representatives of the two sides of industry. The central government establishes the framework and the scale of provisions and has a certain supervisory capacity; it does not however interfere in the day-to-day administration of the scheme. The retention of this administrative structure in 1957 helped, therefore, to allay fears of central Government intervention as well as conforming to neo-liberal theories of decentralization.

It is clearly not in coverage or administration that the pension reform represented a complete break with the past. It is in benefit structure, benefits level and the financial basis of the schemes that a radical change in approach is visible.

The pension insurance schemes continued after 1957, as before, to provide not only old age benefits, but survivors' provisions and disability provisions, a combination which is not uncommon in the countries of the EEC. In the interests of simplicity, however, we shall couch the following discussion in terms of the old age pension alone. It need only be noted that the other provisions follow the same basic pattern with only small variations in the benefit formula.

As has been observed, it had become increasingly difficult in the interim period between the end of the war and the pension reform to differentiate between assistance and insurance provisions. Even before the war the pension schemes had had a somewhat hybrid nature, combining a minimum flat-rate allowance with a supplement based on contributions. It was, therefore, the intention of the

1957 reform to bring about a clear separation of the two objectives:
the provision of minimum incomes financed on a tax-transfer basis
and the replacement of income based on the insurance principle.
The first task, that of protecting the individual against need, was
removed from the pension insurance schemes and became the
responsibility of the public assistance scheme alone, or the social
aid scheme as it later became known. The use of the pension as an
instrument of vertical or horizontal income redistribution was
discontinued. The new scheme had no minimum benefits and no
allowance for the insured's spouse (athough, with some inconsistency, a supplement was to be paid for dependent children).

The pension insurance schemes were allocated the role of
maintaining in old age the status which the individual had attained
during his working life. A fully earnings-related pension was
therefore introduced. In an attempt to provide insurance protection in a manner which would be 'market-conforming' there was
no longer to be any qualitative distinction between income from
work, earned in the market, and income from old age pension
provisions. It was argued that 'work is acknowledged during a
person's active life in the form of wages and other benefits, and
after retirement in the form of pension and other benefits. Wage
and pension are both paid in acknowledgement of work. . . . Wages
and pension are considered on a par, both being designed to pre-
serve the individual's social status'.[1] In short, the principle of a
universal and uniform benefit was firmly discarded in 1957 and
pensions became 'individual'.

The importance of 'status' which pervades the German social
insurance system is doubtless of some sociological interest. We
have already seen some evidence of the status-conscious nature of
the schemes in the differentiation of manual workers and white
collar workers. We shall become aware of it again when looking at
the special pension provisions for that privileged group of employees, the public servants.

If the pension was to be a true acknowledgement of the individual's contribution to the productive process, then it had to take
into consideration not simply the individual's earnings during his
working life but also the length of this working life. Allowance is

---

[1] Professor Dr Kurt Jantz *op. cit.*, pp. 138–9.

made for both these factors in the pension formula. As regards the length of the *insurance record*, it is interesting to note how the framing of pension rights in these terms, that is in terms of contribution to production rather than in terms of a financial contribution to a pension fund, made it possible for a system of accredited periods to be introduced when calculating pension rights. This approach also allowed the introduction of an unfunded system of finance which was to facilitate greatly the process of blanketing-in. Thus, despite the official qualifying period of fifteen years, pensions of a reasonable size could be paid almost immediately after the reform of 1957 without a lengthy transitional period in which pension rights would need to be accumulated. Credit was, and is, given for so-called substitute periods and periods of non-payment[1] when for some reason the individual is not in a position to work or to pay contributions.

With a given insurance record, the status of each pensioner is maintained by means of that part of the pension formula known as the 'personal basis of assessment' (*die persönliche Bemessungsgrundlage*), or the PBA as we shall refer to it. In each year of the insurance period[2] the individual's actual or imputed[3] earnings are calculated as a percentage of the average earnings of all insured in the two general schemes. These percentages are then averaged for the period as a whole, giving an indication of the individual's acquired status, on the implicit assumption, of course, that earnings are in fact a reflection of status. There is, however, a ceiling of 200 per cent of average earnings attached to the level of PBA which may be used in calculating the normal old age pension. Some benefit is paid for any value in excess of this figure, but the calculation is carried out on a much less favourable basis than in

---

[1] Substitute periods (*Ersatzzeiten*) include periods of military service, internment, imprisonment by the Nazis, political imprisonment in the Soviet Zone or the DDR, or periods as a refugee (usually 1945–46). Credit is given for these periods to prevent the individual being placed at a disadvantage for reasons outside his control.

Periods of non-payment (*Ausfallzeiten*) cover periods when the individual is unable to continue in employment, such as during illness, periods of rehabilitation, unemployment, pregnancy, apprenticeship or retraining.

[2] The first five years of the insurance period may be disregarded if this is to the advantage of the insured.

[3] In the case of records of actual earnings being lost, as happened during the war, the insured is accredited with the earnings level corresponding to the average for his occupational group.

the case of the normal pension. Although this implies that there is in fact some element of vertical redistribution in the pension scheme at higher-earnings levels, it does not seem to be considered a departure from the general insurance principle. The existence of a ceiling to the normal pension indicates the level at which it is felt the individual, according to the subsidarity principle, can look after himself.

The length of the insurance period and the personal basis of assessment constitute the 'individual' elements of the pension formula. The base to which they are then applied is a measurement of average earnings prevailing at the time of the pension award. This is the so-called 'general basis of assessment' (*die allgemeine Bemessungsgrundlage*) or G B A. The G B A is a measurement of the average earnings of all insured persons in the two schemes over the three-year period prior to the year preceding the award. In the case of a pension award made in 1972, for example, the earnings values used in calculating the G B A for that year would be those for 1968, 1969 and 1970.[1]

Finally, a predetermined *coefficient* is applied which has the effect of granting a certain percentage of the pensioner's earnings rating (as measured by the application of the P B A percentage to the general basis of assessment) for each year of insurance. In the case of the old age pension in the general schemes, the cofficient is 1·5 per cent, giving a target pension level of 60 per cent of pre-retirement earnings after a standard insurance period of forty years.[2]

The fact that such a high level of income replacement was introduced in the reform may seem surprising. It might instead have been expected that the principle of subsidiary would call for a considerably lower replacement figure through the statutory scheme, to which the individual could add by his own choice of

---

[1] The effect of this fairly substantial lag will be discussed in Section III.

[2] Thus the pension formula is:

$$P_{n+1} = \left[\frac{\sum \left(\frac{w_1}{W_1} + \frac{w_2}{W_2} + \cdots \frac{w_n}{W_n} \right)}{n} \right] \times \frac{nc}{100} \times \left[\frac{W(n-1) + W(n-2) + W(n-3)}{3} \right]$$

where P = the pension, w = individual earnings, W = average earnings of all insured, n = number of years insurance, and c = coefficient applicable to that pension.

personal provision. The argument which was put forward at the time, however, was not in terms of freedom of choice as regards form of provision but rather in terms of freedom of choice in the disposal of pension income. It was felt that the ability to choose to what use the pension should be put would be provided only if the income level was more than sufficient to meet basic subsistence requirements.

The importance placed on freedom of choice for the old person and on the insurance principle is reflected too in the *absence of a retirement condition* attached to receipt of the old age pension when it is paid at the normal pension age of sixty-five (to both men and women).[1] The one exception to this is when the pension is paid to women at the age of sixty. Since this concession has the explicit aim of allowing women who have been employed for a fairly lengthy period to leave the labour force at this age, retirement is a pre-requisite for payment of the benefit. It is of interest that the old age pension is paid at the age of sixty in one other instance, namely when the insured (male or female) has been continuously un-employed for more than one year.

Dynamic pensions. The major changes introduced in the course of the reform concerned not only the setting of the initial pension level. The adoption of this status-linked pension rather than a simple income-replacement target had implications also for the treatment of the benefit once it was in payment. 'Preservation of social status through social benefits is', it was emphasized, 'a dynamic principle. The social status of the individual must evolve in step with changes in the economic situation.'[2] It was therefore considered insufficient to ensure simply that pensions, once in payment, remained fixed in absolute terms or even retained their value relative to prices. In order to maintain the social link between the retired population and the active population, pensions had to be linked to changes in money income. This method of 'dynamizing' pension benefits is one of the most significant features of the German pension reform, both with regard to its direct effect on benefits in Germany itself, and its influence on thinking in the social policy field in other countries.

Pensions are reviewed annually by a specially constituted Social

---

[1] A flexible pension age was introduced in 1973. See p. 95 for details.

[2] Cf. Professor Dr Kurt Jantz, *op. cit.*, p. 138.

Advisory Board.[1] This Board is required to study the case for
pension adjustment having regard to changes in the wage level, in
productivity, in the per capita income of the active labour force
and in other similar variables. Despite this precaution of having
separate legislation for each adjustment, pensions in payment
have consistently been adjusted since the reform in line with
money wages, as expressed in the general basis of assessment, with
the sole exception of 1958, when no adjustment was made
to allow an appraisal of the macro-economic effects of the new
system.[2]

We have seen how the principles of the social market economy
affected the coverage and the form of benefits provided by the
pension insurance scheme. They also exerted considerable influence on the way in which these benefits were financed. The
financial basis of the new pension insurance schemes may, however, be taken to reflect the economic requirements of post-war
Germany as much as the ideologies of the reformers.

During the interim period before the reform of 1957 benefits
were financed to a large extent, as we have seen, from central
Government revenue. This system could not, however, be retained
in the pension reform proposals for two reasons. In the first place
it was too reminiscent of the public assistance scheme. Second, it
was likely to introduce an element of redistribution into the
system which would be at variance with the principles of the
reform. The alternative of financing benefits from pension funds
was also out of the question. The previous pension funds, which had
been destroyed by inflation and the subsequent currency reform,
had never been rebuilt. The rebuilding of such a fund which would
finance benefits from the interest earned on its assets entailed a long
transitional period before pensions of any magnitude could be paid,
whereas such benefits were necessary immediately.

The solution which was adopted to meet the criticisms of
general revenue financing was that no Government subsidies were
to be paid at all to finance old age pensions. It is true that a subsidy

---

[1] The Board comprises four representatives of the insured, four of the
employers, one representative of the Federal Bank and three of the social and
economic sciences.

[2] Since June 1973 there are no longer any statutory criteria which must be
considered in determining whether or not adjustment should take place. Thus it
has been officially recognized that there has never been any year in which they
have been able to influence the adjustment procedure.

was payable to the pension insurance schemes as a whole, but it was explicitly stated in the legislation that this should not be used to finance old age provisions.[1] It was decided that the scheme should instead be financed by contributions borne equally by employers and employees[2] and expressed as a percentage of earnings up to a contribution ceiling set at around one and a half times average manufacturing earnings.

The solution adopted to meet the second point—the difficulty of setting up a pension fund—was that the principle of funding be abandoned, and the new pension scheme financed on a pay-as-you-go basis.[3] The pensions of the current aged population were to be financed directly by the current working population according to the principle which the Germans refer to as 'solidarity of the generations'. There was in other words an implicit social contract in which the working population agreed to finance provisions for the current elderly population in the expectation that future generations would make the same provisions for them. In the words of the official government outline of the system, 'It is not the State which supports the aged from tax revenue, but it is the active members of the population who create the national product in which the workers and those no longer working have a share. . . . That is the solidarity of the generations, whereby the working population supports the elderly population.'[4] In ideological terms this served to reinforce the link between those at work and those in

---

[1] RVO (Pension Insurance Law) 1389, i. No information is available as to how this condition operates in practice. It is conceivable that the distinction is a purely academic one, but at the time of the reform this was considered important in that it emphasized the self-help nature of old age pension provisions and helped to convince the insured that the scheme would be free of state interference or manipulation. The state subsidies help to finance survivors' and disability pensions which, as we noted above, are also provided by the statutory pension schemes.

[2] In the case of voluntary insurance the insured persons had to bear the total cost alone. The employer was to bear the total burden in the case of very low paid workers; the ceiling was, however, set at such a low level that this condition is now virtually meaningless.

[3] In the initial ten-year period a fairly substantial fund was certainly to be built up, comprising, at the end of this period, enough to meet one year's expenditure on benefits. This was a precautionary measure in light of the uncertainty about the possible inflationary effects of the new form of finance. The reserve fund has, however, been run down since 1969.

[4] See Professor Dr Kurt Jantz, *Grundsatzfragen Sozialer Sicherheit, Sozialpolitik in Deutschland*, series No. 31, W. Kohlhammer Verlag, Stuttgart, 1964, p. 12.

retirement on which the benefit formula was based. In practical terms it also meant that pensions could be provided immediately.

At the time of the 1957 pension reform the decision not to rebuild the pension insurance funds gave rise to a considerable degree of concern about the possible implications for total savings in the economy. It was felt that if pensions were provided at such a high level there would be no incentive for the individual to save for his old age. Those fears have not been realized in the post reform period. The immediate effect of the new provisions seems to have been to replace the private support of family and friends on which many old people had been relying.[1] Subsequently, private savings benefited from the new-found ability of the pensioner himself to save part of his pension and from the inherent desire of the German population for security in the form of savings. This was encouraged to some extent by the various savings incentive schemes, based on tax concessions or bonus payments, which had been established in the immediate post-war period.[2] What occurred therefore was not a fall in savings but rather a shift in the form which these savings took.

(b) *Statutory pension insurance : the special schemes*

In the case of the special pension insurance schemes, interest lies not only in the way the schemes reflect the ideology of the social market economists. Instead, interest centres also on the way provisions have been constructed both to meet the needs of the particular population groups and, in some cases, to comply with broader social objectives.

We cannot attribute the existence of these special schemes directly to the 1957 pension reform. The miners, for example, had already had their own special pension provisions since the 1920s, and the artisans had been covered by statutory provisions since before World War II. Both these groups were, however, affected by the reform. Provisions for the miners were granted on the same basis as those in the general schemes, and the independent artisans, since they were incorporated at the time in the scheme for white

[1] Cf. E. von Bethusy-Hoc, *Das Sozialleistungssytem der Bundersrepublik Deutschland*, Mohr Verlag, Tübingen, 1965, p. 57.
[2] See Section V (a) of this chapter.

collar employees, were directly affected by changes in this scheme.
The most important question was: could they remain in existence
in the Social Market Economy structure of provision without
giving rise to charges of inconsistency?

In *the miners' scheme* the way in which the scheme was to be
financed might possibly have been viewed as inconsistent with the
principles reflected in the general schemes. Unlike the equal sharing of the financial burden of old age pensions in the general
schemes by employers and employees, the employers were, in the
miners' scheme, to pay contributions of almost twice the level of
the employees. More importantly, the central Government was to
provide a substantial subsidy, amounting to around 50 per cent of
total revenue.[1] How could this intervention by the state be justified?

The major justification is to be found in the fact that mining,
even in 1957, was a declining industry. The ratio of active employees to pensioners was unfavourable and likely to become worse.
Between 1950 and 1960, for example, there was one pensioner to
each insured person; by 1970 this ratio had deteriorated to two to
one, and was expected to become three to one by 1985.[2] In these
circumstances it would have been impossible to absorb the miners
in the general schemes without compromising the principles of
solidarity of the generations and of non-intervention by the state.
Substantial Government financial aid was necessary and justifiable
if this group of employees were not to suffer.

Germany is, of course, not the only country to be faced with the
problem of providing pensions for members of a declining industry. The case of the railway workers in the USA is a comparable
example.

The miners' scheme differed from the other schemes for
employed persons not only in the financial field, but also in the
benefit structure, which was adapted to meet the particular requirements of this group. The aim of the miners' scheme was essentially
identical to that of the general schemes, namely to maintain the
relative status of the miner in old age through an earnings-related
pension benefit. The nature of mining employment was such,
however, that the status of the miner tended to be threatened not

---

[1] Table 2.2 provides an indication of the different systems of finance in the
various pension schemes.
[2] Cf. Sozialbericht 1971, Bundesministerium für Arbeit und Sozialordnung
(BMfAS), Bonn, p. 149.

only in old age, but also during his working life. Conditions of employment often gave rise to a reduction in earnings in later years when the miner had to move to lighter forms of work. This affected his immediate income and also his future pension rights, since any reduction in earnings would lower his personal basis of assessment. Special pension provisions were therefore introduced for mining employees to compensate for this situation.

Compensation is provided on the one hand through additional benefits to those found in the general schemes. A special miners' pension is paid, for example, to employees whose earnings are reduced owing to an enforced move to lighter tasks. This pension (*Bergmannsrente*) is intended to fill at least in part the gap between the lower and the former earnings level, and is paid up to the point where the miner becomes eligible for the normal old age pension.

Compensation is provided also by adapting the pension formula for the normal old age pension to take the employment pattern for mining employees into consideration. The coefficient which is used in the calculation is fixed for the miners' scheme at 2 per cent instead of 1·5 per cent as in the general schemes. This has the effect of providing a pension equal to 60 per cent of average pre-retirement earnings after only thirty instead of forty years.

Finally, the fact that mining is a declining industry is given explicit recognition in the payment of a special compensation pension to miners over the age of fifty-five who have to leave mining on account of rationalization in the industry. It recognizes the fact that the majority of such men would experience difficulty in finding other employment, since it is calculated in exactly the same manner as the normal old age pension and thus constitutes a premature retirement benefit.

One of the most interesting features of the miners' scheme as a whole is the way in which those factors which could conceivably give rise to hardship for miners in old age were dealt with effectively within the pension insurance system itself. This may be taken to reflect the Social Market Economy idea which is implicit in its criterion for justifying state intervention, namely that socially undesirable consequences should be prevented rather than dealt with once they have arisen.

Even before the 1957 reform, *the independent artisans* had held the rather unusual position of being the only group of self-employed persons to belong to a statutory pension insurance scheme. They were compulsorily insured in the scheme for white collar workers unless they had adequate protection either through complete personal insurance provisions or a combination of statutory and personal provision. The existence of coverage for old age in this form would seem to have had a considerable amount of influence on the way the group was treated after the reform.

One of the major factors in the decision to include them in a statutory pension scheme was the fact that practically all independent artisans were employees at some point in their careers (usually during an apprenticeship), with resulting compulsory membership of an employees' pension scheme. Many, however, would become self-employed without having fulfilled the necessary qualifying period for an employee's old age pension. While most self-employed professions might be in a position to compensate for this loss of pension rights through personal insurance provisions, it was felt that the independent artisan often did not belong to this group. His business was usually small, and income tended to fluctuate to such an extent that a life insurance contract would be difficult to finance. He would, in addition, be faced with relatively high premium charges owing to his age on establishing his own business.

These considerations which had given rise to statutory protection under earlier arrangements, could equally well be used to justify the continuation of this protection in 1957. They complied in fact with the doctrine of intervention where necessary to prevent a socially undesirable situation arising. Difficulties arose, however, as a result of the change in the role of pension insurance provisions in 1957, which made the inclusion of the independent artisans on the same basis and under the same conditions as employed persons impossible. It was, for example, difficult to grant an earnings-related pension to this group since it was extremely difficult to assess the actual value of their earnings at any given time because of wide fluctuations. A further difficulty concerned the system of finance. If pensions were to be granted at the same level to the independent artisans as to the other groups of employed persons, the artisans would require to pay both the employer's and the employee's share of the contribution burden.

The outcome of these problems was a reorganization of provisions for independent artisans in 1962. First, an administrative change was introduced: the artisans, who had previously been covered by the white collar workers' scheme, on the grounds that this was consistent with their 'status' in society, were transferred in 1962 to the manual workers' insurance scheme. This had the aim of affording continuity of coverage, since it would be this scheme to which they would belong during their apprenticeship period as employees. They were, however, to form a separate group of insured within this scheme. Secondly, the basic role of statutory provision was altered for this group. The old age pension was given the task not of maintaining status in old age, but of simply providing a minimum level of income which could be supplemented from other sources. This radical adaptation of the nature of pension provision was to be achieved by limiting the period of compulsory cover in a statutory scheme to eighteen years. (Workers insured in the general schemes are, of course, subject to compulsory membership for the entire period of their employment.) The total eighteen-year period would normally comprise a period in the general manual workers' insurance scheme while employed, then a further period in the special scheme for independent artisans. To avoid the difficulty of evaluating the individual's earnings, it was decided that, while self-employed and belonging to the special artisan's scheme, he should pay a fixed rate of contribution equal to that paid by the average employee in the manual workers' scheme, with the option of limiting payment to every second month if his financial circumstances should warrant this concession.

Thus the regulations in the general schemes were adapted in the case of the independent artisans, as in the case of the miners, to take account of their particular circumstances. One criticism can, however, be levied at the scheme for independent artisans. It is possible to argue that the provision of a minimum pension income through a statutory scheme with supplementation from private provision (unless voluntary membership of the statutory scheme is continued after the minimum period) is inconsistent with the argument put forward in defence of an income replacement figure in the general schemes significantly above a minimum level. It will be remembered that this was justified in that freedom of disposal of an adequate income was given precedence to freedom in the way provision should be made. On the other hand, the difference in treatment could conceivably be justified by the fact that the group of independent artisans would normally have the additional security of their own business which employed persons do not have.

The special scheme for *independent farmers* differs from the two just outlined in that it dates only from the year of the pension reform, 1957. One may therefore be tempted to conclude that its coming into existence was a direct consequence of the new pension doctrine. Like the independent artisans, the independent farmers constituted a section of the self-employed population in need of special protection. In the majority of cases the income earned from the farm was too small to allow for adequate personal pension provision, and for many of this group their only source of income in old age was from the social aid scheme. Unfortunately, many felt that the uptake of this means-tested benefit would indicate a loss of dignity on their part. They opted instead to maintain their independence by retaining possession of their farms and working them even when no longer able to do so efficiently. This situation had clear implications for the structure and efficiency of the whole German agricultural sector.

The special pension scheme for farmers was conceived, therefore, not only in terms of pension policy, but also in terms of general agricultural policy. In 1957 the German agricultural sector was exceedingly fragmented and inefficient. This situation, serious enough in itself, was made more so by the political developments of that year. The establishment of the Common Market made it all the more vital that Germany's agricultural sector should be able to compete with its European neighbours. The restrictions placed on agricultural price policy in the Treaty of Rome, however, made it necessary for other means to be found to improve the agricultural structure. One of the means chosen was that of the special farmers' pension scheme.

This aspect of the pension scheme becomes quite clear when we look at the structure of and conditions attached to the receipt of the old age pension which was introduced in 1957. The pension, which is flat-rate and somewhat less than the equivalent social aid allowance, is financed to a very small extent by flat-rate contributions of the insured. The main source of revenue is a central Government subsidy. Its aim was to enable independent farmers to hand over their farms after they had reached the age of sixty-five (or earlier if they were unable to continue working the farms), and this was in fact the major condition of entitlement attached to the pension. Prior to the introduction of this pension, many felt unable to take this step because they were not able to live on the income from renting out the farm alone, and declined to accept help from the social aid authorities. A further condition regarding the maximum size of the farm if the owner were to benefit from the pension scheme, had the effect of limiting this provision to owners of the smaller agricultural units which were most in need of amalgamation if they were to become efficient.

This policy aim has in fact been considerably strengthened and underlined in the period since 1957 by the introduction of a so called 'transfer-of-land' pension (*Landabgaberente*) in 1969. This is essentially a short-term measure to speed up the process of rationalization. The pension is financed entirely by the central Government and has the aim of encouraging elderly persons between the age of sixty (or fifty-five in special cases) and normal pension age to give up their farms in the interests of structural change. Once again there are restrictions on the maximum size of the farm which will qualify and restrictions on the minimum size of the holding with which it can be amalgamated. It is likely that the introduction of this new measure will increase the success achieved by the earlier provisions. By 1968, Germany had succeeded in lowering the average age of her independent farmers relative to the average in the EEC as a whole. While 55 per cent of farmers in the EEC were over fifty-seven years of age in that year, the figure for Germany alone was only 31 per cent.[1] The rationalization of the farming sector has also had the effect, however, of increasing the number of persons who move out of agriculture to other types of employment. Recognition of the problems regarding provisions for old age arising from this situation has been given as recently as 1971. Since then, extremely generous Government subsidies have been available for ex-farmers (under certain conditions relating to the time spent as an independent farmer) who wish to provide for their old age by payment of back-dated contributions to one of the general statutory pension schemes. Although this move has often been discussed in terms of extending the coverage of the statutory schemes, about which more will be said in Section IV, the fact should not be ignored that this is also a way of encouraging structural change in this sector through removing obstacles to amalgamation of farm units.

Interesting though these schemes undoubtedly are, for the way

---

[1] Cf. *Uebersicht über die Soziale Sicherung*, BM f AS, Bonn, 1970, p. 95.

in which provision is adapted to the needs of the insured and to broader policy aims, they must be kept in perspective. In 1970, around 32 per cent of the total population were insured in the two general schemes. This percentage includes members of the special scheme for independent artisans, whose membership cannot be separated from the total, but it is estimated that they accounted for only about 1 per cent of the total membership of the general schemes of some 19 million. Likewise only about an additional 1 per cent of the total population was insured in 1970 in the two

TABLE 2·1

Social provisions (Sozialleistungen) *for old age*

	1960	1965	1970	1975
Total social provisions[1] as a percentage of GNP (market prices)	21·6	22·4	23·4	24·6
Total expenditure on old age as a percentage of total social provisions	19·2	20·5	22·3	24·3
Total expenditure on old age as a percentage of GNP (market prices)	4·2	4·6	5·2	6·0
Total expenditure on old age (Mrd DM)	12·6	21·2	35·4	57·0
Of Which (Percentage Share)				
Manual workers' pension scheme	35·7	34·4	37·6	38·6
White collar workers' pension scheme	20·6	22·6	24·0	25·1
Public servants' provisions	27·0	26·9	24·3	23·7
Special pension scheme for miners	7·1	7·5	7·3	7·3
Special pension scheme for independent farmers	0·8	1·4	1·4	1·0
Complementary occupational provisions	5·6	4·2	3·4	2·8
Social aid	1·6	1·4	0·8	0·7
Indirect provisions (tax concessions)	1·6	1·4	1·1	0·9

Source: *Sozialbericht* 1971, BMfAS, Bonn, pp. 334–5 ff.

special schemes for miners and independent farmers. Thus, when one takes into account existing pensioners, who comprised some 16 per cent of the population, and dependents of the insured population, amounting to a further 34 per cent, about 83 per cent of the total population in 1970 was protected by some form of statutory pension scheme.[2] Much of the gap in coverage which remains is filled by the special pension scheme for public employees (see below).

[1] 'Total social provisions' includes not only statutory provisions, but also complementary (occupational) provisions and indirect provisions.
[2] *Sozialbericht* 1971, BMfAS, Bonn, p. 98.

(c) Pensions for public servants

Public servants[1] have always enjoyed considerable prestige in Germany, dating from the time when they formed one of the élite groups of Bismarckian society. Since then they have had their own pension scheme, which has exempted them from membership of the statutory schemes.

Both at the time of the 1957 pension reform and in the period since then, the importance of this final form of first tier pension provision has been, in terms of expenditure, second only to that of the general schemes.[2] Its share has declined to a certain extent over this period owing largely to the expansion of provisions by the general schemes, but even in 1970 expenditure on old age pensions for public servants amounted to one third of that on old age benefits from the general schemes. The significance of this becomes apparent when one takes into account the fact that the number of old age pensions paid by the public servants' scheme comprised only about 12 per cent of general scheme pensions in that year.[3]

The pensions paid are extremely generous. After a normal working life, employees can expect to receive a pension equal to 75 per cent of their final salary, a pension which is then dynamized in line with movements in salary levels of a particular grade. The pension is financed by the employer with no explicit contribution from the insured themselves, although this may, of course, be reflected in a lower salary level than would otherwise be the case.

This target pension level for public servants is of interest for pensions policy as a whole. It represents the level at which the statutory schemes for employed persons are aiming through a combination of what are sometimes referred to as the three tiers of pension provision, namely statutory provision, private occupational provision, and personal provision. It is, however, generally true to say that, despite the high income-replacement figure of the statutory schemes, this goal has not yet been attained. One of the main

---

[1] Employees of the central Government, the provinces (Länder), and the municipalities (Gemeinde), religious organizations, the Federal Railway, the Federal Postal Services, professional soldiers, and employees of the social insurance institutes. (*Sozialbericht 1971*, BMfAS, Bonn, p. 155.)

[2] Table 2.1 Social provisions for old age.

[3] About half a million old age benefits were paid in 1970 by the public servants' scheme. The corresponding figures for the two general social insurance schemes was around $4\frac{1}{4}$ million.

reasons for this has been the failure of second-tier occupational schemes to fulfil the role allocated to them. The reason for this will be outlined in the following section.

(d) Occupational pension provisions

We have seen that the 1957 reform introduced a form of statutory pension which had the explicit aim of providing a high level of income replacement for the majority of employees in old age. Occupational provisions were nevertheless given an important role to play as supplements to this basic first-tier provision.[1] It was envisaged that they would fill most of the gap between the statutory pension level and the total target level for income replacement of 75 per cent of pre-retirement earnings. This gap would, of course, be widest in the case of higher paid employees with a significant amount of income above the maximum taken into account for normal pension purposes. Having been given this task, occupational pension schemes have been actively encouraged by the central Government by means of tax concessions on resources allocated for this purpose.

Despite such incentives, occupational provisions have for the most part failed to develop sufficiently to meet these demands. Benefits paid by the occupational schemes have increased in absolute terms over the years, from a total of 0·9 Mrd DM in 1963 to an estimated level of 1·4 Mrd DM by 1973. The importance of this expenditure relative to that of the statutory schemes has, however, declined, falling from 5·4 per cent in 1963 to an estimated 3·1 per cent by 1973.[2] This fall in the relative importance of the occupational pension schemes may in part be attributed to the growth of the statutory pension provisions. It is, however, also indicative of important defects in the structure of the occupational schemes themselves.

Occupational pensions have tended to receive comparatively little public attention in Germany since the pension reform, interest having been centred on the working of the new statutory schemes. At the beginning of 1972, however, some discussion began at last to

---

[1] See *Private Pension Plans in West Germany and France*, by Max Horlick and Alfred M. Skolnik, US Department of Health, Education and Welfare, Research Report No. 36, 1971.

[2] Cf. *Bundesarbeitsblatt* no. 9, 1970, p. 571, and also Table 2.1.

take place about the inadequate coverage of, and inadequate benefits provided by, the majority of occupational pension schemes. A survey undertaken in 1970 at the request of the Federal Ministry of Labour and Social Affairs[1] indicated that, for a large proportion of the working population, occupational benefits were by no means filling the gap between the statutory pension and the ultimate income-replacement goal of 75 per cent of income. Until 1970 there had been very little empirical research done on the coverage of occupational schemes, but an estimated figure of 60 per cent of the employed population with cover[2] had become generally accepted. There was, therefore, some understandable concern following the 1971 survey results, which suggested that the degree of coverage was likely, in fact, to be as low as 30 per cent of the employed population. The survey also showed that the main groups to suffer were those in less well paid occupations.[3]

It also became apparent that, of those who did belong to a private occupational pension scheme, almost two-thirds would lose their claim to an old age pension if they were to leave their firms before reaching retirement age. This had possible repercussions on not only the mobility of labour, but also the level of actual occupational pensions paid out. The main reason for this lack of pension preservation is to be found in the system of finance which is favoured for the provision of these benefits.

The majority of occupational pensions are financed in Germany by means of the so-called 'pension pledge' or 'book reserve' system. This form of provision accounts for around 70 per cent of total expenditure on occupational provision.[4] The pension pledge system is such that the employer promises to provide his employees

---

[1] The results are published in *Bundesarbeitisblatt* No. 10, 1971, pp. 589–93. They are based on a representative sample of 2,000 manual and white-collar workers in private industry, aged between 25 and 65.

[2] See article by Dr Ernst Heissman, in *Der Betrieb*, Sept. 1968: 'Neue Zahlen zur betrieblichen Altersversorgung'.

[3] The survey indicated that while 47 per cent of skilled tradesmen and 44 per cent of higher salaried employees belonged to some occupational scheme, only 21 per cent of unskilled labour and 26 per cent of lower paid white collar workers did so.

[4] The remainder is divided between provident funds, pension funds (supervised by the insurance authorities), direct insurance contracts taken out on behalf of employees, or voluntary additional insurance in the social pension insurance schemes. This last option is, however, not at all popular, as pension benefits earned in this way are not dynamized, unlike normal pensions paid by the statutory schemes.

with an old age pension at a certain age, but allocations for this purpose, instead of being paid into a completely separate pension fund or to an insurance company, are simply book entries set against the assets of the firm. This system has been favoured by employers because of the fact that, not only do they gain tax relief on the sum set aside in this way, but they can also continue to use the sum for the internal finance of the company. This is a practice which is of considerable importance for total investment in Germany. Since the employee does not normally contribute to the scheme in any way he has no direct legal claim on the old age pension until he actually retires. The suggestion has been made that these conditions attached to payment have in fact been used to attract and to keep scarce labour, particularly higher managerial staff.

Occupational pensions are clearly at an interesting stage in their development, since plans are being formulated, following the above-mentioned survey, to extend coverage of occupational schemes and alleviate the difficulties regarding preservation of pension rights arising from existing arrangements. Whatever the outcome of these discussions, however, the role of occupational provisions must remain simply that of supplementing the statutory benefits introduced in 1957.

It is interesting, however, that so little attention has in fact been paid to occupational provisions in the past. Despite the well-developed relations between the two sides of industry—through the so-called *Mitbestimmungspolitik*, or co-determination policy—the trades unions in Germany appear to have shown little interest in campaigning for better occupational pensions. The most likely explanation of this is the general satisfaction with statutory pensions and the recognition of the fact that, given the dynamic features of the statutory scheme, private occupational provision (since benefits are seldom automatically adjusted for price or wage changes) will probably remain an inferior alternative. The survey on attitudes to occupational benefits just mentioned found, for example, that, when asked for an opinion of how pension provisions as a whole might be improved, 68 per cent of respondants favoured the use of the statutory pension insurance scheme while only 18 per cent opted for better occupational provisions.[1] It would

---

[1] Cf. *Bundesarbeitsblatt* 10/1971, p. 591.

D

appear, therefore, that any impetus to improve the occupational pension structure will come not from employees or the trades unions but from the Government itself.

(e) Personal provisions for old age

The neo-liberal economists were, as we have seen, fundamentally in favour of private initiative in the field of social policy no less than in that of general economic policy. Circumstances after the war and leading up to the pension reform were such, however, that reliance on private initiative alone to provide an adequate income in old age was not feasible. The emphasis which was put on the responsibility of the individual in this field is nevertheless reflected in the fact that the statutory schemes which were established in 1957 are often referred to as 'self-help within a statutory framework'.

This importance attached to the self-help principle is to be found even more markedly in the exemption of certain population groups from a statutory pension insurance obligation. It will be remembered that this exemption applied to the majority of the self-employed, the exceptions being the two special groups of independent farmers and artisans, and also to those white-collar employees with income above the affiliation limit. Voluntary insurance may be continued in the statutory scheme in the latter case, but certain qualifying conditions must be fulfilled and the insured would, in any case, have to pay the full contribution rate alone without any assistance from his employer. Personal provision for income in old age has, therefore, always been of considerable importance for those two groups. In addition, it was intended that it should provide an additional tier of protection even for those persons with full statutory pension insurance cover.

The value of old age benefits paid out by the private insurance-based schemes has increased over the period since the reform in both absolute and relative terms. Total expenditure amounted to around 1·3 Mrd DM in 1963, representing some 8 per cent of total social expenditure on old age benefits. It was estimated that it would have increased by 1973 to 4·7 Mrd DM, or around 10 per cent.[1]

---

[1] Cf. *Bundesarbeitsblatt* No. 9, 1970, p. 571.

Various reasons can be suggested for this development. One of the more tangible factors is undoubtedly the changes in the income limit affecting membership of the general white-collar workers' insurance scheme. This limit was not dynamized at the time of the reform, and has been raised only at irregular intervals. After being fixed in 1957 at a level which excluded only some 5 per cent of white-collar employees, it was not raised again until 1965, by which time around 25 per cent of employees were excluded from compulsory membership of the scheme. A further change took place at the beginning of 1968 when the limit was finally abolished completely. In each of these years a large number of white-collar employees therefore became liable once more for compulsory membership of the scheme. It was felt, however, that it would be unfair to compel the groups affected to rejoin the statutory pension scheme as, in the period when they had been excluded from membership, they would have begun personal insurance contracts providing comparable cover for them and their dependents. In this case they were given the choice of opting out of the statutory scheme. Personal insurance provision was chosen by some 65,000 in 1957, 82,000 in 1965 and 220,000 in 1968.[1]

Less tangible factors, however, are also likely to have contributed to the growth of personal provision for old age. One must, for example, take into account the status-consciousness inherent in much of German society. The general standard of living is high, and there is a widespread desire to maintain this standard as far as possible in old age. There is therefore strong motivation to make personal provision for old age whether as a supplement to statutory pensions or as a substitute for them. In the latter instance, expenditure on personal insurance is in fact likely to be higher after the 1957 reform than before as the self-employed not covered by statutory provisions seek to ensure that their income in old age is not inferior to that of the social insurance pension recipients.

These sociological pressures have provided, therefore, an incentive to make such personal provision which has at the same time been facilitated by the substantial rise in real wages and salaries experienced since the 1950s. A study of attitudes to old age provision as a whole in Germany gives the impression that it is this desire to increase one's personal assets which, in addition to

---

[1] Cf. *Uebersicht über die Soziale Sicherung, op. cit.*, p. 43.

financial incentives to savings,[1] has served to bring about an increase in total private savings since the reform despite fears at the time that the introduction of such a generous pension scheme could only lead to a reduction in the savings ratio.

(f) Means-tested benefits

At the beginning of this section on income provision for the elderly we saw that one of the main aims of the 1957 reform was the separation of the two social objectives of income replacement and protect-tion against need. Having discussed the first objective in some detail in the preceding sections, we turn our attention now to the second, protection against need through the provision of a mini-mum level of income. This difference in objectives is reflected first in the fact that minimum provisions are financed from either general or local taxation rather than from contributions, and are paid on the basis of a test of means.

In looking at means-tested provisions, however, two distinct forms of means-tested allowances must be differentiated: first, social aid allowances which in fact represent the accepted minimum subsistence level in society and which may be compared to supple-mentary benefits in the UK, and, second, war-loss maintenance assistance. It must be emphasized immediately that it would be wrong to consider these as simply variations of the same minimum provision. This is not how they are viewed in Germany. There is as much a qualitative difference between war-loss provisions and social aid as there is between social aid and social insurance.

War-loss provisions. The war-loss benefits scheme, known as *Lastenausgleich* or the 'equalization of burdens' scheme, was instituted initially as an emergency measure in 1949, with further legislation following in 1952. Its aim was to provide some form of monetary compensation for those who had suffered material losses as a result of the war.[2] The scheme attempted on the one hand to provide some compensation, either in a lump sum or in the form of a pension, to those who had lost their homes and belongings in or immediately after the war. The value of these payments was

---

[1] Discussed in Section V.

[2] It should be noted that this scheme is quite distinct from provisions for war victims, that is persons suffering physical or mental injury as a result of the war.

directly related to the degree of loss incurred. In addition, the scheme undertook to provide so-called maintenance assistance to elderly persons over a certain age[1] who had lost their savings for their old age in the course of the war or as a result of the 1948 currency reform, and who would, because of their advanced years, be unable to build up pension rights or other forms of support before reaching retirement age. It is this form of provision which is of particular interest in our study of income in old age.

Despite the fact that maintenance assistance for the elderly provided by this scheme is paid on a test of means, it would appear that there is not the usual stigma attached to this particular means-tested benefit. This may be a reflection of the fact that it is paid at a considerably higher level and with more generous disregards than social aid benefits, and that it is regarded as being, not a form of charity, but an indication of the duty of the state to make compensation to persons suffering loss through no fault of their own. The number of persons receiving this allowance has been declining steadily over the years since the end of the war. Some half million persons[2] were, however, still receiving war-loss maintenance assistance in 1970, amounting to a total expenditure of around 1·2 Mrd DM, financed wholly by the central government.

Social aid provisions. In Germany, as in most countries, the last line of income provision is to be found in the social aid scheme. The concept underlying social aid is entirely different from that to be found in the other social provisions already outlined. It is not an insurance-based provision, nor is it any form of direct compensation for losses incurred. It is related rather to the concept of paternalism of the poor laws of the nineteenth century, providing protection against need for anyone with no alternative income sources. The paternalistic undertones of the provisions are visible immediately in the form in which the benefits are provided. There is no national social aid scheme, but assistance is granted and financed solely by the local authorities who still have the power to lower or refuse cash benefits in cases of confirmed 'idleness or

---

[1] Provision under this heading is normally made only to men born before 1 January 1890 and women born before 1 January 1895. In the case of persons who were self-employed the age restriction is slightly less stringent.

[2] This number can be compared to around 4¼ million recipients of statutory old age pensions from the general schemes in that year.

TABLE 2·2

Provisions for old age: sources of revenue in 1970

Scheme	Total benefit expenditure (Mrd DM)	Of which on old age (Mrd DM)	Total revenue (Mrd DM)	Source of revenue—percentage shares			
				Insured	Employers	Public funds	Other
Manual workers' pension scheme	32·2	13·3	32·9	40·1	38·3	19·5	2·1
White collar workers' pension scheme	16·5	8·5	19·0	44·7	42·6	4·7	7·9
Provisions for public servants	19·3	8·6	19·3	nil	90·7	6·7	2·6
Special pension scheme for miners	6·2	2·6	6·0	6·6	13·1	57·4	23·0
Special pension scheme for independent farmers	0·9	0·5	0·9	33·3	nil	66·7	nil
Complementary occupational provisions	n.a.	1·2	n.a.	n.a.	n.a.	n.a.	n.a.
Social aid	3·1	0·3	3·1	nil	nil	100·0	nil
Indirect provisions for old age (tax concessions)	—	0·4	—	—	—	—	—

Source: *Sozialbericht 1971*, BMfAS, Bonn, pp. 252–3.

prodigality', although this prerogative would seem now to be seldom used.

Social aid has, since 1961, been divided into two categories. The first comprises so-called 'help in special circumstances', which provides benefits in kind and social welfare services or once-and-for-all cash payments to meet particular contingencies. Benefits under this heading, which are open to a fairly wide sector of the population (athough on a test of means), are provided at the discretion of the local authorities.

These benefits are intended to provide help for persons whose income is normally sufficient to meet their needs but who require help to meet certain contingencies. Its income test is therefore more lenient than that applicable to the second type of social aid benefit, continuous maintenance assistance.

Although the local authorities have retained a good deal of discretion with regard to 'help in special circumstances' the scope for their discretionary powers has gradually been declining in the case of continuous maintenance assistance payments. All citizens have a right to this benefit, which constitutes the operational minimum income level in society. As we saw in an earlier section, this benefit also constitutes in effect the minimum pension level for the elderly since all minimum elements were removed from the pension insurance schemes for employed persons through the 1957 reform. Although one of the distinctive features of this scheme of cash maintenace allowances is the absence of a unitary scale of benefit rates applicable to the whole country, the spread of rates is not great,[1] and there are clear signs that there is growing harmonization. This harmonization is due partly to the reduction in the importance of regional variations in the cost of living. This follows from the fact that the scale rates are calculated according to the so-called basket-of-goods-approach. Subsistence requirements[2] are defined by an independent national body, the 'Association for Public and Private Welfare', and then evaluated by the social aid authorities in each area according to prices prevailing in their own region.

---

[1] The range of scale rate for the head of the household in 1970 was from 144 DM/month to 162 DM/month and for a married couple over sixty-five from 330 DM/month to 375 DM/month.

[2] These subsistence requirements also include items such as newspapers, tobacco, certain travel costs and similar small luxuries, with the aim of enabling the beneficiary to retain some social contacts.

In our study of the income sources of the elderly it is the continuous maintenance allowance which is of particular interest, since its importance in terms of recipients provides a crude, but useful, indication of the success or otherwise of other schemes of income maintenance. It is therefore significant that there has been a drastic reduction since the pension reform in the number of persons over sixty-five in receipt of this form of assistance. Whereas some 19 per cent of over sixty-fives were receiving this type of allowance in 1955, this had fallen to 3 per cent by 1968 and still further to 2·6 per cent in 1969.[1] Just how low this proportion is becomes apparent when set alongside the comparable figure for the United Kingdom, where some 28 per cent of over sixty-fives (women over sixty) are in receipt of supplementary benefits.

One possible reason for the startling difference in numbers receiving this minimum income level might of course be a variation in the scale of benefit granted by the social aid schemes in the respective countries. If the German rate were, for example, considerably lower than the British one, then the sphere of eligibility of recipients in Germany would be limited. This is not in fact the case. The rates payable for a married couple over the age of sixty-five plus an additional allowance for average rent, are very similar in both countries. In 1970 the benefit rates for this group amounted in both Germany and the UK to around 40 per cent of average manufacturing earnings before tax.

It could also be argued that eligibility for the allowance might be severely restricted in Germany simply as a result of dynamizing pensions while social aid rates remain fixed. This has not in fact occurred. Although social aid rates are not automatically adjusted for wage increases in the same way as pensions, the rates for the elderly have nevertheless risen by slightly more than pension levels over the period 1957 to 1970, indicating that 'poverty' is a relative rather than an absolute concept. Taking the 1957 rate as 100, the average scale rate for a married couple over sixty-five had risen, by 1970, to 260.[2] (This corresponds to a rise in the real value of benefits of about 70 per cent.) Over the same period, pensions in payment had increased from 100 to 228.[3] Neither can the difference

---

[1] Cf. *Wirtschaft und Statistik*, 5/1970 and *Wirtschaft und Statistik*, 1/1971.

[2] Cf. *Uebersicht über die Soziale Sicherung*, p. 239.

[3] See Table 2.3.

be attributed to variations in the level of income disregarded in assessing eligibility. Although disregards are slightly higher in the UK than in Germany, the difference is not sufficiently substantial to account for the gap between the two countries.

A further important factor in limiting uptake of the allowance might be the existence of some stigma attached to the benefit. This is certainly considered to be something of a problem in Germany, where there would seem to be some feeling of personal shame at being poor, but it is unlikely that this is more of a problem in Germany than it is in the United Kingdom. A most interesting suggestion made to us in interview was that this shame in poverty

TABLE 2·3

The development between 1957 and 1973 of the monthly old age pension of a pensioner with forty years' insurance and earnings equal to the average of all insured in the manual and white-collar schemes

Year	Value in DM/month 1	Change over 1957 in current DM (per cent) 2	As per cent of average gross earnings of all insured 3	Per cent change over previous year	
				Pension 4	Average gross earnings 5
1957	214·10	nil	50·9	nil	+ 4·1
1958	214·10	nil	48·2	nil	+ 5·7
1959	227·10	+ 6·1	48·6	+ 6·1	+ 5·1
1960	240·60	+ 12·4	47·3	+ 5·94	+ 8·9
1961	253·60	+ 18·5	45·3	+ 5·4	+10·2
1962	266·30	+ 24·4	43·6	+ 5·0	+ 9·0
1963	283·90	+ 32·6	43·8	+ 6·6	+ 6·1
1964	307·10	+ 43·5	43·5	+ 3·2	+ 8·9
1965	335·90	+ 56·9	43·7	+ 9·4	+ 9·0
1966	363·80	+ 69·9	44·1	+ 8·3	+ 7·2
1967	392·09	+ 83·5	46·1	+ 8·0	+ 3·3
1968	424·50[1]	+ 98·3	46·0	+ 8·1	+ 6·1
1969	459·80[1]	+114·8	45·7	+ 8·3	+ 9·2
1970	489·00	+128·5	44·0	+ 6·35	+12·7
1971	515·90	+141·0	41·5	+ 5·5	+11·9
1972	548·40	+156·0	44·1	+ 6·3	+ 9·3
1972 (July)	600·50	+180·5	—	+ 9·5	—
1973	668·70	+212·3	44·6	+11·35	+10·2

Source- *Bundersarbeitsblatt* 3/4 1973, p. 162.

---

[1] Without deduction of 2 per cent contribution to the pensioners' sickness insurance scheme.

has arisen as a result of propaganda concerning the German post-war 'economic miracle'. The propaganda has been so successful that those who have remained poor have been made to feel that this is a result of their own insufficiency and their failure to contribute fully to the 'miracle'.

The most significant reason for the decline of social aid as a major source of income for the elderly is, in the opinion of most German commentators, the introduction of the new social pension insurance schemes in 1957 and their continued development since then. Sections III and IV will attempt, first, to analyse the way in which the reform has affected the economic circumstances of the elderly in practice, and second, to indicate the current issues in pension provisions and the direction in which the scheme is moving.

III—THE PENSION INSURANCE SCHEMES IN PRACTICE

The discussion of statutory pension insurance provisions has, until now, had a rather theoretical bias. The question remains unanswered: how have the provisions introduced in 1957 affected the income situation of the elderly? We must turn our attention in this section, therefore, to the practical implications of the pension formula, the dynamizing technique, qualifying conditions and the coverage of the pensions schemes. On the basis that the vast majority of the population are covered by the two general pension insurance schemes for manual and white-collar workers and that these constitute the most important source of income for the elderly, the following discussion will be limited to these schemes. The point must, however, be emphasized that the accumulation of various forms of pension or other income is an important aspect of any assessment of the economic circumstances of the aged. Unfortunately, lack of statistical material makes it impossible to judge how extensive this is. It was, however, suggested to us in interview that a significant number of old persons may have as many as four different sources of income. The statutory pension might therefore be regarded as providing only the first tier of support. Any criticism of the system should be viewed in this light.

(a) Implications of the pension formula

The personal basis of assessment. It will be remembered that the pension accruing to the individual pensioner is determined to a large extent by his 'personal basis of assessment' (PBA), which is the measurement of the average ratio of the insured person's income to that of the insured group as a whole over his insurance period. It is by means of this variable that the pensioner is intended to retain in old age his 'status' acquired during his working life.

This technique has the effect of maintaining in the pension distribution the disparities in earnings which exist in the labour market. Statistics show that the distribution of the PBA levels is much as one might expect. There is a wide variation in the average level of the PBA between the manual workers' scheme and the white-collar workers' scheme. Within each scheme women tend on the whole to have a lower personal basis of assessment than men. In 1971 the average PBA for women in the manual workers' scheme receiving old age pensions at the age of sixty-five was only fifty-three, while it rose to ninety-nine in the white-collar workers' scheme. The corresponding levels for men were 108 and 160 respectively. There will, therefore, be a significant variation in the absolute levels of pensions paid to individual pensioners.[1]

It might appear that the white-collar worker fares considerably better than his counterparts in the manual workers' pension scheme. This will almost certainly be the case as regards the absolute level of the old age pension benefit. The position of the white-collar pensioner is, however, less favourable if one considers the fall in income which he is likely to experience on retirement.

In the first place it must be remembered that the level of the personal basis of assessment which is taken into account in the calculation of the normal old age pension is subject to a ceiling. It may not exceed 200 per cent of the level of average earnings prevailing at the time of the pension award. The effect of this ceiling is to limit the proportion of total income replaced by the statutory pension scheme in the case of insured persons with a large proportion of earnings above this level. It is likely that these will be predominantly white-collar employees.

---

[1] See *Bundesarbeitsblatt* 5/1971, p. 328.

Secondly, the fact that the personal basis of assessment is calculated over the whole working life of the insured person is also of significance. This means that in Germany the relative level of the old age pension is not linked simply to the immediate pre-retirement earnings of the individual or even to his earnings in the 'best' ten or fifteen years of his working life as is common in other countries. This whole-of-life approach to the assessment of pension rights has implications particularly serious for the white-collar employee whose income profile is likely to be such that his income will start at a fairly low level but will increase steadily, relative to average incomes, until it reaches a peak just before he retires. The fact that his PBA will, however, reflect his low earnings earlier in life will have the effect of reducing his pension as a percentage of his immediate pre-retirement income. Unless he has taken steps to supplement his statutory pension by private means, he will suffer a drop in income which is likely to be much greater than that experienced by the manual worker whose relative position in the income scale would normally be higher earlier in his working life than just before retirement.

These modifications to the 'status maintenance' principle are, of course, entirely consistent with the principle of subsidarity which, as we have seen, was also a major component of the pension reform. The higher-paid white-collar employee will have to rely on private initiative to maintain his living standards in old age to a much greater extent than the lower-paid worker. One of the major criticisms which is often made of the statutory schemes in this context is that the intricacies of the pension formula tend to make it extremely difficult for an employee in this position to calculate just what level of his immediate pre-retirement income he can expect to be replaced by his statutory pension. He may therefore fail, through no fault of his own, to make adequate personal provision for his retirement.

Some interesting data is also available on the subject of the average length of *the insurance record* of existing pensioners. Although the scheme is officially still in the transitional period, since it began only in 1957, the majority of male pensioners had by 1971 fulfilled the 'standard' insurance period of forty years. There is, of course, no maximum number of years which may count towards a pension, and around 40 per cent had in fact an insurance record of forty-five years or more. Thus the use of the technique of accredited periods, discussed in some detail in Section I I, would appear to have successfully enabled higher benefits to be paid than would otherwise have been the case.

The position of women pensioners tends on the whole, however, to be less fortunate. Of those retired in 1971, the great majority had an average insurance record of less than twenty-five years. Obviously this factor, together with their generally lower personal basis of assessment, will adversely affect their pension level. It would also appear that the tendency for women to have a comparatively short insurance record has had the effect of compelling many to stay on at work until the age of sixty-five, in order to accumulate greater pension rights, instead of opting to retire at sixty.

The general basis of assessment. Let us consider the level of old age pension which the 'average' employee could expect to attain after an insurance period of forty years. In order to abstract from the complications involved in the development of the individual's personal basis of assessment, discussed above, we shall assume that his earnings have always been exactly equal to the average earnings of all insured. In other words his personal basis of assessment is 100 per cent. According to the pension formula he could expect to receive a pension amounting to 60 per cent of the general basis of assessment. Since he has always earned the 'average' earnings level, and since, as we saw earlier, the G B A is by definition the measurement of average earnings prevailing at any given time, one might expect that this individual would receive a pension equivalent to 60 per cent of his pre-retirement earnings. This is, however, not the case. If our average employee had drawn his old age pension for the first time in 1971 then it would have replaced only some 45 per cent instead of the expected 60 per cent, of average earnings in 1971.

The reason for this discrepancy between the pension level in theory and the pension paid in practice is the effect of the time lag built in to the calculation of the general basis of assessment.[1] In periods of rapid growth of earnings, as have been experienced in Germany since the pension reform, this lag can seriously deflate the proportion of pre-retirement earnings which the pension will

---

[1] In the example given, the pension would be based on the level of the general basis of assessment for 1971 which equals the average income of all insured persons in the two schemes over the years 1967, 1968 and 1969.

replace. The position of pensioners receiving payment in 1971 would be aggravated[1] by the fact that the general basis of assessment applicable to that year would still be influenced by the abnormally low level of average earnings in 1967–68 as a result of the economic recession at that time while earnings had again risen rapidly from 1969 to 1971.

(b) The effects of dynamizing

The general basis of assessment affects not only the initial level of a pension, however, but also the movement of pensions after they are in payment through the so-called dynamizing procedure. It will be remembered that all pensions paid by the two main pension insurance schemes (and also the miners' scheme) are reviewed annually and adjusted[2] if there has been a change in average earnings, as measured by the general basis of assessment, of at least 3 per cent.

The fact that adjustment is, in effect, automatic and not governed by political expediency, and that the degree of adjustment is based on an earnings figure which, being an average over a three-year period, is corrected for extreme fluctuations in earnings, has meant that the movement of pensions in payment has shown a very smooth development. This can be seen clearly in Chart 4, included in the Appendix. It is questionable, however, whether the counter-cyclical effects[3] of the lag are being successful in fulfilling the task set them in 1957, namely to prevent the possible inflationary pressures of increases in earnings being aggravated by accompanying increases in pension benefits. Owing to the timing of earnings and pensions increases, however, there have been occasions, notably in 1964–65 and in 1969, when pensions have been rising in response to an earlier earnings peak when earnings have again shown an upward trend.

---

[1] The normal replacement level would be nearer 50 per cent of earnings.

[2] Subject to the advice of a Social Advisory Board. Proposed adjustments have, however, always been sanctioned.

[3] This is in fact the only way in which social pension provisions are used in Germany for counter-cyclical purposes. In comparison with Italy, for example, there have been no discretionary changes in revenue or expenditure regulations. Such counter-cyclical measures have in fact been impossible in Germany as a result of the fact that the pension insurance funds, being administered by various independent pension authorities, cannot easily be manipulated by the Government.

Old age pensions in West Germany have, over the period 1958–72 risen by a much greater amount than would be necessary simply to offset changes in the consumer price index, and have kept pace fairly well over the period as a whole with changes in average earnings. The non-adjustment in 1958, and the fact that the adjustment mechanism is linked to a lagged measurement of earnings had, however, led to a situation where the growth of pensions, in the period of accelerating money earnings between 1957 and 1967, had lagged slightly behind the growth of average earnings. It was only with the recession of 1967–68, when the growth of earnings slowed down, that pensions were able to catch up on the rapid increase in the preceding period. Chart 4, and also Table 2.3, show, on the other hand, that the position had worsened again in 1970 and 1971, with the growth of pensions again lagging behind the growth of current earnings as a result of the fact that the dynamizing formula was still reflecting the low earnings of the recession period. Between 1957 and January 1972, for example, pensions in payment grew by 156 per cent, while the average gross earnings of all insured grew by 223 per cent. The incorporation of this fairly substantial lag in the adjustment mechanism has, therefore, affected the relative income position of pensioners.

Some concern over this situation has been voiced at regular intervals during the period since the 1957 reform, usually at the time of the annual pension adjustment legislation. Until 1972, however, all attempts to introduce a special adjustment procedure to allow pensions in payment to 'catch up' on the adjustment which was not made in 1958 had been resisted by the government. In 1972 the discussions surrounding the pension reform programme (discussed in the following section) gave advocates of this move an opportunity to press for improvements in the income of existing pensioners instead of the reform being confined to improvements in rights for future pensioners.

After a good deal of debate it was decided to effect such an improvement by bringing forward the normal pension adjustment by six months. Thus the increase in pensions in payment of 9·5 per cent which would normally have been implemented on 1 January 1973 was implemented instead in the Pension Reform Law of September 1972 and back-dated to 1 July 1972. In future all adjustments will be made on 1 July, thus reducing to some extent the lag between the rise in earnings and the subsequent rise in pensions.

IV—CURRENT ISSUES IN THE FIELD OF STATUTORY PENSION INSURANCE

(a) *The pension peak*

In reviewing any proposals for the future development of pension provisions in Germany, one cannot help but become aware of the importance which is attached to the phenomenon of the so-called 'pension peak' or *Rentenberg*. This term is used to indicate the deteriorating demographic structure facing the Federal Republic. Demographic forecasts point to a growing top-heaviness in the age structure of the population. While persons over sixty-five years of age accounted for only 14·5 per cent of the population of active age (fifteen to sixty-four) in 1955, this figure had risen by 1970 to over 20 per cent. It is estimated that it will reach 23 per cent around 1980, when the peak is expected to reach its height.

This growth of the elderly population is one of the major reasons why the relative importance of expenditure on provisions for the elderly has grown substantially in the period since the pension reform. In the period between the pension reform and 1970, expenditure on social provisions[1] claimed an ever-increasing share of the national product. Its share has grown from 21·6 per cent of GNP (at market prices) in 1960 to 23·4 per cent in 1970. It is estimated that this trend will continue, with social provisions comprising 24·6 per cent of GNP by 1975. Over this same period the share of expenditure on provisions for old age within total social provisions also increased from 19·2 per cent in 1960 to 22·3 per cent in 1970 (reaching 24·3 per cent by 1975, it is estimated). This expansion of provisions for the elderly has meant that its share of GNP has increased between 1960 and 1970 from 4·2 per cent to 5·2 per cent of GNP.[2] The vast majority of this increased expenditure on the elderly is the result of the growth of expenditure in the statutory pension insurance schemes. This was a cause of some considerable concern to the pension schemes not least

---

[1] The term 'social provisions' includes not only statutory provisions but also complementary (occupational) and indirect provisions (e.g. tax concessions).
[2] See Table 2.1.

because of developments taking place simultaneously which affected the revenue of the schemes. The absolute increase in the number of old persons resulting from the pension peak was accompanied by a decline in the size of the working population on whom the pension schemes depend for their revenue. This was due to a reduction in the birth-rate and to longer schooling and vocational training. Thus, despite the lag of pensions behind earnings to some extent, the expenditure burden of the pension insurance schemes was increasing while the revenue of the schemes was declining.

This problem was partly met by a substantial increase in the rate of contributions to the schemes. The rate[1] had remained constant for both general schemes at 14 per cent between 1957 and 1967, but was then raised to 15 per cent in 1968, 16 per cent in 1969 and 17 per cent in 1970. It has risen again to 18 per cent in 1973. In the special schemes the usual solution to this problem has been to raise the level of central government subsidies.

These across-the-board increases in contribution rates could not, however, help to solve the problem of the growing disequilibrium in the financial structure of the two general pension insurance schemes. A more fundamental change in the financial and administrative relationships of the two schemes was required, which raised the whole question of centralization *versus* decentralization.

(b) The centralization issue

It will be remembered that when the pension insurance schemes were set up in the new form in 1957 they were not directly administered by the state but by autonomous pension institutes. The task of providing pensions for the bulk of the population was divided between the two schemes for manual and white-collar workers. As the pension peak approached it became apparent that some modifications would need to be made to the administrative structure of the schemes if they were to survive the crisis period.

The crux of the matter was that the two general pension insurance schemes were being affected quite differently by this demographic development. While the number of pensioners in both schemes was increasing, the development of the group of

---

[1] That is, the combined contribution rate for employers and employees.

active contributors was different in the two schemes owing to the effects of structural and technological changes in the economy. The definition of what constitutes a manual worker and what a white-collar worker has always been somewhat arbitrary[1] and the retention of the traditional division gave rise to problems in the face of rapid technological development. Large numbers of insured persons have moved from occupations designated as 'manual' employment to what are known as 'white-collar' occupations, resulting in a move from one insurance scheme to the other.

By 1969 the movement of insured persons into the white-collar workers' scheme had resulted in the manual workers' scheme running into severe financial difficulties while the white-collar workers' scheme was building up surpluses. In an attempt to solve the problem, the 'Third Pension Amendment Law' of 1969 abolished the partial funding technique in favour of a purely pay-as-you-go system of finance with reserves comprising only a contingency fund. A system of finance equalization between the two schemes was also introduced. The finances of the two schemes were to be viewed as a whole and if any lack of balance occurred and reserves in one scheme fell below a certain level while remaining high in the other, one scheme (inevitably the white-collar scheme) would be required to transfer resources to the other (the manual workers' scheme). A system of liquidity aid was established at the same time, both these finance equalization measures making it unnecessary for an insurance scheme in difficulty to borrow funds on the capital market.

The result of this collaboration between the two schemes in terms of finance is to make their continued administrative separation seem still more artificial. It was in fact felt by many commentators that the first step towards the formation of a unitary administrative structure[2] was taken as a result of a further change introduced in the 1969 Law, which led to closer co-operation of the

---

[1] The *Bundessozialgericht* or Social Court decreed in 1956 that a manual worker worked in a standing position, but that a white-collar worker carried out his work while sitting.

[2] It is interesting to note in this context that similar trends towards centralization have appeared in other spheres of activity. In discussing developments relating to the banking sector and some sectors of industry, Andrew Shonfield (*Modern Capitalism*, Oxford University Press, 1969, p. 241) says 'There has been a powerful undertow throughout these post-war years which has irresistibly brought together pieces of economic power that were supposed to have stayed apart.'

twenty administrative institutions within the manual workers' scheme. These changes were once more of a financial nature, introducing a system of deficit sharing between the institutions, necessitated by differences in the pensioner density between regions.

There is, however, still some considerable opposition to the amalgamation of the two general schemes, mainly from the side of the white-collar insurance scheme. In part this may indeed be founded in the opinion that, as was claimed in an interview with us, they feel their administrative structure has reached its optimum size and that a larger organization could not be run by one single authority. It is possible, however, that a great deal of opposition stems from the general reluctance to be found in Germany—as elsewhere—to surrender any authority once attained. The white-collar workers' scheme is also reluctant, for reasons of prestige, to lose its identity and combine with the manual workers' scheme. It must be emphasized, however, that in the discussion of any amalgamation of organizations there is no question of the administration being taken over by a centralized government department. The independent self-administrative units would remain, the problem under discussion simply being how to co-ordinate their activities.

(c) Developments in pension provisions

Once the pension schemes were set on a firmer financial footing through these finance equalization measures, the Federal Government felt that the time was ripe to introduce their plans for the future development of old-age-pension provisions. These plans, which were formulated in a 'pension reform programme' in 1971, reflected the major issues of the 1970s.

The political background to the reform programme was the change of government in 1966 when the neo-liberal Christian Democrat Party lost control to a coalition party formed by the Social Democrats (the SPD) and the small Free Democratic Party (FDP). Given that the Social Democrats stand to the left of the Christian Democrats, one might have expected that immediate and fundamental changes in the structure of pension policy would result. The proposed changes were hailed by some commentators as representing a departure from the pensions policy based on the social market economy approach and a move towards what is often referred to as a 'welfare state' type of policy. In practice, however, the distinction between these two principles is not always clear-cut. The Social Democrats certainly proposed changes in provisions where they considered this to be necessary, but they tended to take up a more pragmatic than doctrinaire approach to the question. As a result, the interpretation of trends is far from easy. While concessions to a welfare state type of policy might well have been made, they were not so radical as to preclude their being interpreted as continuing to reflect in broad terms the neo-liberal ideology.

The major reform proposals concerned the improvement of pensions for the self-employed and for women, and the introduction of a flexible pension age. The majority of the 1971 proposals have now found their way on to the statute books after a rather hasty passage through Parliament at the end of the sixth legislative period in 1972. Most of the principles underlying the proposed changes had considerable all-party support, but, as we shall see, there was some difference of opinion as regards details of the changes.

Improvements in provisions for the self-employed. In its pension reform proposals[1] the German Government stated that it was its intention to open membership of the statutory pension insurance schemes on a voluntary basis to all self-employed persons who were previously denied membership as a result of the neo-liberal restrictions on membership. Groups affected by this change would be those members of the professions not previously covered[2] and the self-employed working in trade and commerce, together with members of their families assisting in the business. It is estimated that this would comprise some three-quarters of a million self-employed and around two million family assistants.

This proposal was implemented in the Pension Reform Law (*Rentenreformgesetz* or RRG) of 21 September 1972 (in force from 19 October 1972). The Reform Law introduced the possibility of membership of the statutory pension insurance scheme for those

---

[1] See *Bundesarbeitsblatt*, 1/1972.

[2] Some members of the professions were previously covered to a certain extent by the statutory schemes, but this coverage was by no means universal or uniform.

not previously covered. Membership is now possible for these groups on a purely voluntary basis *or* they can apply for compulsory membership (*Pflichtversicherung auf Antrag*). In the case of voluntary membership, the insured is free to choose the level of contributions he wishes to pay. In the case of compulsory membership on application[1] the insured must pay the total contribution rate applicable for the scheme on his actual level of earnings. Since this might prove a heavy burden, especially for those just setting up in business, the insured is required to pay contributions only every second month for up to three years after he joins the scheme.

It is interesting that this development has come about largely as a result of the demands of those concerned, who felt that they were at a disadvantage through not belonging to one of the statutory pension insurance schemes. There are, for example, tax advantages in contributing to a statutory scheme rather than simply accumulating private savings or entering into a private insurance contract. Many of those excluded appeared to feel also that the statutory arrangements, particularly with respect to the provisions for dynamizing pensions in payment, were superior to the majority of personal insurance contracts which tended not to guarantee to maintain in the post-retirement period the real value of the pension relative to wages.

The way was in fact opened to these demands in 1968 when the affiliation limit applicable to members of the white-collar employees' pension scheme was abolished. The impetus for this development was provided partly by the financial problems facing the scheme. The other reason given, however, was one of solidarity, that all white-collar employees—regardless of their income—should be allowed to benefit from the social insurance provisions for old age. Once the principle was established that a high income from work did not necessarily guarantee security in old age, then the very basis for the exclusion of the self-employed had been destroyed.

It cannot be denied that the change is a significant one and that it does indeed alter the basis of the pension insurance scheme envisaged by the neo-liberals. The fact that membership of the scheme is open to these new groups on a voluntary basis, however, would tend to imply that the shift towards a welfare state concept is only a partial one. It could indeed be argued that the principle of

---

[1] Application must normally be made within two years after becoming self-employed, or—in the first instance—by 31 December 1974.

subsidarity remains intact, that the will of the state is still subsidiary to the will of the individual, but that attitudes have changed to such an extent that the individual now demands not freedom to make his own personal provision for old age, but rather the freedom to choose to belong to the statutory scheme. Some commentators, clinging to the neo-liberal concept, claim that Germany is simply setting its existing scheme on a broader base. The question of interpretation remains open.

Improvements in pension arrangements for women. The most radical and far-reaching of the reform proposals concerned new provisions for housewives and improvements in the pension regulations for women as a whole. These formed an attempt to meet some of the problems resulting from the existing regulation of pension provisions.

We saw in the previous section on pension insurance schemes in practice that women are often in a much less favourable position than men as far as their right to an old age pension is concerned. The two main reasons for this are their shorter insurance record and their low personal basis of assessment, reflecting low earnings during their period in employment.

On the whole it is probable that the shorter insurance period accruing to women can be attributed at least to some extent to their leaving the work force at intervals to have children or for a longer period to care for their family. Pregnancy itself is treated as an accredited period for the purpose of insurance contributions and therefore this does not adversely affect the woman's insurance record. There has, however, been some concern about the possible disadvantages facing a woman who wishes to return to the work force soon after her child is born. There may be not only personal difficulties, but also difficulty in finding employment without delay.[1] The German government, in its pension reform proposals, took cognisance of this fact and proposed that all women should be accredited for pension purposes with an extra so-called 'Baby-Year' for each child they have. This proposal was, however, one of those defeated by the opposition parties in the course of the Bill's passage through parliament. But another, probably more

---

[1] It is interesting that the same problem is recognized in Sweden, where employers are under a legal obligation to keep a woman's job open for her for a certain length of time after the birth of her child.

important, measure did receive the parties' approval, that is the introduction of a pension based on a minimum income (*Rente nach Mindesteinkommen*). Although this measure is not confined to women, they form the group most likely to benefit from the new regulations.

The Pension Reform Law introduced a scheme to improve the pension rights of at least some women by establishing a minimum level of personal basis of assessment[1] in the calculation of pension rights. It is the intention by this means to provide a minimum benefit for those with a full working life behind them, but who nevertheless have a totally inadequate pension as a result of low wages during their working life. Persons who have an insurance record of at least 25 years and whose personal basis of assessment used in the calculation of their pension is less than 70 per cent will be granted a pension based on the 70 per cent figure.[2]

This change involves the adoption of a weighted benefit type of formula which was rejected by the neo-liberals in 1957. When one turns one's attention to the reasons underlying this new proposal, however, it would seem that it may not, in fact, be completely at variance with the social market economy concept. The proposals do not suggest a basic universal minimum of the same type as the British or Swedish old age pension which would indeed indicate a move towards a welfare state system. The conditions attached to its payment indicate that it is intended instead to compensate for the undervaluing of some forms of employment in the labour market.[3] Another method which could be employed to meet the same ends would be some regulation of low incomes which, it is believed, are received by many women in the labour force and, to a lesser extent, by employees in forestry and agriculture. Any action now in this field would, however, fail to provide assistance to those

---

[1] It will be remembered that the PBA is a measure of the relationship of the individual's earnings to the average earnings of all insured persons in the two general pension schemes.

[2] In the original pension reform proposals it was intended that a minimum level of PBA should be set to qualify for this concession in order to exclude those whose earnings could in any case not have provided a subsistence income (it was assumed that they would have other income sources and thus other ways of earning pension rights). This condition was, however, abolished with the result that even those in part-time employment will now benefit from the change. The original qualifying period of insurance was also reduced from thirty-five years to twenty-five years.

[3] See *Bundesarbeitsblatt* 3/4 1973, p. 147, for an outline of the argument underlying this reform.

already at or near pension age, and thus more direct intervention at the stage of calculating the pension itself has been favoured. One could, therefore, justifiably argue that this is yet another example of intervention aimed at alleviating social problems arising from the free working of market forces. Some indication of the likely importance of this proposed change is given by the fact that, if it had been in force in 1971, around 220,000 women in the manual workers' pension schemes would have benefited from an increased pension benefit.

Important though these changes may be for the groups affected, they do nothing to improve the income situation in old age for those women who have either never been employed in the labour force or who have not worked for a sufficiently long period (the minimum period is fifteen years) to qualify for an old age pension. This group will be formed in the main of non-employed housewives.

The married woman without rights to an old age pension on her own insurance record has two alternative sources of income in old age. First, she may be supported by her husband's old age pension. Since this does not, however, include a supplement for a wife, it may be insufficient in some cases, if the husband was in a low paid job, for example, to provide adequate support. Second, if her husband is dead the woman will normally have a right to a widow's benefit. The inadequacy of this benefit is, however, widely recognized. The husband's old age pension does not pass to his widow in full. In most cases (that is if she is at least forty-five years of age or if she has a child to support), she will receive a pension equal to 60 per cent of his pension or the pension to which he would have been entitled. The problem of women whose husbands have been divorced is particularly acute. The former wife has a claim on part of the already inadequate widow's benefit if she was maintained by her former husband.

The solution which has finally been adopted to meet the problem of inadequate income for women in old age is the opening of membership of the statutory pension insurance schemes on a voluntary basis as was outlined above. It is hoped that non-employed housewives will be one of the main groups to benefit from this. As was noted they will be able to choose the level of contributions they wish to pay and thus the value of the pension rights which they can accumulate. They and all others opting to join the statutory pension scheme will also be given the opportunity to build up rights rapidly by back-dating contributions to 1956.

This reform, which has the effect of opening the insurance scheme to some seven million non-employed housewives, constitutes an even greater move away from the traditional image of German pension insurance with its emphasis on the protection of the worker. It is perhaps indicative of the widespread realization that it is hardly just to penalize a woman in financial terms for choosing to devote her attention to her family instead of entering the labour force. It remains to be seen, however, whether many will in fact take advantage of the opening of the pension schemes in this way. Although a great deal of discussion has taken place in Germany on this radical reform, no one seems to be risking an estimate of the extent to which it will in practice improve the economic circumstances of women.

(d) Flexibility in pension age

Another issue which has received considerable attention in the 1970s—and not only in West Germany—is the question of a gradual withdrawal from the labour force instead of a complete and sudden break at a given age.[1] The issue has tended to arise partly as a result of the upsurge of interest in the ageing process and particularly in the emotional disturbances which can result from the sudden change from employment to retirement.

In addition there has been a growing awareness of the tendency for older workers to find themselves transferred to lighter, and less well paid employment,[2] or to be made redundant as they approach normal retirement age. This trend becomes accentuated in recessionary periods. If he is made redundant, the individual has the choice, in the absence of other sources of income, of applying for social aid assistance,[3] or claiming disability pension from the pension insurance schemes. Although it is not officially recognized as such, it is likely that the disability pension (both partial and total disability) in Germany is widely used as a form of early retirement

[1] See the discussion of pre-pension provisions in France, for example, p. 298.

[2] It is interesting that this problem has been recognized for some time in the miners' pension scheme, where special provision is made to compensate for this transfer to less well-paid employment.

[3] One of the main groups of persons receiving continuous maintenance assistance is comprised of persons between the ages of fifty and sixty-five.

pension. At the beginning of 1968 for example (the latest figures available), around 40 per cent of both partial and total disability pensioners in the manual workers' scheme and between 35 and 40 per cent in the white-collar workers' scheme were in the sixty to sixty-five age group.[1]

Unlike the situation in Italy, where the more lenient qualifying conditions for a disability pension as opposed to an old age pension have given rise to some apparent abuse of the system, this is not considered a problem in Germany, although the same difference in qualifying periods exists. There is concern rather with the possible disadvantages facing the elderly person who is forced into the position of having to make use of the disability provisions in this way.

In the case of total disability pensions the benefit level is calculated in the same way as the old age pension and the insured would therefore be in the same financial position as if he had retired normally. The partial disability pension on the other hand is calculated on a less favourable basis (using a coefficient of 1 per cent instead of 1·5 per cent) on the assumption that the beneficiary will be able to accumulate some additional earnings from part-time work.[2] This is, however, not always possible, owing to the lack of such job opportunities, particularly in the light of the fact that there would seem to be some correlation between claims for disability pensions and the condition of the labour market.[3] In any case, the elderly person is subjected not only to financial loss, but also to a medical examination, which many appear to find degrading.[4]

The enormity of this problem of premature retirement became apparent only after results of a survey undertaken in 1970 were published.[5] These showed that 30 per cent of old age pensioners

[1] *Uebersicht über die Soziale Sicherung*, 1970, BMfAS, p. 63. Taking both forms of disability pension together, these accounted for some 483,000 persons in the manual workers' scheme and some 94,000 in the white collar schemes.

[2] In both cases the beneficiary automatically becomes eligible for an old age pension at the age of sixty-five.

[3] See *Uebersicht über die Soziale Sicherung*, 1970, BMfAS, p. 61.

[4] See *Bundesarbeitsblatt* 1/1972, p. 2.

[5] See *Bundesarbeitsblatt* 1/1972, p. 19, 'Die Einführung einer flexiblen Altersgrenze in der Meinung der Versicherten.' The survey was undertaken by the Institut für angewandte Sozialwissenschaften in Bad Godesberg between August and October 1970 at the request of the Ministry of Labour and Social Affairs. A representative sample survey technique was employed.

covered by the survey had left work at sixty-five, only 7 per cent at a later age, and no less than 58 per cent before the age of sixty-five. The main reason given for this early retirement was declining physical capabilities. At the same time there was a growing realization that old people cannot be regarded as a homogeneous group, particularly as regards their ability to continue in employment. The result of these pressures was urgent discussion at the beginning of the 1970s of the possible introduction of a flexible pension age. The discussions culminated in the Pension Reform Law of 1972. This law made it possible, from the beginning of 1973, for elderly persons with an insurance record of at least thirty-five years to draw their old age pension from the age of sixty-three, with no actuarial reduction in the benefit level. The disabled or severely handicapped may draw it even earlier, at the age of sixty-two. While this change was passed with little difficulty, the parliamentary parties found it impossible to reach agreement on whether or not there should be any limitation on the level of income which could be earned in addition to the early pension. The Government, which was in favour of limitation, was without a parliamentary majority at the time the Pension Reform Bill was being discussed, and was defeated on this issue, the opposition succeeding in introducing an amendment to the reform proposals allowing the pensioner to earn an unlimited amount in addition to drawing his early pension. The situation did not, however, stay like that for long. As soon as it was returned to power, the SPD/FDP coalition introduced the 4th Pension Amendment Law (4.RVAG) to reintroduce its original proposals. The 4.RVAG became law on 31 March 1973 with retrospective effect from 1 January 1973. It introduced a limitation on earnings allowed while drawing an early pension. Additional earnings are possible only if they are temporary in nature (i.e., limited to three months or seventy-five days in any one year) *or* if they amount on average to no more than 30 per cent of the contribution rating limit per month (i.e. to no more than 690 DM a month in 1973). Since the limit would thus be equivalent to just less than half average manufacturing earnings, this would enable the pensioner to continue in some form of part-time employment.[1]

---

[1] These regulations apply also to women. It will be remembered that, at present, if a woman wishes to draw her old age pension from the age of sixty a condition of payment is that she must withdraw from the labour force. Under

After the age of sixty-five there will, as formerly, be no limit to the level of income which can be earned, although, as we have just seen, this lack of a retirement condition would not appear to provide a great incentive for old persons to continue working. Other physical or social factors appear to be of more importance in influencing the retirement decision. It is estimated that, following the introduction of flexibility into the pension age, no less than two thirds of the insured meeting the necessary conditions will opt to draw their old age pension at the age of sixty-three.[1]

The Pension Reform Law introduced flexibility not only in a downward direction, however, but also in an upward direction. A system of supplements was introduced for the postponement of a pension claim. Under the Reform Law supplements of 0·4 per cent of the original pension level were to be payable for each month between the ages of sixty-three and sixty-seven for which the pension claim was postponed, without contributions to the pension scheme being payable during this period. Once again, however, the SDP/FDP pledged itself to change this situation, arguing that a supplement should be paid only in exchange for postponement of a pension claim after the age of sixty-five. If paid from sixty-three it would provide a positive incentive for the insured to continue working, and thus his choice of whether or not to draw an early pension would be dependent more on material factors than on his own capabilities or inclinations. The 4.RVAG therefore introduced an amendment, whereby a supplement of 0·6 per cent a month is paid for the postponement of a pension claim between the ages of sixty-five and sixty-seven. Furthermore, the new law requires the continuation of contributions to the pension scheme if a supplement is to be granted.

Whether or not a large proportion of insured will continue in employment after the age of sixty-five or will supplement their early pension with part-time earnings will depend very much on the labour market situation. There was some concern in the Federal Republic at the end of the 1960s about the lack of employ-

---

the new regulations she can earn an amount equivalent to about one quarter average earnings, in addition to her pension, between the age of sixty and sixty-two. After the age of sixty-three the same arrangements would apply as in the case of other insured persons.

[1] See *Bundesarbeitsblatt* 1/1972, p. 25.

ment opportunities for elderly persons,[1] probably accentuated by the fact that, as we have already mentioned, older employees had been the first to be made redundant during the recession of 1967–68. This concern resulted in provision being made in the 'Furtherance of Employment Act' (*Arbeitsförderungsgesetz*) of June 1969 for subsidies to be paid in certain circumstances to employers willing to employ older persons. It would appear, however, that this programme has proved to be of little significance.[2]

(e) Summary

These then are the current issues affecting pension insurance provisions for the elderly. There is no doubt that the future development of the pension schemes along the lines summarized above will bring about an improvement in the economic circumstances of those population groups who did not benefit from the 1957 legislation. It is not without interest, however, that the emphasis appears to be on extending the existing pension provisions. Despite the change in government since 1966 there has been no attempt to alter fundamentally the basic structure of the schemes as it affects the vast majority of the population.

This situation underlines one of the main features of the German provisions which distinguishes them from those in the United Kingdom. The reform of 1957, with its dynamic system of calculating and adjusting pension levels, resulted from a lengthy period of all-party discussion. Thus there is a fair amount of consensus of opinion between the parties resulting in the removal of pension insurance provisions on the whole from the main political arena. The approach of all political parties would appear to be a pragmatic one, based on what is best for the elderly as a group in the light of changing social and economic circumstances. This is reflected too in the use of independent research organizations to test general opinion on major proposed changes. These factors tend to give the impression of an essentially stable pension insurance system designed to meet the requirements of this particular section of the population.

---

[1] In 1965 (the latest figures available) only 11 per cent of the over sixty-fives continued to receive income from employment. (See *Wirtschaft und Statistik*, Feb. 1969.) Two thirds were self-employed or professional people.

[2] See *Bundesarbeitsblatt*, 6/1973, p. 284.

V—OTHER SOCIAL POLICY MEASURES
AFFECTING THE ELDERLY

Although there is considerable justification for placing the emphasis
in our discussion on the pension insurance provisions for the
elderly, the picture would be incomplete without a brief survey of
other measures which, although not intended solely for the old,
are likely to influence either their income level or their quality of
life in old age. Under this heading come property and savings
policies, housing provisions, health provisions and, finally, services
for the elderly.

(a) *Property and savings policies*

The main features of property and savings policies introduced after
World War II are based, in a similar way to pension insurance
provisions themselves, on a mixture of ideology and economic
necessity. From the conceptual viewpoint the neo-liberals, and
indeed all the political groups and forces in Germany after the war,
were, for varying reasons, committed to a policy of private ownership of capital. Capital was defined in its broadest sense as including shares in enterprises, personal savings and property. This
policy was not unconnected to policy for the aged. On the principle
that the ownership of capital gave the individual not only greater
security and increased freedom during his active life, but also in
his old age, an attempt was made to promote the will and the
ability of the working population to save.

At the same time, it should be noted that in the immediate
post-war period there was an urgent need for investment capital
for the industrial reconstruction programme and for investment in
building to alleviate the severe housing shortage. It was, therefore,
of some urgency that the private sector should be encouraged to
save despite the economic hardship of the post-war period. Any
form of forced savings approach was, however, firmly rejected as
being politically unacceptable and the emphasis was placed instead
on the use of tax concessions and direct bonus payments for
specific forms of savings and investment to stimulate personal
savings.

The measures adopted after the war in an attempt to increase the propensity to save of households differentiated between two forms of savings: general savings such as those deposited in savings accounts or investment trusts, or used for the purchase of stocks, bonds or debentures, and savings directly connected to house building.[1] These two types of saving were covered by two separate pieces of legislation.

In the immediate post-war period, general savings were encouraged simply by the use of income tax concessions. However, there was soon growing discontent with this type of incentive since, by its very nature, it did not benefit the less well-off members of society who were exempted from paying income tax. The issue became crucial in 1958 when a reform of the income tax system raised the tax threshold. An important change took place in 1959, therefore, with the introduction of the Savings Bonuses Act (the *Sparprämiengesetz*). In place of tax concessions, this Act introduced a system of bonus payments by the central Government (in addition to normal interest payable) on the specific forms of saving mentioned above if these were deposited for at least five years. The bonuses amounted to 20 per cent of the deposits, with a maximum level set which varied according to family circumstances. This maximum meant that married couples and larger families could have larger amounts of savings eligible for the bonus payment, but there was in fact no limitation of the scheme to lower or middle income groups. This lack of restriction gave rise to considerable criticism and as a result a system of additional bonuses for low income groups[2] was introduced in 1969.

As regards the second form of savings, the features of the Dwellings Construction Bonus Act (das *Wohnungsbau-Sparprämiengesetz*) of 1952 (amended in 1960) were essentially similar.[3]

---

[1] Deposits with home savings and loan associations, money used to purchase shares in construction and housing co-operatives, and home savings accounts with credit agencies and housing and development corporations.

[2] The supplementary bonuses are payable to single persons with an annual income (before savings) of not more than 6,000 DM and a married couple with income of less than 12,000 DM (i.e. around half average earnings and average earnings respectively in 1970).

[3] It should be noted that this incentive to house savings is quite separate from, although supplementary to, Government schemes aimed at directly promoting house building through loans, etc. These direct provisions, which were used in the main for the provision of low-cost 'social housing', will be discussed in the following sub-section on housing provisions. The incentives outlined here were intended to enable people to save towards the purchase of their own house.

Bonuses were again payable, varying between 25 and 30 per cent of deposits depending on family circumstances, with a maximum level set at 400 DM. Since 1969 an additional bonus for low income groups has also been payable. In this scheme, however, the saver could choose between the bonus and a tax concession. It would obviously be to the advantage of higher income earners to choose the latter option, since this would mean that he could set the amount of his savings against his taxable income.

Although there was general agreement in political circles on the need for such incentive schemes, there was a considerable amount of discontent during the 1950s at their apparent lack of success. It was felt that, although a fair number of persons were making use of the provisions, these were people who would have saved in any case. There had, therefore, been little increase in the distribution of total savings or in the general propensity to save.

New measures were required to bring new groups of the population within the 'savings orbit' by increasing their ability, as opposed to their will, to save. These measures were contained in the 'Act to Promote Saving and Investment by Employed Persons' (*Das Gesetz zur Förderung der Vermögensbildung in Arbeitnehmerhand*) of 1961, which has subsequently been revised in 1965 and 1970. In its original form this law provided tax concessions and exemption from social security contributions for both employers and employees who entered into an agreement for either part of the employee's normal wage or an addition to his wage up to a limit of 312 DM per annum[1] to be allocated for some savings purpose. As in the case of the two measures already mentioned, this allocation would, to qualify for the concessions, have to be blocked for a specific period. Savings made in this way could be allocated either to the two savings schemes outlined above,[2] or they could be used for the construction of a dwelling, used for the purchase of the stock of the enterprise (at preferential rates) or lent to the enterprise in return for a given rate of interest.

The same criticisms were, however, levelled at this scheme as at the others. The use of tax concessions tended to provide a relatively

---

[1] Or 468 DM per annum if the employee had three or more children.
[2] In which case they would qualify for the bonuses under these schemes, as well as for the tax concessions and social contributions exemptions.

greater benefit for the better off,[1] and the reduction of income liable for social security contributions was not a net gain because this led to a reduction in the level of social benefits to which the employee was entitled. The major amendments to the law in 1970 introduced therefore a system of bonuses amounting to 30 per cent of the savings which was to replace the previous system in 1971. At the same time the maximum amount which could benefit from the incentives was doubled from its previous very low level of 312 DM and the scheme was limited to employees in the middle or low income brackets.[2]

How successful have these measures been in increasing the number of savers in the population? In 1969 it was estimated that almost 10 million persons were participating in either the Savings Bonuses scheme or the Housing Construction Bonuses scheme, with bonuses amounting to some 6 Mrd DM being granted under the first scheme between 1959 and 1968, and 15 Mrd DM in bonuses or tax concessions under the second between 1950 and 1967.[3] These 10 million people account for about 20 per cent of the population over eighteen years of age, and can be taken, therefore, to represent about 40 per cent of households.

Perhaps the most striking success is to be found, however, in the development of savings by employed persons since the new law of 1970. The record of these provisions until 1969 had been very disappointing indeed: in 1969 only 5·7 million employees were participating in the scheme and the level of savings concerned amounted in that year to only around 1·6 Mrd DM. By the end of 1971, however, the number of employees with contractual agreements of the type laid down in the Act had more than doubled to 14·5 million, while the level of savings during 1971 had risen to 6·3 Mrd DM.[4] This improvement has meant that two-thirds of all employees are now participating in the scheme. Savings undertaken through this incentive scheme also increased from only about

---

[1] It was in fact estimated that about 4 million employees were excluded from the incentive scheme by the use of tax concessions.

[2] Single persons with income of less than 24,000 DM per annum, and married couples with an income of less than 48,000 DM (i.e. about twice and four times average earnings in 1970).

[3] See 'Die bisherigen Massnahmen zur Spar-und Vermögensförderung', by Dr Rolf Schwedes in *Bundesarbeitsblatt* 12/1969, pp. 746–47.

[4] See 'Die Belastung der Wirtschaft bei voller Ausschopfung des 624-DM-Gesetzes', by Dr Günter Halbach in *Bundesarbeitsblatt* 3/1972, p. 160.

E

3 per cent of total private savings in 1969 to around 11 per cent in 1971. It is clear that the growth of this and the other schemes is severely limited by the low ceilings on savings eligible for bonuses and on the bonuses themselves. If the schemes, and particularly that aimed at increasing savings in the hands of employees, continue to grow at their present rate, however, then it is to be expected that a large proportion of employed persons will, in the future, be able to look forward to not only a substantial statutory pension, but also additional income in their old age from capital and savings. These provisions can be seen therefore to constitute an important part of long-term policy for the aged.

(b) Housing allowances

The measures which have just been considered are to some extent part of housing policy as a whole since they contain some incentives to encourage savings towards personal home ownership. In the immediate post-war period, however, the housing market in Germany was in such chaos that it would have been impossible to rely solely on private initiative and private savings to bring about a rebuilding programme. Despite its general dislike of direct state participation, this was one area where the neo-liberal Government at the time was compelled to intervene. Not only did the homes destroyed in the war have to be rebuilt, but there were an additional nine million or so homeless refugees requiring some form of shelter.

The policy measures adopted in the light of the severe housing shortage were, first, the imposing of rent controls on all pre-1948 housing and, second, the payment of large Government subsidies to builders willing to build low-cost 'social housing'. The result was that some five million dwellings were built in the course of the 1950s, almost two-thirds of them being financed by means of these subsidies.

This direct intervention by the central Government could, however, remain compatible with neo-liberal doctrine only for as long as such intervention was justified by the market situation. When, at the beginning of the 1960s, the housing shortage became less severe, the neo-liberals attempted to revert to a free market situation through the lifting of rent controls and the abolition of social housing grants. In their place housing allowances were to be granted in cases where this change of policy resulted in hardship. A complete and sudden transition from the post-war interventionist policy to a *laissez-faire* approach proved to be impossible, however, on account of strong political pressures. Gradual changes were accomplished nevertheless in the mid-1960s, with a substantial reduction in expenditure on social housing and removal of rent controls in some areas, depending on the housing situation in the area.

In conjunction with this relaxation of rent restrictions, the role of individual housing allowances, which had previously been very limited, was to be extended. Until 1965, when the Housing Allowance Act or '*Wohnungsgeldgesetz*' was introduced, the most important form of allowance which had existed was that paid by the social aid authorities (paid in addition to the maintenance allowance, and very much at the discretion of the local authorities). The new Act introduced a comprehensive scheme of allowances, however, with conditions of eligibility and the level of the benefit determined at a national level. Despite the change of government in 1966, soon after this Act was introduced, housing allowance provisions have continued to develop, owing to the fact that the Social Democrats, although opposed to the reduction in social housing, were largely in favour of the substitution of allowances to those in need for general rent controls. The basis of the housing allowances scheme was essentially that households should be required to pay only a certain percentage of their income for housing costs, the exact proportion dependent on family size; this included both rent payers and owner occupiers. Subject to certain conditions regarding the size of the dwelling and the level of the rent or the cost burden, assistance would be provided (financed by the central and the local government) if this proportion were exceeded.[1] In order to provide assistance to those most in need, there was a family means test attached to payment of the allowance, with the conditions being determined in such a way that all households with an income approximately equal to the average earnings would be eligible.

These features were largely retained in the second Housing

---

[1] In order to distinguish this allowance from the rent allowance paid to those receiving continuous assistance from social aid, the individual householders did not, however, receive the full housing costs from the scheme; they had to meet a proportion of the costs themselves.

Allowance Law which came into force in 1971. The new law did try, however, to simplify to some extent the conditions of eligibility as well as bring the limits applicable to income as well as to the level of the rent or housing burden more into line with the current situation. It is questionable whether it was the fact that these variables remained static between 1965 and 1971, while incomes and housing costs were rapidly rising, or whether it was the general complexity of the scheme which gave rise to the disappointingly low uptake of the benefit. In 1969 only 850,000 households, accounting for about 3 per cent of total households or 2·7 per cent of the population, were in receipt of an allowance from the scheme. The number had risen in 1971 to some 7 per cent of households as a result of amendments to the law and the fact that recipients of social aid became eligible for the allowance from 1970, instead of receiving their rent allowance only from the social aid authorities. Nevertheless, response has been lower than that anticipated by the Government on the introduction of the scheme.

However limited the effect of the scheme has been, it is true to say that the elderly have been one of the main groups to benefit from the allowance. Pensioners accounted in 1969 for 56 per cent of all beneficiaries and 65 per cent of those receiving rent allowances.[1] The allowance has above all, it would seem, had the effect of preventing this number of old persons from having to seek, not continuous social aid, but occasional assistance with rent costs. In doing so, this allowance system has helped to establish an interesting trend in social provisions in Germany. Whereas residual means-tested benefits of the traditional kind, namely social aid, have been declining in terms of expenditure relative to other social expenditure, new methods of means-tested allowances aimed at directing allowances to those most in need have been introduced with the effect of reversing this trend and bringing about a rise in means-tested provisions as a whole.[2]

(c) Health provisions for the aged

We have already seen that the vast majority of old persons in Germany receive some form of pension from the two main pension insurance schemes for manual and white-collar workers. These pen-

---

[1] See Third *Wohngeldbericht.*
[2] See *Sozialbericht 1971*, BMfAS, p. 71, para 16.

sioners are automatically insured, without payment of contributions,[1] in the general statutory sickness insurance scheme. Thus access to medical care is free, and they are also completely exempted from all prescription charges. The miners too have their own quite separate medical care scheme, in which recipients of miners' pension provisions are covered.

Those old persons who do not receive pensions from these schemes may, on the other hand, have to meet the cost of voluntary medical insurance coverage themselves, either in the statutory scheme or a private sickness fund. Most of them do, however, have protection of some form, and it is only some groups of self-employed persons, predominantly the independent farmers, who have been the cause of some concern in the past owing to their lack of insurance. In cases of need, they could of course always rely on assistance with medical costs from the social aid authorities.

It is likely, however, that this position will alter considerably in the course of the next few years. In the first place, the Government has already announced in 1972 that a special compulsory sickness insurance scheme for independent farmers is to be set up. Secondly, the extension of membership of the general pension insurance schemes to additional groups in the population[2] will mean equally an extension of the special pensioners' sickness insurance scheme and thus the removal of remaining gaps in the present system.

One of the main areas in general medical care for the elderly which is, however, causing some concern in the 1970s is that of geriatric provisions. The reasons for this state of affairs require some consideration of services for the elderly as a whole, which will conclude this section.

(d) Services for the elderly

When considering services for the elderly in Germany, it is not only the type of provision which is of interest, but also the way in which provision is made. The two are, of course, interrelated. We have already seen that social aid, based as it is on a concept of individual need, has been left in the hands of local bodies instead

---

[1] Between 1968 and 1970 pensioners did have to contribute 2 per cent of their pension towards the cost of medical care, but this decision was repealed in 1970 and contributions paid in this way have since been reimbursed in full.

[2] See Section IV.

of being administered at a centralized level. Provisions to be made at such personal level have tended, it would seem, to be regarded as being outside the competence of central Government. In the field of community services responsibility has likewise tended to remain in the hands of charitable organizations, which may be either of a religious or a non-denominational nature.

Voluntary associations in Germany enjoy a somewhat privileged position. Although they are subsidized to a large extent by the local authorities in whose areas they work, and for whom they often carry out tasks on a contract basis (the remainder of their finance coming from donations or from a share in the compulsory church tax), they are on the whole entirely responsible for the setting up of and administration of the majority of hospitals, old peoples' homes, children's homes, community services, and provisions such as meals on wheels and home helps, as well as special flats for old persons.

This situation has meant that, although services in some areas may indeed be excellent, this depends very much on the initiative of the voluntary organizations. Provision is, as a result, not at all uniform throughout the country owing to the lack of a general plan for the best allocation of resources. Geriatric provisions which, as mentioned above, appear to have been neglected to a large extent, stand witness to the shortcomings of the system.

Some attempt is being made by the Federal Government at the beginning of the 1970s, however, to remedy this and similar situations through its taking some initiative in the establishing of services. It is not the intention of the Government to take over the running of the services itself—the opposition on the part of the voluntary organizations would be immense. It has, however, expressed its readiness to provide both the initiative and the initial financial assistance to establish new provisions.[1]

It is of importance for our general discussion that the particular types of provision which the Government has in mind in making these proposals concern the elderly. As in many other countries, attention has turned to the social and psychological problems of the elderly as opposed to their financial problems, and emphasis has moved to community care services to enable the elderly to maintain an independent existence in their own homes for as long

---

[1] Cf. *Sozialbericht 1971*, BMfAS, p. 37.

as possible and to alleviate at the same time feelings of isolation and loneliness. It is the Government's intention in Germany to promote an increase not only in residential accommodation for the aged in the form of old people's homes or nursing homes, but also in special dwellings constructed with the needs of the elderly in mind. It is intended that there should be an increase in the provision of meeting places and day centres, social counselling services, meals on wheels, films, and even special large-print library books, all of which would help the old person to maintain his or her social contacts.

VI—CONCLUSION: A LOOK TO THE FUTURE

In the past, Germany has often been hailed as being in the forefront in the field of income maintenance in old age. We have seen that, for the vast majority of old people, this is indeed the case. Looking to the future, then, it would appear that Germany is well on the way to consolidating this position which she achieved by the pension reform in 1957. Through the so-called second pension reform of 1972 pension insurance coverage has been extended to new groups of the working and non-working population, thus filling in the gaps which previously existed in pension provisions. Important developments are taking place too in other fields. Housing allowance provisions, for example, which are, at the beginning of the 1970s, still relatively undeveloped, will, in all probability, be extended to provide wider cover and more generous benefits; capital formation policies are also on the verge of expansion. Services for the elderly too are, we have seen, emerging from a period of relative neglect and are likely to undergo vast development in the course of the next decade. These changes, together with the greater freedom of choice for the elderly which will accompany the introduction of the flexible pension age, should greatly improve prospects for future generations of pensioners.

CHAPTER THREE

The Netherlands

I—INTRODUCTION

The Netherlands stands apart from its neighbours in the EEC in the field of pensions in so far as it has retained a minimum flat-rate benefit, whereas other members of the original Six have tended to turn to provisions reflecting the earnings of the beneficiaries. It would, however, be rash to infer that the elderly population in the Netherlands is likely to be experiencing hardship in comparison to the elderly in the other countries we have studied. The elderly population in the Netherlands, comprising at the beginning of the 1970s about 10 per cent of the total population, is in fact a highly favoured group, with over 30 per cent of total social insurance expenditure being devoted to the statutory old age pension system.[1] There is general concern that everything possible should be done to improve the lot of the aged, both in material and social terms. In the seventies, because of severe economic pressures, the rate of growth of public expenditure is being cut back in the Netherlands (with proposals for restricting family allowances and introducing cost-sharing health insurance), yet policy for the aged is continuing to move forward with little reduction in its expenditure programme foreseen for the next planning period. The attitude seems to be that any economies which have to be introduced cannot be allowed to impinge on this group of the population. On the contrary, there are plans to improve the financial position of

---

[1] See Table 3.1.

the aged considerably through structural changes in the basic pension benefit.

TABLE 3.1

*The development of expenditure on old age pensions
as a percentage of GNP, 1960–70*

Year	Gross national product (current market prices), Mrd guilders	Social insurance[1] expenditure as percentage of GNP	General old-age insurance as percentage of social insurance	General old age insurance	Public servants pensions	Comple-mentary[2] pension benefits
				As percentage of GNP		
1960	42·7	7·7	33·3	2·6	0·7	0·3
1961	45·3	7·7	33·4	2·6	0·7	0·4
1962	48·5	8·3	34·5	2·9	0·7	0·4
1963	52·9	10·0	31·6	3·2	0·9	0·4
1964	62·1	10·1	32·2	3·2	1·0	0·4
1965	69·4	11·3	36·9	4·2	1·0	0·4
1966	75·4	12·1	35·7	4·3	1·0	0·4
1967	83·0	12·6	34·7	4·4	1·1	0·4
1968	91·9	13·4	31·8	4·3	1·1	0·4
1969	102·3	14·2	31·7	4·5	1·1	0·4
1970	113·1	14·8	31·2	4·6	1·1	0·4

In addition to the first-tier state pension, which all residents receive at the age of sixty-five, a large proportion of Dutch employees in both the public and private sectors are also eligible for some form of second-tier occupational provision. Occupational schemes in the private sector are organized either on an enterprise or an industry-wide basis, and have always been viewed in the Netherlands as an important and integral part of the total pension structure. While the state has provided a basic minimum pension, it has been considered the responsibility of the occupational schemes to supplement this flat-rate benefit.

The whole system of pension provision in the Netherlands is

---

[1] Social insurance comprises old age pensions, general widows' and orphans' pensions, children's allowances, health fund insurance, unemployment and redundancy benefits, sickness benefit insurance, incapacity for work insurance (before 1967 accident insurance and disability pensions).

[2] Includes only risk-bearing occupational funds and excludes re-insurance. Approximately 80 per cent of this figure, which includes all forms of pensions, can be attributed to old age pensions.

poised on the brink of a new period of development in the 1970s, in which it is likely that the occupational schemes will be integrated more formally with the state schemes. An outline of the issues involved is given in Section III. The proposals being considered foresee a considerable expansion of occupational provisions and a standardization of the amount and type of supplementary provision to be afforded by the schemes, resulting in all employed persons having a claim, on retirement, to a total pension (inclusive of the state benefit) of 70 per cent of their final gross earnings (up to a ceiling). More could, of course, be provided by private provision on a voluntary basis.

These developments would clearly have a significant effect too on the importance of residual public assistance provisions, which are considered in some detail in Section IV of the chapter. In this area, the apparent stringency of the qualifying conditions for assistance, probably a relic of the 'poor law' character of the scheme until its recent reform of 1965, affords a contrast with the generosity of the benefits provided. Although the Netherlands scheme has a certain similarity to the British scheme in that the assistance benefit is, as in the UK, retained at a higher level than the old age pension, there is little similarity in the level of the benefit itself. Whereas the rate for a pensioner couple (inclusive of an average rent allowance) in the UK was, in 1970, around 40 per cent of average male manufacturing wages, the Dutch rate, at almost 60 per cent, is half as high again.

Section IV also deals with the question of housing provision for the elderly. Not only does the Netherlands have places in residential accommodation for 10 per cent of the elderly (compared with around 2 per cent in the UK), but it is active in the provision of special houses and flats suited to the requirements of elderly persons. A study of these, welfare services and health provisions, serves to round off this survey of the nature and extent of provisions for the elderly in the Netherlands. A brief summary in Section V concludes that the Netherlands, although attracting relatively little attention from social commentators in other countries, has emerged as being one of the most advanced welfare societies as regards care of the aged.

II—PENSION PROVISIONS FOR THE AGED

(a) The statutory old age pension scheme

Historical background. Like its neighbours in the EEC, the Netherlands had traditionally confined compulsory coverage of social security schemes to employed persons. When its first old age pension scheme was introduced in 1913, the non-contributory pension was paid only to those who had a certain employment record. This restriction was maintained in 1919 when the first pension insurance provisions were introduced in the Disability Act of that year, providing coverage for old age, survivors and disability. Membership of the scheme was limited to manual and white-collar workers with income below a certain affiliation limit, who received, on reaching the age of sixty-five, an old age pension based on the value of their contributions to the scheme. This scheme was admittedly supplemented, also in 1919, by a voluntary old age insurance to which the self-employed could belong, but it seems that few were able to afford the contributions required for membership.

Discontent with this system of provision began to make itself felt shortly before World War II, but war broke out before any major reforms could take place. The circumstances in the immediate post-war period merely served, therefore, to intensify feelings about the need to extend compulsory statutory coverage for old age provisions to the whole population. Those elderly persons with no insurance cover were in a particularly needy position after the war since many had lost their possessions and their family and thus their whole means of livelihood. Those who received a pension under the 1919 Disability Act were in fact little better off, since benefits were fairly low and needed to be supplemented by personal provision which was, in many cases, no longer available. In 1947 an Emergency Interim Act was passed to provide immediate assistance to the elderly in need. For the first time this provided pensions, subject to a means test, to all persons over the age of sixty-five whether or not they had been employees.

This reliance on means-tested old-age benefits was, however, to be nothing more than a short-term measure. As in Germany, where a very similar situation existed after the war, a long-term solution to the problem of provision for the aged was required. The similarity between Germany and the Netherlands was carried still further by the long delay before an acceptable solution could be found and implemented. The year 1957 was chosen by both countries to bring into force new pension insurance legislation, but it is here that the similarity ends. Political pressures pushed pension insurance in quite different directions in the two countries. Whereas Germany set up a graduated pension scheme, the Netherlands opted for flat-rate official pensions. It must be said at once that this choice was based on quite good grounds of principle but the making of the choice was also influenced, as we shall see, by institutional arrangements in Holland.

The influence of the two sides of industry. One of the main factors giving rise to the delay just mentioned, and one which is of the utmost importance for an understanding of the development of provisions for the elderly in the Netherlands, was the prior existence of established pension schemes administered and financed by individual firms and industries. These had begun before World War II and had developed greatly in the immediate post-war period as a result of the continuing close co-operation between the two sides of industry initiated during the occupation. These individual occupational pension funds were not inclined to surrender any of their autonomy.

The existence of these occupational provisions was, it was suggested to us in interview, the major reason that an employment based, earnings-related scheme, such as was introduced in neighbouring West Germany, also in 1957, was rejected in the Netherlands. Instead, in the General Old Age Act (*de Algemene Ouderdomswet*), or *AOW* as it is known, the Dutch legislature introduced a pension scheme providing universal coverage[1] on the grounds of residence. The benefit to be provided was to be a flat-rate one. The occupational funds thus won their fight to limit statutory provision to a basic level of allowance and to retain their right to supplement this through their own pension provisions.

The influence of the two sides of industry on social policy has

---

[1] It is interesting that the principle of universal protection is gradually being extended in the Netherlands to cover the major risks (such as survivors' provisions, and long-term sickness costs) although schemes for employed persons only still exist.

been making itself felt in the Netherlands since the beginning of the century. Each new piece of social legislation was surrounded by heated discussions as to whether its administration should be in the hands of government or industrial organizations. The Old Age Act was no exception. In the case of the employment-based insurance schemes such as had been the norm prior to the introduction of the AOW in 1957, the administration had predominantly been entrusted to 'occupational associations'. These had been established on the initiative of the two sides of industry and were composed of representatives of employers and employees. The demand of these associations to be allowed to administer the AOW also was rejected as incompatible with a universal social insurance scheme. Its administration was delegated instead to the Social Insurance Bank in Amsterdam and to twenty-two regional Labour Councils (*Raden van Arbeid*) throughout the country. The Social Insurance Bank is composed of a Chairman, appointed by the Minister for Social Affairs, and fifteen members, one third of whom are representatives of employers, one third representatives of employees and one third appointed by the Minister. This body is responsible for supervising the Labour Councils which consist of a Chairman appointed by the Crown, and six members appointed by the Minister, of whom three represent the employers and three the employees.

This compromise between the Government on the one side and the industrial organizations on the other permeates the whole of the field of social administration in the Netherlands. It manifests itself too in policy-making, where Government decisions are normally based on consultation with independent advisory bodies such as the Foundation of Labour (*Stichting van de Arbeid*) and the Social and Economic Council (*Sociaal-Economische Raad*). The Foundation of Labour was officially established in 1945, although its genesis can be traced back to the years of occupation. During this time, Dutch employers and employees, working together in the underground movement, made a pledge to continue to work together after liberation to maintain industrial peace and discipline in the Netherlands and to raise the living standards of the Dutch population. It has been the practice of the Government to consult with this organization of employers' and employees' representatives on issues affecting wages and working conditions. The Foundation, in its turn, set up a number of permanent committees to handle matters referred to it, such as committees on wages, on social insurance, public health, health insurance, and industrial training. For some time this was the main advisory body to the Government on social policy matters. Its place now seems to have been taken, however, by the Social and Economic Council. This latter body came into existence as a result of the Industrial Organization Act of 1950. Its task was to establish a comprehensive statutory organizational framework for management–labour relations. Over time, however, the function of the Council has tended to shift in emphasis and scope, until it has become the most influential advisory board on social and economic policy to the Government. It is composed of an equal number of representatives of employees' organizations, employers' organizations, and independent experts or 'Crown members'. It responds to Government requests for advice on specific matters and also has a mandate to investigate and advise the Government on any social and economic issues which it feels ought to be brought to the Government's attention. Its advice must by law be sought before any significant changes in social policy legislation are introduced, and, although the Government is under no obligation to accept its advice, it tends on the whole to do so.

It is against this background of pressure by the two sides of industry that we must now turn to consider the form which pension provision for old age takes in the Netherlands of the seventies.

Pension provision under the AOW. As has already been mentioned, the AOW introduced in 1957 a universal flat-rate old age pension.[1] In the first instance, the level chosen for the pension was that equivalent to the highest benefit payable (these had differed according to region) under the emergency interim provisions which had been in force from 1947 to the introduction of the AOW. This new benefit was no longer means-tested as was the case under the interim act, but was payable to all residents as of right and with no retirement condition at the age of sixty-five.

Conditions attached to the payment of the old age pension are, in practice, very few. In the law of 1957 there is mention of a so-called 'contribution condition' which states that 'a full old age

---

[1] Provisions payable under both the 1919 Pension Acts continued to be paid after the introduction of the new scheme, but these are small and the schemes are gradually being phased out.

pension will only be paid to persons who have been insured from the age of fifteen to the age of sixty-five and have not deliberately avoided paying their contribution'. A 2 per cent reduction in the pension benefit is envisaged for each year of non-payment. Although this may appear an excessively long qualifying period, the fifty-year insurance period has in fact little significance in practice. Persons who were over fifteen years of age when the scheme came into force and who cannot therefore fulfil the qualifying period are accredited, during the transition period, with having paid contributions from the age of fifteen. Those already over sixty-five in 1957 also received the full pension. 'Blanketing-in' has been a simple matter.

The main reason for the 'contribution condition' is really the prevention of an accumulation of various pension rights by persons who move between countries (e.g. within the EEC) and thus earn a claim to benefits for the time spent in these other countries. A reduction in pension claims will also be made, of course, for any persons failing to pay contributions when they are liable to do so. In effect, since contributions to the pension schemes are levied in conjunction with the general income tax system, non-payment of contributions is a very rare occurrence. Evasion of payment is simply not felt to be a problem in the Netherlands.

Between the introduction of the scheme at the beginning of 1957 and the end of 1973, the pension level has increased by over seven-fold in current money terms in the case of a single person and by over six-fold in the case of a married couple. In real terms the value of the old age pension has increased by some 360 per cent and 300 per cent respectively. (It should be noted that in the Netherlands, as in the UK, the pension for a couple is payable only when the man reaches the pension age of sixty-five. His wife, if she is older, receives nothing until her husband qualifies.) The movement in benefit levels can be accounted for by two distinct and separate mechanisms: first, the AOW has, since its introduction, been related to general wage developments by a so-called *dynamism mechanism* and, second, several *structural changes* have been made with the aim of raising the level of pensions relatively to income from work.

First, the procedure for dynamizing pensions in payment in the Netherlands takes account not only of changes in prices, but also of movements in wages. Thus the relative position of the pensioner in the general income structure is guaranteed. The index used to adjust pensions is a combined index of negotiated wages and salary rates for adult employees in all categories of employment. A Royal Decree is required before any adjustment can take place. Until 1972 the adjustment process was initiated when there was a rise in the wage index of at least 3 per cent. There was no significant lag incorporated in the adjustment formula, and a movement of the specified magnitude in the wage index always resulted in an immediate announcement that the pension would be adjusted accordingly. There might, of course, be an administrative lag of three to four months before the revised pension was payable, but it seems that the new level was then back-dated to the time when the initial index change occurred.

The fact that each adjustment process requires a separate Royal Decree would tend to suggest that the Government is retaining the power to recommend, if the general economic situation were to warrant it, that no adjustment should take place. Theoretically it seems it has the power to do this, but those closely involved in this field in the Netherlands have emphasized strongly in interview that such a decision would be politically impossible. Whatever curtailments may have to be made in public expenditure as a whole, provisions for the aged are most unlikely to be affected. This is one point on which all the political parties appear to be united.

As a rule, changes have occurred once or twice a year, but the frequency of pension adjustments has been increasing, reflecting the rampant price and wage inflation causing concern in the Netherlands at the beginning of the 1970s. The pension level rose no less than four times in 1971. This has given rise to obvious administrative difficulties and also to a great deal of confusion and uncertainty among the elderly population as to what pension they are actually entitled to. From the beginning of 1972, therefore, it has been decided to standardize the adjustment procedure to twice a year. Pensions will be reviewed on 1 January according to the wage index at the end of October and on 1 July, using the wage index for the end of April.

The second factor in the development of pension levels is that of *structural change*. The effect of these adjustments can be clearly seen, for example, in the fact that the pension for a married couple has risen from some 32 per cent to over 48 per cent of average gross wages of men in industry between 1958 and 1973, while the pension for a single person has similarly increased from 20 per cent to some 35 per cent of average gross wages.[1]

The largest structural change during this period was that in 1965, when the pension index (1957 = 100) rose to 263 from the 1964 level of 207 in the case of a married couple and from 224 to 306 for a single person. This development was a result of the decision to raise the pension from what might be termed a subsistence minimum to a so-called 'social minimum', which would allow the old person some small comforts over and above what he required simply to survive.

It is interesting that an attempt was made to determine the level of this 'social minimum' in an *objective* manner. The choice was based on an investigation of minimum requirements carried out by the Central Planning Office, in conjunction with the Social and Economic Council. This study suggested that the social minimum for a married couple should be set at 70 per cent of the minimum guaranteed gross income of an industrial worker. At the same time it was decided that the pension accruing to a single person should be 70 per cent of that of a married couple. This brought about a greater relative increase for the single person, as is reflected in the index figures. The pension for a single person had previously varied between 60 per cent and 65 per cent of that for a married couple. Although the social minimum was determined in this way, it has not been regarded as static but has subsequently been raised in line with earnings.

Despite this significant increase in benefit levels in 1964 further increases in the basic pension level have been introduced to try to satisfy demands for a still higher income for the elderly population. The principle has been accepted by Parliament that the pension level for a couple should be raised by around 20 per cent over the 1965 level to 100 per cent of the *net* minimum wage. This would be equivalent to approximately 85 per cent of the gross minimum wage. Since the gross minimum wage itself is at a level of about 70 per cent of average gross manufacturing wages, which is fairly high relative to most other countries, this would really

---

[1] The AOW pensioners also receive a holiday supplement, payable in the month of May and equal, since 1971, to 6 per cent of the pension benefit.

It should be noted that, since the beginning of 1973, the income tax threshold has, for both single persons and couples, been set at such a level as to entirely exempt old age pensioners with no additional income to their basic state pension from payment of tax. (See *Op Leeftijd*, 10/1972, pp. 31–2.)

provide the Dutch pensioner with a high position in the international league of pension levels. The initial target date for
attainment of this goal was January 1973, but it now seems unlikely
that this target will be met before 1975.[1] The pension has, however,
approximated very closely to the net minimum wage since 1 January
1973 when the 5 per cent gap which existed between the pension
level and the net minimum wage was significantly reduced by a
4 per cent structural rise in the pension.[2] At the same time,
however, the minimum wage itself underwent a 3 per cent structural
rise.[3]

It should perhaps be noted at this point that widows in the
Netherlands, as well as the elderly, benefit from the generosity of
the provisions just outlined. After the first step towards the separation of social insurance provisions for the old, survivors, and the
disabled had been taken with the introduction of the old age
pension insurance in 1957 (it will be remembered that the 1919
insurance scheme had a multi-functional character), the next step
was the introduction of a completely separate insurance scheme
for widows and orphans towards the end of 1959. This was the
so-called *Algemene Weduwen—en Wezenwet* (AWW). This had
much in common with the old age scheme. It too provided universal flat-rate benefits. In comparison to equivalent benefits in
many other countries, widows' provisions in the Netherlands
appear to be generous, and there would certainly appear to be relatively little concern about poverty among this group. For example,
a benefit equal to the old age pension for a single person is paid
to widows between the age of forty and sixty-four. If there is a
child under the age of eighteen, the pension is paid from the age of
thirty-five and is equivalent to the old age pension for a married
couple.

The financial structure of the AOW pension scheme. The general
financial principle of the AOW scheme is one of pay-as-you-go.

---

[1] See *Op Leeftijd*, Oct. 1972, p. 5.
[2] See *Op Leeftijd*, Dec. 1972, p. 39. From Jan. 1973 the pension amounts to
5,910 guilders (single) and 8,370 guilders (married) constituting a total rise of
about 10 per cent over its previous level, through the combination of the structural and the normal wage-related increase.
[3] The minimum wage is adjusted according to the same index and at the same
time as pensions to prevent the situation arising where pensions might rise above
the minimum wage.

This universal flat-rate benefit is financed mainly by the contributions of the insured with only a small subsidy from general revenue. Everyone with an income above a very low floor is obliged to contribute a percentage of his income (up to a ceiling) to the pension scheme. Both employed persons and the self-employed are obliged to contribute.

If the individual has an income below the floor, which, in 1973, was set at 1,800 guilders per annum in the case of a single person, or 2,400 in the case of a married person, he is completely exempt from payment of contributions. In practice it is unlikely that this floor will have any great significance. It has not been adjusted upwards since 1965 and so has decreased greatly in importance. It should, for example, be compared to average industrial earnings in 1973 which amounted to some 18,000 guilders per annum. If the individual has an income between this floor and 3,420 (for a single person) or 4,020 (for a married person) and if his social security tax is not deducted at source, his contribution rate is reduced. This will normally apply to self-employed persons. The Netherlands tax system is such that a wages tax is deducted at source from the income of all employees. An income tax is levied in addition at the end of the year if he has had any additional income. At the same time he may have to pay additional social security contributions. Self-employed persons who do not pay a wages tax pay their social security contributions together with their income tax.

In the case of employed persons, the contribution is collected through the normal wage-tax mechanism. The contribution is payable on income between the floor and an income ceiling, which is equivalent to approximately one and a half times average industrial earnings. The ceiling too is dynamized and is linked to the same wage index as governs the movement in pensions. By dynamizing the contribution ceiling in this way, the Dutch have avoided the danger of creating an imbalance in the system which inevitably occurs when a dynamic benefit structure is linked to a non-dynamic system of finance.

When the new old age pension scheme was introduced in 1957, the contribution rate was set at 6·75 per cent of earnings. This rate was in fact reduced between 1960 and 1962 to compensate for the additional contribution burden resulting from the introduction of the general widows' and orphans' pension scheme in 1960, then regained its original level in 1963 and 1964. The contribution

rate then rose substantially to 8·7 per cent, reflecting the decision
to raise the old age pension to the level of a social minimum. This
rate remained fairly stable for a few years, but subsequent structural changes in the pension and a deteriorating age structure have
necessitated further increases. In 1971 the rate rose to 9·9 per cent,
then to 10·3 per cent in 1972, and to 10·4 per cent in 1973. It is to
rise still further to 10·6 per cent in 1974.

The Netherlands differs from most of its neighbours in that the
total contribution is levied on the insured person alone. The
employer does not contribute directly to the old age pension
scheme. The whole complicated issue of the incidence of social
security taxes is raised, however, by the fact that there is an *explicit*
assumption in the Netherlands that the employer will increase wage
levels to compensate for this burden and that any further increases
in the contribution rate will be reflected in higher wage rates.
Whereas there is often a tendency to assume that whoever pays the
contribution bears the cost, the fallacy of this belief is generally
recognized in the Netherlands. It is true that this in itself does not
solve the problems of incidence, but at least it poses the question.

The contributions of the insured comprise almost the total
revenue of the scheme, and it is interesting to note the extremely low
level of state participation in the financing of the scheme. In 1973,
for example, the state subsidy to the AOW scheme represented
less than 3 per cent of total revenue. The purpose of the subsidy is,
first, to meet the cost of pensions for low-income recipients who,
as mentioned above, are totally or partially exempt from payment
of contributions and, second, to meet any temporary deficit which
may result from short-term fluctuations in either revenue or
expenditure. At times the state subsidy has also been used to
prevent too large and too sudden an increase in contribution rates.
This explains the substantial rise in the subsidy between 1964 and
1966 when it rose from 1 per cent of total revenue to 5·4 per cent.
The level of the state subsidy is linked to the wage index and
therefore rises automatically. It is likely to become a falling proportion of the total by this method, however, since, although
moving with the wage level, it will not take into account the
growing burden of pensioners.

As a result of the combination of an earnings-related contribution system and a flat-rate benefit, there would seem to be a
significant degree of vertical income redistribution incorporated in

the system, albeit limited by the existence of the contribution ceiling. There is, however, little opposition to this situation in the Netherlands. The need for such a form of financial organization appears to be widely accepted. It was pointed out in interview that the question of redistribution must in fact be considered over the lifetime of the individual. Those with higher than average incomes often enter the labour force at a later age and therefore the relatively shorter period of insurance compensates in part for the higher contributions payable. In addition, the extent of the redistribution is limited by the existence of the contribution ceiling. There would seem to be more concern about the variation in the relationship of contributions paid to benefits received between single and married persons. A report published in 1970.[1] has suggested that some adjustment should in fact be made in the contribution rate for single persons over a certain age. It would seem unlikely however that, because of the growing pressure on financial resources, any such amendment would be contemplated in the immediate future.

The pension burden. Although the Dutch pension scheme is not affected by a growing financial burden resulting from the maturing of pension rights, such as faces graduated schemes with long transitional periods in other countries, it is nevertheless affected, as are its neighbours in the EEC, by an increasing proportion of elderly persons in the total population. The ratio of over-sixty-fives to the total population is expected to increase from its 1970 position of 10·1 per cent to 11·1 per cent by 1990 and the ratio of over-sixty-fives to the population of working age (fifteen to sixty-four) from 16·2 per cent in 1970 to 17·6 per cent in 1990.[2]

It is, however, generally accepted in the Netherlands that, if financial disequilibrium were to appear in the pension insurance scheme as the result of a growing elderly population, it should be countered, not by a decrease in the rate of growth of benefits, but rather by an increase in contributions. 'In view of the necessity of making a choice between raising the contributions, revising the conditions for granting certain benefits, or raising the Government's contributions, the social security schemes in the Netherlands

---

[1] See *Commissie Premiedruk in de sociale verzekering*, Stâatsuitgeverij, The Hague, 1970.
[2] These are 1970 projections which are rather more favourable than the previous (1967) estimates.

have always decided in favour of the raising of the contributions. Thus the problem of the financial equilibrium has changed into a problem of an increasing burden of contributions.'[1]

It seems that the Netherlands intends to achieve its stated aims regarding the expansion of certain social security benefits, in particular the setting of the old age pension equal to the net minimum wage, while at the same time limiting the growth of the financial burden, by implementing offsetting cost reductions in other policy areas. It has been suggested, for example, that any necessary increase in the old age pension contribution rate could be offset by trying to lower the contribution rate in the child allowance insurance scheme (by freezing the allowance for the first and second child) and in the sickness fund scheme (by introducing an element of participation in costs). Much depends, of course, on the priorities attached to the various branches of social policy.

(b) Second-tier occupational pensions

The preceding section will have shown that there is a close similarity between the Netherlands and the United Kingdom in the structure of their basic flat-rate pension schemes. The role which has been allotted to second-tier occupational provisions in the Netherlands is also very similar to that outlined for occupational pension schemes in the United Kingdom in the 1973 legislation. We might, therefore, usefully consider whether any lessons might be learned in Britain from the experience of the Dutch.

In both the Netherlands and the UK, the extent to which official first-tier old age pensions have been supplemented has, by tradition, depended on private initiative. The outcome of this policy has, however, been very different in the two countries. One of the main factors giving rise to this difference is the active interest in pension provision which has tended to be shown by the two sides of industry in the Netherlands. Employers' and employees' organizations were, of course, involved in the administration of the statutory pension schemes before the introduction of the General Old Age Pension scheme in 1957, as well as being active in initiating private occupational arrangements. Thus a sound basis existed for the role which was given to them in 1957 of supplementing the basic old age pension.

---

[1] M. de Korte, *'A Criterion to be Applied when Increasing Social Expenditure'*, unpublished paper, 1971.

A further important factor in the development of second-tier pensions in the Netherlands is that the outcome of the 1957 pension reform in fact represented a victory for the occupational pension funds. They actively campaigned for the right to provide all pension income above the official basic level; this was not simply a task imposed on them by a Government which was unwilling or unable to provide an adequate pension on a statutory basis. This interest shown by industry in the provision of pensions for its workers was, of course, not simply a sign of their altruism. In many cases, it represented a way of circumventing the wage freeze in the post-war period. Nevertheless, whatever the reason for the existence of occupational pension schemes, it is true to say that they have developed much more fully in the intervening period in the Netherlands than they have in the United Kingdom. This does not mean, however, that all the problems connected with this form of pension provision have been solved. We shall see that there are still some major issues giving rise to concern and much discussion in the Netherlands during 1973. It is nevertheless true to say that the development of occupational pensions in the Netherlands has also taken place in a more orderly fashion than in the UK largely due to the acceptance of a scheme of statutory supervision of occupational schemes which had the aim not of superseding private initiative, but of supporting it. This showed an early recognition of the need to have a common policy on certain issues and, above all, the need to protect the individual by ensuring the viability of the individual schemes. In the initial period of their development, occupational pensions agreements were completely private bargains which took place at the level of the undertaking or the individual industry. Gradually, however, dissatisfaction grew with this situation. Difficulties arose because of the completely different regulations governing each individual pension scheme, and it was felt that such collective agreements were only temporary in nature and unsuited to providing permanent pension provisions.

The Industry Pension Fund Act. The next stage in the development of occupational provisions was, therefore, the setting up of a statutory framework for *industry-wide schemes* by means of the Industry Pension Funds Act (*Bedrijfspensioenfondsenwet*) of 1949. This law empowered the Minister for Social Affairs, if requested to do so by representatives of employers and employees, to make participation compulsory for all persons, or certain categories of persons, employed in the industry concerned. It should be noted that the Minister cannot compel an industry to establish a pension fund; it must first be set up by the industry itself, which can then apply for the introduction of a compulsory participation order. Before making a decision, the Minister must consult the administrative organization responsible for the industry in question, the Social and Economic Council, and the Insurance Board (*Verzekeringskamer*), which is responsible for the supervision of occupational pension provisions. It must be determined further whether the asking body is in fact representative of the two sides of industry. Their request must be accompanied by an actuarial study of the pension fund, its revenue, the investment of funds, and the rights of beneficiaries. If participation in a fund is declared obligatory it is then placed under the supervision of the *Verzekeringskamer* or Insurance Board.

These regulations apply only to industry funds. At the beginning of 1972 there were eighty-six such industry-wide funds in existence, sixty-five of which had compulsory membership. Within industries, however, exemption from membership of such industry-wide funds can be granted to individual enterprises if they have their own pension funds providing at least equivalent benefits, and if these funds are run on recognized lines and if the rights of the insured are guaranteed. This right to claim exemption is based on the principle that what is already in existence must be respected. Many enterprises had their own pension funds long before the advent of industry-wide funds.

This second type of occupational pension fund, the *enterprise fund*, is also subject to some statutory control through the Pension and Savings Fund Law (*Pensioens-en Spaarfondsenwet*) of 1954 which applies to both the industry and enterprise funds. This law is basically concerned with the organization and administration of pension and savings funds, with the aim of ensuring their viability. Although the actual administration of the individual pension fund is left in the hands of the organization concerned, a certain amount of supervision is exercised by the Ministry of Social Affairs through the Social and Economic Council and the Insurance Board.

In general terms, the object of the pension and savings funds law is to ensure that, once an employer has given a pension commitment to his worker, the benefit promised will be paid. The employer must therefore choose between four alternative ways in which the provision will be made. He may (*a*) participate in an industry pension fund, (*b*) establish an enterprise pension fund, (*c*) establish group insurance contracts for his employees, or (*d*) give assistance in setting up such group contracts.

If he opts to make provision through either an industry or enterprise pension fund, the statutes and rules of the proposed scheme require the approval of the Ministry of Social Affairs. The Ministry is particularly concerned with such details as the proposed composition of the board of management, the income and investment of the fund and the estimated value of claims to be paid by the fund. The board of management of an Industrial Pension Fund must, for example, be composed of an equal number of representatives of the employers' and employees' federations. That of an Enterprise Fund or a Savings Fund must be composed of at least as many representatives of employees participating in the fund as of employers' representatives.

No direct restrictions are imposed on the investment of the pension funds, the only requirement being that 'the investment of the available means of a pension or savings fund must be made in a sound manner'.[1] It appears that in practice a large proportion of investment (particularly in the case of the larger enterprise funds) flows into the real estate market. There is no restriction on the purchase of equities, and this option appears to be gaining in importance at the beginning of the 1970s.[2] There is, however, a restriction, which affects enterprise and savings funds, on the proportion of revenue which can be used as a form of self-finance within the firm. In 1972, a maximum of 10 per cent could be employed for this purpose, but proposals to amend this ratio to a level of 5 per cent were already before Parliament. There is apparently some concern about the possibility that too great a proportion of finance may be diverted into the enterprise leaving the fund in some cases in a position where it is unable to make the necessary pension payments.

---

[1] See *Pensioens-en Spaarfondsenwet*, Article 14.

[2] This form of investment may well provide the pension funds with a hedge against inflation in the long run, depending on the exact nature of the investment. It may, on the other hand, give rise to timing problems, unless the fund succeeds in developing its assets extremely smoothly. See '*Ondernemings-pensioenen*', N. Samson NV, Alphen aan den Rijn, 1972 V-9-1.

In addition to supervising these aspects of the organization of industry and enterprise funds, the Insurance Board also has the task of checking the actuarial soundness of the funds. Their balance sheets must be presented to the Board annually for approval. If the enterprise chooses to provide occupational pensions for its employees by means of group contracts with a life insurance company, the approval of the Ministry of Social Affairs is not required before such schemes can be introduced. Firms must nevertheless present to the Insurance Board an annual report of resources allocated for this purpose. According to Article 22 of the pension and savings funds law, the *Verzekeringskamer* has at all times the right of access to books and documents of a pension fund or of an employer in so far as they relate to insurance contracts.

Finally, the law of 1954 contains regulations appertaining to the preservation of pension rights. If an employee belongs to either an industry-wide or an enterprise fund for more than one year but less than five, he is entitled, on leaving the fund, to reimbursement of his contributions to the old age pension fund. A person who has an insurance period of five years or more must, unless his pension rights are very small, be given a paid-up claim on the pension benefits due to him on the basis of his contributions or contributions made on his behalf. There was, however, some considerable concern in the Netherlands that the minimum period of membership before preservation of pension rights is guaranteed was too long. Proposals being discussed in 1972 for amending the pension and savings funds law contained a clause which would reduce the five-year minimum contribution period for a paid-up claim to a period of one year. This would therefore completely abolish the procedure of reimbursement of contributions and the ensuing loss of pension rights.[1]

These regulations have, therefore, gone some way towards providing a basic framework within which the occupational pension schemes could operate. The decision to supplement the state pension in this way has, nevertheless, not been without its difficulties. Some of these problems have furthermore become more acute and have attracted more attention over the years as attitudes have changed as to what constitutes an adequate old age pension.

---

[1] In 1973 a law was passed, reducing the minimum period for preservation of pension rights to one year. Although this is not to be compulsory until 1 May 1975, it seems that many funds are applying the new rule immediately.

Coverage. The coverage of occupational pension schemes is undoubtedly more widespread in the Netherlands than in the United Kingdom. The problem of incomplete coverage does, however, remain.[1]

It is estimated[2] that, in 1971, some 2·3 million persons were covered by some form of occupational pension scheme, whether an industry-wide fund, an enterprise pension fund, or an insurance contract sponsored by the enterprise. It was suggested to us in interview that this implies that some 200,000 or 300,000 employees who might be expected to be covered by some form of occupational pension schemes are in fact without cover of any sort.[3] It is thought that the majority of this number will be members of the retail trades where the formation of pension schemes has lagged behind that in other sectors. One interesting point which came to light in discussions in the Netherlands is that membership of private occupational schemes is ceasing to be the prerogative of employees. It appears that there is a growing tendency for independent workers to set up their own occupational pension funds. Examples of those groups of self-employed who have already done so were given in interview as blacksmiths, independent electricians, barristers, and notaries. The doctors are also pressing for membership of an occupational fund, largely because of the greater tax concessions which they could expect to receive by so doing.

While membership of occupational pension schemes has expanded significantly since the pension reform of 1957, the fact that the majority of schemes have come into existence only since 1945 and the fact that the control of preservation of rights was implemented only in 1954 has meant that many of those at present retired have little or no pension rights.[4] At the beginning of 1972, for example, a total of some 490,000 pensions were paid by occupational pension schemes, around 122,000 from enterprise schemes and 370,000 from industry-wide schemes. This number comprises not old age pensions alone, but old age pensions, widows'

---

[1] We are extremely grateful to Mr G. O. J. van Tets, Director of 'Progress' (Pensioenfonds Unilever Nederland) for providing a great deal of information on the subject of occupational pensions in the Netherlands.
[2] See Stichting van de Arbeid, *Interimrapport inzake het Pensioenvraagstuk*, The Hague, 1971, p. 1.
[3] This would represent about 15 per cent of the active working population.
[4] It is estimated that, in total, approximately 40 per cent of those already retired in the early seventies have no pension cover other than the state pension.

benefits and disability pensions. In the case of the industry-wide schemes it is possible to extract the numbers of old age pensions from the total; they amounted to 236,000. If one may assume that roughly the same proportion of total pensions in the enterprise schemes is devoted to old age benefits, then a total of some 306,000 old age pensions would be paid by both forms of occupational pension schemes. This number would in fact over-estimate the number of persons involved owing to the possibility of the accumulation of more than one pension. At best, however, the number of occupational pensions in payment at the beginning of 1972 accounted for less than one third of those paid by the General Old Age Pension scheme in that year.[1] The position is, of course, improving as pension rights mature and coverage is extended, but a great deal of concern is being voiced about those employees without adequate occupational benefits.

The structure and level of occupational old age pensions. The question of adequacy relates not only to coverage, of course, but no less to the structure and level of benefits. Despite the attempts at statutory regulation of some aspects of the pension schemes as outlined above, the choice of the structure of the old age pension and the level at which it is to be paid has always been left to the individual pension schemes. As a result, the variation in procedure is immense.

In the case of the *industry-wide funds*, which are much more extensively documented than the enterprise funds, the majority of schemes have, in the past, adopted a flat-rate benefit structure in which a set sum would be paid for each year of employment. This was in fact still the situation in over half the eighty-eight industry-wide funds in existence in 1970. In some of these cases the flat-rate amount may be adjusted over time to keep pace with changing economic circumstances, but this is by no means guaranteed. The pensions paid by this type of scheme are likely to be low.

The trend, however, is away from this type of benefit and towards one which relates the old age pension to the earnings of the employee. The majority of employees are in fact likely to benefit from this type of provision since the newer and largest industry funds have adopted or are in the process of adopting this

---

[1] In addition, one must take into account the 200,000 or so pensions paid by the special scheme for public servants.

technique. In this case it is a certain percentage of earnings for each year of service which determines the pension level. In a few cases a pension structure has been adopted which co-ordinates the occupational old age pension with the pension from the AOW scheme. The aim in these instances is to provide a combined pension after a period of forty years of about 70 per cent of pre-retirement earnings. As we shall see later, there is pressure to extend this type of benefit structure to cover all occupational schemes.

As regards actual benefit levels, it is estimated[1] that the average pension paid by the industry funds in 1970 amounted to between 500 and 1,000 guilders per annum (4 and 8 per cent of average earnings). Claims for employees still in employment were, however, considerably higher, averaging between 1,000 and 3,000 guilders per annum.

In the case of the *enterprise pension funds*, very little published information is available regarding the structure or level of benefits. From information obtained in interview with persons closely concerned in this field, however, various general features can be outlined. Benefits paid by the enterprise schemes are generally considerably higher than those paid by the industry scheme. They also tend to be related to the earnings of the individual. Total expenditure on old age pensions by the enterprise funds amounted in 1971, for example, to approximately 274 million guilders, while that by the industry funds amounted to 185 million guilders. In the same year, however, the number of pensions paid by the enterprise funds was only slightly less than one third of those paid by the industry schemes. Average pensions in payment to members of the enterprise schemes amounted in 1970 to around 2,500 guilders per annum (or just under 20 per cent of average earnings), with pension rights accumulated by those still in employment averaging about 4,000 guilders.[2]

The main reasons for this disparity between the two types of schemes can be explained in part by the fact that the enterprise funds have generally been in existence longer, and they often include higher-paid workers. The most important factor, however, is that the enterprise funds usually correspond to the largest

---

[1] See 'Social Security in the Netherlands', in *International Social Security Review*, 1, 1970, p. 56.
[2] See 'Social Security in the Netherlands', *ISSR*, 1, 1970, p. 57.

companies in the economy, most able (and willing) to make adequate provision for their employees. On more than one occasion the comment was made in interview that many of the large companies have tended to use pension provisions as a way of attracting and retaining scarce labour. It would seem that this was one way around the wage control policy in the post-war period. At that time, it would seem that it was a common feature of most enterprise pensions that benefits were lost completely on transferring to another job.

This lack of uniformity applies not only to the choice of the initial benefit level, but also to the treatment of the pension once it is in payment. In both the industry-wide and enterprise schemes there would seem to be no guarantee that benefits, once in payment, will be revalorized in line with either movements in prices or wages. Most of the industry schemes and the larger enterprise schemes do, however, apparently attempt to adjust pensions regularly to some extent. This has largely been possible through the real rate of interest actually earned on the assets of the funds being greater than the actuarial rate of interest assumed. The average rate of interest earned on investments was above 5 per cent[1] during the second half of the 1960s while the actuarial rate of interest assumed for the same period was around 3·5 per cent.[2]

There has been a certain amount of discussion of the possible regulation of pension adjustments. The Government consulted the Social and Economic Council on this matter in 1958. Advice was given in 1961 regarding the possible adoption by occupational schemes of a pay-as-you-go system with the creation of a fund for equalization of burdens between schemes. It was thought, however, that this would be difficult to realize, particularly since none of the schemes wanted to subsidize other schemes, and the proposals were not put into practice. As an alternative the Social and Economic Council therefore proposed the raising of the basic national old age pensions, and this the Government did by lifting it to the new 'social minimum' in 1964.

Although the idea of guaranteed dynamizing of private occupational schemes was abandoned at the beginning of the 1960s, the question has regained prominence a decade later. Full dynamizing in line with wages is, of course, well established in the basic

---

[1] See *Verslag van de Verzekeringskamer 1966–69*, p. 28.
[2] See *ISSR, op. cit.*, p. 56.

statutory pension scheme. This has lent force to the idea that the total pension received by an individual, of which the occupational benefit is an integral part, should retain its value during retirement relative to wages paid to the active population. As a result, attempts are being made to find a way of bringing occupational provisions as a whole into line with state provisions.

The finance of occupational pensions. The financial bases of occupational pension schemes in the Netherlands are subject to almost as many variations as are the benefits themselves. The practice which all schemes do have in common, however, is that they are financed on a funded basis. In both types of scheme, contributions are paid by employers and employees. In the *industry-wide* schemes, contributions may be either flat-rate or related to earnings, according to the type of benefit which is provided by the particular scheme. Although it is not possible to show the distribution of the financial burden between the employer and the employee at the level of the individual fund, it would seem from global statistics that employers pay about half as much again as employees.[1]

In the case of the *enterprise* schemes the bias is much more towards greater contributions by the employer. Total contributions by employers have tended to amount to about four times the total contributions of employees. It seems that there has in fact been a tendency to suppress the part of the contribution burden to be borne by employees since 1965, when the contribution rate to the AOW scheme, paid only by employees, underwent a substantial rise. We must, of course, remain aware of the problems involved in trying to ascertain the real incidence of these contributions. Despite the fact that the employer is directly responsible on the whole for the actual payment of contributions, it is more than likely that the employee's wages may be lower as a result than they may otherwise have been. It is nevertheless of considerable interest that occupational provisions are encouraged to such an extent by employees' federations in the Netherlands.

Payment procedure. One of the problems inherent in any system of occupational pensions where provision is made through

---

[1] See *Sociale Maandstatistiek*, August 1973 (CBS), p. 470.

completely independent pension funds is that of claiming the various benefits due from each period of employment on reaching pension age. In the Netherlands the onus is on the individual to make application for whatever pensions are due to him when he nears retirement age.

Some system of co-ordination is in force as far as the industry-wide funds are concerned. Since the late 1960s a system has operated whereby the individual applies for his pension to the industry fund of which he was a member at the time of his retirement, giving details of his past employment and membership of other industry funds. It is the duty of this last fund to determine and pay the pension and then reclaim the amounts payable by other pension funds. There is, however, a good deal of discontent surrounding this system. Some of the larger and more generous industry funds want to be allowed to pay out their pension provisions separately in order that the employee may appreciate the generosity of his employers. A further complication is to be found in the agricultural sector, which wants its occupational pensions to be paid out through its own banks.

In the case of the enterprise funds, there is no co-ordinating procedure in operation. Each enterprise is completely autonomous as regards the payment of its pensions, and the individual must make separate application for payment to each enterprise fund with which he has been associated. It is obvious that these procedural difficulties as well as the differences in the benefit structures of individual schemes will make it difficult for the individual to assess the final pension level which he will attain. It also renders it impossible to estimate with any accuracy the average size of occupational benefit which an employee can hope to attain over his working life through an accumulation of pensions from various sources.

The uncertainty facing the individual as to the level of income which he can expect in his old age has thus given rise to some discontent with the existing pension structure in the Netherlands. It would be wrong to say that the Dutch are disillusioned with private pension schemes. They do apparently feel the need, however, to take a fresh look at the occupational pension structure and find a means of providing a more uniform level of pension for the whole working population. All employees should, it is felt, be guaranteed a certain level of income replacement in old age, regardless of the enterprise or industry in which they have been employed. The proposals which have been formulated to meet these demands and solve the problems outlined above are of particular interest to the United Kingdom at this time and are, therefore, outlined in the following section. The two countries have broadly similar objectives and face broadly similar problems. Their choice of action is not, however, identical.

III—THE FUTURE DEVELOPMENT OF STATE AND OCCUPATIONAL PENSIONS

There is little doubt that the major topic of discussion in the field of old-age pension provisions in the Netherlands at the beginning of the 1970s concerns the future relationship and development of state and private occupational pensions. The proposals—and it must be emphasized that at the time of writing in 1973 these are no more than preliminary ideas—are to be found in a draft report by the Foundation of Labour presented to the Government in April 1971.[1] Although these proposals are receiving a great deal of attention, it is far from clear what the outcome of the debate will be.

The first point which must be made is that the proposals do not affect the AOW pension at all. The structure of this benefit would remain unchanged except, as mentioned earlier, that its level (for a married couple) would be raised to 100 per cent of the net minimum wage. The proposals are concerned, rather, with the development of occupational provisions in the private sector.

The proposals suggest, first, that, in order to meet the problem of non-universal coverage, obligatory occupational pension schemes for all employees should be introduced. Employers and employees agreed on this principle in 1969. It is indicative of the attitudes towards occupational provision that there was little opposition from either side of industry. The proposals would mean that only employed persons would benefit, while the self-employed would continue to receive only the basic state pension. The assumption is, however, that they could be expected to have additional income from continued employment, or from the sale of their business when they retire, or from personal savings.

---

[1] See Stichting van de Arbeid, *Interimrapport inzake het Pensioenvraagstuk*, The Hague, 1971.

F

Secondly, it is proposed that the level of the total pension, inclusive of the AOW benefit, should be a specified percentage of final income for all employees.[1] The suggested average percentage is 70 per cent, with possibly an increased percentage for low-income recipients and a slightly lower one for higher-income recipients. This, it is felt, would serve to rationalize and streamline the whole pension system, by integrating formally the state and occupational provisions. It should be noted here that some of the industry-wide funds have already introduced such a system and it is one which has been established for some time for public employees. The proposals suggest that such an income-related pension should be calculated according to a 'standard final pay system' in order to simplify the administration of the scheme. The pension would indeed be based on final salary, but calculations of back-service which had to be taken into account would be based on the assumption that the employee reached his final pay by way of the wage trend. Thus the revalorization of past income would be standardized, which would make it unnecessary for each employer to have to trace each individual's actual earnings back over the span of his working life.

With regard to the second major problem facing the occupational schemes—the dynamizing of pensions—the committee considering the pension system were concerned about the fact that this does not occur more frequently or on a more substantial scale. They agreed that the new statutory regulations must make provisions for pensions which are at least *stable in value*. To allow adjustments in line with the cost of living index the proposals suggest that the system of finance, though basically one of full funding, should also contain pay-as-you-go elements which would provide the finance necessary to make adjustments in benefit levels in payment. The exact way in which these two techniques are to be combined has still to be disclosed.

The report outlining the proposals states that there is also growing concern that the problem of *labour mobility* which may lead to the loss of pensions is becoming more critical. This concern is particularly justified since structural changes in industry (especially in the textile industry, agriculture and mining) are

---

[1] This replacement level would apply up to a certain income ceiling which is likely to be fixed at between one-and-a-half and twice average manufacturing earnings.

making labour mobility necessary. The report is concerned not only about the effect which a change of job might have on labour mobility if it leads to the loss of pension rights[1] or to inferior pension provisions, but also the effect on mobility resulting from an enterprise with good pension provisions favouring a younger rather than an older worker because of the difference in costs.

The proposals have tried to counter this tendency to favour younger workers because of relative pension costs in the system of finance which it suggests. The obstacles to labour mobility resulting from loss of pension rights or the change to an inferior pension scheme would, of course, be met by lowering the minimum pension period to qualify for preservation of rights and by introducing compulsory occupational provisions at a uniform level. As regards the second obstacle, the report puts great emphasis on the use of what it calls the 'years of life principle' (*levensjarenbeginsel*). This means that the pension benefit to be paid by each employer depends on the age of the employee and the income earned while actually with the employer. Thus the employer is not burdened with the task of paying up pension claims for persons who have since left his employment. The final pension rights are therefore built up evenly during the whole period up to the pension age of sixty-five. In this way there would not be a rapid accumulation of rights in the last few years before retirement, which, it is feared, often discourages an employer from engaging an older worker.

Before the proposals were formulated there was a great deal of indecision as to the best *administrative form* to be adopted. Obviously, with so many interested parties, this is essentially a political question. The committee have decided in principle, however, that there should be no one centralized administrative body. Instead they have preferred to rely on the 'know-how' of the organizations already so active within this field, and have advocated the adoption of a so-called 'pluriform' system of administration.

It would appear that it is generally accepted that the administration of schemes already in existence should remain as they are. There is however a suggestion that the number of industry funds should be greatly reduced, from its 1970 level of eighty-eight to twenty-six, which would correspond to the number of occupational

---

[1] This would happen if he had not fulfilled the five years membership of a scheme necessary to guarantee the preservation of pension rights.

associations. The problem is how to make provision for those not belonging to an occupational pension scheme, and three alternatives have been suggested. These are the setting up of a 'residual' industry fund, the possibility of establishing additional industry funds, or the insuring of those without provisions with private life insurance companies. With regard to the third option, the life insurance companies, anxious to participate in this new field of activity, have said that they are willing to undertake this pension coverage on a non-profit basis, if they could be given a guarantee of continuity.

The committee in their report mention that they are aware that the 'pluriform' system may have disadvantages, particularly with regard to the possibility that pensions may be paid out from various sources. It is felt, however, that the advantages of competitiveness and experience in the field will outweigh the disadvantages. In addition, they suggest that some sort of clearing system could be set up to avoid the problem of paying the final pension from several sources.

Finally the report argues that if it is to be made compulsory for an industry or enterprise to provide pensions at a certain level, it is necessary to set up a framework within which pensions can be provided without giving rise to too great differences in cost. This is also essential if labour mobility is not to be hindered. The report therefore puts forward suggestions for a system of either complete or partial equalization of costs (depending on the degree of solidarity which is wanted) arising from differences in the age or wage structure between industries or enterprises. It is envisaged that some form of Central Equalization Bureau would be set up. A tariff norm would be established, with the enterprise or industry contributing to the Equalization Bureau if its burden were lower, and receiving compensation if it were higher.

As mentioned earlier, no decision was taken in 1973 as to which if any, of the tentative suggestions of the Foundation would eventually be adopted. The general opinion seems to be, however, that, even if these specific Foundation of Labour proposals are not accepted, some development of pension provisions along broadly similar lines is inevitable. The principle has been accepted; only the practicalities still require to be determined. It is felt, however, that it will take some time to implement the proposals, and estimates suggest that no change is likely before about 1975. The introduction of the new system would also require to be spread over a period of some ten years.

Assuming that these, or similar, proposals are implemented, they would serve to provide all employees in the Netherlands with a level of income replacement in old age comparable to that enjoyed by the *public servants*.[1] In the Netherlands, as in Germany, provisions for this group have been taken as the target at which the general schemes are aiming.

The public servants' pension scheme, with its benefit level reflecting final earnings, its dynamism, and its total integration with the A O W Scheme, embodies the major elements of the Foundation of Labour proposals. It is perhaps significant that there is little dissatisfaction with the working of this scheme. The authorities may well be justified in looking to this as the ultimate goal in pension provisions.

IV—OTHER PROVISIONS FOR THE ELDERLY

(a) General public assistance

The Netherlands has been slow to develop its public assistance measures in a modern form. The Public Assistance Law (*De Algemene Bijstandswet*) came into force only in 1965, replacing legislation stemming from the poor laws at the beginning of the century, which required needy persons first of all to seek financial assistance either from members of their family or from private or religious charitable organizations before turning to public aid bodies.[2] In 1965, however, the Government took over total responsibility for cash provisions, becoming committed to providing assistance as of right to any Netherlands citizen who is unable or is in danger of being unable to provide for himself. He is no longer under an obligation to seek aid first from the family or

---

[1] The General Pension Fund for Public Servants covers personnel of the central and local Government, and employees of some nationalized industries such as the gas, electricity, and water industries.

[2] By the time the 1965 law came into force, it was in fact only formalizing a situation which had already existed for some time. By that time the Government was meeting 90 per cent of the cost of financial assistance, since the voluntary and religious organizations were simply unable to carry out this task as well as provide welfare services (discussed in Section IV c).

140 Pensions, Inflation and Growth

charitable institutions. The assistance is granted subject to a test of means. The amount which can be provided in assistance is thus individually determined, taking into account the total resources of the claimant, his opportunities and circumstances.

The means test. The basic principle of the Public Assistance Act is that provision must be made on the basis of need. The family means test involved is becoming more standardized and the scope for discretion at the local level is becoming limited. Some apparently very stringent conditions, are however, still attached to the means test, probably representing a relic of the days of the Poor Law, There are, for example, virtually no disregards of income or savings. If the claimant was a house-owner he could at one time be compelled to sell his house if in need of finance. Although the sale of the house is no longer implemented, he must take out a credit mortgage on the house with the public assistance authorities who provide aid subject to the undertaking that repayment will be made when the claimant dies or when his house is sold. The general feeling seems to be that this is a perfectly just condition and a perfectly reasonable way of providing assistance. With this exception, no recipient of public assistance is expected to repay any assistance in retrospect in the event of his personal circumstances undergoing a significant change.

The administration and finance of public assistance. The administration of the public assistance provisions is in the hands of the eleven provinces in the Netherlands and their 800 or so local authorities. In the past these local bodies have enjoyed a great deal of autonomy in the administration of provisions for which they are responsible, with the result that there have been significant variations in both the level and type of assistance provided. There would seem, however, to be a tendency at the beginning of the 1970s to reduce the discretionary powers of these authorities. This has the aim of not only introducing a greater degree of harmonization in benefits and services supplied, but more particularly of exerting more effective control over expenditure on these provisions. It should be emphasized that the Government realizes such changes must be accomplished gradually since any attempt to impinge on their areas of competence is fiercely resisted by the local authorities.

Although the administration is entirely in the hands of the local authorities, public assistance benefits are financed mainly from general central Government revenue. This is due to the fact that there are no significant local taxes levied in the Netherlands, and therefore the local authorities are not in a position to provide a large proportion of the finance themselves. The finance is supplied either directly by the Ministry responsible for the public aid scheme, or through a 'municipal fund' consisting of grants to the local authorities from the central Government. It is the long-term policy of the Dutch Government to change over to a more uniform system of finance where the total cost would be met directly by the Ministry responsible. It is hoped by so doing to give the central Government a greater degree of control over the ways in which the money is spent.

Expenditure on public assistance. Total expenditure on public assistance grew quite significantly between 1965 and 1967, rising from 536 million guilders to 911 million guilders, or from 6·8 per cent to 8·7 per cent of total social insurance expenditure. A sudden and substantial drop in public assistance expenditure in 1968 in both absolute terms (to 738 million guilders) and in relative terms (to 5·4 per cent of social insurance expenditure) can be attributed to the introduction of the Special Sickness Expenses Insurance or AWBZ, as it is known. This new Act, which provided coverage for long-term illness expenses, was to be of considerable importance for the elderly, as we shall see. It also took over a task formerly carried out in many instances by the public assistance authorities. Expenditure has continued to show an upward movement again since 1968 and it reached the level of 1,100 million guilders in 1970.[1]

The most important reasons[2] for the continuing rise in public assistance expenditure are, first, a rise in the public aid benefit rate as a result of a reappraisal of the level of necessary subsistence costs. Secondly, it is felt to reflect the lack of adequate occupational pension provisions for a large number of aged persons. Expenditure is influenced thirdly by the increasing claim on benefits by one-parent families and fourthly by the fast-rising cost of care in old people's homes. It is clear, that with the exception of aid for

---

[1] See *Statistiek van de Algemene Bijstand 1970*, CBS, The Hague, 1973.
[2] *Nota over de Inkomensverdeling*, Bijlage 15, Miljoeneta, 1970, p. 69.

one-parent families, these factors have a bearing on the position
of the elderly.

Public assistance benefit levels. According to the regulations
of the Public Assistance Act as they were first formulated in 1965,
the Government had to provide assistance according to the living
standards of the individual claimant. This meant the benefit level
differed according to his previous income or standard of living.
Each municipality set its own rules and some were more generous
than others. Costs were, however, tending to rise sky high as a
result of the flexibility in the regulations, and it was felt that a more
objective criterion for determining benefit levels in the public
assistance scheme was required. Since 1968 the Ministry has
therefore laid down rules for the calculation of assistance benefits,
with the result that all municipalities now pay more or less the
same rate. Discretionary powers still exist, but these relate not to
the benefit levels but rather to the conditions attached to the payment of benefits to some groups. The elderly are, however, not
affected by this factor.

Since 1968, benefit levels have been related to the legally fixed
minimum wage. The basic assistance level for a couple is equivalent
to the net minimum wage after deduction of tax, social insurance
contributions and expenses connected with employment. As in the
pension scheme, the allowance for a single person is 70 per cent
of that for a married couple. In most cases an addition would be
made to the basic rate for the actual level of rent paid by the
claimant. In practice, this results in an average assistance rate,
inclusive of the rent allowance, which is considerably higher,
relative to average manufacturing earnings, than the equivalent
rates in either the UK or Germany. The Netherlands rate for an
elderly couple was equal in 1971 to almost 60 per cent of gross
average manufacturing wages, compared to ratios of around 40
per cent in both the UK and in West Germany. The most significant feature of the public assistance benefit level is the fact that the
average rate, because of its generosity, is slightly above the basic
AOW pension level, a situation similar to that in the UK. As a
result, those without occupational or other supplementary old age
provisions should be entitled to maintenance aid from the public
assistance authorities.

The elderly as recipients of public assistance. In 1970 about 160,000 persons, or about 12 per cent of the over sixty-fives, received public assistance, some 55 per cent of them living in their own homes, and about 45 per cent living in residential accommodation. This percentage of old persons in receipt of public assistance benefits must however be compared to the number who, according to official estimates, have no sources of income other than their AOW pension and would therefore appear to have a right to supplementary assistance. The officially accepted figure is given as between 25 per cent and 30 per cent of the over sixty-fives. As a result of the discrepancy in the numbers apparently eligible for public assistance and the numbers of elderly actually receiving it, the Dutch are concerned at present about the problem of non-uptake of public assistance benefits. A publicity campaign emphasizing that all citizens have a *right* to these benefits was undertaken, but the response was felt to be discouraging, resulting in only an extra 10,000 or so claimants. Part of the blame for the problem is attached inevitably to the existence of a feeling of stigma as regards public assistance. This is perhaps hardly surprising since until 1965 the concept of assistance was based on poor-law principle. Elderly people still tend to cling to the notion that the immediate source of help should still be one's family, although it is true that the church has now become less important in this field.

It is considered probable, however, that at least some of those who appear to have a right to assistance may in fact have additional sources of income which they are unwilling to disclose. The most likely source is that of income from letting part of their house. As will be shown in the following section on housing provisions, a large proportion of old people in the Netherlands live in large old houses, highly suited to this purpose.

The number of elderly persons receiving or eligible to receive continuous public assistance benefits, however, is likely to decline over the next few years. This will be a result both of the proposed extension of occupational pensions, and of the structural changes foreseen in the state pension itself. Indeed, the raising of the pension level to that of the net minimum wage has the aim of making it unnecessary for most of the old people to turn to public assistance provisions. It is worth mentioning perhaps that the minimum wage, the AOW pension and public assistance rate are now all linked to the same wage index. A rise in the pension level as a result of wage movements does not therefore affect the pensioner's right to public assistance since this rate too will have increased.

When the pension is raised to 100 per cent of the net minimum wage, this will not, of course, prevent the pensioner from still having a claim to 'incidental assistance', which constitutes once-and-for-all payments to cover necessary expenditure on furnishings, medical costs and such like. This can be paid in addition to continuous assistance or as a quite separate item. It must be stressed, however, that this form of assistance is provided entirely at the discretion of the local authorities. They are under no obligation to provide assistance, and therefore no regulations exist as to its level.

Assistance to persons in residential homes for the aged. While a total of about 100 million guilders was spent in 1970 on public assistance payments to 90,000 old people living at home, the 70,000 living in old people's homes received no less than 300 million guilders.[1] Between 9 and 10 per cent of persons over sixty-five in the Netherlands live in residential old people's homes and no fewer than 70 per cent of these receive help in meeting the cost of their board from the public assistance authorities. This is understandable when one considers that, in the newer homes, the cost of care can be approximately double the level of the basic state pension. The person with only an AOW benefit would pay this total sum to the residential home, and the difference in cost would be met by the public assistance authorities. In addition the public assistance scheme provides a small personal allowance.

The rate of growth of costs in residential homes was in 1972/3 running at between 15 and 20 per cent per annum, which can largely be attributed to fast-rising labour costs, accounting for about 60 per cent of the total costs of the homes. This trend is giving rise to a great deal of concern in the Government, and attention has turned to ways in which the cost of accommodation can be kept under control and the limited accomodation used most efficiently.

In order to understand the problem facing the authorities in this matter, it is necessary to look briefly at the organization of residential homes in the Netherlands. The vast majority of homes are

---

[1] The figures were provided in interview at the Ministry of Culture, Recreation and Social Welfare, The Hague.

non-profit making, providing about 80 per cent of total beds. These are owned largely by religious or other voluntary organizations (although under the supervision of the local authorities as a result of the Homes for the Aged Act of 1963) who have traditionally enjoyed a great deal of independence. The autonomous position of the authorities of the homes means that they can admit whomsoever they wish. As a result, many old people, who are still in a position to look after themselves quite adequately, apply for, and gain, admission to homes, in their anxiety that they may not be successful when eventually they are really in need of residential care. This has meant on the other hand that some old people in need of care have been unable to gain admission to the homes and have had to be put on the waiting list.

In an effort to allocate these scarce resources more fairly the Ministry of Culture, Recreation and Social Welfare has proposed to the home authorities that admission should take place through a 'Council of Admission'. This Council would be established by the local authority and comprise a doctor, an independent person and a social worker, who would, on the basis of 'points of urgency', advise on the type of accommodation most suited to the applicant. These points of urgency would include his physical and mental capabilities, his social position and his family contacts. The need to introduce change gradually, because of the fact that the boards of the residential homes are reluctant to relinquish any of their independence, has meant that, in the first instance, the councils would be able only to give advice, but not to make their recommendations compulsory.

The organizations running the homes seem to be voicing some opposition to this proposal. One of their main complaints is that the restricting of admission to the most needy cases would have the effect of increasing the personnel required. They feel that the current ratio of staff to residents of 3 to 10 would have to increase to one of 4 to 10.

A further point of issue in the field of residential accommodation for the aged concerns the question of who should finance the cost of care in the homes. As mentioned above, those who are unable to meet the cost themselves are, under current regulations, granted public assistance. The Ministry of Culture, Recreation and Social Welfare, which is responsible for this provision, is, however, dissatisfied with this situation and feels that the cost should be covered by the AWBZ, the special sick-care expenses act. This insurance-based provision meets the cost of care in approved nursing homes, i.e. in homes catering for those who are physically or mentally handicapped, but does not cover residential homes. A clause was in fact included in the original AWBZ (Article 6) which stated that residential homes might eventually be brought under the Act. It appears, however, that this is being removed from the new version of the Act.

One of the arguments in favour of financing through the AWBZ is that this would reduce the stigma felt by the old person on account of his dependency on public assistance provisions. This is certainly true. It is possible, however, that this argument might decline in importance as a growing proportion of those in residential homes receive assistance from this source.

In the light of the attempts to restrict admission to residential old people's homes to those who really need this service, it is necessary to consider what alternatives are to be provided. This will be dealt with in the course of a brief survey of the housing conditions of the aged in the following section.

(b) Housing conditions of the elderly and assistance with housing costs

In 1969 about 18 per cent of old persons were living in some form of accommodation specifically intended for the aged.[1] Of this number, 108,000 old people or 8·2 per cent lived in residential homes coming under the Old People's Act (that is, those providing care for more than five old people), 29,000 or about 2·2 per cent were in nursing homes, 15,000 or 1·1 per cent lived in service flats for the aged, and 87,000 or about 6·6 per cent of the total number of old people lived in special houses for the elderly.

Homes for the aged and nursing homes. A distinction is drawn in the Netherlands between residential homes for those among the elderly who are still in good health (whose importance was discussed in the previous section) and homes providing accommodation for persons who are mentally or physically incapacitated. The latter belong to the category of nursing homes. Although these provide beds for over 2 per cent of the elderly population, it has been estimated that

---

[1] See Ministerie van Cultuur, Recreatie en Maatschappelijk Werk, *Nota Bejaardenbeleid, 1970*, Staatsuitgeverij, The Hague, 1970, p. 14.

this is insufficient to meet requirements and therefore an additional 10,000 beds are to be provided by the end of 1974.

The cost of care in officially recognized nursing homes, that is those conforming to regulations regarding size, provisions and personnel, is met by the previously mentioned AWBZ law on special sick care costs. Prior to this law coming into force in 1968, any person requiring long-term care and unable to meet the cost could receive help under the General Public Assistance Act. Those who have not been in a position to contribute to this new contributory insurance scheme will, of course, continue to receive assistance from the public aid authorities; their numbers will, however, decline.

Service flats. Service flats for the aged are a fairly recent phenomenon in the sphere of housing for the elderly. These usually have a resident caretaker, and possibly additional provisions such as meals and domiciliary aid, but in most cases there is no provision for nursing services in the event of illness. The percentage of elderly living in this type of accommodation is exceptionally small, mainly as a result of the fact that those flats could normally only be bought and not rented. They were expensive and inhabited, therefore, only by persons in the upper income groups. Some rented service flats are, however, now becoming available and this field has, at least to some extent, been opened to the less well off.

Special houses for the elderly. The figures show that this is one of the most important forms of special accommodation for the elderly. In providing accommodation for 6·6 per cent of old people, it is second only to care in residential homes. This category comprises homes for independent families, containing one or two rooms, kitchenette and bathroom. These houses provide accommodation particularly suited to the needs of old people, and have the effect of enabling them to retain their independence for as long as possible.

This is likely to be the fastest growing category of accommodation for the aged in the future. It is favoured by both the Government, worried as it is about the cost of care in residential homes, and also the National Federation for the Care of the Aged (the NFB) which is particularly concerned with means of enabling old persons to remain in their own homes for as long as possible.

The current plan is to build an additional 12,000 of these special dwellings per annum.[1] The stock at the end of 1969 amounted to about 51,000 dwellings. It is felt in some quarters that even this proposed rate of growth of this form of housing is not large enough to meet the demand. These special houses are built by either the local authorities or housing associations, with subsidies from the Ministry of Housing available under certain conditions.

The elderly in 'normal' housing. Despite the growing importance of the types of accommodation outlined above, the vast majority of old people still live in ordinary dwellings. Most of them are likely to live in rented accommodation. Only 35 per cent of the total housing stock in the Netherlands is owner-occupied, and it seems that very little of this will be in the hands of the aged since, particularly in the inter-war period, one had to be fairly rich to be able to afford to purchase a house.

The vast majority of the elderly, it would appear, tend to live in old dwelling-houses mainly because of the nature of the rent control regulations. After the war, old houses were subject to very strict rent restriction as a result of the wage freeze, and the rents of these properties have continued to lag behind those of newer dwellings. It is, for example, the case that the rent of a new social dwelling (i.e. one built with state assistance) can be as much as three or four times that of an old dwelling. An attempt has been made to 'harmonize' the rents of old and new dwellings by raising the rent of old houses by 6 per cent in 1970. The result of this vast differentiation in rents is, however, that many elderly people living in large old dwellings are unwilling to move to newer, smaller dwellings more suited to their needs, because of the difference in costs. In consequence, as mentioned earlier, many of the old people in these houses sub-let part of their dwelling to obtain an additional source of income. Some local authorities have attempted to encourage people to move by granting subsidies in order to make the roomier accommodation available for larger families, but this does not seem to have been very successful.

Personal housing allowances. It is estimated that the average rent payable by elderly people living in old dwellings amounts to about

---

[1] Critics of the Government feel that this number is totally inadequate and estimate that an additional 35,000 to 40,000 homes per annum are required. (See *Op Leeftijd*, April 1972, pp. 7–9.)

10 per cent of a couple's state pension. In such cases, it is generally felt that the rent burden for the old person is not a problem. The situation of old people living in newer and more expensive dwellings is, however, causing some concern. If the burden is too high, two possibilities of assistance are open: the Ministry of Housing individual rent subsidy or General Public Assistance.

The introduction in 1970 of the *Ministry of Housing rent subsidy* is the first experimental step in a long-term plan to replace 'subsidies to the stones' by rent subsidies payable to individuals. It has the aim of limiting the proportion of their income which those in lower income brackets and in certain types of housing must pay in rent.

Between July 1970, the date of introduction of the scheme, and March 1971, 28,209 of those allowances were paid. Of this number, 8,728 were paid to persons over 65. This is of no small significance, since this 30 per cent representation must be viewed in the light of the fact that only 7 to 8 per cent of over-sixty-fives live in new dwellings covered by the Act. It would seem therefore that the elderly are benefiting a great deal from the scheme.

Those persons who do not fall within the regulations laid down for the Ministry of Housing allowance and whose rent burden is too high for their income, may apply to the public assistance authorities for aid. Conversely, persons who are in receipt of continuous assistance under the Public Assistance regulations are not eligible for the Ministry of Housing subsidy. Those with an income in the region of the maximum income level applicable for public assistance and who live in a dwelling covered by the Housing Ministry subsidy can choose which of the two forms of benefits they wish to claim.

The Ministry of Housing subsidy is financed from general taxation. It seems there has been some evidence of a reluctance among some people to take up the allowance, particularly among the elderly. One disincentive may be the clause in the regulations which states that the allowance may be reduced if the claimant could move to cheaper accommodation. This is in fact merely a form of safeguard to make it possible for local authorities to induce persons to move if they are obviously in unnecessarily expensive accommodation *and* if a dwelling can be offered by the authorities which is more suited to their financial position and their requirements. In practice, however, this has not yet been implemented, and it is unlikely that it will be because of the difficulty in controlling the availability of cheaper accommodation.

(c) *Domiciliary and other services for the aged*

As a result of the increasing emphasis being placed on the need to make it possible for old persons to retain their independence for as long as possible, attention has turned in the Netherlands towards the provision of services for those old persons living in their own homes. It is unnecessary to give details of all the services available, such as meals on wheels, health visitors, home helps and so on, since most of them are common to most advanced societies. Attention should be drawn, however, to one of the most recent innovations in provisions for the elderly, and one of which the Dutch are immensely proud—*the service centre.*

Statistics show that, of the 80 per cent or so elderly persons living in ordinary housing, about three-quarters live in one-family dwellings, while one-quarter live with, or provide accommodation for, others. One of the most urgent problems facing elderly persons therefore is felt to be that of isolation. It was in an attempt to overcome this problem that the building of service centres was initiated at the beginning of the 1960s, with the aim of enabling old people to continue living in their own homes. The main functions of such centres are to provide contact with other people of the same or different age groups, to organize recreational activities in which the old person can participate, to provide social guidance and advice (on social security matters, for example), and to co-ordinate the various services available to the old person in his neighbourhood.

The services provided in the individual centres differ widely, but they all have the aim of enabling the old person to participate in the social life of the community. The Netherlands Federation for the Care of the Aged (the NFB) has been campaigning against the idea that old age must necessarily be equated with both poverty and infirmity. The NFB stresses that 80 per cent of old people are in need of forms of assistance other than finance or nursing care. They require mental and physical stimulation to keep them alive and alert, and it is in this area that it is felt the service centre can play such an important role.

By the beginning of 1972 there were already more than 100

service centres in operation in the Netherlands. They are to be found either in new buildings or buildings adapted for this use. They are usually established by the local authority, but financial assistance is also available in most cases from the state. The number of service centres is increasing rapidly as a result of the target building plan of fifty additional centres per annum between 1970 and 1975. The estimated cost of central Government assistance to this programme over the five-year period is over 32 million guilders (without allowing for increases in wages and prices). This, together with an increase in the extent of home help services (it is hoped to attract an additional 45,000 workers into the service by 1974) and the district nurse service, are to be the main areas of expansion in services for the elderly during the next planning period.

(d) Health provisions for the elderly

All persons domiciled in the Netherlands who are sixty-five years and older can, on application to the sickness fund, voluntarily join the health insurance scheme provided that their annual income does not exceed a ceiling laid down in the Act. This amount is about 5,000 guilders higher than the benefit fixed for a couple under the General Old Age Pensions Act, and follows the development of this pension level.

Those entitled to Old People's Insurance pay a contribution which is much lower than would be necessary to cover the real cost of providing medical services for them. The actual rate of contribution varies according to the individual's income.

Not all persons belong, however, to this special scheme. Alternatively they may belong to the general compulsory insurance scheme if their income is above the ceiling for the old people's insurance scheme but below that for the general scheme. The number of old persons belonging to this group is small and is likely to be comprised of persons still in employment.

The second possibility is that the old person may continue his membership of the voluntary sickness insurance fund. This is particularly to the advantage of single persons who were in the voluntary scheme before the age of sixty-five. Their contribution, which differs as between married and single persons, is likely to be lower than it would be in the special old people's insurance scheme where there is only one rate (except in the top income group).

In any case, whatever the form of insurance to which they belong, it seems to be generally accepted that all old persons and their families are covered by some form of sickness insurance cover. If any person did not have cover, the public assistance authorities would, of course, meet the cost of medical treatment. This seems, however, to be a very rare occurrence.

The contribution costs are the only expenses which have to be met by the old person. Medical fees are paid by the sickness funds direct to the medical personnel concerned without extra payment by the insured person. The cost of medicines too is paid to chemists by the funds and at the moment there are no elements of direct cost-sharing in the system. The cost of up to one year's stay in a hospital is met by the sickness fund. The cost of stays in excess of this period is met, as mentioned previously, under the scheme for special sickness expenses.

V—SUMMARY AND CONCLUSIONS

In the field of pension provisions for the elderly, two main trends are clearly visible: the movement of the state flat-rate pension towards the net minimum wage level, which is likely to be achieved within a few years, and the proposed developments in the occupational pension field. The proposed integration of the two tiers of pension provision is of particular interest from the point of view of the UK, since it reflects in many ways broadly similar lines of thought to those in the 1973 Social Security Act. In both countries funded occupational pension schemes would supplement flat-rate state pensions financed by graduated contributions. One of the main differences, however, is to be found in the administrative structure of the second-tier scheme. No form of state reserve scheme is contemplated for the Netherlands. Instead membership of an occupational pension scheme will be made compulsory, thus preventing the need for the state to become directly involved at all in the provision of second-tier pensions.

There is no doubt that the proposed developments in the Netherlands will greatly increase the average pension income of the elderly population. In the long term the Dutch scheme might well be considered as one of the most generous in Western Europe. The problem remains, however, of the uneven incidence of occupational provision at the present time, and the choice of a funded occupational pension structure means that it will be some time before the target income level is reached for all employees. The problem is certainly less severe in the Netherlands than in the UK, where the new 1973 legislation's approach also requires a long period of transition. The Dutch basic pension is, in the first place, more generous than its British counterpart in terms of income replacement, and thus the gap to be filled by occupational pension is smaller. In addition, the majority of employees in the Netherlands are already covered by some occupational scheme and have therefore already accumulated some pension rights. Those who will suffer most severely are employees who are as yet without cover of any sort.

The Dutch proposals differ from the British plans in that they contain a slightly more general commitment to dynamize the occupational pensions in payment despite the funded basis of the schemes. This might well encourage the occupational pension funds in the UK to be more optimistic or at least more forthcoming as regards this issue, given that the demographic structure is likely to become more favourable in the UK before it will in the Netherlands.

If we turn our attention from pension provisions to public assistance provisions, the main trend which has been visible in this field is that of a gradual movement towards a more centralized administrative structure. This has been achieved to a certain extent by the general standardization of the benefit rate. Discussions are currently in progress to standardize also the conditions attached to entitlement and compel the various local authorities to adopt a common policy on such matters. The final step towards which there has already been some progress is the complete centralized control of the finance of the scheme.

There is as yet no sign of any relaxing of the conditions of eligibility attached to payment of social assistance benefits, which seem in the context of international comparison to be somewhat stringent. This is perhaps not of great importance in practical terms, however, because of the high level of the assistance rate itself. It is also likely that this assistance scheme will in the future, as a result of the extension of pension provisions, take on a very residual function indeed in the field of provision for the aged. This trend will be accentuated if the demands of the public assistance authorities for the inclusion of homes for the aged under the special sickness expenses act are successful. Practically all the over sixty-fives would then no longer be in need of assistance provisions. In any case, means-testing does not appear to be so great an issue in the Netherlands as it is in the UK.

Provisions for the aged in the Netherlands have therefore undergone a gradual but continuous development during the past decade. With the final policy objectives in the field of pension provisions likely to be achieved with the introduction of the new proposals surrounding the occupational schemes, there are perhaps signs that the emphasis is now turning towards the provision of housing and services for the aged. This is certainly an area in which there is a great deal of interest in the 1970s, reflecting a trend which has become apparent in several of the countries studied in this book.

CHAPTER FOUR

Sweden

I—INTRODUCTION

Sweden's 'wealth and welfare' state is commonly looked upon as a model of its kind. At the beginning of the seventies, Sweden had, it is true, the highest per capita income of any of the countries studied in this book. It may, however, be a little surprising to find when we come to the comparative analysis of chapter 8 that she is not at the top of the 'league table' for expenditure on the social services and, more specifically, that her pensions were less generous and her pension targets less ambitious than those of some of her rather less affluent neighbours. This is not to belittle the extent of her achievements. Sweden was a relatively poor, predominantly agricultural, country long after Germany, France and Belgium had largely completed the process of industrialization. Her first old age pensions, and very meagre ones at that, date only from 1913 and her pension structure is still not in full operation. The massive developments in her social services are by and large the product only of the last quarter of a century during which her national output has more than trebled. On the other side of the coin, she has been spared the devastation of two world wars, the political upheavals and post-war currency crises which have shaken some of the other countries with which this volume is concerned. Peace and stable government should have made it easier for her to develop her welfare provisions as output rose.

Sweden, in common with most Western countries, has an ageing population. In 1970 the elderly formed nearly 14 per cent of the population as compared with $12\frac{1}{2}$ per cent a decade earlier. On present projections this figure will reach a peak of $16\frac{1}{2}$ per cent in 1990. This has meant rising expenditure on pensions and other provisions for the elderly which now account for over a quarter of the social service budget. The major concern, however, is not so much with the pension 'burden' as it is in some of the other countries studied in this book as with the rapidly escalating cost of the health services which in the early 1970s absorbed between two-fifths and one half of total social service expenditure. The position may change as the pension peak is approached and as the pension schemes described below reach maturity. However, the schemes have been so devised as, hopefully, to cope with these changes without imposing too heavy a strain on the active population. Sweden has a three-tier pension scheme of flat-rate and supplementary, earnings-related national pensions and occupational pensions which 'top-up' the national provisions. Apart from the basic flat-rate benefits the pension schemes are some considerable way from maturity and the income prospects of the 'new' pension population will be substantially better than those of the older generation of pensioners. The three pension tiers lie on top of each other, and national and occupational alike are closely integrated to form a single, if somewhat complex, pension pyramid.

In the process of developing this pension structure since the first *folkpensioner* were introduced in 1913, Sweden has been ahead of many of her neighbours in thinking about pensions, although more recently she has been overtaken in some respects by events elsewhere. As early as 1913 the Swedes based their first pensions on the principle of universality. The *folkpension* as its name implies is a citizen's pension and today, if not originally, the same basic pension rights are available to all Swedish citizens, guaranteeing everybody at least a minimum of income in old age, something for which some continental countries are only now beginning to see the need. Sweden was one of the leaders in introducing automatic inflation proofing and also in providing a link with rising real incomes from work, although the latter has subsequently been dropped. She has experimented with various combinations of universal and selective pension benefits in an attempt to meet pensioners' needs effectively and economically; some of these, such as the housing supplements to the basic pension, merit close attention. So too do the Swedish 'national' occupational pensions, which at least solve some of the problems of transferability of rights that beset many such schemes.

The national pension schemes have two sets of objectives. The basic *folkpension*, largely financed out of general tax revenues, aims at providing every Swedish citizen as of right with a flat-rate pension designed to ensure a modest but adequate standard of living, what is often called a 'decency and dignity' standard. This may be increased, on a means-tested basis, by various supplements to take account of the varying needs of pensioners. The *national supplementary pension scheme* provides a second-tier pension which aims at replacing in retirement a proportion of peak earnings during working life. The two schemes together will, on maturity of the supplementary scheme, provide the great bulk of the working population coming up to retirement from then onwards with a pension equal to about two-thirds of their previous earnings up to the pension ceiling. The supplementary pension scheme is nominally pay-as-you-go but there was limited blanketing-in and large funds have been accumulating and supplying useful sources of credit for the capital market.

On top of this *occupational pension schemes* are designed to do two things: to provide an early temporary pension for employees wishing to retire before the late national pension age of sixty-seven and to give all pensioners a third tier of income in addition to the two national pensions from sixty-seven onwards. Occupational pension plans for public servants and some private salaried employees date back to the beginning of the century but the main developments came in the early 1960s. For manual workers they were introduced only in 1973 and the scheme will not reach maturity until the year 2000. An interesting feature of the occupational pension schemes is that the majority of employees are insured for the same benefits under two general pension plans, one for white-collar and one for blue-collar employees, which are operated by centralized insurance institutions. They are, in effect, 'national' occupational pensions and there is little of the multiplicity of schemes found in many countries which give rise to such thorny problems of transferability of rights. These pensions are funded, although there are interesting arrangements for credit insurance, and the pensions when in payment are, like the national pensions, adjusted for price increases, but not for rising earnings.

In what follows an attempt will be made to describe very briefly some of the events in the historical development of this pyramid and to present as clear a picture as possible of what the pyramid means to the pensioner in the early 1970s, with some tentative projections to the time when the schemes reach maturity. Housing allowances form part of the basic pension scheme so something must be said about these and the role, however small, played by residual social assistance in helping the pensioner also needs to be looked at. Health care and other services provided by central or local government will be touched on briefly to give a more complete picture of the total resources available to the pensioner. The financing of pensions and the respective roles played by state, insured persons and employers will be examined. The final section will look at pensions in a critical light in an attempt to assess their adequacy and to consider some of the implications for the economy as a whole of the expenditure of these vast sums on pensions and of the methods used to raise the money. A concluding note will say something briefly about the remaining controversies in the pension field.

II—THE EVOLUTION OF THE PENSION PYRAMID

The first national pension legislation in Sweden dates from the period prior to World War I which witnessed a series of important social reforms. Prior to this the elderly no longer able to work had been dependent on savings, family resources or means-tested assistance. Few, and these mainly public servants, had rights to pensions. Assistance was the responsibility of the local communes, the poor had no rights to help and what the communes could afford or chose to give was often barely enough to provide a very meagre level of subsistence. The position would have been even worse had Sweden not still been a predominantly agricultural society, and many old people were able to scratch some sort of livelihood from the soil.

The first decade of the century saw important political and social changes. Developments in neighbouring countries in the fields of pensions, industrial safety, sickness and unemployment insurance and so on, highlighted the relative backwardness of Sweden in many of these respects. A series of parliamentary committees were set up to study and report on the possibility of reforms. At this time too the Social Democrats were establishing themselves as a Parliamentary party and the conflicts between the Conservative and Liberal Parties gave them the opportunity to consolidate their position. The extended franchise reform of 1909 and the consequent increase in their representation in the *Riksdag* opened up for the Social Democrats the possibility of influencing the reform of society from within by parliamentary methods. The failure of the general strike in 1909 had shown that the Party was not strong enough or well enough organized to take over power by revolutionary means. The Social Democrats became, and have remained, a party of reform, not of revolution. Soon they had members on the various parliamentary committees looking into questions of social reform and the foundations were being laid for the government by concensus which has become so marked a feature of Swedish politics.

One of the most important fruits of the reforming zeal of this period was the introduction in 1913 of the first national *folkpensioner*, compulsory, contributory, and universal in coverage. It was a bold move for a relatively poor country to go straight for universalism, and the presence of the Social Democrats on the committee which drew up the proposals for these early pensions undoubtedly influenced the decision. But, advanced though they might be in principle, the first pensions were very limited in scope. No government subsidies were forthcoming; the pensions were intended to do no more than supplement other forms of income. Contributions were related to income and pensions depended on the actual contributions paid. Incomes and contributions were low, the scheme was funded and it would take fifty years to build up rights to a full pension. In the meantime the pensions actually payable were small indeed. The inadequacies of the scheme were apparent from a very early stage and the central Government had to come to the help of the poorer pensioners with supplements of various kinds, financed out of general tax revenues, which dominated the pension itself. Social assistance continued to play a large residual role and local finances were sorely pressed by the demands made on them. This system dragged on for nearly a quarter of a century. Although various Pension Commissions recommended rationalization of this hybrid and complex system of universal earned pensions, selective supplements and local assistance, reform did not come until 1937.

In that year pension finances were reorganized and pensions henceforth were to consist of two parts: a fixed amount financed on a pay-as-you-go basis and a variable amount paid from an accumulated fund and dependent on contributions actually paid. The pension increases which this new system initially permitted were soon overtaken by rising prices and resort was again had to various types of *ad hoc* supplements, mainly means-tested: cost-of-living bonuses, regional allowances and such like. Supplements continued to provide a greater part of the pensioner's income than the pension itself and general social assistance was still helping large numbers of old people.

In the wave of social reforms which followed World War II another attempt was made to rationalize and simplify the system and to get rid of some of the more distasteful elements of selectivity. The reforms had, of course, been the subject of years of deliberation by one of the commissions which by now had become so marked a feature of the Swedish political process. The aim of the new pension legislation of 1947 was to provide the pensioner with an income which would guarantee an *adequate* level of subsistence without recourse to social assistance. Pensions were still to be universal in coverage. The two-part pension of 1937 was now to be replaced by a single flat-rate pension benefit. There are obvious affinities to Beveridge's thinking here: national, universal, contributory, subsistence pensions provided by one unitary system. But Sweden, of course, had embraced most of these principles thirty years earlier, which is not to say that in the post-war revision of her social security systems she was uninfluenced by Beveridge's thinking.

The post-war years might have been thought to be the time to go for a single, but larger, pension which by itself would have provided the adequate income which was the overall objective for the pensioner. This, however, would have been costly and selective supplements were retained as a more economical way of helping those pensioners most in need. The income limits were set relatively high, over half the pension recipients were at once eligible at least for a housing allowance, and the combination of universal and selective benefits was accepted, and has continued to be accepted, by the pension population with little or no questioning. The 1947 scheme abandoned even partial funding, pensions were now to be financed on a completely pay-as-you-go basis. Pension contributions, however, were low and central and local government revenues provided about four-fifths of the total finances. This position has not changed substantially up to the present day.

The Pension Commission, on whose findings the 1947 legislation was based, had made the quite revolutionary proposal for the time that pensions in payment should be automatically indexed for rises in the cost of living. This recommendation was not adopted at once because of fears of possible inflationary effects. Almost as soon as the new scheme came into operation, however, the rising cost of living brought up this issue again and once more Sweden took the lead and adopted a form of *automatic indexing* as early as 1950. The early techniques used, however, were perhaps somewhat clumsy and repeated attempts were made over the years to refine them. The rise in the special pensioner price index required to trigger-off an adjustment in the pension was lowered from the original 5 points to 3 points, and annual supplements in the form of Christmas bonuses were replaced by monthly payments. The real weakness of the system, however, was the fixed 50 SW.kr. supplement which was added to the pension when a rise was justified and which did not necessarily compensate for the actual increase in prices. Indeed, it did so increasingly less as the rate of rise in the pensioner price index gathered momentum and the supplement itself stayed fixed.

Large numbers of pensioners were still applying for assistance in spite of these arrangements and it was becoming increasingly obvious that pensioners' incomes were not keeping pace with the rapidly rising earnings and standards of living which were being enjoyed by the working population. Once again Sweden took the lead and in the mid 1950s brought into operation a system of '*standard supplements*' to the pension with the aim of allowing the pensioner to have some share in increasing prosperity. Like the 'index supplements' these were fixed sums but they were not automatically linked to rises in earnings and legislation was required each time a new supplement was thought necessary. To employ the terminology used elsewhere in this volume, successive structural changes were made to the pension in addition to the automatic adjustments for rising prices.

In the meantime more radical measures were under consideration both to rationalize this somewhat complex structure of the basic pension and to bring Swedish pensions as a whole more into line with the movements in neighbouring countries towards earnings-related pensions. A new method of calculating the basic pension was introduced in 1957. The pension was now to be a percentage of a *base amount*, fixed in 1957 and to be automatically indexed for rises in the consumer price index. This base amount was also to be the reference point for the new *supplementary earnings-related pensions* then under discussion. The basic pension was to relate to income below the base amount and the supplementary pension to replace a smaller percentage of earnings above the base (up to a ceiling of pensionable earnings – see below). In this way the universal flat-rate citizen's pension and the graduated employment pension would be integrated and the total pension provision would be somewhat slanted in favour of the lower income bands. It was hoped to bring as many as possible of the lower-paid and part-time workers within the graduated scheme so the base amount above which earnings count for earnings-related pension was set relatively low in 1957 at 4,000 Sw.kr. or about a third of average male industrial earnings at the time.

The base amount merits a word of explanation and comment both for the important part which it plays in the pension structure and for its intrinsic interest as a tool or technique of social policy. This was a hypothetical figure fixed in 1957 as a device for simplifying the basic pension structure and for providing a means of co-ordinating the two national pensions. Since then, as we shall see below, it has taken on other functions in relation to both the national and to occupational pensions. The indexed base amount would provide automatic indexing for both types of pension and could also be used to maintain the standard of the pension *vis-à-vis* earnings. It was, therefore, decided in the late 1950s that the basic pension as a percentage of the basic amount should go up by stages from 60 per cent until it reached a target of 90 per cent (for a single man) in 1968, with a corresponding development of pensions for married couples. At that date the structural increases ceased and pensions were subsequently adjusted only to match rising prices. Thus Sweden put herself out of line with most of her European neighbours whose pensions had increasingly come to be related to rising earnings. This does not appear to have raised much comment at the time although the issue was one of the items put on the agenda of the new Committee on Pensions set up in 1970.

So far we have been concerned mainly with the basic pension.

We must now go back and look in more detail at the developments which had led to the introduction of the second tier of the pension pyramid at which we have only hinted. Several Pension Commissions had been considering the possibility of introducing graduated pensions throughout the 1950s and various sets of proposals had been put forward and thoroughly debated. There was in fact considerable general agreement over this new concept that pensions should in some measure reflect earnings during active working life. Thinking did not go as far as in Germany where pensions are entirely related to earnings with no minimum pension. Sweden clung to the idea of a citizen's pension that would guarantee everyone a certain basic income in old age; earnings-related pensions would supplement this universal pension but would not replace it. There was another consideration here—the numbers of elderly were growing and would continue to grow for many years ahead. Any substantial increase in the basic pension, financed as it was to a large extent out of general tax revenues, would be likely to increase the already high rates of taxation.

A new source of revenue was thought to be desirable; the employers who had hitherto contributed relatively little in the way of social security taxes, and nothing to the basic pension, were thought to be the most ready source of extra finance, especially if pensions were to be related to income from work. The major divisions of opinion centred on whether or not the new pension scheme should be a compulsory, state-controlled scheme and financed on a pay-as-you-go basis which would allow pensions to be paid quickly. The main alternative to this proposal of the Social Democrats was the suggestion put forward by the Conservative and Liberal parties and the Confederation of Employers for a voluntary system, funded and handled by private insurance companies and introduced on the basis of collective agreements. This seemed quite feasible in a country where the employers and workers were well organized and their federations were accustomed to work together on issues such as this. The self-employed were particularly opposed to compulsory insurance and their pressure groups fought hard to maintain the voluntary principle; the existing occupational pension schemes were no less worried about their future.

Perhaps an even more important issue throughout this controversy was the possible repercussions any new pension scheme might have on the supply of credit which is a perennial cause of worry in Sweden. If employees no longer needed to make private provision for old age would the supply of private savings dry up? Moreover if the employers had to pay large contributions into either a Government or private fund would this cut into their own working capital? There was the further fear of the Conservatives that a national pension fund might be used by the Government to enlarge its control over industry. In the event, as will be discussed below, these fears proved not to have been unfounded. At the time, however, the pension issue was the subject of an unusually heated controversy for Sweden. A plebiscite was held in 1957, Parliament had to be dissolved in 1958, new elections held, new committees of enquiry appointed, and new legislation drafted, until finally the Social Democrat proposals, having had a relatively easy passage through the Upper House, scraped through the Lower House in 1959 with a bare majority of one. The struggle over, the new proposals were accepted with little question. This appears to be one of the great advantages of the Swedish type of consensus government. Ample opportunities are available at the stage when proposals are under discussion and legislation is being drawn up for views to be expressed and for the interested parties to have a say in the policy-making process. When legislation is eventually put on the statute book, even after such an unusually heated debate as in the case of this particular reform, there is some feeling at least of joint responsibility for what it contains.

Some particular worries had been dealt with during the period of discussion and negotiations. The self-employed emerged with the right of voluntary membership of the new scheme as far as their earnings from self-employment were concerned. Having established this point of principle they turned round and joined up in large numbers. The doubts of the occupational pension interests had also been set at rest. Among the largest and most influential of these groups were the public employees, central and local government civil servants, the armed forces and the teachers. Many of these, and in particular the central Government civil servants, were already enjoying very favourable pension rights; the position was rather different for some of the local government employees and for some members of private occupational plans, many of which were providing pension rights inferior to those proposed in the new scheme. The new national earnings-related pensions and the existing schemes were not seen as alternatives but as complementary to each other, and special agreements were negotiated in order to co-ordinate them with the national plan and thus to ensure that those who were already covered by pension arrangements superior to the new arrangements should retain these advantages. In these cases the members of the schemes were to be brought into the new national scheme but have their national pension rights made up to the levels they already enjoyed. Some pension schemes with inferior rights were discontinued.

Perhaps the most interesting development in this field was the growth in occupational schemes, at least for salaried employees, after the introduction of the national graduated pension scheme. A model occupational plan was worked out by the organizations representing employers and salaried workers to replace the diverse private schemes already in existence. It was then open to individual industries to adopt this plan by collective agreements and between 1962 and 1970 the numbers of employees covered or actually receiving such pensions nearly doubled.

The new official supplementary pension legislation came into effect in 1960. The first contributions were paid by employers in the same year and first (part) pensions paid out in 1963. Nominally the supplementary earnings-related pension scheme (ATP)[1] is pay-as-you-go but in practice full pensions are not payable until thirty years contributions have been paid, reduced to twenty years in the case of pensioners retiring in the transitional period. In the meantime, of course, basic flat-rate pensions, which still remain as the first-tier, continue to be the main source of income for most pensioners. But year by year after 1963 more pensioners were retiring with some graduated pension rights and this began to give rise to differences between older and younger pensioners, which were not thought to be acceptable. The answer was a new pension supplement (the *pensionstillskott*) for the pensioner with few or no rights to supplementary pension. This came into operation in 1969 for a ten-year period and, once again, the base amount was used as the reference point for calculating the size of the supplement each year.

There was still one major gap in the pension pyramid—the virtual lack of any *third-tier occupational pension for the blue collar worker*. It is perhaps surprising that pressure from the strong

---

[1] Allmänna tilläggspensioner, National Supplementary Pensions.

Trade Union Organization (*Landsorganisation*-LO) for collective
pension agreements has only grown up in relatively recent years,
and long after the introduction of national supplementary pensions, might have been expected to do away with the case for
occupational provisions. In Britain there had been big developments in the coverage of occupational pensions from the 1950s
onwards but then, of course, there was no national move comparable to the introduction of the supplementary pension scheme in
Sweden. Apart from the fact that the flat-rate pension was replacing
a higher proportion of his previous earnings for the manual worker,
the LO appeared to have had other priorities for its members—
higher earnings, longer paid holidays, a shorter working week, etc.
Much had been done to satisfy these demands; new causes could
be taken up. One of these is the movement to narrow the remaining
differentials in conditions of employment between white and blue
collar workers. Occupational pensions, and the lower retirement
age which the salaried employee could enjoy because of his occupational pension, obviously put the white collar worker at a considerable advantage. These occupational plans had grown rapidly
since the re-organization of the schemes in the early 1960s so the
gap had become more obvious. Perhaps too the new graduated
pensions whetted the appetites of the workers for a more comfor-
table retirement income. The employers agreed quite readily in
principle when the Trade Union Organization (LO) put forward
a case for occupational pensions; the delay in reaching final agreement centred largely on the issue of a funded or a pay-as-you-go
scheme. The LO strongly favoured the latter to enable pensions to
be paid as quickly as possible. A compromise was finally agreed
upon in 1971 and came into operation in 1973.[1]

III—THE PENSION SYSTEM IN THE 1970s

So much by way of a preliminary historical summary of developments. The pattern which has emerged is complex with pensions
payable on three different levels with different arrangements for
both benefits and contributions. We shall now review the current
position in each case and try to indicate how provisions are likely
to develop in the future.

---

[1] See below, p. 180.

National basic pensions (AFP)[1]

One of the interesting features of the Swedish pension arrangements is the breadth of coverage of the first-tier flat rate *folkpension* which is paid as of right to every Swedish citizen resident in Sweden (or registered for census purposes in Sweden between the ages of fifty-seven to sixty-two) on reaching the age of sixty-seven. With virtually no exceptions every one is entitled to at least a basic income for old age. Further there are no retirement or other conditions, such as exist in the U K and elsewhere, to stand between the citizen and his pension. On the other hand the pension age, at sixty-seven, is high.[2] This has been regarded as a major weakness of the scheme and has caused difficulties particularly for the elderly worker in heavy industry or in regions of declining employment. Special measures of the kind described below have had to be introduced to help in such cases.

The scheme is nominally contributory but heavily subsidized— as to two-thirds of actual expenditure on pensions in the early seventies—out of central and local government general tax revenues. Contributions take the form of a tax, in 1973 5 per cent, on taxable income with a ceiling of 1,500 Sw.kr. per year on the maximum contribution payable. This is in fact a hypothecated tax, but it is very small and is paid along with other taxes so is barely recognized for what it is. It may be questioned why it should be kept apart rather than merged in general taxation, or conversely, why it should not be raised so as to cover the whole or a large part of the cost of pensions.

The pension payable is calculated as a percentage of the *current indexed base amount*—90 per cent for a single pensioner, 140 per cent for a married couple when both are of pensionable age. We have already explained above the history of the base amount and its importance as a reference point for the three tiers of pension and for other social security benefits. The base amount is reviewed every three months and if there has been a rise in the consumer

---

[1] Allmänna folkpensioner.

[2] The pension may be drawn on special application at the age of sixty-three or payment may be delayed until the age of seventy. In the one case the pension will be reduced, in the other case increased, by 0·6 per cent (in perpetuity) for every month involved. As from 1972 it may be paid in full from the age of sixty-three, or even earlier, to the unemployed person who has exhausted his rights to unemployment insurance benefits. See below, p. 187.

G

price index of at least 3 per cent the amount is raised, but in relation to the price level two months earlier, thus incorporating a
small built-in anti-inflationary time lag. Pensions are then adjusted
in line with the base amount. It is possible for the base amount,
and so pensions, to be raised more than once in any one year. In
fact pensions were raised three times during 1971. The pension is
thus very much more sensitive to price changes than are earnings
increases which are negotiated on an annual basis. This is a point
which deserves to be stressed. The Swedes appear to have overcome the administrative difficulties of frequent adjustments in
pensions which have so often been put forward in the UK as the
justification for our biennial, or more recently annual, increases in
benefits which, in times of fast rising prices, undoubtedly cause
hardship for the pensioner. In Sweden this sensitive inflation
proofing may account in part for the relative lack of concern
about the absence of indexing for rising earnings.

The basic pension may be supplemented in various ways. The
most important are the *means-tested allowances* for wives between
the ages of sixty and sixty-seven, and, especially, the *housing allowances*.[1] (There are no allowances at all for wives under sixty unless
there are young children or the husband needs care; otherwise
they are considered to be fit enough to earn their own livelihood.)
It is important to note how these two selective supplements work
as this has important implications for their acceptability to the
pensioner. Entitlement to the supplements is incorporated in the
pension legislation and the income-qualifying conditions are laid
down at national level,[2] although the income test is applied by the
local municipalities who also decide the actual amounts of the supplements to be paid. The same *wives' supplement* is paid as a rule
by all municipalities and these are financed by central Government. The *housing allowance*, which is financed out of local
taxation, may be calculated by the local municipalities in one of

---

[1] Non-means-tested allowances are paid for dependent children and disable-
ment allowances for severely disabled pensioners.

[2] Full housing and wives' supplements are paid where income other than the
pension, sickness benefit or family help, does not exceed 2,000 Sw.kr. per year
or 3,000 Sw.kr. in the case of a married couple. These figures have not been
raised for some years, a point which in itself is favourable to pensioners (as was
the raising of the property disregards in the early 1970s to 50,000 Sw.kr. and
80,000 Sw.kr. for single persons and married couples respectively). Reduced
supplements are paid where income or property exceeds these amounts.

three ways laid down by central Government but the actual amount payable is left to the municipalities themselves:

(*a*) A general allowance may be paid to all qualifying pensioners without regard to the cost of housing (this applied to over 40 per cent of pensioners in 1970) and may be anywhere between 700 and 2,000 Sw.kr. per year;
(*b*) The allowance may be related to the actual cost of housing;
(*c*) The allowance may be given in two parts, one to all qualifying pensioners, the other part related to the actual income of the pensioner.

There are local variations in the way this scheme is administered and the size of the allowance paid but some important general points emerge. First, the means tests appear to be liberal—over half of all pensioners every year have been receiving housing allowances since they were first introduced. Second, it is safe to generalize that the allowance paid will cover the total cost of housing for the pensioner with no income other than his pension.[1] Third, means-testing can be generally acceptable if it is attached to a specific service and provided for a specific category in the population and if, furthermore, the income limits are high enough to bring in a large proportion of that category. Even a pensioner with two pensions, basic and supplementary, may be eligible for a housing allowance as supplementary pensions are still low for most pensioners although this no doubt will change as the supplementary scheme approaches maturity.

In addition to these means-tested supplements the pensioner may be entitled to a *pensionstillskott*, the new supplement introduced in 1969 to help the pensioner with no rights, or poor rights, to an earnings-related supplementary pension. This again is related to the central reference point, the *indexed base amount*. The first full supplement payable as from July 1969 was 3 per cent of the current base amount and it is to rise automatically in 3 per cent stages each year until it reaches 30 per cent of the base in 1978, to take account of the increasing maturity of the graduated pension. The actual supplement payable to the individual pensioner depends

---

[1] If the allowance does not cover the full cost the pensioner may apply for additional help from general social assistance and many local authorities will give this. In only very rare cases will the authority refuse if it thinks the rent unduly high.

on the amount of supplementary pension he is receiving, if any, and the maximum supplement is reduced kronor for kronor so that his income from ATP pension plus supplement does not exceed 30 per cent of the current base amount.[1] Gradually, of course, fewer and fewer pensioners will be eligible for these supplements. At the same time average supplementary pensions will become larger each year and the *pensionstillskott* will do less and less to narrow the differentials between different groups of pensioners. Nevertheless an important point of principle has been conceded here and some attempt made to tackle a problem which inevitably arises when pensions are related to previous earnings. The basic pension, made up of these various components, would at 1 October 1971, for example, have looked like this:

	Single man	Pensioner couple both aged sixty-seven
Basic pension	100	100
Housing supplement (estimated)	19	25
Pension supplement	10	13
	129	138

National Supplementary Pensions (ATP). All earnings above the current base at any point in time up to a certain ceiling are compulsorily insured for the *earnings-related* pension, except for earnings from self-employment. Nine out of ten of the self-employed, however, have exercised their option to insure their earnings from self-employment. Pensionable earnings then are earnings which lie above the current base up to a ceiling of 7·5 times that base. We shall have more to say later about the floor and ceiling for pensionable earnings. Contributions are payable by employers alone on all the pensionable earnings of their work force

---

[1] An example may help elucidate. The supplement at 1 July 1972 was 12 per cent of the base amount, that is 876 Sw.kr. A pensioner with no ATP income would receive the full supplement; a pensioner with ATP income of 1,200 Sw.kr. would also receive the full supplement (1,800 + 876 Sw.kr. did not exceed 30 per cent of the current base amount); a pensioner with ATP income of 1,500 Sw.kr. would have received a reduced supplement of 800 Sw.kr. (1,500 Sw.kr. + 876 would exceed 30 per cent of the base by 76 Sw.kr. and his supplement would be correspondingly reduced).

and have risen steadily from the original rate of 3 per cent in 1960 to 10·75 per cent in 1973. We shall look at what this means for the pension funds below.

An ATP pension is payable after a qualifying period of 3 years of insurance but *full* pensions are payable only after thirty years of insurance, or twenty years in the transitional period up to 1980. The scheme is nominally pay-as-you-go but there was limited blanketing-in and pensions actually paid before maturity of the scheme are full pensions reduced proportionately for every month short of the full qualifying period. The aim of the scheme is to provide on maturity a full pension equal to 60 per cent of pensionable earnings averaged out over the fifteen 'best' earnings years, in this way relating pensions to the most active years of a man or woman's working life. The ATP pension is payable in addition to the basic pension and the two pensions together will for the majority of pensioners provide an income of about two-thirds of former earnings. The actual replacement factor will, of course, depend on the pensioner's individual earnings record.

The mature supplementary pension can be expressed in terms of a deceptively simple formula:

$$\frac{60}{100} \times \frac{P}{15} \times \text{Current base amount}$$

where P equals the total pension points earned in the fifteen 'best' earnings years. Each year the employee earns a certain number of *pension points* which are calculated on the basis of the relationship between his pensionable earnings and the prevailing base amount (a man earning 24,000 Sw.kr. in a year when the base amount was, say, 6,000 would have a pensionable income for ATP of 24,000 minus 6,000, i.e. 18,000 which would be three times the base amount and therefore give him three pension points for that year). Given the ceiling to pensionable earnings the formula gives a maximum number of pension points in any one year of six-and-a-half. On retirement the pension points earned in his fifteen 'best' earnings years are averaged and multiplied by the base amount at the time he retires; a full pension would equal 60 per cent of that sum.[1]

---

[1] A simple example may best illustrate: an employee reaching the age of sixty-seven in 1980 who had earned, say, five pension points for each of ten years of the period 1960–80, four points in five other years and three in the remaining

The supplementary pension when in payment is automatically indexed for rises in the cost of living in the same way as the basic pension but, in common with the basic pension, not for rising earnings. These pensions are payable at the age of sixty-seven but may be drawn at an earlier date or deferred when they will be proportionately reduced or increased in the same way as the basic pension.

A number of comments need to be made at this point. The first relates to the population coverage of the scheme. The floor for pensionable earnings for ATP was set low in order to bring in as large a proportion of the working population as possible. The ceiling on pensionable earnings was at the same time put high so as to cover the great majority of all earnings. It appears to have gone a long way to achieving both these objectives. In 1966[1] some 97 per cent of workers had all their earnings covered for pension purposes. The ceiling, however, which is indexed for rising prices but not for rising earnings may, at some future date, begin to cause difficulties, as has been the experience in many countries. The classic example perhaps is the USA. Changes in the American ceiling require legislation and are infrequent. There was, for example, a period of six years between the adjustments in 1960 and 1965 during which time average earnings rose by 20 per cent. The ceiling in the USA in any case is low and only 76 per cent of workers had all their earnings covered for pension purposes in 1966, compared with the 97 per cent in Sweden and 88 per cent in Germany. The Swedish pension ceiling has in fact fallen from the original level of about two-and-a-half times average male earnings in manufacturing in 1960 to about twice such earnings. This is the target figure in Germany and Austria but in these countries the ceiling is adjusted for rising *earnings* rather than prices. In Sweden, where this is not the case, thought is already being given to the possible future need for change and this is another of the

---

five would select for calculation of his pension ten years by five points and five years by four points, giving a total of seventy points. His ATP pension would then be:

$$\frac{60}{100} \times \frac{70}{15} \times \text{base amount 1980.}$$

[1] See 'Role of the Contribution Ceiling in Social Security Programs: Comparison of Five Countries', by Max Horlich and Robert Lucas, in *Social Security Bulletin*, February 1971, US Department of Health, Education and Welfare, Washington.

issues under consideration by the Pensions Committee appointed in 1970.

Another point to be looked at is the pension formula itself and in particular the device used to relate pensions to earnings during active working life. Other schemes may relate pensions to earnings over the whole working life, others to terminal earnings. The latter tends to favour the salaried workers who reach their peak earnings at the end of their working lives but puts at a disadvantage many manual workers whose earnings tail off in their fifties and sixties. The Swedish formula seems to cater for all patterns of working life. It would seem too to favour labour mobility as the worker will have every incentive, present and future, to move in search of higher earnings.

ATP is still some distance from maturity. How many of the present generation of pensioners are in fact receiving these pensions and what do they add to their income from the basic pension? The proportion of all pensioners drawing the second-tier pension slowly increased over the 1960s until by 1970 it had reached nearly 30 per cent of the total pensioner population. At an average level of some 2,300 Sw.kr. it was by then adding something like 20 per cent on to the basic pension in the case of a male pensioner. One might add here the not unexpected comment that women as a whole are faring less well: only about 20 per cent of all ATP pensioners in 1970 were women and their average pensions were only in the neighbourhood of 60 per cent of the average male pension, reflecting lower female earnings and intermittent work records.

National disability and survivors' pensions

Something must be said at this point about disability and survivors' pensions if only because a number of the 'elderly', who are our major focus, are being helped by one or other of these pensions. The pattern of these pensions follows much the same lines as that for old age pensions, a basic pension as of right, a supplementary pension based on employment record[1]—which may be that of the husband in the case of widows or orphans—and in some cases a

---

[1] The disabled person claiming a supplementary pension is helped by the fact that he is credited with 'assumed' points for years in which he is unable to earn because of his disability and the pension is then calculated on the basis of what he would have received as retirement pension at sixty-seven.

third tier of occupational pension, yet to be discussed. Basic disability, or early retirement pensions as they are often called, are paid to any disabled person whose earning capacity is permanently reduced by not less than half. A full basic pension, at the same rate and with the same supplements as the old age pension, is payable where working capacity is almost entirely lost (up to about five-sixths) or where work has never been possible, two-thirds pension where loss of capacity is between five-sixths and two-thirds and half pension in other cases. The important point here is that the disability *folkpension* is payable as of right irrespective of whether or not the disabled person has ever been able to work, which at once gives the congenitally handicapped a much superior status, and more generous income, than his opposite number in Britain. For all disability pensioners (not only war and industrial injury pensioners as in the UK) it is possible to draw a part disability pension and earn, although only a small proportion of all disability pensioners are in fact doing so. The vast majority are too incapacitated or too old and suitable part-time employment is scarce.

In 1970 and again in 1972 the arrangements were liberalized to help the older unemployed worker who has difficulty in finding employment. It is now possible as we have mentioned above to draw a full early retirement pension at sixty-three, or even earlier, if the claimant has exhausted his rights to unemployment insurance benefits. The late pension age of sixty-seven has in the past posed problems for many elderly workers, particularly in heavy industry and in areas of high unemployment, and it will be interesting to see how many older workers will be helped by the new dispensation. It may, of course, be that increasing numbers of elderly workers have already been helped in this way and this may account for some of the 32 per cent increase in the numbers of disability pensioners between 1966 and 1971. The income prospects of the disabled who have worked are, of course, improved by occupational pension rights. Up to 1972 this applied only to salaried employees but from then on the new AGS[1] Sick Pay Scheme for manual workers will make up the national disability pensions to 90 per cent of net earnings. This is a generous arrangement, but an unintended side-effect will be to increase the income disparities between different groups of pensioners.

---

[1] AvtalGruppsjukförsäkring.

Where *survivors* are concerned it is interesting to note that up to 1960 widows' pensions were payable only after a test of means. This now applies only to women widowed before 1 July 1960 who must pass an income test[1] to qualify for the benefits which are available as of right to more recently widowed women. These benefits vary according to the age at which the woman is widowed and whether or not she has dependent children. A full widow's basic pension which equals the old age pension (and includes the same supplements) is payable to a widow aged fifty at the time of her husband's death or to a widow with children under sixteen living at home. A reduced pension is payable to widows without children if under fifty but over thirty-six at the time of the husband's death. At the age of sixty-seven, whatever her previous pension rights, she becomes entitled to a full single person's old age pension. The pensions for children were much improved in late 1973 and are now calculated at the rate of 40 per cent of the indexed basic old age pension for each child. The widow and her family are also entitled to supplementary pensions, which are related to the amount of the retirement pension earned by the husband by the time of his death.[2] The majority of widows and orphaned children are now receiving supplementary pensions.

It is an interesting feature of the Swedish arrangements that unmarried women or divorcees have the same basic, but not supplementary, pension rights as the legal spouse if they have been cohabiting with a man at the time of his death, or have been married to him or had children by him at some time in the past. On the other hand conditions attaching to eligibility for supplementary pensions are quite stringent; the widow must have been married for not less than five years and the marriage contracted not later than the sixtieth birthday of her husband.

Occupational pensions

Closely integrated with the two national pension schemes are the occupational pension arrangements which form the *third tier* of the pension pyramid. The most generous of these arrangements are

---

[1] The same as applies for the housing and wives' supplements (see p. 168 n, above).

[2] The widow is entitled to 40 per cent of this if she has no dependent children; if she has children she herself receives 35 per cent and a further 15 per cent goes to the first child and 10 per cent each to subsequent children.

the pension provisions for *public employees*. Civil servants, the armed forces, local functionaries of different kinds are generally the first groups in any country to be looked after when their working life is over. Sweden is no exception. Public pensions date from the 19th century and although these schemes have now been co-ordinated with the national schemes retired 'public servants' still have the edge on practically any other group of retired persons. Central and local government (and certain other 'public' employers like the various semi-official National Boards) insure their employees in the national schemes and they make up the two national pensions which the retired employee will receive so that his total retirement income will in general equal 65 per cent of his salary over the last five working years (provided in general he has worked for thirty years or longer). The majority of public employees reach their peak earnings at the end of their working life and there is no ceiling on pensionable earnings. These factors at once put them in an advantageous position. The majority of public employees enjoy the further advantage of a flexible retirement age which has been a considerable bonus with as high a national pension age as sixty-seven. Moreover, pensions in payment are supposedly kept in line with increasing salaries, not merely prices. This appears not to have worked very well in the past but renewed and more successful attempts have been made since 1966 to keep pension increases more directly in line with salary increases. Again this puts the public servant pensioner in a class apart.[1] It is estimated that nearly 175,000 retired people are drawing various types of 'public' retirement pensions (plus a further number of widows of pensioners which it is difficult to put a figure to). This may mean that perhaps up to one in three retired persons are enjoying a 'public' pension which brings them above the basic or even basic plus supplementary pension level.[2]

Occupational pensions in *private industry* were a relatively slow growth until the 1960s, perhaps not surprisingly in a country

---

[1] There are other signs of favoured treatment; thus public employees are exempt from prescription charges for medicines, the only group to be treated in this way, unlike the position in the UK where children, the elderly, low-income families, etc., enjoy this treatment.

[2] This estimate must be treated with caution. In comparing 'public' pensioners with all basic pensioners it is not known how many more of the former have retired before sixty-seven than is the case for ordinary pensioners, and so the 'public' and total pension populations are not strictly comparable.

where industrialization was comparatively late in developing, the small enterprise has continued to be the norm and economic growth is a relatively recent phenomenon. The real movement in private occupational plans, as we have already seen, came after the introduction of the national supplementary pension scheme in the early 1960s, which had brought up the whole question of unifying such schemes as already existed and coordinating them with the national pensions.[1]

A general plan (ITP)[2] was worked out and agreed in 1962 by representatives of employers and salaried employees covering old age, invalidity and survivor pensions. At first it was left to employers and employees to make voluntary agreements to adopt the plan. Increasing numbers did so now that earnings-related pensions had become so much part of the pension scene and as from October 1969 these agreements were changed into collective contracts. Where a firm has not introduced the plan, it is up to the employees, or their organization, to require the firm to do so. If the firm is a member of the Employers' Federation (SAF)[3] then the plan is legally binding on it. Such is the strength of the organizations on both sides of industry, that there has never been any question of an employer refusing to come into line. (The general plan in theory relates only to firms where the employers are members of SAF but it has in fact been used as a model by non-member industries such as insurance, banking, the co-operative societies and the merchant navy.)

One of the arguments often advanced in favour of occupational pensions is that they allow for diversity of pension arrangements to meet individual needs. In Sweden with the adoption of a general uniform plan it might be thought that something had been lost. The general plan has, however, advantages in simplifying administration and in easing transferability of pension rights. Employers can, and many do, make voluntary arrangements to provide additional benefits—the icing on the cake—to suit individual needs and to attract staff.

The general aims of ITP are twofold: first, to provide employees

---

[1] The number of employees and retired employees covered by such arrangements increased from 177,000 in 1957 to 317,000 in 1962 and by 1970 had grown to 540,000.

[2] Industrins tilläggspensioner.

[3] Svenska Arbetsgivareföreningen.

with full temporary pensions at sixty-five[1] which will enable
them to retire before the official pension age of sixty-seven, and
second, to provide additional pensions from sixty-seven onwards
which will complement the national basic and supplementary
pensions. (Naturally there are also arrangements for complementary disability and survivors' pensions.) The target in either case
is a total pension from national and occupational sources equal to
65 per cent of final salary up to a ceiling of ten times the base
amount used for computing national pensions, and 32·5 per cent
of final salary between ten and fifteen times the base amount. In
this way occupational pensions are coordinated with the national
schemes and pensions provide a different level of replacement income at different parts of the income structure, the whole system
being slanted in favour of the lower income groups. It follows that
the relationship which the individual's *actual* pension will have to
final salary will depend upon the pensioner's position in the salary
scale and may be above or below the 'target' replacement figure of
65 per cent. These are, of course, full pensions and require thirty
years membership of the scheme (as do national public employee
pensions)[2] and pensions are reduced proportionately for 'missing'
months of service. The great majority of salaried employees have
only been accumulating these pension rights since the early 1960s
so it will be many years before the retired white collar workers as a
group will be enjoying fully mature pensions.

The present pensioners will be concerned, of course, not only
with the size of their starting pension but with the retention of its
value over the years both in relation to rising prices and in relation
to the rising earnings of those still at work. The protection of
pensions in payment against inflation has often been claimed to
present well-nigh insuperable difficulties if a scheme is funded, as
is essentially the case with the Swedish occupational schemes. The
Swedish experience is, therefore, of relevance here. Pensions in
payment are not *automatically* indexed but in fact have kept in line
with rises in the retail price index. The possibility of going beyond
this and adjusting pensions in order to take account of rising incomes of the working population has not been seriously considered

---

[1] It is interesting to note that originally the age for female employees was
sixty-two but this was raised to sixty-five as from 1 January 1971.
[2] Special rules apply for calculating years of service for employees who had been
members of older schemes before the introduction of the general plan in 1960.

for occupational pensions—and it is not even the practice, as we have seen, for state pensions. There were particular circumstances in Sweden which might have been expected to militate against indexing even for price rises. There are strict government regulations on investment of occupational pension funds (see below) and only 10 per cent are 'free' to be invested in equities or real estate which might be expected to yield the sort of rate of return needed for dynamizing of any kind. What has happened is that the bonuses have been paid out of surpluses which have arisen because of 'pessimistic' assumptions about interest yields, mortality rates, etc., on which the original premiums were based and because the number of pensioners is still relatively small in relation to the total number insured. The actuarial basis of the scheme is so arranged, however, that this type of indexing will continue to be possible even when the relationship between the numbers of pensioners and non-pensioners changes.[1]

Undoubtedly the centralized administrative and financial arrangements for occupational pensions have made indexing of this kind easier; this type of arrangement might, of course, only be possible in a country like Sweden where both employers and employees are so strongly organized and the organizations have been so ready to work together on issues such as this. The Swedish Staff Pension Society (SPP)[2] which centralizes the arrangements was first established in 1917 by the Federation of Swedish Industries and the unions of salaried employees as a friendly society to coordinate the various occupational pension schemes which had been growing up in a sporadic way over a number of years. In 1929 it became a mutual assurance company with some indirect Government control exercised largely through restrictions on the operation of the society's trust funds. This was the obvious institution to handle the much greater volume of insurance that was likely to follow the introduction of the general plan (ITP) in the early 1960s. All firms who are members of the Swedish Employers' Federation handle their disability and survivors insurance through SPP and the small firms use it for retirement pensions too.

---

[1] Changes in pension payment are limited to rises in the retail price index and by the condition that the expected future surplus of the existing insurance stock should be sufficient to give bonus additions in future to both existing and future pensioners.
[2] Svenska Personal-Pensionskassan.

The larger firms, however, instead of taking out joint policies with SPP for retirement pensions may use two other institutions, the Pension Guarantee Mutual Insurance (FPG) and the Pension Registration Institute (PRI), set up in 1961. This arrangement enables the larger enterprises to transfer each year to an 'allocated for pensions' account in their own books, the amounts equivalent to the SPP premiums. No tangible assets have to be transferred but as a guarantee that the money will be there to fulfil pension obligations when emploeeys retire these employers are required to take out guarantee insurance with FPG; the size of the premium they have to pay depends upon FPG's rating of the financial standing of the individual employer.[1] PRI handles all the administrative work of keeping employers' records and paying out pensions. This arrangement appears to have met with general satisfaction and the employers concerned feel that it gives them greater freedom over the use of their assets. All these various institutions work together closely and are administered jointly by the organizations representative of employers and salaried workers —a typical example perhaps of Swedish participative administration.

A major advantage of these arrangements is, of course, that they facilitate transferability of pension rights. This is particularly the case if the employee transfers between two firms using SPP; it is more complicated if one firm operates through SPP and one through FPG/PRI but arrangements are being made between the different institutions to iron out these difficulties in the future. No complete solution has yet been found, however, where employees transfer between completely different systems, e.g. private and government employment.

Occupational pensions for *manual workers* are, as we have already seen, a very recent innovation. The principles of a general plan (STP)[2] were agreed in 1970, more detailed plans were then worked out and adopted by collective agreements between employers and employees and came into operation in 1973. The STP plan follows the broad lines of the ITP plan for salaried employees. This is part of a general move, favoured alike by government circles, employers and employees, to lessen the differentials

---

[1] There were nine cases of insolvency during 1970 but no pension rights were jeopardized, because of the FPG arrangement.
[2] Särskilda tilläggspensioner.

between white and blue collar workers where fringe benefits are concerned. (The new sick pay plan for manual workers (AGS) to be introduced at the same time is another step in the same direction.) As with the white collar scheme, the two aims of the new arrangements for manual workers are to provide full temporary pensions between the ages of sixty-five and sixty-seven (STP 1) and a third tier of pension income complementary to the two national pensions from the age of sixty-seven (STP 2). The arrangements for early retirement pensions at sixty-five (STP 1) would appear to be relatively liberal. All workers reaching the age of sixty-five after the scheme comes into operation will be entitled to full pensions if they have long enough employment records as they will be back credited with employment prior to 1970. For the older workers there are also special arrangements to reduce the normal requirement of thirty years service. These pensions aim at providing a pension equal to what the worker could expect to receive from the national basic and supplementary pensions if he worked to age sixty-seven.

The STP 2 pension aims in broad terms at adding another 10 per cent of income to the national basic and supplementary pensions, which is comparable to the arrangements for salaried employees. Full pensions will be payable only after thirty years membership of the scheme although proportionately reduced part pensions will be payable from 1973. These pensions will be related to the current base amount and the same ceiling on pensionable earnings will operate as for the national supplementary pension so that they will be closely integrated with the national pension schemes. The qualifying period of thirty years, it may be noted, is shorter than is the case in other countries. There is, however, no provision for blanketing-in apart from the three years insurance units with which workers are to be credited when the scheme comes into operation. Full STP 2 pensions will not be payable until the year 2000. The earnings on which these pensions will be based are those in the best three out of the last five years of employment up to a national ceiling on pensionable earnings. This will relate the occupational pension quite closely to final earnings and also bring total pension rights a little more in line with terminal wages. Whether or not this will benefit the individual worker will, of course, depend on the period in his working life at which he reaches peak earnings. Another point to be noted relates

to indexing. It would appear that again the manual workers'
scheme will follow the lines of the white collar workers' scheme.
Whilst there is no formal undertaking to index pensions in payment either for rising prices or rising earnings nevertheless it is
implied that any surplus arising from the insurance arrangements
will be used primarily for raising pensions in payment to compensate for increases in the cost of living.

The methods chosen for financing and administering the scheme
would appear to have a number of points of interest. The temporary pensions, STP 1, will be financed on a pay-as-you-go basis
out of the payroll tax to be paid by employers; which allows for
full pensions at sixty-five to be introduced at once. STP 2 pensions,
however, are to be funded, hence the long delay in reaching
mature pensions. The method chosen for sharing the cost of
pensions by all employers, irrespective of age or other characteristics of their labour force, puts all workers on an equal footing.
National finance and administration of occupational pensions
through various institutions to be set up through the Swedish
Pension Organisation (SPP) also means that there will be no
problem of transferability of pension rights on change of employment, a point to which we in this country might give some thought.
Employers are going to have a similar option as under the ITP
arrangement not to pay current premiums, which will take the form
of a payroll tax, but to buy credit insurance to cover their liabilities.
This will have the advantage of releasing working capital that
would otherwise be used for premium payments. The great
majority of the pension population will in future have three sets of
pension rights, although for some years to come the basic flat-rate
pension will continue to be the major source of income for the
majority of pensioners, and for many who have never worked it
will always be the sole source of income. It is important that we
should try to assess the adequacy of the basic pension arrangements and to this we will turn later.

IV—OTHER PROVISIONS, IN CASH AND IN
KIND, FOR THE ELDERLY

Pensions are of course the major source of income for the elderly
non-active members of the population but other assistance is
available which may help the old person with special needs or

which, more generally, may add to his total resources. The importance of the *housing allowance* which forms part of the basic pension has already been touched on. Over half of all pensioners have been receiving this allowance for many years. On a rough estimate, it adds some 20 to 25 per cent to the basic pension and covers the whole cost of rent where the pensioner has no other source of income than his pension. One may speculate as to the future of the housing allowance when more and more people come to receive graduated pensions and larger ones than at the time of writing. So far graduated pensions on average have not been large enough to take many pensioners without private sources of income above the income qualifying limits for the allowance. Presumably, however, the numbers eligible for the allowance will decrease as the earnings-related scheme comes to maturity but presumably again it will remain as an additional source of help for numbers of pensioners with poor or no ATP pension rights.

Rent controls are an additional source of help to many old people who are living in the older apartments which have not been freed from controls. This brings its own problems, however, as these apartments are often cramped and of poor amenity and in the decaying down-town areas of the larger towns and cities. In the rural areas, too, old people may be living in cheap but often poor quality property. The growing numbers of old people, the poor housing conditions in which many live, and the high cost of building new houses have in recent years caused many local authorities to give priority to the needs of the elderly in their housing programmes. Special housing units for the elderly have been built in increasing numbers and loans made available for improving old property. It is estimated that about one in six of the pensioner population are now living in purpose-built housing or in housing constructed or improved with the help of these special loans.

For good or ill, a relatively large number of the elderly population in Sweden are not living in their own homes but in *residential accommodation* of various kinds. This is the responsibility of the municipalities to provide. Capital subsidies from the central Government have helped the local communes to increase and improve their stock of homes and it is estimated that about one in twenty old persons are catered for in this way (as compared with less than one in fifty in the UK). Charges are made in all homes. Although the system used varies from commune to commune, in all cases the residents are allowed to keep part of the pension for personal expenditure.[1] The weakness of family ties and the relative under-development of *community care services* until very recently may be two of the factors accounting for the large number of old people in residential homes. There is little detailed information except for the Home Help Service. This has received a special government subsidy (35 per cent of the cost of wages) since 1964 in order to promote its growth. The subsidy has had considerable success and the numbers of the aged and handicapped population receiving the service more than doubled over the years 1965–70.[2] About one in five of the elderly are now receiving the service but the amount of help they get averages less than three hours per week. Charges are made for the service but in the majority of areas the pensioner with no income other than his basic pension receives it free.

Health care and housing are no doubt the most important sources of additional help for the elderly. The national health service provides for all the population a wide, but not completely comprehensive, range of health services, heavily subsidised, but not free at time of consumption. The pensioners are exempt from the health insurance contributions but not from the charges levied at time of use unless they can prove need and obtain an exemption certificate from their local Social Welfare Board. This means that for out-patient medical care a pensioner is liable to pay a charge of 15 Sw.kr. for every consultation with a doctor; this includes the cost of X-ray and any other specialist services needed.[3] Medicines are free in a limited range of 'life-saving drugs' but normally the patient has to pay a charge which averages half the cost of the prescription (which may include several items) with a

---

[1] The pensioner may keep 30 per cent of the basic pension plus 20 per cent of all other net income. In the UK the personal allowance is equivalent to rather less than 20 per cent of the standard pension.

[2] Based on Table 294, *Statistical Abstract of Sweden*, 1971 National Central Bureau of Statistics, Stockholm. The comparable figure for Britain in 1970 was about 6 per cent. The average amount of help given per week was probably only two to three hours. See *Social Trends* No. 3 1972, Central Statistical Office, London.

[3] If he chooses to go to a doctor in private practice, in order to jump the queue for public health service doctors or for reasons of personal choice, he will be refunded 75 per cent of the cost according to a prescribed tariff, and will have to pay the remaining 25 per cent of the tariff plus any part of the fee above the official scale.

maximum charge of 15 Sw.kr. Public ward in-patient hospital care is free but in the case of the elderly only for 365 days, after which his pension is reduced for each extra day.[1] Dental treatment is available at reduced fees for the elderly at some hospitals and clinics, and municipal grants may help the less well-to-do with the fees. Waiting lists for dental treatment are, however, long and the elderly may have to have recourse to private treatment, which is costly.[2] Ophthalmic care is not available at all under the national health service but the old person may apply for social assistance with this and with dental costs. There is not much evidence that many do in fact apply for such assistance or that medical charges are a burden for the pensioner.

A limitation of another kind may in some cases prevent the pensioner from obtaining all the health cover he should have. The health insurance legislation provides only for *curative*, not *preventive*, medicine. Screening services and health check-ups not necessitated by illness but which may detect medical conditions at an early and treatable stage, are not available under the health service and this is considered to be one of the major weaknesses of the health service as a whole. For the old person the relatively poor quality of much in-patient geriatric care is another problem, although steps are now being taken, in Sweden as in many other countries, to concentrate resources on improving conditions in geriatric and psychiatric hospitals.

Few pensioners, only 3 per cent in recent years, have recourse to *local social assistance*. When they do, this is mainly for special purposes such as health charges, exceptional housing costs, or for once-for-all grants for renewal of major items of clothing or household equipment, removal expenses and the like. There is no doubt that the increases in pensions, and in particular the housing allowance, together with heavily subsidized health care, have largely done away with the need for help with the general costs of living. The old person shares the same rights to social assistance as the population generally but as the basic pension is used by some municipalities as the standard by which claims are assessed, or at

---

[1] Health Insurance Societies have funds from which they may help the pensioner in these cases if need be.

[2] The introduction of national dental insurance in 1974 will greatly help the elderly; three-quarters of the cost of major dental treatment (including dentures) will be refunded.

any rate is thought to be the standard which should be aimed at, there would be little chance of the pensioner being eligible for help with the *general* costs of living. This is very different from the situation in the UK where some 28 per cent of old age pensioners had their national insurance pensions supplemented in 1972. This, of course, is possible because the means-tested supplementary pension is higher than the insurance pension, largely because it makes provision for housing costs. In Sweden this latter item is covered within the national pension arrangements and this appears to be a more acceptable method of helping the pensioner, even if the housing allowance is means-tested. How claims made by the Swedish person for extra assistance are dealt with depends on the local municipalities which are responsible for the administration and most of the finance of assistance. There may be delays in getting claims settled and there are pensioners who are ignorant of, or too independent to claim, their rights but by and large there seem few complaints about the treatment they receive.

V—THE ELDERLY UNEMPLOYED

The unemployed person who is elderly but not yet old enough to draw a national old age pension has been rather a special problem in Sweden, partly because of the high pension age and partly because of the concentration of unemployment in the older age groups in recent years. In 1969, for example, over 40 per cent of the unemployed were over sixty years of age. Many of these had been employed in contracting industries like farming and lumbering and especially in the declining northern regions. Many are too old to make the move to central or southern Sweden where they might find jobs. Many have exhausted unemployment insurance rights, and others have never been eligible.[1]

Special measures were introduced from 1968 onwards to help the elderly unemployed. Unemployment benefit periods were extended, readjustment allowances were introduced, retraining faci-

---

[1] Unemployment insurance was voluntary in Sweden and organized on a trade union basis. Agriculture and other traditional industries are not highly unionized and so workers in these industries have not been covered for unemployment. By 1970 coverage had reached a figure of 70 per cent of the labour force. The position will change with the introduction of compulsory unemployment insurance in 1974.

lities and loans made available to set up in private business, central Government subsidies to help finance local assistance were made more generous. By mid 1969 some 4,000 elderly persons were being helped by support measures of different kinds, about 60 per cent of them living in the northern counties. In 1970, and again in 1972, the arrangements for paying full disability, that is early retirement, pensions were made more liberal. Under the later reforms of 1972 a *full* pension is payable at age sixty-three, or sixty in special circumstances, to anyone who has exhausted his unemployment insurance rights or has been in receipt of a re-settlement grant for eighteen months. The big growth in the numbers of disability pensioners over the 1960s suggests that these pensions had already been helping a considerable number of elderly workers. As from 1973 the position will be further eased when full temporary pensions become payable at sixty-five under the new occupational pension arrangements. In these various ways the pension age is in fact being lowered without the question of the national pension age having to be tackled in a more basic way.

VI—THE FINANCING OF PENSIONS AND OTHER PROVISIONS

The number of pensioners in Sweden has increased dramatically in recent years, by some 20 per cent between 1963 and 1970 in absolute numbers. More importantly the numbers in relation to the total population have risen from 10·2 to 11·7 per cent. Nevertheless the figures appear to show that Sweden spends less on pensions than many of the other countries studied in this book. In 1970 her total expenditure on cash benefits for the elderly and survivors amounted to only some 5·0 per cent of her GNP. We must not overlook the fact, however, that at the same time she is making massive provisions for future pensioners. Payments into the funds for national supplementary pensions from contributions and income on investments in 1970 amounted to some five times actual expenditure on benefits. Both these aspects are relevant and if taken together Sweden is providing for the present and future generations of pensioners on a scale nearly comparable with Germany and the Netherlands who head the league tables in this

respect. The motives, of course, may not have been entirely un-
mixed; these accumulating pension funds have been playing a
very important part in priming the credit market. We must remember too that the provisions made for the elderly do not stop at
cash income; publicly financed health and welfare services add
substantially to their total real incomes.

The basic pension is, however, at the present time the main
source of income for the majority of old people. In 1970 some
947,000 elderly persons and 100,000 widows were drawing the
folkpension supplemented for over 50 per cent of them by means-
tested housing allowance. Nearly 30 per cent of these old age
pensioners (and over three-quarters of the widow pensioners) had
rights to supplementary pensions and these, on average, were increasing the basic (single male) pensions by some 20 per cent.
Nearly nine out of ten old people and six out of ten widows were
drawing the (small) pension supplement if they had no, or poor,
supplementary pension rights. In all the basic pension, with the
housing allowances and pension supplements, accounted for some
90 per cent of national expenditure on pensions. Again we must
add the caution that the position changes from year to year as
more and more people retire with rights to supplementary pensions.
How then is the *folkpension* financed? This is essentially a contract
between state and citizen and the great bulk of the finances—
nearly 70 per cent in 1970—comes out of central and local government general revenues. A small pension tax of 5 per cent on
taxable income with a maximum annual contribution of 1,500 Sw.
kr. provides the remainder. There has been a move on the part of
the central Government over recent years to push more of the
burden on to the insured person by putting up the pension tax
and by 1970 it covered 30 per cent of total expenditure as compared with 15 per cent in 1953.

A number of interesting points may be touched on here. The
basic pension is a flat-rate benefit financed, in part at least, by a
proportionate contribution. In Britain the Crossman proposals
considered that graduated contributions would only be acceptable
if pensions too were graduated. The Conservative plan set out in
Strategy for Pensions, which formed the basis for the National
Insurance legislation of 1973, is closer to the Swedish model.
Graduated contributions in return for flat-rate benefits involves, of
course, some measure of vertical redistribution. In the Swedish

case the pension tax is small and it is paid along with other (very much more substantial) taxes, so passes more or less unnoticed. Where the major redistribution takes place, is through the general tax system. Three-fifths of basic pension expenditure comes out of general revenues, which rely heavily on the steeply progressive national income tax. But here pensions are only one of many items which have been pushing up public expenditure, and so taxation, in recent years. We have raised elsewhere the question as to why the Government doesn't put still more of the cost of pensions on to the hypothecated pension tax which appears to be a more acceptable method of raising money. Another interesting point to note is the not insubstantial part played by *local* government, which provides 10 per cent of the total finances for pensions. This is because of the housing allowance. The local municipalities are in a relatively strong financial position with the right to raise a local income tax, which takes precedence over the national income tax in that it is deductable from taxable income before national income tax is levied. The local income tax, however, is proportionate to income, not progressive like the national tax, and is generally thought of as much less of a burden. This has given the counties and municipalities considerable freedom to develop certain local benefits and services. The housing allowances for the pensioner are one such benefit; hospital and other medical services on a generous scale are another.

The employers play no part in financing the basic pensions of their workers but the earnings-related supplementary pension scheme, although national in coverage and administration, is essentially employment-based and is financed entirely by the contributions of the employers and the self-employed. Nominally it was designed as a pay-as-you-go scheme. This would have enabled pensions to be paid out in the early days of operation. As the scheme has been managed, however, there has been little blanketing-in and enormous pension funds have grown up since its inception. By 1970 these funds accounted for 30 per cent of the total supply of funds to the credit market and this is expected to rise to nearer 50 per cent by 1975[1]. The lending of the funds has

[1] There are three separate funds—one for contributions for public employees, one for large enterprises and the third for small enterprises. In this way it was hoped to avoid too large a concentration of control over the capital market. The funds had grown from some 1,190 million Sw.kr. in 1961 to over 10,000 in 1965, and nearly 48,000 by the end of 1971.

to a large extent taken the form of housing credits, the purchase of Government bonds and loans to communes.[1] The funds have largely solved the serious difficulties encountered in these sectors in the 1950s in finding long-term finance. They have done less in a direct way for private industry but the commercial banks and other private credit institutions, relieved of some of their responsibilities to the public sector and housing, have been freer to help private enterprise. The employers have also the right to borrow back in any year 50 per cent of the contributions paid in the previous year. This facility has, however, been relatively little used owing to the complexities of the way the system operates. Employers have on the whole preferred to use the commercial banks and other credit institutions to supply their credit needs. The pattern of lending has undoubtedly changed, but, writing in 1968 Borje Kragh could say that 'all in all, neither the fears of the Conservatives nor the hopes of the Socialists that the fund would be used as an instrument for planning and Government intervention can be said to have materialized during the initial period of its existence.'[2]

But this position is starting to change. The *Riksdag* was taken by surprise in the spring of 1973 by a proposal from the Social Democrat Government that the pension funds should be given the power to acquire shares in Swedish industry. This appears to have been the result of pressure from the Confederation of Trade Unions and, although opposed by the opposition parties of both the left and right, it was accepted by the *Riksdag*. A Commission set up by the Finance Ministry will start to purchase stock in 1974. At first only 500 million Sw.kr. (roughly 1 per cent) of funds will be used in this way but this is generally thought to be only a beginning and, according to political persuasion, is welcomed or feared as nationalization by the back door. There are, of course, possibilities here for the Government to acquire a substantial holding in Swedish industry. The funds will continue to grow until the year 2010 even although mature pensions will have been paid long before that. The funds will then begin to be run down, but slowly, and it is not planned that contributions and payments

---

[1] In 1971 total assets held were some 47,500 million Sw.kr. Of these 9 per cent were Government funds, 50 per cent housing credits, 10 per cent loans to municipalities, 24 per cent loans to industrial enterprises, 6 per cent loans to premium payers.

[2] Sweden's National Pension Insurance Fund, Borje Kragh, the *OECD Observer*. No. 33, April 1968.

should be in balance before the middle of the century. How far the government will be able to use this position for political purposes is another matter. The shortage of equities on the Swedish stock exchange may make this difficult unless more radical methods of extending the government interest in industry are devised.

We can only just mention other possible effects of forced savings of this magnitude. It had been feared when the supplementary pension scheme was under discussion in the 1950s that one consequence would be a decline in both *private and public savings*; individuals would no longer feel the need to save when so much was being done to provide for their old age, firms would be unable to save when faced with such large compulsory contributions. This is not a field into which we can venture except to say that savings by both individuals and firms have remained buoyant throughout the 1960s and 1970s. The *incidence* of a payroll tax, in particular when levied on the employer, is another interesting question and one which it is notoriously difficult to answer. Is the tax passed forward in the form of increased prices to the purchasers of the product, or backwards to the worker in the form of lower wage increases than might otherwise have been given. During the pension negotiations in the fifties it was recognized that one or other of these things would happen. It is now generally assumed that contributions come out of wages and this factor is taken into account when the collective wage agreements are being negotiated each year.

Occupational pensions are financed entirely by the employers in the first instance, but the incidence of the premium contributions, through their effect on prices, is hard to assess. Given the fact that only salaried workers were covered until 1973, the immediate burden on the employer has probably not been unduly great; they are estimated to cost between 8 and 9 per cent of pensionable earnings. The interesting thing again is what happens to the funds which have been building up, particularly since 1966, as the membership of the schemes has increased more rapidly than the number of beneficiaries. Ninety per cent of these funds must by law be invested in central and local Government bonds and comparable securities, and the Bank of Sweden also can, and does, make recommendations. By 1970 the funds were making available some 9,600 million Sw.kr. in total. The Swedish Pension Society, however, finds it difficult to exercise its rights to invest its 10 per cent 'free' funds because of the shortage of Swedish equities and the rigid control which is exercised over the real property sector in which it may also invest. This control obviously keeps down the rate of return on the investment of the funds, but, in spite of this, as we have already seen, the SPP manages to keep occupational pensions in payment in line with rising prices out of interest on investments and surpluses on the business of the fund. The employers themselves have accepted these controls more or less philosophically although there has been some talk of the Government wanting 'to create capital without creating capitalists'.

But this is not the whole of the picture where public provision for the elderly is concerned. National pensions, public servant pensions and occupational pensions together put some 8,136 million Sw.kr. of spending power at the disposal of old people and widows in 1970. Many old people were cared for in residential homes, paid for largely out of local government finances and very large numbers would at some time or another make some use of the national health services. These two items alone would add some 1,220 million Sw.kr. and an estimated 3,000 Sw.kr.[1] to the money incomes of the elderly, an increase of about 50 per cent in their total real incomes. Local authority welfare services would put this figure up still further, although probably not significantly so, but separate figures for expenditure on the elderly are not available. Whilst admittedly rough and ready, a simple exercise such as this has its uses in helping us to get a fuller picture both of the total resources of the elderly population and the part which is played by public money in determining their overall standard of living.

VII—SOME APPRAISAL OF POLICIES FOR THE ELDERLY

Many of the most important questions to be asked about the pension provisions of any country centre round the question of

---

[1] This figure is arrived at as follows: Expenditure on medical care was some 10,750 million Sw.kr. in 1970. Calculations made by the Office of Health Economics for the UK estimated that persons of sixty-five and over absorbed 28 per cent of national health service expenditure in 1966. If this figure is applied to Swedish expenditure on health care we arrive at the, admittedly crude, estimate of 3,000 million Sw.kr.

'adequacy'—but adequacy on a number of different counts: the population covered, the conditions attaching to payment of pensions, and the size of the benefits themselves and the arrangements made to maintain their value, i.e. the issue of dynamism. Here absolute figures say very little and bench-marks have to be found against which to set the pension. The annual disbursement of vast sums of money on pensions and the accumulation of large pension funds raise other issues mainly of a macro-economic nature: pensions and cyclical policy, pensions and the capital market, pensions and inflation and growth, pensions and the distribution of incomes. Some of these questions have been touched on already in the description of the schemes but their full implications have not been brought out. It would also be an interesting exercise to know how pensioners (present and to be) view the pension arrangements; but unfortunately no consumer research has been undertaken on this question.

First, the question of adequacy; the Swedish basic pension arrangements are possibly as universal in coverage as any pension scheme can be. Only in very exceptional cases is any Swedish citizen likely to find himself or herself without a full basic pension after reaching the official retirement age (e.g. if he had been living abroad for a considerable time). The supplementary earnings-related pension scheme also seems as broad in coverage as such a scheme can be. As we have seen above, the Swedish scheme was deliberately designed to bring in as many low-paid workers as possible and to cover for pension purposes the total earnings of the vast majority of the working population. Only the self-employed may opt out and that only for earnings from self-employment. There is no doubt that the broad coverage of Sweden's basic pension has done much to relieve her of the problem of 'the poor pensioner' which besets so many countries. But wide coverage would not be enough, as we know to our cost in the UK, if the pension were not providing adequately for all those it covers. By 1980 the great bulk of the working population will have two pension incomes and increasing numbers three pensions. The two national pensions aim to provide on average a target pension income in the neighbourhood of two-thirds of peak earnings during working life, occupational pensions are beginning to add a third tier which eventually will increase national pensions by 10 per cent.

For the majority of the present generation of pensioners, however, the basic pension is what matters most; targets for 1980 or 2000 mean little to them. Does the *folkpension* provide the 'decency and dignity' standard which was expected of it? What a flat-rate pension such as this means to the pensioner differs of course according to the income which he earned before retirement. Therefore it is logical to compare the pension with the income to which the pensioner was accustomed during his working life or which he might be receiving if he continued in work. The most usual—although admittedly crude—way of doing this is to put the pension alongside gross average male earnings in industry. This, of course, does less than justice to a flat-rate pension as many pensioners will never have earned up to that level, and even if they have done so at some time in the course of their working life their earnings in the years prior to retirement would be less in the case of virtually all manual workers. The pensioner too is likely to have a tax advantage. In principle his pension is taxable but if he had no income other than the basic pension he would be below the tax threshold.

In the following rounded figures 1971 pensions have been related to gross industrial earnings in the preceding year (revalorised for changing prices). The basic pension includes the housing allowance and pension supplement.

	Single man (*per cent*)	Married pensioner couple (*per cent*)
Basic pension in relation to average earnings	30	45
Basic pension in relation to 75% average earnings	40	60
Basic pension in relation to 50% average earnings	60	90
Basic plus average supplementary pension in relation to average earnings	40	55

Nearly one in three pensioners were receiving the second supplementary pension by 1971 and for these the two pensions, as we see, would give a relatively high rate of income replacement for the average earner with average supplementary pension rights. For the low income earner, especially if he has a pensioner wife, the basic pension with its various supplements guards him against any dramatic fall in income on retirement. The housing allowance is important here; for the single man it has added 5 per cent, and for the married couple 10 per cent, to the replacement value of the pension at average earnings; for the low earner it has obviously done much more. If we go on to look at pensions in relation to *net* pre-retirement earnings the Swedish pension scores high. For our average pensioner couple with basic and supplementary pension, the replacement factor is as high as 75 per cent. Swedish direct taxes are high and steeply progressive but the average pensioner as yet is unlikely to have much in the way of taxable income after the tax-free allowances have been deducted from his pension.

All this, of course, raises the whole question of the income which the old person needs in old age. Full pay on retirement would be unduly costly and not necessary: family commitments are less, work expenses have no longer to be met and other needs may be less. How big a drop in income is acceptable is another question. The ILO Social Security Convention No. 128 of 1952 set a target of at least 45 per cent of the previous earnings of the married breadwinner. The standards of 1952 are perhaps somewhat outmoded. For some time half pay on retirement was a popular slogan. This in its turn has become out of date and most of the countries studied in this book set their pension targets at 60, 70 or even 80 per cent of former earnings. The present generation of pensioners, however, are not always doing as well as this. Sweden has gone further than many in providing today's old people with a reasonable competence.

The national pension, of course, is not the whole of the picture. In making any overall assessment on this question of adequacy a number of other factors have to be taken into account: income from occupational pension or savings, 'income' in the form of subsidized health care and other services, the expectations of the pensioners themselves. Many pensioners have income in addition to their basic pension. About a third of basic pensioners were drawing supplementary earnings-related pensions in addition to their basic pension in 1971 and every year more and more people will retire with two pensions. Between a fifth and a quarter of pensioners are ex-public servants and about a tenth have occupational pensions. Unfortunately it is impossible to say how many pensioners in total

have more than one pension. Clearly there will be a considerable
amount of overlap between the different types of additional pensions and many pensioners will have two national pensions and
one public servant or occupational pension or perhaps both an
'official' and 'unofficial' occupational pension. Nevertheless it does
mean that large numbers of workers and an even higher proportion
of salaried employees are receiving a total pension income much in
excess of the basic pension. Personal savings probably play an important part too. Unfortunately there is little information about
small savings in Sweden but it would appear that in 1970 about
one in ten men and women over sixty-seven were living in households with private property of more than 100,000 Sw.kr. which is
a not inconsiderable proportion. Many of these, however, are
likely to be the same people who are already drawing multiple
pensions. Subsidized health care and other welfare services as we
have already seen increase the total pension income of the elderly
by about 50 per cent.

Can we get any other insights on the economic circumstances of
the elderly? The Family Expenditure Survey of 1969[1] tells us one
or two perhaps surprising things on this score. Figures for average
expenditure *per capita* on consumption, after making allowance for
differences in family size, show retired persons with no income
other than their pensions in a more favourable position than farmers; and pensioners with other sources of income emerge with
higher figures than workers:

Average per capita expenditure on consumption: 1969

Farmers	100
Wage-earners	133
Salary-earners	181
Retired persons with pensions only	117
Retired persons with income in addition to pensions	141

Pensioners on average appear from this, and on previous evidence,
to be enjoying relatively high standards of living. Many of the
present generation of pensioners were accustomed to comparatively

[1] This covered a representative sample of some 3,200 families of all socio-
economic groups. See *Statistical Abstract of Sweden, 1972*, pp. 213–16.

low earnings in working life, in agriculture perhaps or other poorly paid occupations; some will have memories of the meagre pension levels of earlier years. Their expectations for old age may not have been unduly high and the pension in many cases may exceed these expectations. The present generation of workers, whose expectations may be higher, have more generous pensions to which to look forward.

Undoubtedly another important factor which contributes to this apparent satisfaction with pensions is the fact that, as we have seen, they are protected against the effects of inflation in such a way that pensions may go up two or three times during the course of a year in times of rapid price inflation. This, and the growth of supplementary pensions in the late 1960s and early 1970s, have perhaps masked the fact that Swedish pensions no longer take account of rising earnings. This question of dynamism is another item on the agenda of the Pensions Commission appointed in 1970 and may, of course, come up more seriously as earnings continue to forge ahead of pensions.

Some other points should perhaps be made in trying to assess the adequacy of Swedish pensions. One is the fact that virtually no one is without expectations of at least a basic pension on reaching sixty-seven or even earlier; another is the relatively short period for which an employee must be insured for earnings-related pensions before he acquires full supplementary pension rights—thirty years reduced to twenty in the transitional period. That there should be even as long a maturity period as this in what is nominally a pay-as-you-go scheme may seem surprising. This appears to have met with little criticism in Sweden itself. Another point here is the question of the ceiling for pensionable earnings. When this was set in 1959 the ceiling represented two and a half times average male industrial earnings; by 1971, indexed as it is for rises in prices but not for earnings, it had fallen to just less than twice average earnings. Nevertheless only about 4 per cent of total earnings are above the ceiling. This is a question to which some thought must be given in future if the graduated pension is not to lose too much ground and is another of the items to be dealt with by the Commission on Pensions, although it is not at the present a pressing question.

A little must now be said, however briefly, about some of the possible effects on the economy as a whole of the pension set-up.

A problem encountered in other countries studied in this book, and notably perhaps Germany, is the effects that occupational pensions may have on the *mobility of labour* through the non-transferability of pension rights (ch. 2, p. 70). In Sweden this has not been a problem so far. The occupational pension schemes are run on what is virtually a national basis and, as we have already seen, whilst there may be complications in the case of some salaried workers on transfer from one type of fund to another these are in the main sorted out between the various pension institutions and the employee is not impeded in his freedom of movement. The difficulties arise only on transfers between public service and private industry. The new arrangements for manual workers appear to take adequate precautions against problems of this nature arising. The possible effects of pension and other social security benefits on *cyclical policy* have been a matter of more concern in Sweden. The mechanism for the adjustment of pensions to rising prices has incorporated into it a three-month lag as a counter-inflationary device; at the same time the frequent adjustment of benefits which the mechanism allows may, as well as helping the individual pensioner, also help maintain purchasing power in times of recession. Conversely, of course, the relatively sensitive adjustment of pensions to prices, even with a time lag, may have inflationary effects in times of rapidly rising prices, particularly when pensioners have a high propensity to consume. Pensions, however, account in total for only some 8 per cent of personal incomes so perhaps the effect either way would not be unduly large. This last fact too puts in some perspective the effect which pensions, largely financed out of general Government revenues as the basic pensions are, may have on the *distribution of incomes*. Some vertical redistribution of incomes there must undoubtedly be, and also some inter-generational redistribution, but the net effect must be comparatively small. The old-age pensioner too is at least helping to pay for his own pension, given the high rates of indirect taxation in Sweden.

Social security payments have also played a part in *regional and structural policy*. The recent move to allow unemployed elderly persons to draw full pensions at an early age is in fact a recognition of the limitations of policies to move the elderly from the northern and other regions with poor employment prospects to the more prosperous areas of central and southern Sweden. If it is thought

desirable on political or other grounds to keep these regions popu-
lated, then social security benefits may be as good a way as any to
finance those left behind and are certainly cheaper than the public
work projects which have at times been mounted to create
additional jobs.[1] We have already looked at pensions and *the capital
market* and the important part played by the funds of both the
national and occupational pensions schemes in providing money
for central and local government investment and for the housing
market. The new occupational scheme for manual workers is likely
to be a new source of funds.

What then is the unfinished business? The official pension age
remains high but by various means, as we have seen, more and
more people from now on are going to be able to retire on full
pension at sixty-five, in some cases even earlier. The present
generation of pensioners are better off than a casual examination of
the pension arrangements would suggest. The 'poor pensioner' is
largely a problem of the past. Plans have been laid to ensure
future generations of pensioners an even better deal. This 'new deal'
may not aim as high as the targets which some other countries
studied in this book have set themselves but the national plans will
at least become a reality by 1980. Blue collar workers have now
attained parity of treatment with white collar workers where
occupational pensions are concerned, although it will be many
years before they receive their full rights. When it is eventually
mature the Swedish national and occupational pension structure
will provide a three-tier income for the great majority of pensioners
which will provide a different level of replacement income for
different bands of the earnings structure, the whole being slanted
in favour of the lower income groups. We have seen how this will
be brought about by an ingenious use of a common reference point,
the base amount. Women are still in an inferior position as regards
pension income but the cure for this lies not so much in pension
policy as in the wage system, in improvements in the female labour
market and in the attitudes of women themselves to gainful employment. Pensions in payment are not adjusted for growth and

---

[1] It has been estimated, for example, that in 1967 the cost per head of providing
public relief works in Sweden for the unemployed was between two and three
times as much as paying unemployment benefits. See Santosh Mukherjee,
Making Labour Markets Work—a Comparison of the UK and Swedish Systems,
PEP Broadsheet 532, January 1972, p. 129.

this is probably the Achilles heel of the Swedish pension structure. If and when the need for dynamizing demands urgent attention it should not, however, be beyond the capacity of the Swedes, with their gifts for innovation and good management, to find a feasible and workable solution to this problem.

CHAPTER FIVE

Italy

I—INTRODUCTION

One cannot judge a country's pension or other social security policies without taking into account the economic and political context within which these policies operate. There are four relevant features of the Italian economy which deserve immediate mention. First, Italy is still a relatively poor country. International comparisons of income per head are notoriously unsatisfactory but the statistics suggest that Italy is among the poorest countries in Western Europe and the poorest of the countries covered in this book. In 1970 Italian income per head was about 70 per cent of that in the United Kingdom, around 56 per cent of Germany, 59 per cent of France and about 42 per cent of Sweden. Second, it is a country that is undergoing what can only be described as a structural revolution with quite enormous outflows of people from agriculture—about half in the 1960s. This change is carrying with it a great urban explosion. A plausible estimate is that while in 1961 37 per cent of Italians were living in centres of more than 110,000 population, this will rise to 49 per cent by 1981. In absolute terms these centres will need to accommodate an extra 9 million people over this twenty-year period.[1] This movement into the larger towns has been of serious proportions for the whole of the post-war period, and has created great demands for social investment in the form of schools, housing, roads, etc. Third, Italy is still a dual economy. In the spatial or regional sense, the economic disparities between North and South are greater than elsewhere in Europe.

---

[1] S. Cafiero and A. Busca, *Lo Sviluppo Metropolitano in Italia*, Giuffrè, Rome, 1970.

The South has a net income per head only slightly more than half of that in the North, annual net emigration equal to $12\frac{1}{2}$ per thousand of the population during the 1960s, and heavy unemployment and underemployment. One aspect of this dualism is the large number of workers in small plants in the South who are often poorly paid and have poor social benefits. Another is the large number of independent workers (self-employed)—about a third of the labour force in 1970.

All of these features make for problems in the evolution and operation of a social security scheme. The great occupational changes require a system which is capable of allowing workers to transfer their social security rights, and the large numbers of self-employed provide problems as these are a notoriously difficult group in any social security system. Then, the social investments in the rapidly expanding cities and the impoverished South might be expected to detract from expenditure in the social security field. If nothing else, these features, combined with the relative poverty of Italy, might have been expected to result in a cautious approach to pensions and social security generally. But the Italians have been bold and have aimed at evolving schemes which cover virtually the whole of the labour force, cater for occupational transfers without loss of rights, have been generous with blanketing-in arrangements and have drawn up pension formulae which can replace a high proportion of pre-retirement income—higher than in most of the other countries covered in this study. Unfortunately, as with many aspects of Italian life, there is a contrast between objectives and current reality. This is particularly true of pensions which, because the majority of workers have an inadequate contribution record, are generally well below the high target levels. Over time, and as more workers fulfil the necessary contribution record, this gap will slowly narrow, but at present the vast majority of Italian pensioners are on a low means-tested minimum. There is much poverty among pensioners in Italy as there is indeed among workers generally.

In one respect at least the Italian pension system structure is simpler than in the other countries covered in this book. There is not a number of different tiers as for example in Sweden, with its basic flat-rate pensions, its second-tier official supplementary pensions and its third-tier occupational pensions. In Italy, the pensions are nearly all on one tier. But the complexity of this one tier is formidable not least because of the large number of schemes involved, all operating under a multiplicity of conditions. What is said in this chapter relates to some twenty-five or so of these—although it may be wise to add at once that these are not analysed in detail! These schemes can be divided into six main groups—the general obligatory scheme for dependent workers, the independent worker schemes, the social pension scheme, the special dependent worker schemes, the public employees schemes and the free profession schemes. The first four of these groups are managed and administered by INPS (*Istituto Nazionale della Previdenza Sociale*)—an autonomous public agency with its key posts being filled by state nominees. In total nearly 90 per cent of Italian pensions are paid by schemes within the INPS organization.

By far the biggest scheme is the general obligatory scheme for dependent workers. In 1970 it was paying out some 6·24 million direct (old age and disability) and indirect (survivor) pensions—about 61 per cent of the total. The independent worker schemes cover three groups: first, farmers, tenant farmers and sharecroppers with 1·8 million pensions; second, artisans with 280,000; and third, small traders with 215,000. Together, the independent worker schemes cover about one-fifth of Italian pensioners. The public employee schemes (local and national and including the railway workers' schemes) were, in 1970, paying slightly more than a million pensions and accounted for about one-tenth of total Italian pensions. The social pension is a recent innovation and paid to citizens over the age of sixty-five with no rights to any other pension. There were some three-quarters of a million social pensioners in 1970. The remaining two groups of schemes are, in terms of number of pensions or insured, not very important and although their various features are covered in the chapter we have tried to avoid complicating the exposition too much and have not treated them in any great detail. The special dependent worker schemes cover eleven groups of workers ranging from public transport workers to aircrews, from miners to telephone workers, and pay around 120,000 pensions. The majority of these schemes are complete substitutes for the general scheme but four are integrated with it. These four enjoy the basic conditions of the general scheme though in many aspects give more generous treatment with correspondingly higher contributions. (The substitutive schemes are, as the name suggests, not openly linked with the general scheme. Again contributions and pensions are relatively high.) As with most of the Italian pension schemes, the major contributor to the special schemes is the employer. The smallest group of all is that of the free profession schemes. There are ten such schemes covering, among others, architects, engineers, lawyers and surveyors, paying some 45,000 pensions. In total these six main groups of pension schemes account for virtually the whole of Italian pensions in payment.

II—AN HISTORICAL SURVEY[1]

As with many other countries, the Italian pension system has its origins in a variety of friendly societies, employers' pension schemes and trade-union benefits. Pensions and other assistance paid by these bodies were generally small and the proportion of the population covered was slight. The state neither encouraged nor contributed to these schemes, but in the final years of the nineteenth century, the increasing wealth of the country and the growing force of the trade unions pushed the Government towards recognizing that it could not for much longer delay the development of some form of social security. A bill for the creation of a workers' insurance fund to cover old age and disability became law in 1898. Membership was voluntary and the scheme was financed by voluntary employer and employee contributions plus a small state contribution. Compulsory membership was introduced at the turn of the century but only for some groups of workers. Moreover, although this fund may be seen as being the predecessor of the later social insurance schemes, the numbers insured remained small.

The end of World War I saw increasing pressure on the Government to extend its activities in the field of social security and in particular to extend compulsory insurance. The outcome was the introduction in 1919 of an obligatory (at least in principle) scheme for dependent workers to be run by the workers' insurance fund. The scheme covered agricultural as well as industrial workers,

---

[1] The major sources of information for this section are INPS, *Settant'Anni dell'Istituto Nazionale della Previdenza Sociale*, Rome, 1970, and R. Campopiano, *La Previdenza Sociale*, Rome, 1971.

though few of the former joined. Indeed, by no means all industrial workers became members. The scheme was funded and, as in
the earlier private schemes, the pensions were graduated. The
state contribution was in the form of a small annual sum to those
who were in receipt of pensions. The contingencies covered were
extended subsequently to include unemployment, family allowances, etc., and in 1933 the workers insurance fund received its
modern title of *Istituto Nazionale della Previdenza Sociale* (INPS)
to reflect its involvement in these broader issues.

These insurance schemes, with their accumulated funds, were
shattered by the inflation of World War II and its aftermath.
The funded element had become less important and with the
steady post-war inflation was dropped altogether in 1969. In 1952,
after a series of post-war interim measures, contributions were made
by employers, employees and the state and set at 50, 25 and 25 per
cent respectively, with the employer and employee contribution combined being 9 per cent of earnings. This latter percentage was steadily raised over the years as pension provisions
were improved and by 1970 was some 20 per cent of earnings with
the employee paying a third and the employer two-thirds. This, it
need scarcely be said, is a very high payroll tax. It must be added
that these figures cover pension scheme contributions only. Total
employer contributions to all social security schemes in 1970
amounted to 52 per cent of earnings while employee contributions
were 7 per cent.

The 1950s saw considerable improvements in the lot of the
general obligatory pensioners. Free health treatment was introduced
in 1955, the minima were raised in 1958 and pensions were revalued in the same year. It would be misleading, however, to give
the impression that the only pension developments in the 1950s
were with the general obligatory scheme. A number of schemes for
the free professions were developed in this decade, while some of
the older professional schemes were strengthened. The public
employee schemes, which had existed and paid generous pensions
for many years, continued in the forefront of pension provision. A
major development in the 1950s was, however, the introduction of
schemes for two major independent worker groups, particularly
important in Italy, which had been without earlier pension arrangements. Independent workers throughout Europe have always been
the last to enjoy social security provisions; largely because of the

administrative problems involved combined with a view that, being independent, they should provide for themselves—a view which has now largely collapsed. In Italy the first scheme, in 1957, was for independent agricultural workers (farmers, tenant farmers and sharecroppers) while, in 1959, the artisans were given a similar scheme. The introduction of pension schemes for these groups of workers meant that, by 1960, the great majority of the Italian working population was contributing to a pension scheme. The coverage was virtually complete when the scheme for small traders, the last of the major independent worker groups, was started in 1966. The 1950s, in addition to seeing the development of these independent worker schemes, also saw two new special dependent worker schemes developed—one for gas industry workers in 1955 and the other for electricity workers in 1956. These added to the other special dependent worker schemes which had been developed in the inter-war period. After the electricity workers' scheme in 1956 there was only one more special scheme developed—that for air-crews in 1965. The special schemes, not quantitatively important as we have already seen, were intended to cater for worker groups which by the nature of their work or by tradition required better pensions or a different pensionable age from that set in the general scheme.

In 1962 a Commission on Social Security was set up with important consequences in the field of Italian pensions. Legislation introduced in 1965 owed much to the Commission's work. The minima for pensions were raised, pensions in payment were revalorised and 'seniority' pensions were introduced. These latter were paid to dependent and independent workers after thirty-five years' contributions irrespective of age. The major reform was, however, the creation of a Social Fund which was to pay a uniform basic pension to all INPS pensioners[1] of 12,000 lire per month for a thirteen-month year with the pension funds being responsible for the difference between this figure and the actual pension paid. Thus, a pensioner receiving say L30,000 per month would have L12,000 of this paid by the Social Fund and the remaining L18,000 by the fund to which he belonged. The Social Fund was largely financed by the state, the aim being that it would eventually, by 1976, be wholly state financed. The earlier system

---

[1] Apart from pensions paid by the special substitutive dependent worker schemes.

whereby the state paid into the pension funds a proportion of the workers' earnings was therefore dropped and the moneys used in the past for this were diverted into the Social Fund. Thus the state now largely paid for a basic pension instead of contributing to graduated payments. The earlier system had favoured the more highly paid workers. The new system was considered to be more equitable.

Not all of the results of the 1962 Commission were incorporated in the 1965 legislation but much of what remained was included in laws passed in 1968 and 1969. These two years saw great reforms of Italian pensions and pension systems. A major driving force behind these reforms was the trade unions, who used industrial action to secure their demands. For many trade unionists the pension system, paid for largely by the employers, must have seemed a case of something for nothing, a point to which we return later. The laws of 1968 and 1969 included the usual increases of minima and pensions in payment but beyond this there were five major changes. First, the 1968 legislation introduced a change in the method by which the general obligatory pension values were calculated. The earlier system of pension values, determined by revalorized contributions (to take account of inflation), was abolished and a new system was introduced whereby pensions were paid at the rate of 1·625 per cent of average earnings in the last three years of work for every year of contributions up to a maximum of forty years.[1] The maximum pension was therefore 65 per cent of terminal earnings. In 1969 the formula was changed again and pension values were set at 1·85 per cent of average earnings in the best three years' earnings during the final five years of work. The maximum pension therefore became *74 per cent* of terminal earnings so defined. The 1969 legislation committed the Government to raising this maximum to *80 per cent* (based on the best three years' earnings in the final ten years of work) by the end of 1975. Secondly, *social pensions* were introduced in 1969. This was a much needed move. The social pension, 12,000 lire (about £8)[2] per month for a thirteen-month year, is paid to Italian citizens of sixty-five or above with an income of less than 156,000 lire per annum. For those with an income above this, the social pension is reduced lira

---

[1] The independent worker schemes continued to be based on revalorized contributions.
[2] The exchange rate used in this and subsequent calculations in this chapter is 1,500 Lire to the pound sterling.

for lira. The social pension is paid by the Social Fund mentioned above and by 1971 some three-quarters of a million people were in receipt of this pension. Although the social pension is small it does represent modest improvement over the earlier system under which these people had to rely wholly on their savings, family assistance or *ad hoc* aid from their local authorities. Thirdly, under the 1969 legislation, the general scheme and independent worker pensions were tied to the cost-of-living index with changes in pensions for every 2 per cent change in the index. Earlier changes with respect to the cost of living had been *ad hoc*. Fourthly, a firm commitment was given that the Social Fund would be wholly financed by the state by 1976. Finally, the general obligatory scheme was made entirely pay-as-you-go. This was not a particularly drastic move. As mentioned earlier, the funded element in the scheme, being fixed absolute amounts, had diminished continually after the war while the pay-as-you-go element grew. It was no great problem, therefore, by the end of the 1960s, to drop the funded element completely.

Over the post-war period, then, the Italian pension system has developed considerably. The coverage has been extended as new schemes have developed for those outside the system, pension values have risen rapidly, pensions have been introduced for those people already retired and without any pension rights, and pensions can replace a very high proportion of terminal earnings. These improvements have been all the more laudable, perhaps, in that they have taken place in the face of demographic changes (a falling birth and death rate) which have increased the proportion of elderly in the Italian population.

The improvements in the Italian pension system, including its greater coverage, have inevitably resulted in increased pension expenditure. The actual extent of this increase is, however, quite startling. In real terms the increase has been some 1,000 per cent between 1952 and 1970. Thus, pension expenditure has risen much faster than National Income. Limiting ourselves to INPS pensions (representing 90 per cent of Italian pensions), expenditure has risen from 1·51 per cent of GNP in 1952 to 5·66 per cent in 1970. To some degree, the growth of expenditure on pensions has resulted from the increased coverage of the schemes and in particular the extension to independent workers. But the greater proportion of the increased expenditure is accounted for by increased pensions per pensioner. Something like a quarter of the increased expenditure has arisen because of the increased number of pensioners and the remaining proportion reflects the increased value of the pension.

III—THE ITALIAN PENSIONS SCHEMES—MAJOR CHARACTERISTICS

A prime feature of the Italian pension system, reflecting the manner in which the system developed, is the great number of schemes operating under a variety of conditions. This section, by examining the major features of the pension system, is aimed at illustrating this diversity. The section is largely descriptive and the major issues which arise both from the general features and the diversity are discussed in detail in Section VI, below.

The various Italian pension schemes have quite different *pensionable ages*, reflecting a variety of factors—the date when the scheme was founded, the hazards and arduousness of the occupation and the inclinations of the members. For the majority of Italians, however, those in the general schemes, the pensionable age is sixty for men and fifty-five for women—one of the lowest in Europe. The point is often made that considerable savings could be achieved by raising the pensionable age, both in terms of savings on pension expenditure and by increasing the supply of labour, though this latter point is perhaps not of great relevance in the case of Italy with its considerable labour surpluses.[1] Something like one-third of old age pensioners are between sixty and sixty-five (men) and fifty-five and sixty (women). No doubt in an attempt to cut down on costs, the schemes for independent workers have pensionable ages of sixty-five for men and sixty for women. The integrative special schemes for dependent workers normally adhere to the general obligatory pensionable age, except for mineworkers with a pensionable age of fifty-five, and gas industry workers with a pensionable age of sixty for both men and women. The substitutive schemes show a variety of pensionable ages ranging from fifty-five for air personnel to seventy for clerics. The pensionable age (and retirement age) for state employees is

---

[1] For a discussion of the effect of pension provisions on the supply of labour see Commissione delle Communità Europée, *Incidenze Economiche della Sicurezza Sociale*, Bruxelles, July 1968.

generally sixty-five but with a number of exceptions, e.g. magistrates. The local employee scheme has a pensionable age of sixty for both men and women. The pensionable age for the free profession schemes is generally sixty-five with no male/female distinction.

Pensions are only paid by a scheme if a specified *minimum number of contributions* have been made by the applicant. The contribution record covers both actual and figurative contributions. These latter include the period in military service and periods of unemployment and illness. The minimum contribution condition is important in that if fulfilled the applicant is at least eligible for a minimum pension (discussed below). The minimum contribution conditions differ between pension types (old age, disability, survivor) and schemes.

The minimum contribution requirement for an *old age pension* in the general and independent worker schemes is fifteen years. This is waived for the transitional period of the independent worker schemes though the insured must have contributed since the founding date of the scheme or must be able to show that he was in the relevant sectors before the schemes were created. The fifteen years' contribution record also applies to the great majority of the special dependent worker schemes. The public employee schemes generally require a longer period of contributions than the INPS schemes—twenty years for state employees and between fourteen-and-a-half and twenty-four-and-a-half years (depending on various conditions) for the local authority scheme. The free profession schemes show a great range of qualifying conditions of between ten and twenty-five years.

The minimum qualifying conditions for a *disability pension* are generally less than those for an old age pension. Five years of contributions are required for the general obligatory and the independent worker schemes with the former paying a disability pension after one year of contribution if the disability results from an accident at work. The majority of the special dependent worker schemes follow the same lines as the general obligatory scheme with respect to disability pensions as do the free profession schemes though some are as low as two years, and one is as high as ten years. The public employee schemes are not generous with respect to disability pensions. The state employee scheme only pays if the insured is disabled at work (when there is no minimum contributory period) while the local authority scheme has a fifteen years' minimum contributory period. The definition of disability has given rise to considerable trouble for the various pension schemes. The free profession and public employee schemes are usually unequivocal and disability pensions are generally paid when the member is unable to do his job. The special dependent worker schemes and the general and independent worker schemes have differing definitions. In the general scheme a disability pension is paid when ability to earn is permanently reduced to less than one third of previous earning ability if the insured is a worker and to less than one half if he is a white-collar worker.[1] For farmers, tenant farmers and sharecroppers and for artisans, ability to earn must be permanently reduced to less than one third of the previous level while the proportion for small traders, for reasons which are difficult to appreciate, is less than half. The real problem is the vague criteria used to measure reduced earnings capacity. By all accounts the criteria are applied in a lax fashion, with the result that members of the general and independent worker schemes who do not have sufficient contributions to claim an old age pension appear to have easily been able to secure a disability pension. This explains the large numbers of disability pensions paid in Italy. Something like a third of all INPS pensioners are in this category.

In the general obligatory and the independent worker schemes, *survivor pensions* can be paid on condition that a minimum of five years' contributions have been made. In the special dependent worker schemes there is some variability but normally the survivor pension minimum contribution conditions are the same as those for the disability pensions from these schemes. This is common also in the free profession schemes. In many schemes, survivor pensions are paid with much reduced contributions (one year is normal) where death of the insured results from an accident at work. In the public employee schemes, there is no contribution requirement where death results from an accident at work. On the other hand, the public employee schemes have quite a stringent minimum contribution requirement for normal survivor pensions —fifteen years in the case of local authority employees and twenty years with state employees.

---

[1] The distinction between workers and white-collar workers in respect of disability pensions has recently been removed and replaced by the white-collar proportion for both groups.

Assuming that the minimum contribution requirements have been met, the actual pension paid is determined by specific, even if varied and complicated, *pension formulae*. In general terms, however, the position for *direct pensions* (old age and disability) is as follows. The general scheme and the special worker schemes pay pensions calculated by taking into account both terminal earnings and the number of years of contributions. The general scheme for example pays a pension equal to one-fortieth of 74 per cent of average earnings in the best three years of the last five years' work for every year of contribution up to a maximum of forty-fortieths. The special dependent worker schemes generally pay a higher proportion per year of service, and never lower, so that the maximum is reached after fewer years of contributions. They also pay on the basis of higher proportions of terminal earnings, up to 100 per cent in some instances. The free professions show great variety. Some base pensions simply on contributions, others give a fixed pension as long as qualifying conditions are met, others give a fixed amount plus additional fixed amounts for every year of contribution above a set number. The independent worker pensions are calculated in the same way that the general obligatory scheme was calculated up to 1968 with pensions being paid on the basis of revalorized contributions. The public employee schemes give pensions which are dependent on the number of years of contributions and terminal income and are more generous than the general obligatory scheme. Two final points need to be made. First, and discussed in more detail later, most schemes operate a minimum pension, paid where the pension would otherwise be below the minimum and on condition that the minimum contribution requirements have been met. The major exception to this is the public employee scheme. Second, the general and independent worker schemes, as well as the public employee schemes, give a dependents' allowance on top of the pension. This is paid for spouse and for children and adds about 15 per cent to the pension for each dependent. The dependents' allowance is not so common in the special dependent worker schemes and, where operative, generally only applies to dependent children. Ten per cent for each dependent child is the normal figure. Dependent family allowances do not appear to be common among the free profession schemes.

Indirect (survivor) pensions are paid as a proportion of the pension or pension rights of the deceased. The general obligatory scheme pays 60 per cent to the surviving spouse without dependent children and the same figure for a dependent orphan. For each dependent child with the surviving spouse, 20 per cent is paid. The maximum survivor pension is 100 per cent of pension or pension rights of the deceased. The independent worker schemes, and most of the special and professional schemes, have similar conditions. The local authority employee scheme and the state employee scheme both pay 50 per cent of pension or pension rights to the surviving spouse. In addition, the local authority scheme pays 10 per cent for each dependent child up to a maximum for spouse and children of 90 per cent while the state employee scheme pays 25 per cent for each child with a maximum of 100 per cent for spouse and dependent children.

On condition that minimum contribution requirements have been met, the insured is eligible for a *minimum pension*. The minimum pensions are important in the Italian pension system not least because the majority of the general obligatory scheme pensioners and the independent worker pensioners are at the minima. (See Section IV, below.) In the general obligatory scheme the minima differ according to age, and in 1971 were L313,000 (£209) p.a. for direct pensioners below sixty-five and L340,600 p.a. for those above sixty-five. Survivors of such pensioners receive the proportions of the deceased's pension or his pension rights mentioned above. Standard dependent family allowances are paid on top of the minima. There is no clear statement available on the criteria used to fix the general obligatory minima. The sums are, however, similar to what the *average* industrial worker would secure with fifteen years of contributions. It is generally recognized that the minima are not adequate to meet minimum income requirements where the pensioner does not live with his children or does not have another source of income (see Section VI, below). The independent worker minima are below those in the general scheme and do not vary according to age. The 1971 direct pension minimum for the independent worker schemes was L245,050 p.a. with the standard dependent family allowances paid in addition. The integrative special schemes for dependent workers pay minima which are generally equal to the general obligatory minima while the substitutive schemes show a considerable variety. The free profession schemes generally operate on the basis of flat-rate minima which are normally above those of the general obligatory scheme and rarely differentiated by age. Finally, the public employee schemes have no set minima except for the local authority employee scheme and this is only for survivor pensions.

In the general obligatory and the dependent worker schemes, *contributions* are based on earnings with the employer paying much more than the employee. The total employer and employee contribution to the general obligatory scheme is 20·8 per cent of earnings. The majority of the special dependent worker schemes have contributions above this level. The proportion paid by the employer to the general obligatory scheme is about double that of the employee. The integrative schemes generally have similar proportions. The substitutive schemes normally have a lower employee contribution and a higher employer contribution than the general scheme. The schemes for independent workers, always a problem, are financed through a flat-rate contribution which is not tied to earnings. Contributions to the local authority scheme amount to 23 per cent of earnings with the employee paying about one quarter. The employee pays 4·8 per cent of his earnings to the state employee scheme with the state paying what is required to comply with the pension agreement with its employees. The free profession schemes are financed in a variety of ways. The standard method is a flat-rate payment plus a charge on work done or income received. The free profession schemes do not receive any contributions from the state, nor do the substitutive schemes for dependent workers. The state does, however, make quite substantial contributions to the general obligatory scheme, the schemes for independent workers and the mineworkers' integrative scheme. The state aid primarily comes through the Social Fund, mentioned above, though in addition the state also contributes directly to the individual schemes. Only in the case of the independent worker scheme for farmers, tenant farmers and sharecroppers, however, is this of any great significance.[1] The state, through its contributions to the Social Fund and its direct subsidies, accounted for about 30 per cent of total INPS pension expenditure.

---

[1] In 1970 the state gave L158 milliard to the farmers' scheme. At the same date, the contribution by production and 'other' sources was a mere L17·3 milliard. The desperate financial state of this scheme is a result of Government reluctance to change the contributions, which have remained fixed since 1957, a diminution in the numbers insured as people leave the land and a growing proportion of pensioners relative to the insured.

As we have seen, the general obligatory scheme is now wholly *pay-as-you-go*. The independent worker schemes still retain an element of funding though it is slight. The special dependent worker schemes differ considerably. The integrative schemes have an element of funding involved in the integrative part of the pensions and the substitutive schemes are generally more funded. In general, however, the trend has been for the special dependent worker schemes to move more and more on to a pay-as-you-go basis. Without this, they would undoubtedly not have been able to increase pensions in the way that they have over the post-war period. The free profession schemes are generally funded though with a pay-as-you-go element involved. The state employee scheme is entirely pay-as-you-go while the local authority scheme still has an element of funding.

Since 1969, the general obligatory and the independent worker schemes have been tied to the *cost of living*. Before this, changes were *ad hoc*. There is now an automatic revaluation of pensions with every 2 per cent change in the cost of living index. The special schemes for dependent workers are similarly tied though the percentage change required before the pensions are adjusted is greater, except for the mineworkers' scheme, which has adopted the general obligatory dynamizing system. The cost of living index has to move by between 10 and 15 per cent before pensions are adjusted in the other special dependent worker schemes. Considering that many of these schemes are both generous and forward looking, it is strange that they are so poorly dynamized. The local authority employee pension scheme is tied to the cost of living but changes are made on an *ad hoc* basis. The state employee pensions are tied to the cost of living and adjusted annually. There is no automatic tying of pensions to the cost of living in the free profession schemes. The normal system with these schemes would be that pensions are changed in the light of cost of living changes and other factors. Most of the free profession schemes review their situation in some detail each year.

IV—ITALIAN PENSIONS IN PRACTICE

By setting down, as we have in Section III above, the various provisions of the Italian pension schemes, and particularly those concerned with replacement of earnings, it is too easy to gain an exaggerated view of Italian pension values in practice. This section tries to correct this by presenting and discussing the average value of Italian pensions, their distribution around the mean and their growth over the post-war period for each of the major Italian pension groups.

(a) The general obligatory scheme

Table 5.1 shows the average annual values of pensions in payment by the general obligatory scheme at the end of 1970. The numbers receiving general obligatory scheme pensions are also given. Finally, the table shows the average values of new pensions (paid for the first time in 1970) and the numbers involved, and sets their average values against the average value of pensions in payment.

TABLE 5.1

General obligatory scheme : Pensions and average annual pension values ('000 lire)

	Old age	Disability	Survivor
Pensions in payment (1970): average values	471·1	384·5	288·3
Pensions in payment (1970): numbers	2,635,235	2,175,826	1,425,987
New pensions (1970): average values	542·2	402·6	264·0
New pensions (1970): numbers	150,301	165,557	159,855
Average values of new pensions (1970) in relation to pensions in payment (the latter = 100)	115	104	92

Source: INPS, *Rendiconti dell'Anno 1970*, Rome, 1971.

A number of points arise out of this table. The first is that the average value of pensions is low by British standards. The old age pensions in payment amount to around £315 per annum while the disability and survivor pensions are some £257 and £186 per annum respectively. Second, the average value of the old age pension is about 33 per cent of gross manual worker industrial earnings and therefore well below the target of 74 per cent. New pensioners, at some 38 per cent, are not much better placed. The reason for these shortfalls is principally that the pensioners have not fulfilled the forty years of contributions required for a full pension—a point to which we return later. Third, the large number of disability pensions in payment is perhaps surprising by British standards. Disability pensions account for over a third of the total number of pensions paid under the general obligatory scheme. Similar proportions hold for many of the other pension schemes in Italy. The major reason for this high proportion is because—as we have already observed—a large number of pensioners, on reaching near retirement age, are unable to show the necessary number of contributions for an old age pension (fifteen years) but yet generally have enough for a disability pension (five years). For many of those with an adequate number of contributions, the pension likely to be received will only be at the minimum or near the minimum even if they continue to work to the normal pensionable age, so that by retiring on disability grounds they lose little in terms of pension values and yet can continue to work or enjoy early retirement. Furthermore, and related, the criteria for disability are so vague that most who apply seem to be accepted. A final point of interest arising from Table 5.1 is that there is not a great deal of difference between the average value of pensions in payment and the average values of new pensions. This reflects two factors. First, most Italian pensioners are on a minimum pension and these pensions have been increased considerably during the 1950s and particularly the second half of the 1960s. Second, and the other side of the coin, it reflects the fact that the great majority of those retiring have been in the scheme for much less than the full period required to obtain the quite substantial proportion of income which is replaced after forty years' contributions.

The point has already been made that the great majority of general scheme pensioners are on the minima. This is quantitatively confirmed in Table 5.2, which gives the 1970 distribution pattern of general scheme pensioners in the form of the proportion of pensioners in various average monthly pension bands.

Table 5.2 illustrates well the bunched distribution pattern of the general obligatory scheme with the majority of pensioners being at or below the upper minimum (for those aged sixty-five or above) of L25,000 (£16.00) per month.[1] About 55 per cent of the old age

---

[1] Old age and disability pensioners can receive a pension below the minimum when they have an alternative source of income above a set level. Survivor pensioners receive a specified proportion of the spouse's pension and, of course, this can place them below the minimum.

TABLE 5.2

General obligatory scheme: pension distribution pattern (1970)

	Old age proportions	Disability proportions	Survivors proportions
Percentage :			
Below the minimum	1·46	0·99	29·26
At minimum of L23,000	12·30	40·47	22·69
At minimum of L25,000	41·12	36·25	29·65
Above minimum and up to L40,000	21·28	14·03	14·74
From L40,001 to L60,000	14·14	5·52	2·78
From L60,001 to L80,000	5·43	1·06	0·59
L80,001 and above	4·27	1·68	0·29
Total	100·00	100·00	100·00
Total number	2,473,052	2,075,504	1,357,560

Source: *Rendiconti dell'Anno 1970*, Rome, 1971, p. 345.

pensioners have pensions at or below L25,000 per month.[1] Some 78 per cent of the disability pensions are at or below L25,000 per month—not surprising in view of the point made above that disability pensions are often a form of early retirement or a way of evading the old age pension fifteen-year contribution requirement. About 30 per cent of the survivor pensions are below L23,000 per month and some 82 per cent are at or below L25,000 per month.

Low though the average general obligatory pensions may be, it is important to recognize that their value has risen considerably during the 1950s and 1960s. Indeed, the increases have been among the highest in Europe and this in spite of the continuing rapid growth in the number of pensioners mentioned earlier. Between 1952 and 1970 average old age pensions at current prices increased 5·5 fold and disability and survivor pensions by 4·8 and 4·4 fold respectively. The major increases came in the late 1950s and 1960s with old age pensions rising some 4·6 fold between 1957 and 1970 while survivor pensions and disability pensions increased about 4 fold. The rise in general obligatory pensions has been well above the 80 per cent rise in the cost of living between 1952 and 1970, and also the increases in average industrial hourly earnings—around 160 per cent between 1952 and the end of 1968.

---

[1] Table 5.2 includes seniority pensions (see p. 206, above) in the old age pension group but these pensions tend invariably to be above the minimum and some 65 per cent are in the band L40,000–L80,000 a month. The number of seniority pensioners is, however, so small that their exclusion would barely affect the figure of 55 per cent mentioned in the text.

(b) Schemes for independent workers

It will be recalled that there are three schemes for independent workers—one for farmers, tenant farmers and sharecroppers, another for artisans and a final one for small traders. These schemes, started in 1957, 1959 and 1966 respectively, were, in 1970, still in a transitional phase with the inevitable result that by far the greater proportion of pensions paid by these schemes are at the minimum—a minimum which at L 18,000 per month is below that for the general obligatory scheme. As one would expect, therefore, average pensions are of a lower value.

There are four further points to note about the independent worker schemes. First, the differences in pension values between the old age, disability and survivor groups for all three independent worker schemes, are small. Second, the average values are well below those for the general obligatory scheme. Old age pensions are slightly more than a half of those in the general obligatory schemes, disability pensions are about two-thirds and survivor pensions about three-quarters. Third, the average value of pensions does not differ much between the three independent worker schemes. Fourth, new independent worker pensions are virtually the same as the average value of pensions in payment. The reason for all four of these characteristics is that virtually all the pensions paid by these schemes, because they are still in their transitional phase, are at the minimum—a minimum which is the same for all three independent worker schemes. In 1970, over 90 per cent of independent worker pensions in payment were at or below the minimum, a much higher proportion than with the general obligatory scheme.

There has been a tendency for the average value of independent worker pensions to rise more rapidly than pensions in the general obligatory scheme.[1] This reflects the rapid growth of minimum pensions in the late 1950s and throughout the 1960s. The differentials between the independent worker pensions and the general scheme pensions, though still considerable, are therefore less than when the independent worker schemes were first set up.

---

[1] Tables showing the average values of the general obligatory and independent worker pensions, and indeed all INPS pensions, over the period since the various schemes were created and up to 1968, can be found in INPS, *Settant'Anni, op. cit.* These can be brought up to date using INPS, *Rendiconti dell'Anno.*

In 1970, for example, the average value of the independent workers old age pension was some 50 per cent of the general scheme pension while in 1961 the farmer and artisan schemes were paying old age pensions having an average value equal to about 40 per cent of the general scheme old age pensions. Independent worker disability and survivor pensions have shown a similar tendency to those for old age.

(c) The special schemes for dependent workers

The special schemes for dependent workers, reflecting the great variety of conditions and regulations under which they operate, have quite differing pension values. All the dependent worker special scheme pensions are above those of the general obligatory scheme. The miners' scheme comes closest to the general obligatory pension values, but even this scheme has pensions which are 76 per cent higher. The special scheme for flight personnel gives the highest pensions—about 9·5 times the average value of the general obligatory scheme pensions. The weighted average old age pension in the special schemes was, in 1970, some three times that of the general scheme old age pension, while the weighted average of the disability and survivor pensions were 2·8 times and 1·8 times the general scheme respectively.

The major reasons for the higher pensions in the dependent worker schemes are: the earnings of employees in these schemes are normally higher than those in the general obligatory scheme; the minimum pensions are generally higher; the proportion of final income paid as a pension is often higher; the payment of a pension which is tied to terminal earnings has been the pension formulae for more years than under the general obligatory scheme; the number of years of service required in order to receive the full old age pension is often less than under the general obligatory scheme; the proportion of pension or pension rights in the case of disability or survivors is generally higher than under the obligatory scheme. Finally, and associated with many of these points, the contributions to the special schemes are usually higher than in the general scheme, thereby allowing higher and more generous pension rights.[1] We have already noted that new pensions under the general

---

[1] Further details on all these features can be found in Section III, above.

obligatory scheme are not much different from the average value of pensions in payment and that the differences for the independent worker schemes are negligible. This is not the case with the dependent worker special schemes where quite substantial differences exist. The reason for this is that while the great majority of both existing and new general scheme pensions are at the minima, this is not the case with the dependent worker schemes where the distribution is far more even and less bunched towards the lower end of the pension range. Thus, while the rapid increase of minima in the general scheme, and the continuingly inadequate contribution record of those newly retired, has meant little difference between old and new pensions, this is not found to anything like the same degree in the dependent worker schemes. Moreover—though less important—the special schemes are, as we have seen, much more poorly dynamized with respect to the cost of living than the general scheme—often requiring a 10 per cent or more change in the cost of living index before they are adjusted.

It will be recalled that the general obligatory scheme and the schemes for independent workers were characterized by a bunching of pensioners at the lower end of the pension scale. This was particularly strong with the independent worker schemes, where over 90 per cent of pensioners had a pension which was at or below the minimum; but even the general obligatory scheme had some 55 per cent of old age pensioners at or below L25,000 per month and 75 per cent or more of the disability and survivor pensions were at or below this level. The special schemes for dependent workers have a more even distribution with some bunching at the lower end of the pension bands though not nearly as serious as with the general and independent worker schemes.

The more uniform distribution of the special dependent worker schemes relative to the general scheme[1] is a result of four major factors. First, the special schemes, for a long time, have had more complete coverage than the general scheme. This means that greater proportions of pensioners have contributed for the required period. Second, in a number of the schemes, the contribution

---

[1] The heavy bunching at the minima of the independent worker scheme is, as explained earlier, very largely a result of the fact that these schemes are still relatively new.

period for a full pension is less than in the general scheme, with the result that the probability of getting above the minima is greater. Third, a point which has already been mentioned earlier, the special schemes are often poorly dynamized with respect to the cost of living so that new pensions paid are above the average pensions and this tends to stretch the distribution. Fourth, the minima for the special schemes appear not to have been increased as rapidly as with the general scheme where rapidly rising minima have tended to create bunching at the lower pension range.

Although the special schemes still have higher pensions than the general obligatory scheme, the differentials have been narrowing as a consequence of the more rapid growth in the value of the general scheme pensions. During the 1960s the general obligatory scheme saw a growth in average pension values which was more rapid than with any of the special schemes except for the seamen's disability and survivor pensions. The great changes in the general scheme in the 1960s, pushed by the trade unions, is undoubtedly the major reason for the relative improvement. Looking at the whole period from 1950 to 1970, the general scheme again does well in terms of the growth of pension values relative to the special schemes. Old age, survivor and disability pensions for consumer and direct tax collectors rose faster than the general scheme (though from a relatively low 1950 level), as did the disability and survivor pension for telephone workers, but the obligatory scheme did better than the remaining special schemes.

Factors which have played a part in determining the growth of pensions in the various special schemes include the relative bargaining power of workers in the various industries, the number of pensioners relative to the number of insured and the financial state of the schemes. It needs to be recalled that the special schemes are to varying degrees still funded, while the general scheme has in the post-war period been financed very largely, and now wholly, on a pay-as-you-go basis. The general scheme has thus been better placed to increase its benefits though the point needs to be made that the special schemes, faced with increased pension demands, have also tended to reduce the funding element and to move increasingly towards pay-as-you-go. Our view is that the major reasons why the special schemes have not been able to keep pace with the general scheme are, first, because of the greater pressures which have been operating in favour of increased general scheme pensions. Because the special schemes had (and still have) such high pensions relative to the general scheme, the pressures to increase these pensions were not so strong. Second, the special schemes have been much more poorly dynamized relative to the general scheme.

(d) Pension schemes for the free professions[1]

Very little information is available on these schemes. In part this reflects the fact that the schemes are not administered by INPS, with the result that information is not co-ordinated, and in part the fact that quantitatively they are not important. About 288,000 people were, in 1969, insured under the free profession schemes and about 45,000 pensions (direct and indirect) were being paid. We have no information on the distribution of pensions within the schemes—though many are so new that there will be considerable bunching around the minima.

Although the free profession pensions normally have a value above the general scheme pensions and some of them, e.g. solicitors, are high by any standards, they do not in the main stand out as being particularly high. The weighted average of free profession pensions, at L699,064 p.a., is below that for the special dependent worker schemes (L988.025) even though well above the independent worker weighted average (L241,175) and the general scheme average of L385,550.

A number of points need to be kept in mind when considering the value of free profession pensions. First, many of the free profession schemes are of recent origin and, as a result, are not well organized and still going through a transitional phase.[2] Secondly, some of the members will be receiving pensions from other sources. A number of midwives and doctors, for example, will be insured for pensions by the state health group, INAM. Third, one suspects that many of those in the free professions expect to continue working well into old age and then to live either on their capital or on the basis of income from private pension arrangements.

---

[1] The information in this section is taken from an unpublished paper prepared by Dr Enrico Grossetti of INPS. All information refers to 1969.

[2] Although many of the free profession schemes are obligatory, there can be little doubt that the newer schemes do not cover all potential members.

(e) Public employee schemes

As with the free profession schemes, there is little published information available on the growth and distribution of pension
values in the major public employee schemes. Information is
available on the average value of pensions in the two major public
employee schemes (for state employees and for local authority
employees) for 1969. The figures are not broken down into the
three groups of old age, disability and survivor pensions. As one
would expect, given the fairly high earnings in the public sectors,
the fact that the schemes are long standing and, most important,
have generous pension provisions, the public sector pensions are
above those paid in the general scheme and above most of the other
INPS schemes. In 1969 the average direct and indirect pension
value in the state employee scheme was L921,520 p.a. and L882,688
in the local authority scheme. These are well above comparable
figures for the general independent worker and free profession
schemes. They are slightly below the weighted average for the
special dependent worker schemes.

(f) Other pensions

Formidable though the list of pensions so far discussed may appear
to be, we have not covered them all. Because of lack of data we
have not discussed a number of schemes run by some Italian
banks for their employees, the scheme for industrial managers and
other minor schemes. Our discussion has also excluded the much
more important social pensions. It will be recalled that these have
been paid since 1969 to Italian citizens of sixty-five or above who
have no other income (including pensions) in excess of L156,000
p.a. Any income above this sum means a reduction in the social
pension by the amount of that income. Few social pensioners
appear to have other sources of income since the average social
pension paid in 1970 was L153,927 p.a. as against the theoretical
maximum of L156,000. It is not particularly useful to show the
distribution pattern of these pensions nor, since they were only
introduced in 1969, their growth over time. The social pension is
the lowest of all Italian pensions. In 1969, the number of social
pensioners was 470,856 and rose to 766,027 in 1970. In this latter
year 8 per cent of total INPS pensioners were on the social

pension. More social pensions can be expected to be paid as knowledge about the schemes reaches more people. There can be little doubt that the uptake is still well below the number eligible for the social pension. In 1970, the social pension was a pitiful 11 per cent or thereabouts of gross industrial earnings.

V—OTHER AIDS FOR PENSIONERS

So far, this chapter has been primarily concerned with pensions. Although these are the main items determining the well-being of pensioners, there are other factors and payments which need to be taken into account—payments made in addition to pensions, the costs of health treatment, how pensions are considered for tax purposes, rights to work and still receive a pension, housing subsidies, etc. This section briefly examines these factors as well as financial concessions paid to families who have pensioners within their household.

Many of the pension schemes in Italy include *a dependent family supplement* though it is rare in the free profession schemes. It is generally paid for dependent children up to eighteen years of age (twenty-one if at secondary school and twenty-six if at university) and no age limit for incapacitated children. In view of the large numbers of disabled pensioners in Italy, the dependent child's allowance is not unimportant though in so far as the disability pension is often a substitute for an old age pension, we would not want to exaggerate this point. In addition to the child's allowance in the general and independent worker schemes, a supplement is paid for the pensioner's wife (or the husband of a female pensioner if the male is disabled).[1] The supplement for the spouse is sometimes conditional upon the spouse not enjoying an income above a specified sum—L21,000 per month in the general scheme or L30,000 if the income arises solely from pensions.

The value of the supplement and the system for calculating it vary from scheme to scheme. The supplement for those in the general scheme is equal to the family allowance for industrial workers—L4,160 per month for the spouse and L5,720 per month for each dependent child. The supplement for independent workers

---

[1] None of the special schemes for dependent workers pays a supplement for the spouse though supplements for children are normal.

is 10 per cent of the pension but with a minimum of L2,500
for each dependent per month. As the majority of these independent workers are on a minimum pension of less than L25,000 per
month, they would be receiving the L2,500. Dependent family
supplements are not paid to social pensioners.

The head of a family can receive *a family allowance for dependent
members* (including pensioners) who fulfil specified conditions. In
particular, they must not have an income of more than L21,000
per month or L30,000 if this arises solely from pensions. For both
dependent parents the combined income can be up to L32,000
per month or L54,000 if the income arises solely from pensions.
The allowance is L2,340 per month for each parent. The family
allowance paid for pensioners is not unimportant in Italy where it
has been estimated that some 35 per cent of pensioners live with
their children.[1]

Retirement indemnities have a long history and go back to 1919
when legislation established for salaried workers with twenty-two
to twenty-eight years' service a grant which was equal to half of
the monthly salary multiplied by the number of years service on
condition that the amount did not exceed one year's salary. In 1926
the law laid down that the amount must be *at least* a half of monthly
salary multiplied by the number of years of service. The system
was slowly extended to workers in the pre-war period. The post-
war years saw changes, pushed by the trade unions, which increased the indemnity for salaried workers and extended it to
more wage earners. Employers are now obliged by law to make
provisions for the payment of indemnities to workers who leave
their employment whether this be because of retirement or because
they leave voluntarily before retirement age. The financing of the
indemnities is the sole responsibility of the employer and is
normally done through private insurance companies. The value of
the indemnities vary from industry to industry and between
worker groups but in general the current position is that white-
collar workers receive one month's income for every year of service,
blue-collar workers receive a similar indemnity but only after a
specified period of service (generally between five and ten years).
Manual workers receive an indemnity which varies from a minimum of six days of income for every year of service to around

[1] 'Pensioni e limiti di eta del pensionamento', in *Bolletino della Doxa*, June–
July 1972.

fifteen days. There are, of course, exceptions. ENI chemical and petroleum workers, for example, receive an indemnity which can reach a month of income for every year of service after fifteen years with the company, telephone workers receive the same indemnity treatment as the white-collar worker in that sector, while the private petroleum companies pay twenty-six days of earnings for each year of service when the worker has been in the company for ten or more years.[1] Six weeks of pay for every year of service is not uncommon for managers. There is a tendency for the worker indemnity treatment to be brought in line with that for white-collar workers. It will be obvious that retirement indemnities are not unimportant and their value is often high. If nothing else, the indemnities do provide an income for the pensioner while he is waiting for his pension to be paid. It can take anything up to six months (or even longer) after retirement before the pensioner receives his first pension payments.

The great majority of Italian pensions are not liable for the main Italian *income tax* (*Imposta di Ricchezza Mobile*) and stamp duty is not payable on INPS pension payments or documents. The income tax concession is not as generous as it might seem at first sight, for the income tax is only levied on incomes (net of social security contributions) in excess of L660,000 per annum (L50,00 per month). The great majority of Italian pensions are, as we have seen in Section IV, well below this. The income tax rates for incomes above L50,000 per month are not high by British standards, rising from 4·4 per cent for incomes of between L50,000 and L90,000 to 20.25 per cent for incomes above L1,716,668 per month. Although not subject to income tax, pensions are liable for the 'complementary' (family) income tax. However, for the majority of pensioners, not living with their children, the complementary income tax, because it is only imposed at high income levels, will be irrelevant. Similarly most families whether they have a pensioner living with them or not, will have a family income which is so low that they are not liable for the complementary tax or, alternatively, pay it at a low rate.

Retirement indemnities are not subject to income tax as long as they do not exceed 1 million lire. Above this, further exemption is granted on L40,000 for each year of service, with standard income

[1] See G. Ammassari, 'Le Differenze di trattamento tra operai e impiegati', *La Retribuzione nell' Industria*, Franco Angeli, 1970, p. 109.

tax rates applied on sums above this. White-collar workers are liable in addition to pay the complementary income tax. The average manual worker would pay very little or no tax at all. Even quite substantial indemnities are not heavily taxed. A white-collar worker, for example, with an income of L2 million per annum with twenty years service and an indemnity of a month for every year of service thereby giving an indemnity of L3·3 million, would only pay around 2·5 per cent of the total indemnity in tax.

The Italian *health system* is financed on the insurance principle with employers and employees paying specified proportions of earnings into a sickness fund. The greater part of the contributions are made by the employer. In 1970 the employer contribution into the main dependent worker scheme (INAM) was 14·6 per cent of earnings with the employee paying a mere 0·15 per cent. As with the pension system, there are a considerable number of health insurance funds but the main ones are INAM covering most dependent workers, ENPAS for state employees, INADEL for local authority employees, plus three schemes covering farmers, artisans, and small traders. The free professions and a number of other groups have separate schemes. Most of the Italian schemes cover the insured for a very high proportion of doctors' fees, hospitalization, and drugs, and in addition pay a set percentage of earnings as sickness compensation. Normally, the schemes cover dependents as well as the insured himself. Pensioners (direct and indirect) continue to receive medical assistance, excluding sickness compensation, from the schemes to which they or their spouse belonged when working but they pay no contributions. The great majority of pensioners are therefore covered in this way and a high proportion of the remainder will be covered by their children's insurance contributions as long as the pensioner is living with his children. The main group excluded from the health scheme is the social pensioner unless claiming on his children's insurance. He has to rely on medical assistance, usually of a poor standard, from the local authority. One would hope that this will change in the near future perhaps with the social pensioners being covered by INAM.

How are pensions affected when pensioners *continue to work*? It is difficult to say with respect to the special schemes for dependent workers, public service employees or for those who were in the free professions. For the general scheme, however, and for independent worker pensioners employed by a third party the position is as follows: first, pensioners who take up work abroad or as agricultural workers do not suffer any loss of pension if they work; second, those receiving survivor pensions may work without any loss of pension; third, those on an old age or disability pension only receive the minimum pension plus a half of the remaining part of the pension. In total they cannot receive a pension which is in excess of L100,000 per month.[1] Few would pretend that the system is either equitable or rational. Seniority pensioners cannot work and at the same time receive a pension unless the pension originates from a date before the end of April 1968 when the system for general scheme pensioners, described above, is applicable.

Evidence suggests that a quarter of pensioners work after retirement, though few of these work for a third party. It was estimated that in 1969 some 17·2 per cent of pensioners continued to work on their own account while only 7·7 per cent worked for a third party.[2] The self-employed workers would largely be those on an independent worker pension. Of those who continued to work, half worked regularly. One suspects that few of those working for a third party would declare their activities to the authorities so the 7·7 per cent mentioned above is probably an understatement. Those working on their own account will generally be independent worker pensioners and probably on the minimum pension so their pension will not be affected by the fact that they continue to work. The estimate of pensioners working on their own account is therefore probably accurate.

There are a number of other forms of aid for Italian pensioners which should at least be mentioned. First, *private pensions*. A number of firms are known to pay these, second-tier, pensions though detailed information is not available. In general, few firms operate such schemes, and the pensions involved are small. With improved general scheme pensions they have diminished yet further in

---

[1] An example might help to clarify this point. Assume that we have a general scheme pensioner who is less than sixty-five years of age and has the right to a monthly pension of L150,000. During the period in which he works he can only receive the minimum pension (L24,100 a month) plus a half of the difference between L150,000 and L24,100 (L62,920). In total therefore he receives L24,100 plus L62,950, i.e. L87,050.

[2] *Bolletino della Doxa, op. cit.*

importance. Few observers expect any extension of the schemes. Second, pensioners in need (or any citizen in need) can apply to their local authority for assistance. The degree of generosity and the criteria for granting assistance vary between local authorities. In general, assistance is paid only to meet basic needs and is not of a continuing nature. Local authorities can provide lodgings, though again this is not on a continuing basis. Similarly, much of the aid from the various religious bodies to pensioners and indigent citizens is not of a continuing character. Third, mention should be made of ONPI (*Opera Nazionale per i Pensionati d'Italia*). This body, financed by worker contributions, was created in 1948 and gives subsidies for burial, financial aid to needy pensioners and their families, financial aid for the education of the children of needy pensioners and, most important, in recent years has built and managed hostels for pensioners. It has twenty-nine hostels and is aiming to bring this to thirty-seven (10,000 beds) over the next few years. The hostels are extremely well run, service is of high standard and the tariffs are related largely to what the pensioner can afford. All pensioners can apply for admission. Finally, on a negative tack, Italy has virtually no form of domestic assistance for its elderly nor are there any relevant housing allowances.

VI—ITALIAN PENSIONS: SOME ISSUES

The aim of this section is to consider a number of the more important issues raised by the Italian pension system and other forms of aid for the elderly. Five issues are covered. The first is the degree to which Italian pensions are 'adequate'—a difficult topic but one on which, in the Italian case, we believe that firm conclusions can be reached. Second, it will be recalled from Section II that the Italian population structure has been characterized for many decades by an increasing proportion of elderly people. We must now examine some of the population forecasts and try to analyse what these forecasts and other anticipated changes in the pension system mean for expenditure on pensions. Third, we want to look in a little more detail at the systems whereby the Italian pension schemes are financed and the economic implications of these systems. Fourth, in view of the large number of Italian pension schemes, we want to examine the arrangements made for workers who change jobs and schemes. Finally, we shall consider the interesting way that the Italians have used their pension and social security schemes as counter-cyclical and regional development measures.

(a) The adequacy of Italian pensions

This discussion of adequacy is limited to INPS pensions because these are the only ones where information on the distribution pattern of pensions in payment is readily available. It will be recalled, however, that the INPS pensions cover some 90 per cent of the total number of Italian pensioners.

Table 5.3 gathers together information covering *all* INPS schemes in 1969 and shows average annual pension values and the proportions of pensioners in various monthly pension value bands.

TABLE 5.3

INPS pensions: average value and distribution pattern (1969)

	Old age	Disability	Survivors
Average annual value ('ooo lire)	375	330	293
Percentage at or below L18,000 per month	45	33·8	42·3
Percentage at or below L25,000 per month	89	86	81
Percentage at or below L40,000 per month	89	86·5	81

Note: The schemes covered in this table are the general obligatory scheme, the schemes for independent workers, the special schemes for dependent workers and the social pension scheme.
Source: INPS, *Rendiconti dell'Anno 1969*, Rome, 1970.

Table 5.3 shows the great majority of pensioners having a pension which is below L25,000 per month (increased by about L4,000 if the pensioner has a spouse). Since most Italian pensions are paid on the basis of a thirteen-month year, the L25,000 is equal to around L27,000 per calendar month. Even so, by British standards, this is very low—£18.0 per calender month for a single pensioner and £20·7 for a couple. But such simple comparison is an unsatisfactory guide to adequacy. Exchange rates do not reflect at all well the cost of living difference between countries. For example, the simple use of exchange rates means that the Italian

I

pensioner became 14 per cent better off after the British devalua-
tion in 1967 and this is obviously misleading.

There are a number of possible ways in which the adequacy of
Italian pensions can be judged. A comparison with average earnings is one. In 1969, average gross industrial earnings, including
family allowances, tips, holiday pay, and thirteen-month premium
were around L100,000 per calendar month. On this basis INPS
old age pensions are some 30 per cent of earnings, while disability
and survivor pensions are 27·5 and 24·5 per cent respectively.
Eighty-five per cent of all INPS pensions are at or below 25 per
cent of gross industrial earnings.

A large proportion of Italian pensioners live with their spouse,
an estimated 45 per cent in 1969.[1] Some of these would also be
living with their children, but ignoring this for the moment, and
viewing the pensioner and wife as a family, the average income of
this pension family (from pension and wife's allowance) would be
around L410,000 per annum if the pension was for old age. It is
interesting and relevant to compare this with the Italian consumer
expenditure figures for a normal two-unit Italian family. In 1968,
annual expenditure on food was L280,000 *per member* of such a
family while their non-foodstuff expenditure was L93,000 per
member.[2] These figures exclude housing expenditure. About 34
per cent of Italian householders over the age of sixty-five rent their
houses and the average rent for families whose total income is less
than L600,000 per annum is around L120,000 per annum.[3] Even
excluding housing costs, it can be seen that the per capita income of
the average pensioner living with his wife is less than the average
annual Italian expenditure on food alone for a family of comparable
size. The point need hardly be made that the majority of pensioners
(living on an income below L325,000 per annum) have an income
which is well below the average Italian expenditure figure for
food.

About 35 per cent of Italian pensioners live with their children.
Where the pension recipient is the only person living with the
family, his pension, if it is about average, would be enough to
cover expenditure on food for him by the family. Average annual

[1] *Bollettino della Doxa, op. cit.*

[2] ISTAT, *Annuario Statistico Italiano 1969*.

[3] 'Risparmio e Struttura della Ricchezza delle Famiglie Italiane nel '69', in
Bolletino della Banca d'Italia, 1970.

expenditure on food *per member* in a four- to five-member family is about L220,000. Even those on the minimum pension of between L234,000 and L325,000 per annum would, with their pension, be able to cover the expenditure on food incurred on their behalf and, indeed, at the latter figure some other items would also be covered. Their pension would not, however, be adequate to cover any additional housing expenditure and is completely inadequate where both the pensioner and his wife live with the family. Family ties are extremely strong in Italy but it is interesting to note that an estimated 8 to 10 per cent of families having a pensioner or pensioners living with them found the pensioner a burden and over 50 per cent said that this burden could be resolved by an increase in pensions.[1]

Another, more subjective, way of measuring the adequacy of pensions is to ask those who are still at work what they consider an adequate pension to be. In a recent survey[2] 62 per cent of those interviewed considered an adequate pension to be between L40,000 and L90,000 per month (39 per cent gave the figures L60,000–L90,000), 18 per cent thought that a pension over L90,000 per month would be adequate and only 10 per cent saw a pension of below L40,000 as adequate. The relevant figure is, of course, this latter and means that 80 per cent of Italian pensioners are living on a pension which is considered inadequate by all but 10 per cent of the labour force at large.

All the methods used above, although giving an indication of the adequacy of Italian pensions, are subject to a number of criticisms. The subjective element in some of them is large, calculations on the basis of average consumer expenditure fail to differentiate between pensioner consumer expenditure and non-pensioner consumer expenditure, while the method which relates pensions to earnings, though perhaps interesting for the purposes of international comparison, does not tell us very much about adequacy in any explicit manner.

A good measure of adequacy, though not completely free of criticism, is to relate pensions to some quantitative measure of the minimum income required to live. The subject of minimum incomes has not received a great deal of attention in Italy. In 1970, however, a conference was held in Rome which discussed this

---

[1] *Bollettino della Doxa, op. cit.*
[2] *Ibid.*

topic. One of these papers was particularly interesting in that it presents the quantitative results of an attempt to measure the minimum income requirements in Alto-Adige.[1] The basic conclusion was that the minimum income requirement of a pensioner living alone was about L26,000 per month plus rent and heating costs of around L11,000 per month. The minimum income requirement for a pensioner living with his wife, and assuming the same rent and heating costs, would be L55,800 per month. The minimum income requirement of a pensioner living with his family is L18,900 per month with no allowance for rent and heating.

In sum, according to this study, the minimum pensions, on which most Italian pensioners live, are not adequate to cover the minimum income requirement of the pensioner who lives alone. They are certainly not adequate where the pensioner has a dependent wife. Where the pensioner lives with his family, the minimum pensions are just about enough to meet his minimum requirements but not adequate if both he and his wife live with the family. In all this it must be stressed that the minima used in the calculations were very spartan.

Our conclusions, then, are that Italian pensions in payment, by most standards, are generally inadequate in value and that large numbers of the population, on minimum pensions, are having to survive on sums which are completely inadequate or else are imposing a financial burden on their families. The plight of the social pensioner on L12,000 per month needs no further comment except to stress again that there are three-quarters of a million social pensioners in Italy.

(b) Population and pension expenditure forecasts

It will be recalled from Section II, above, that the Italian population structure is characterized by a growing proportion of elderly. This is a trend which has been operating for a hundred years or so and is expected to continue into the future. One estimate anticipates that the proportion of the population aged sixty-five or over will rise from the 1966 level of 10·2 per cent to 13·45 per

---

[1] 'Studio per la determinazione del minimo vitale nella regione Trentino Alto Adige', Istituto per gli Studi di Servizio Sociale, *Lo Standard Garantito*, Rome, 1970.

cent in 1981, 13·52 per cent in 1991 and 14 per cent in 2001.[1] The proportions in the more relevant age group of sixty or over (the male retirement age is sixty) are expected to rise from 15·4 per cent in 1966 to 17·8 per cent in 1976, 18·3 per cent in 1986 and 19·3 per cent in 2001. The absolute numbers aged sixty or over are expected to increase by 28·1 per cent between 1966 and 1986 and a further 8·8 per cent between 1986 and 2001.[2]

Ideally, we want forecasts for the age groups which coincide neatly with the normal pensionable age for men and women (sixty and fifty-five respectively). These are indeed available up to 1981.[3] It is estimated that females aged fifty-five and above will account for 24·5 per cent of the total female population in 1981 as against 22·3 per cent in 1967. The male proportions (for the age group sixty and above) are expected to rise from 13·2 per cent to 14·6 per cent over the same period. As a proportion of the male labour force it is anticipated that the males aged sixty and above will represent some 27·5 per cent in 1981 as against 23·1 per cent in 1967. In 1967 the number of females aged fifty-five and above was already 112·8 per cent of the female labour force and was expected to rise to 133·5 per cent in 1981. The increasing proportion of the population in the pensionable age groups relative to the working population means, other things being equal, that pension expenditure will rise and become a higher proportion of GNP—trends which have anyway been noticeable over the post-war period and indeed, as we have seen, pension expenditure as a proportion of national income has grown quite spectacularly. In 1952 INPS pension expenditure amounted to 1·5 per cent of gross national income and by 1970 the proportion was up to 5·7 per cent. This rapid increase is all the more remarkable when account is taken of the rapid growth of Italian national income—among the highest in the world. The increasing importance of pension expenditure reflects improvements in pension provisions, the increased coverage of the schemes over the period (particularly the extension of pension schemes to independent workers) and the increasing proportion of the Italian population in the elderly age groups. The major factor in the 1950s was probably the increased coverage while improved

---

[1] *Settant'Anni, op. cit.*
[2] *Ibid.*
[3] G. de Meo, 'Evoluzione e propettive delle forze di lavoro in Italia', *Annali di Statistica*, Series VIII, vol. 23, ISTAT, Rome, 1970.

pension provisions has been the major factor in the 1960s. Although the growing proportion in the elderly age groups is a continuing trend it accounts for only a small proportion of the increased expenditure on pensions over the post-war period, probably less than 1 per cent, and, in consequence, is a relatively minor factor in explaining the increasing proportion of pension expenditure relative to national income.

It can be expected that pension expenditure will rise substantially during the 1970s and that this too will principally result from improved pension provisions rather than increased coverage (or the increasing proportion of elderly in the Italian population). Improved provisions will come about as a consequence, first, of an automatic element resulting from the fact that pensions will rise as the schemes become more mature and more people receive higher pensions because they have contributed for a longer period. The fact that old age pensions newly paid in 1970 under the general obligatory scheme were some 37·5 per cent of average industrial earnings indicates how pension expenditure could increase as average contribution records rise and as more people reach the number of contributions required for the maximum 74 per cent of terminal earnings. We have no detailed information which would indicate when the greater number of new pensioners will be at this latter level but suspect it more likely to be in the 1980s rather than the 1970s. Even then, of course, the majority of pensioners will be on pensions below this level. New pensions always represent only a minority of pensions in payment. In 1970, for example, newly paid pensions (direct and indirect) in the general obligatory scheme were only about 7 per cent of total general obligatory pensions in payment. It is fairly obvious that the increasing maturity of the schemes, though like the demographic factors forcing a continuing and not to be underestimated upward movement of pension expenditure, is not likely to be a major factor in increased pension expenditure during the 1970s.

The point has already been made that the major factors affecting pension expenditure during the post-war period have been increased coverage of the schemes and increased pension provision. The former will not be important in the future, and indeed was not particularly important during the 1960s. The major element in the increased pension expenditure has not hitherto been the increasing maturity of the schemes but their increasing

generosity as a result of trade-union-pressured Government decisions and in particular the constant increase in minimum pensions. In addition, the tying of pensions to the cost of living in
1969 has increased the monetary value of the expenditure. One
can expect that these factors will also play a major role in the future.
The actual effect they will have upon expenditure is, however,
quite impossible to predict, depending as it does on the pressures
exerted by the trade-union movement and/or the willingness and
inclination of the Government to increase pensions. In 1971 the
trade unions pushed for substantially increased pensions and
largely secured their demands in 1972.[1] Further increases are
likely. The Government has already agreed that in 1976 each year
of contribution to the general obligatory scheme will secure a
pension of 2 per cent of terminal earnings instead of the current
1·85 per cent, though this will of course only affect pensions first
paid in 1976 and beyond.

It is difficult to imagine that a country which is part of Western
Europe can continue to have such large proportions of its elderly
population living in what can only be described as dire poverty.
Any attempt to give meaningful help to these people, because of
their numbers and their current low standards, must increase
pension expenditure substantially. In 1970 the average value of
all INPS pensions (direct and indirect) was L344,158 p.a. and
equal to a mere 23·8 per cent of average industrial manual worker
earnings. If these were raised to some 45 per cent of earnings
(giving pensions which even then would only just be adequate in
the 'minimum income' sense discussed earlier) INPS pensions
would account for more than 11 per cent of GNP. If all INPS
pensions were to rise to the general obligatory target of 74 per cent
of earnings they would be equal in total to nearly 17 per cent of
GNP. On top of this would be the non-INPS pensions. Of course
these sums give an exaggerated picture of the incidence of pensions
under the 74 per cent rule not least because the pension is 74 per
cent of earnings in the best three of the last five years of labour.
Assuming that the last three years are the best three and that earnings are growing by some 6 per cent per annum, the pension would
be equal only to some 68 per cent of earnings in the last month
(grossed up to an annual figure) of earnings. But beyond this, as

---

[1] See pp. 248–9, below.

long as pensions are not dynamized with earnings, only a minority (the new pensions) will be receiving this percentage of earnings. Furthermore, we have assumed that INPS survivor and disability pensions are equal to the target per cent of earnings and this is either unlikely or not possible on the standard pension formulae. Nevertheless one can see that even an attempt to push pensions to reasonably adequate levels will mean that pensions take a substantial part of GNP. It can only be expected that as increasing numbers of workers are eligible for greater pensions simply because they have a better contribution record, pension expenditure in relation to GNP is likely to rise slowly but steadily.

(c) *Finance*

The most important of Italy's pension schemes are financed on a pay-as-you-go principle and hold reserves which are much more in the nature of contingency provisions than funds. In 1970, for example, the general scheme held reserves equal to about one quarter of total annual expenditure. The INPS special schemes exhibit a variety of conditions in this respect. In some, the value of reserves is such that a substantial element of funding still remains. The gas workers' scheme has reserves which are eight times the total annual expenditure, the aircrew scheme reserves are fifteen times expenditure and the telephone workers' scheme has reserves which are some seven times expenditure. The transport workers' scheme on the other hand has reserves which are about three-fifths of total expenditure while the seamen's scheme reserves are around one-fifth. The free profession schemes are completely funded while the public employee scheme is entirely pay-as-you-go.

The fact that the major Italian schemes are pay-as-you-go has been a factor allowing the rapid improvements in pension provisions over the post-war period. Fully funded schemes, without quite massive increases in contributions, would not have been able to pay such increases nor would they have permitted the wide-scale 'blanketing-in' of the population which has taken place.

One of the most interesting aspects of Italian pension finance is the high contributions paid by production (employers and employees). We have already seen in Section III that contributions into the general scheme by production are some 20 per cent of the employee's earnings. Most other schemes have similar proportions or even higher. The greater part (two-thirds or more) is paid by the employer. In addition to pension contributions the employer (and to a very limited extent the employee) has to contribute to the health schemes, unemployment schemes, industrial injuries schemes and family allowance scheme. In total these contributions amount to a substantial proportion of the employee's earnings. In the case of general scheme employees, for example, production's contribution into these various schemes is equivalent to some 59 per cent of earnings. Of this, the employee contribution is around 7 per cent of earnings while that of the employer is about 52 per cent. Similar proportions, or even higher, also operate for most other working groups. Both the total contributions (as a percentage of earnings) and the employer contributions are easily the highest in the EEC while the employee contributions are among the lowest. Over the post-war period the social security contributions by the employer have risen considerably to pay for the improved social security benefits.

There can be little doubt that the Italian system of financing the social security schemes largely through employer contributions has been an important factor leading to continuing pressures for improved social security benefits. The cost of improvements in a direct sense is very low for the employee. It must, to many Italians, seem to be a case of something for nothing. The drawbacks, however, are obvious. First, it has led to a degree of irresponsibility on the part of the various pressure groups and particularly the unions, with the result that labour costs have been pushed higher than would otherwise be the case. Inevitably, in a situation of fixed exchange rates, this has had its effects on Italian export performance and on employment. It has reduced the employment opportunities in industry and limited the prospects of labour switching from the low productivity sectors. Dr Lutz, in her major work on the Italian economy, laid great stress on the dualistic nature of the Italian labour market arising out of high wages in the 'protected' (large scale) industrial sector, and the consequences of this for growth and employment.[1] The social security contributions have worsened this situation not least because the protected sector, quite different from the small-scale sector, has little opportunity

[1] Vera Lutz, *Italy: A Study in Economic Development*, Oxford University Press, 1962.

or inclination to evade social security contributions. There can be little doubt that the heavy Italian inflation and balance-of-payments problems in 1970 and 1971 were in part a consequence of the social security improvements and increased contributions in the second half of the 1960s. In the early 1970s the inflationary situation, coupled with balance-of-payments problems, forced the Government to deflate the economy. The effects of this policy, combined with the slower growth of exports resulting from Italy's diminished competitiveness in international markets, had a marked effect on economic growth, which indeed was negligible in this period. The switching of resources from low to high productivity sectors, which has been an important source of Italian growth, requires favourable demand conditions if it is to operate. The higher social security contributions, through their effects on exports, have seriously diminished the growth of demand, and through this national growth. Secondly, although it is not possible to calculate exactly the incidence of the Italian form of social security and pension finance, a proportion of the employers' contributions will be passed on in the form of higher prices and thereby represents a very inequitable form of indirect tax.[1] Thirdly, the heavy employer social security contributions, representing a fixed element in labour costs, have diminished the potential attractiveness of the South as a location for industry, and the competitiveness of industry already in that region, in that they reduce the possible degree of labour cost flexibility; though admittedly much of the labour-cost advantage in the South had already been whittled away through successful trade-union pressures to reduce inter-regional wage differentials. At the present time, indeed, such differentials are negligible in big firms. Furthermore, the Government has tried to use concessions on social security contributions as an incentive for Southern industrial development and this is a topic to which we return later. Even so, the increased labour costs in the South resulting from a basically uniform wage and social security contribution system have deterred the movement of industry into that region and a number of Italian firms have gone to underdeveloped countries to secure their labour rather than the South. Fourthly, the high employer contributions are undoubtedly a factor explaining attempts by employers to evade their responsibilities in the social

---

[1] For a good discussion and analysis of the incidence of social security contributions see *Incidenze Economiche della Sicurezza Sociale, op. cit.*

security field. In spite of severe penalties, a considerable number of workers are not insured in the various pension, sickness, unemployment, etc. schemes. The high contributions are also one factor explaining the quite large numbers of under-age workers in Italy—workers for whom no social security contributions will generally be paid and whose wages are also very low. Such abuses are perhaps inevitable in the relatively slack labour market conditions of Italy. Our point, however, is that they are worsened by the high employer social security contributions.

Many of these problems could, of course, be eliminated or reduced in importance if the state were to take over a larger share of financing the social security system though the point does need to be made that in the Italian context, and in many other European countries, some of the problems would remain. The difficulties of raising finance through direct taxes are so severe in Italy that additional state financing would probably need to come through indirect taxes though these could be more progressive than the results of the current system.

We have already made the point earlier in this section that pension and social security expenditure can be expected to rise substantially during the 1970s if trade union pressures continue and if Government commitments are honoured. It is virtually inconceivable that these improvements could take place without a substantial increase in Government expenditure in this field—not only in absolute terms but also as a proportion of total social security expenditure. Without this, there is the danger of doing damage to the national economy. The industrial goose has up to now continued to lay golden eggs. With the, justifiable, demands now being made to improve pensions, and the social security system generally, there is a real danger of injuring even if not killing the goose unless the system of finance is changed. Beyond increases in employee contributions, the only alternative is more state intervention.

(d) Inter-scheme transfers

A social security system, such as that in Italy, with a large number of schemes is not without its advantages, in particular the fact that it is more likely to reflect the needs, working conditions and inclinations of members than one single homogeneous scheme. This is a point which is so frequently forgotten in the current European mania for harmonization, though this is not to say that within Italy there is no need for some further harmonization. Many of the differences between schemes reflect more the historical circumstances of the period when they were set up than any differences of need or working conditions. But a major disadvantage of a variety of schemes operating under a multiplicity of conditions can be that they impede the movement of labour between occupations or industries, and/or give rise to a loss of pension rights when such movement takes place. The existence of such transfer problems would be both undesirable from the individual's viewpoint and also from the viewpoint of national growth since the switching of resources between sectors is an important ingredient of economic growth.

The transfer problems in Italy, in spite of the large numbers of schemes, should not be exaggerated. First, the great majority of the work force is insured with the general obligatory scheme and any change of job which does not require the employee to leave this scheme is not, of course, detrimental to his pension rights. Second, a large number of workers stay in the same industry or sector throughout their working life so that pension transfer problems do not arise. Third, transfers between the general scheme and the INPS special schemes for dependent workers have never been difficult, with payments into one scheme capable of being transferred and accredited to the insured if he moves to employment which requires insurance under another scheme.

Even so, problems have arisen when the worker was not within any of these three categories and it was only in the late 1950s that legislation was introduced which resolved the problem. In 1958[1] it was laid down that workers insured outside the general scheme and who left without securing the right to a pension would have their contributions transferred to the general scheme and, on the assumption that they fulfilled the general scheme conditions, would be eligible for a pension based on these contributions and the norms of the general scheme. In other words the general scheme became something akin to a marshalling point in this context. This move, though welcome, still did not cover those people, admittedly few, who had contributed but were not eligible for a pension under

---

[1] Law of 2 April 1958, No. 322.

the general scheme but, because of a change in occupation or place or work, were eligible for a pension under one of the non-general schemes. In other words there was no system for transfering contributions out of the general scheme (except to the INPS special schemes). It was not until 1962 that legislation was introduced to correct this problem.[1] The procedure adopted was that the insured could request a supplementary pension from the general scheme based on his revalorized contributions.

The transfer systems adopted by the Italians are simple but effective. The use of the INPS general scheme as a clearing house for pension rights is particularly interesting from the United Kingdom viewpoint. It is a function which could, perhaps, be adopted by the proposed Special Reserve Scheme and in this way avoid the transfer problems already present between United Kingdom occupational pension schemes; and which are likely to grow in the future as these schemes increase in number and importance.

(e) *Social security in countercyclical and regional policy*

We come now to the final issue to be considered in this section—the way in which the Italians have used pension and social security benefits and contributions as a means of controlling the economy. These benefits and contributions are now such an important element in the economy that even minor changes can have substantial effects. It is almost inevitable, therefore, that national economic consequences are taken into account when changes are under consideration and, more positively, that thought should be given about how desirable national objectives might be secured through a manipulation of the social security system. The point does perhaps deserve to be made at the start that social security systems are generally countercyclical even where no positive effort is taken to make them so in that benefits are often higher (and contributions lower) during depressed economic conditions and vice versa when the economy is buoyant.[2]

There can be little doubt that in Italy, as in other countries, improvements in the pension and social security system have generally taken place in periods when it was felt that the economy

---

[1] Law of 12 August 1962, No. 1338.
[2] For a further discussion of this point see *Incidenze Economiche della Sicurezza Sociale, op. cit.*

could carry the burden. The improvements in minimum pensions, in 1965 for example, coincided with a period when additional demand could be easily met and was indeed welcome. It would, however, be wrong to overstress this point, for improvements in the social security system have also been a consequence of pressure by various groups, and in particular the trade unions. There is a case for saying that the relative neglect of the social security system in Italy during the 1950s, at least in terms of the value of the benefits, coincided with a period when the trade unions, over-involved in political issues, were weak. The stronger trade unions of the 1960s and their growing interest in social security, almost as part of the wage bargaining process, resulted in greatly improved pension and social security provisions. On the other hand, the placing of social security within the realm of interest of trade unions and wage bargaining means that social security improvements may run counter to the national interest. The wage explosion in 1969 together with improved pensions and social security gave rise to inflation and economic difficulties which, even in 1973, had not been fully resolved.

Beyond the incidental cyclical effects of the social security system, social security contributions have also been used as purposeful countercyclical measures in Italy though the policy was only adopted in the early 1960s. It was first used in 1964 when the economy was depressed and the balance of trade in serious deficit. A law presented in mid-1964 transferred a portion of social security contributions to the state; initially for the period 1 September to 31 December 1964. In the context of the general obligatory pension scheme this reduced the employee contributions by 0·35 percentage points—from 6·35 per cent of earnings to 6 per cent. This concession was continued in 1965 and 1966. In addition, in March 1965, further legislation aimed at stimulating the economy was introduced which reduced the employer contribution by a large 3 percentage points from 12·65 per cent of earnings to 9·65 per cent for the period April 1965 to March 1966 initially and then extended to December 1966. It was generally agreed that these measures, particularly as they accompanied improvements in pension values, had a substantial reflationary effect and were particularly useful in a situation where heavy unemployment coincided with inflation and balance of payments problems. In 1970–1 these conditions occurred again and, belatedly as a result of political difficulties, legislation was introduced in July 1971 which granted social security concessions to artisan and small (less than 300 employees)[1] industrial firms equal to some 5 per cent of earnings. The concession is financed virtually half and half by the INPS unemployment fund and the state. The preamble to the legislation does not speak specifically of the need to stimulate the economy, as did the earlier legislation, but without doubt this was its purpose. It is perhaps worthwhile stressing the point that in the Italian context the potential use of social security as a countercyclical measure is particularly valuable. Italy is a country where fiscal policy, so useful in demand management in other countries, has played a very limited role, partly because on the expenditure side, the administrative system is such that expenditure cannot be rapidly changed. Indeed, a major problem in Italy is for the administration to spend the money allocated to it.[2] In these conditions the potential role of social security in short-run demand management is very great.

The second area in which the social security system has been used as a means of securing Government economic objectives is in the field of regional development policy. A common feature of European incentives aimed at regional industrial development is that they are generally oriented towards capital, e.g. grants, depreciation allowances, loans at subsidized interest and equity finance. Few countries give labour subsidies in spite of the fact that labour is normally the surplus resource in the backward regions. The UK, through its Regional Employment Premium, and Italy are the major exceptions. In Italy the labour subsidy operates through the social security system. The first move in respect of this policy came in mid-1968 when legislation granting a social security concession was introduced for industrial firms employing more than thirty-five employees and operating in the South. The concession was set at 12 per cent of earnings net of overtime payments. The cost of the concession was to be borne half by the unemployment scheme and half by the state. These

---

[1] In August 1971 this limit was dropped for the textile sector which was going through a particularly critical period.

[2] For a very good discussion of the inability of the administration to spend the funds allocated to it and the subsequent shortfall in public expenditure which arises, see Ministero del Bilancio e della Programmazione Economica, *Programma Economico Nazionale 1971–75*, 'Allegato Secondo, Programma 1966–70: obiettivi e risultati', Rome 1972.

concessions were intended to run through to the end of 1973. The legislation was changed somewhat in October 1968, limiting the period of operation to the end of 1972, extending the concession to artisans and industrial firms irrespective of size, and reducing it to 10 per cent of earnings instead of the original 12 per cent. Furthermore, the concession, which previously had been paid solely to the employer, was now divided between employer and employee with the former receiving 8·5 percentage points of the 10 per cent and the latter 1·5 percentage points. In addition, and very important, a further supplementary 10 per cent of earnings was conceded to the employer on the earnings of all employees taken on after the end of September 1968 and which increased the total number of employees relative to that date. The system of financing these new concessions remained largely as before. The total cost of the concessions was estimated at some L933 milliard —nearly L300 milliard per annum over the life of the scheme. This is a substantial sum by any standards but its value can probably best be illustrated by the fact that the annual allocation to the *Cassa per il Mezzogiorno* (the main Southern development body) for industrial development purposes was, in the late 1960s, only some L111 milliard.

We have concentrated on the social security concessions for Southern concerns. The point does perhaps need to be made that when the Southern legislation of October 1968 was introduced virtually identical concessions were legislated for the depressed areas of the North. The concessions were, as in the South, 10 per cent of earnings, covered the same industry groups and time period, and were financed in the same way. The concession for additional labour was also the same as that in the South.

Further legislation for the South giving even more generous concessions was introduced in July 1972. This extended the basic 10 per cent concession to the end of 1980 and raised the supplementary concession (for additional labour taken on after 1 January 1971) from 10 per cent to 20 per cent of earnings. Southern firms were also eligible, if in the relevant size group, for the national 5 per cent concession, mentioned earlier, on top of the specifically Southern concessions.

In brief, the current situation in the South is that all industrial and artisan firms receive the equivalent of an annual grant of 10 per cent (or 15 per cent if they have less than 300 employees) of their wages bill net of overtime payments. New firms receive 30 per cent (or 35 per cent) while expanding firms receive 10 (or 15 per cent) plus 20 per cent for wages paid to additional labour taken on after 1 January 1971. Ten percentage points of all these concessions is guaranteed to 1980 while the supplementary payments for additional workers will remain until the next piece of legislation setting new dates for the calculation of 'additional' workers. On past experience this will probably be in 1974.

The regional social security concessions have resulted in a substantial improvement in the value of Italian regional development incentives and are probably greater in value than all the other Italian regional incentives put together. The concessions certainly make the British Regional Employment Premium, indiscriminate between existing and new employment and originally equal to about 7 per cent of earnings and now much lower, seem very weak.

VII—POSTSCRIPT AND SOME CONCLUSIONS

Italian provisions for the elderly, and particularly pensions, have developed rapidly in the post-war period. The extension of pension arrangements to independent workers and the increased coverage of dependent workers now means that virtually the whole Italian labour force is covered by a pension scheme. Pensions have risen rapidly in value and this, combined with increased coverage, has meant a rapid rise in total pension expenditure. On paper, the Italian pension schemes are among the most advanced in Europe. Most pensions are related to terminal income and replace a substantial proportion of earnings. Almost all pension schemes are dynamized for cost-of-living changes.

The Italian pension system has developed under a number of pressures including a genuine political desire to improve pension arrangements but, most important of all, the trade unions have been a major force in pension reform, and indeed social security reform in general. This trade-union pressure has been particularly strong since the mid-1960s. A succession of weak governments, combined with a trade-union movement which was prepared, and organized, to take comprehensive industrial action to secure its aims, are important explanations of recent pension reforms. The Italian trade unions are becoming increasingly concerned with developments

outside the factories. The view that there is no point in improving
conditions in the factory if they are not matched by conditions outside is one which is common among trade-union leaders.

Although the Italian pension schemes are advanced it is expected that the next five years will see further changes. The Government is already committed to increasing the percentage of terminal
earnings replaced by pensions in the general obligatory scheme
from the current 74 per cent to 80 per cent by 1975; but beyond
this the trade unions were, in late 1971, pressing for further reforms and improvements including a change in the system for
the award of the minimum pensions which, as we have seen, differ
according to whether the pensioner is less or more than sixty-five
years of age. The unions wanted this difference abolished. In addition, and more substantial, they wanted the minimum pension
raised to L50,000 per month by 1975 in steady steps, a substantial
revaluation of pensions first paid a number of years ago, and the
tying of pensions to earnings and not only the cost of living.
Pressures for dynamizing pensions with respect to earnings seem
a general European phenomenon. The point need hardly be made
that these demands, if met, would have resulted in an enormous
increase of pension expenditure. The union demands only applied
to the general obligatory schemes though it was expected that if
successful the other pension schemes would, as in the past, follow
suit.

The union demands came during the first quarter of 1972 at a
time when the Government was weak and indeed premature
general elections were held in the spring. No doubt in part an
election measure, the Government drafted a bill on general obligatory pensions which met many of the union demands and became
law in Summer 1972. The main changes introduced were four in
number. First, as from 1 July 1972, the minimum pension was
raised to L32,000 per month for those aged sixty-five and above and
to L30,000 for those below sixty-five.[1] It will be recalled that these
were previously at L26,200 and L24,100 per month. Second, and
much needed even though not included in the union demands, the

---

[1] During the summer of 1972 the minimum pensions for independent workers
were also raised from L18,850, per month to L24,000 per month to take effect
from 1 July 1972. At 1 July 1975 it is intended that the minimum pension for
independent workers will be equal to that in operation at that date for the
general scheme workers.

social pension was increased from L 12,000 to L 18,000 per month from 1 July 1972. From 1 January 1973 the social pension, like the general scheme pension, has been tied to the cost of living. Third, it was agreed to revalorize earlier pensions along the lines suggested by the unions. Pensions paid for the first time before 1952 were to see an increase of 40 per cent, those paid in 1952 38 per cent and coming down by two percentage points per annum until 1968 with an increase of 6 per cent. These increases are, however, not as generous as they might seem at first sight. Many of these pensioners will be on the minimum pension and the percentage increases apply to the pensions before being integrated with the minimum pension. Some pensioners will move above the minimum as a result of these increases but probably the majority will find their positions unchanged, i.e. they will still be at the minimum. The increases will be more important for survivor pensioners than for those on direct pensions. Fourth, the income allowance before pensions are affected was increased as from 1 July 1972 by around 30 per cent per person.[1] and it is intended that this income allowance will in future be increased in line with changes in the cost of living. The income allowance for social pensioners will be similarly treated in respect of the cost of living provision and was raised from L156,000 p.a. to L234,000 p.a. The unions' proposals for dynamizing pensions with respect to earnings have not been accepted though they must nevertheless be reasonably pleased with the new provisions. Few would claim, however, in spite of the Government's generosity, that Italian pensions are still anywhere near adequate. The new provisions do not persuade us to change our conclusions on adequacy in Section VI above. There can be little doubt that the unions will push for further pensions improvements over the next few years.

The Italian pension schemes have numerous features which are different from those in the United Kingdom—an inevitable result of different political, social, historical and economic factors. The pensionable age is lower, most of the schemes have been openly tied to the cost of living for a number of years, payment of pensions is generally made once every two months, the form of the state contribution is fairly unique to Italy, there are heavy contributions made by employers, and disability pensions are an important part

---

[1] See p. 229 for the previous position with respect to income and its effect on pension rights.

of the pension scene. The use of pensions and social security concessions in regional development policy is particularly interesting. These and other features of the Italian schemes, together with the differences between schemes, have been discussed in earlier sections.

The Italians are renowned for the extent to which they criticise, and some would say abuse, their public and semi-public bodies and systems. The pension system and the various pension agencies are not immune from this criticism. Allegations of corruption and misuse of funds are not rare while the criticism of excessive bureaucracy in the administration of pensions is common both in the press and among recipients. The lack of consistency in small details in the various documents required to receive a pension can mean delays which would never be tolerated in the United Kingdom.

At a more substantial level, however, there are a number of major drawbacks and shortcomings of the Italian pension schemes and assistance for the elderly with which we want to end this chapter.

First, the minimum pensions, on which the majority of pensioners have to live, are low by most standards, close to subsistence level if the pensioner lives alone and below it where the pensioner has to live with a dependent. The allowances for a dependent are derisory. To all intents and purposes, the man and wife have to live on the man's pension. It is, perhaps, surprising that attempts have not been made to increase the dependent's allowance substantially or to adopt the United Kingdom scheme of awarding a pension which is considerably higher for a married, as opposed to a single, pensioner. Many Italian pensioners do, of course, live with their children and, seen in this context, the minimum pension becomes more reasonable. It does, however, generally mean that the family has a serious financial burden. Beyond this, the point needs to be made that the massive urbanization of Italian society anticipated over the next decade and the growing proportion of the population living in flats will diminish the extent to which families are capable of taking pensioner parents into their homes without incurring severe difficulties.

Second, nearly three-quarters of a million people are currently having to live on the social pension. With the recent increases, this is now L 234,000 p.a. but still well below what could be considered as adequate. Social pensioners are still not eligible for free medical treatment. The trade unions do not seem actively interested in this group. It is all the more laudable therefore that the Government, in its recent pension proposals, decided to increase the social pension substantially and to tie it to the cost of living. The lot of the social pensioner is nevertheless still miserable and it is not putting it too strongly to say that it is a disgrace that this state of affairs should exist in any Western European country. Of course in time the number of social pensioners is likely to fall since they are largely a reflection of the poor coverage of earlier pension schemes, and particularly the lack of comprehensive independent worker schemes until quite recently. Nevertheless it is likely to be decades until the social pensioner disappears completely.

Third, we have seen that the greater proportion of pension, and indeed social security expenditure in general, is financed by employer contributions. Although opinions differ about the final incidence of these levies they can represent a most inequitable form of indirect tax and, without doubt, have affected Italy's foreign competitiveness. In that they are a nationally uniform levy on labour, they represent a deterrent to the movement and expansion of industry in the South even though this is partially offset by the Southern social security concessions mentioned earlier. Moreover, in that the contributions raise the cost of labour in the 'protected' sector, they impede the eradication of labour market dualism in Italy. The state is intending to take over a larger proportion of pension expenditure. There would be substantial advantages in speeding up this process, not least because as the pension schemes become more mature and larger numbers of workers contribute for longer periods and are therefore eligible for bigger pensions, expenditure on pensions is likely to increase substantially.

Fourth, although the Italians have made considerable improvements in their pension arrangements in the post-war period, they have made few advances in the other aspects of aid for the elderly. A variety of aids which are now well established in the United Kingdom—housing allowances, heating allowances, geriatric hospitals, home helps—are either non-existent in Italy or very poorly developed. The financial problems of Italian local government severely limit the aid that it can give to the elderly. The secular aid bodies which exist in the United Kingdom and which, among other things, help the elderly are very rare in Italy. The religious bodies, though doing good work, are generally recognised as being poorly organized and co-ordinated. It is hoped that over the next few years the service element of state assistance for the elderly will be developed considerably. Whether, after years of neglect, this can be organized in a short period must be open to question. As with many other Italian problems, it is the organization of change rather than the financing of it which often makes for the greatest difficulties.

CHAPTER SIX

France

I—INTRODUCTION

France's pension arrangements are particularly interesting for the light they shed on a question which is central to British policy-making, namely, how to supplement an inadequate state scheme by means of occupational pension schemes. Her occupational or *complementary* schemes have attracted a lot of attention abroad,[1] and they continue to fascinate both the actuary and the social policy-maker. They have, as we shall see, achieved notable success in eliminating many of the problems commonly associated with occupational schemes.

If Italy has the most complex system of pensions in Europe, her closest rival in this respect must surely be France. For not only are there several tiers of pension provision, but each of these tiers comprises numerous schemes covering different occupational groups.

The *General Scheme*—the title represents not so much a fact as an aspiration—provides basic pensions for employees in the private sector of industry and commerce, and for agricultural employees, whose scheme has been almost fully integrated with the General Scheme. For the *self-employed* there are four separate organizations and one of these, which covers the liberal professions, is further subdivided by profession into fifteen schemes. To complete the basic tier there are over *120 special schemes* for employees, predominantly in the public sector. Table 6.1 illustrates in numerical terms the relative importance of these statutory schemes, which

---

[1] The author has benefited greatly from reading Tony Lynes, *French Pensions*, Occasional Paper on Social Administration, No. 21, Bell, London, 1967.

had 20·6 million contributors and 8·3 million pensioners at the beginning of 1970. Of these, 12·2 million were contributing to the General Scheme and 3·2 million were drawing General Scheme pensions.

TABLE 6.1

Coverage of basic pension schemes, 1 January 1970

Scheme	Number of contributors (*1000*)	As per cent of total	Number of pensioners (*1000*)	As per cent of total
General scheme	12,240	59·5	3,183	38·1
Agricultural employees	801	3·9	507	6·1
Sub-total	13,041	63·4	3,690	44·2
SNCF (French railways)	301	1·4	423	5·1
Miners	164	0·8	348	4·1
EGF (electricity and gas)	121	0·6	96	1·1
RATP (Paris transport)	37	0·2	39	0·4
Merchant seamen	79	0·4	81	1·0
Civil servants	1,130	5·5	390	4·7
Military	335	1·6	448	5·4
Local authority staff	497	2·4	189	2·2
State workers	99	0·5	99	1·2
Other special schemes	60	0·3	25	0·3
Special schemes: sub-total	2,823	13·7	2,138	25·5
CANCAVA (artisans)	567	2·8	324	3·9
ORGANIC (traders and small businessmen)	877	4·3	559	6·7
L'beral professions	169	0·8	60	0·7
Farmers	3,090	15·0	1,572	18·9
Self-employed: sub-total	4,703	22·9	2,515	30·2
Grand total	20,569	100·0	8,343	99·9

For those who are covered by the General Scheme there is a second tier consisting of *complementary schemes*. (Special scheme pensions are normally adequate in themselves and the self-employed may make complementary provision within their own statutory schemes.) Two national giants dominate the complementary pension field: AGIRC (*Association Générale des Institutions de Retraites des Cadres*) covers managerial and technical staff in the private sector of industry and commerce, while ARRCO (*Association des Régimes de Retraites Complémentaires*), a federation of some twenty-six schemes, covers workers in this same sector. Certain occupational groups have their own complementary schemes, e.g. foremen in the metal and steel industry, employees of social security organizations, temporary or unestablished state employees, commercial travellers, and bank staff. Agriculture has a complementary structure similar to that in industry, but less complex: one scheme covers managerial and technical staff, another covers agricultural workers and a third provides pensions for employees of the agricultural social security schemes. All these complementary schemes are compulsory. In the autumn of 1972 it was announced by the Government that the complementary system would be extended to cover the small group of private sector employees who still get only one pension. These people number about 0·6 million and are mainly in domestic service.

The third tier comprises *optional complementary schemes* which may take one of two forms. First, firms and employees belonging to one of the complementary schemes mentioned above may choose to contribute more than the compulsory minimum rate. Second, top executives and their employers may also contribute to another type of scheme whose function is to provide pensions based on earnings higher than those covered by the General Scheme or even by AGIRC.

The pension arrangements in France thus ensure that the bulk of the population will have two graduated pensions which will replace substantial proportions of the incomes of those with mature claims. For a variety of reasons there are, however, people with only partial claims or with no claims at all under any of the basic schemes. There are other arrangements designed to provide a floor below which the incomes of the aged should not fall. These arrangements, all of which are means-tested, are complicated. First of all there is the AVTS[1]—an allowance of declining importance but one which is still provided under the General Scheme. Similar allowances are also provided under other basic schemes. These allowances, however, are payable only to those with a record of twenty-five years employment. Second, there is the *special allowance* payable on the same scale as the AVTS to those who have no claims at all under any of the basic schemes. The third arrangement is now the most important quantitatively. This is the provision of *supplementary allowances* which are added to very low pensions in order to lift them to what is described as the

---

[1] See p. 258 below, and 286–7.

social minimum. This is means-tested and administered by the central Government.

Assistance for particular services is also disbursed according to statutory rules by the local authorities: for example, assistance with home helps, residential accommodation, etc. These forms of assistance are collectively described as 'social aid'. Until recently assistance with housing also fell into this category but this in future will be administered centrally. Pensioners are entitled to free medical insurance and social aid helps to meet medical costs not covered by the insurance schemes. It is not easy to put figures on benefits of these kinds, but it is of interest to record that about a quarter of the elderly in France rely wholly or partially on means-tested assistance from central or local Government. Even after a large rise in the autumn of 1972 this means-tested assistance remains modest.

As regards the level of pensions in the various schemes we have mentioned, the situation may be briefly summarized: special scheme pensions in the public sector are extremely good, providing 75 per cent of final salary after thirty-seven-and-a-half years' service; pensions for employees in the private sector are less high but are growing very rapidly with the expansion of the complementary schemes in the 1960s and with recent improvements in the General Scheme; pensions for the self-employed remain very low but reforms have been announced which, it is hoped, will help to rectify this situation. Table 6.2 illustrates the position in 1970: the special schemes, given the number of pensioners they had, accounted for a disproportionately large percentage of total benefits, while a disproportionately small percentage went to the self-employed and to the recipients of the special allowance.

While the *ancien régime* did not have an active social policy it must none the less get credit for France's first official pension fund, set up by Louis XIV for the benefit of retired seamen. It was only after the Revolution that further developments began to take place: an act passed in 1790 created a scheme for civil servants and by 1850 there were also schemes covering the military, the actors of the *Théâtre Français*, employees of the *Banque de France* and of the *Imprimerie Nationale*. At the beginning of the twentieth century schemes were set up for the miners and the railwaymen. It was not until 1948 however that the whole of the working population was covered by pension schemes.

TABLE 6.2

Benefits received by the elderly, 1970
(contributory and means-tested)

Category	No. of pensioners as per cent of total	Benefits as per cent of total	Benefits in millions of francs	Benefits as per cent of GNP at factor cost
Private sector Employees	43·0	44·0	22,677	3·17
of which: General scheme		25·6	13,182	1·84
Complementary schemes		18·4	9,495	1·33
Special schemes	24·9	42·0	21,657	3·03
Self-employed	29·3	12·6	6,463	0·90
Others[1]	2·8	1·4	712	0·10
Total	100·0	100·0	51,509	7·20

Sources: Unpublished figures from the *Commissariat Général du Plan*, OECD National Accounts Statistics.

The first bill proposing compulsory pensions was laid before the Assembly in 1901. At this time the legislature was torn between two conflicting principles: to extend non-contributory means-tested assistance, or to create a system of old age insurance with contributions from employers, employees and the state.[2] The former principle was embodied in the 1905 Act on Assistance for the Aged and Chronically Sick; over 350,000 people, or 15 per cent of the population over seventy, benefited from this measure. An attempt was made in 1910 to apply the second principle when the compulsory Social Insurance Act set up the '*Retraites Ouvrières et Paysannes*' (ROP), to provide pensions for workers and peasants. This measure met with very fierce opposition: for some it was an attack on private property, for others an intolerable burden on producers. The system suffered as a result and never fully recovered from the disruption of World War I.

After the war a durable solution was all the more necessary, as the border territories which France won back from Germany already had had the latter's social insurance system. Although a bill

[1] Those receiving the special allowance. In most cases they also receive the supplementary allowance, and the benefit figures take this into account.
[2] Joseph Flesch, *Les Régimes de Retraite Presses Documentaires*, Paris, 1967.

was laid before the assembly in 1921, it was not until 1930 that a social insurance scheme was finally set up for workers in industry and commerce. The scheme had a contributions and affiliation ceiling; this was approximately equal to the earnings of a skilled worker, and all employees who earned more were excluded from the scheme. Its financial basis was a mixture of funding and pay-as-you-go.

When World War II broke out, pension rights in the new scheme were far from mature, while inflation and disruption were soon to add to the problems of the elderly. In order to help those most in need the Vichy Government introduced in 1941 the *Allocation aux vieux travailleurs salariés* (AVTS), a flat-rate means-tested allowance which was conditional upon twenty-five years' employment.

Shortly after the war ended, pension arrangements were overhauled. Under the terms of an Ordinance published in October 1945, the social insurance scheme set up in 1930 was replaced by a new General Scheme; the agricultural scheme and the special schemes were to remain in existence. The new General Scheme was wholly pay-as-you-go and financed largely by employers' contributions. It had a contributions ceiling, but unlike its predecessor, did not exclude those who earned more. In May 1946 an act was passed whereby the General Scheme was to be extended to the whole of the population. However, this project was abandoned in 1947 'in the face of hostility from the middle classes (i.e. self-employed) and from the right-wing press and political parties'.[1] Separate schemes for the self-employed were not set up until 1948.

The self-employed were not the only group to have reservations about the General Scheme. Civil servants and others covered by special schemes, while not opposed in principle to the idea of 'national solidarity', were certainly not prepared to give up their existing rights for something inferior. Highly paid employees in the private sector would only agree to come into the General Scheme on the express condition that they could set up their own scheme in addition. For if the General Scheme had a low ceiling on contributions and benefits it could not give managerial and technical staff pensions proportionate to their earnings. Some

---

[1] Jean-Jacques Dupeyroux, *Sécurité Sociale*, Dalloz, 1971, p. 275.

of the special schemes also had a ceiling on contributions and benefits, notably that of the miners. Various complementary schemes were subsequently created to compensate for this, covering mining engineers (1948), salaried staff (1949) and miners (1960).

The growth of complementary schemes started in 1947 when AGIRC was set up by national agreement to cover managerial and technical staff. The agreement was signed by the *Conseil National du Patronat Français* (CNPF) and by the various trade unions concerned; its provisions were subsequently rendered compulsory by Government decree in all branches of industry represented in the CNPF. Consequently firms had to honour the agreement even if they were not actually affiliated to the CNPF through an employers' federation. They were free however to join the pension 'fund' of their choice or to set up their own, provided that it was approved by AGIRC and by the Ministry. AGIRC consists of sixty 'funds' or institutions, most of which group together several firms in one or more branches of industry. The scheme is unfunded and its creation opened up a whole new field of actuarial theory and practice.

Complementary pensions were gradually extended to other categories of employees in the private sector, the aim being not so much to compensate for the effects of the General Scheme's ceiling as to make up for its low level of income replacement (maximum of 40 per cent at sixty-five). In 1955 an agreement was signed by unions and management at Renault, an enterprise which since the war has been constantly a pioneer of change. Further developments came in 1957 when a national agreement set up the *Union Nationale des Institutions de Retraite des Salariés* (UNIRS). There was no Government decree making this scheme compulsory but it soon became the largest of the complementary schemes. The final breakthrough was an agreement in 1961 between unions and the CNPF making complementary schemes compulsory in all sectors of industry covered by the CNPF. Like the AGIRC agreement of 1947, this was backed by government decree. The 1961 agreement did not in fact set up a pension scheme but it created the *Association des Régimes de Retraites Complémentaires* (ARRCO), whose role was to control and co-ordinate the finances of both new and existing schemes catering for non-staff employees. AGIRC—the scheme

for managerial and technical staff—remained separate from
ARRCO.

The post-war period has also seen important developments in
national means-tested provisions for the elderly. Minimum allowances similar to the AVTS were incorporated in each of the
various statutory schemes, payable only to people who had worked
for a certain number of years in the sector covered by the scheme.
In 1952 the Special Fund was set up in order to ensure that old
people not eligible for the AVTS, etc., did receive some assistance.
All these allowances were low and their inadequacy was recognized
in 1956 when Mollet's 'Republican Front' Government created a
'*Fonds National de Solidarité*' to pay supplementary allowances
to all elderly people in need.

In 1962 the Laroque Report[1] emphasized the poverty which
many of France's old people still had to endure, and made radical
recommendations on how to improve the situation. While progress
during the 1960s may be noted in many spheres concerning the
elderly, some of the Laroque Report's recommendations were
ignored, so that various criticisms made in 1962 remain valid in the
1970s.

II—PENSIONS FOR EMPLOYEES IN THE PRIVATE SECTOR

People who have retired from employment in the private sector[2]
may receive *two* pensions, one from the General Scheme and one
from a complementary scheme. A small proportion of employees
in the private sector are not yet covered by complementary schemes,
notably domestic servants.

The general scheme

Pensions in the General Scheme are graduated and their value
depends basically on three factors: the age at which the pension is
drawn, the length of time the individual has been insured, and his
pre-retirement earnings. They are not subject to any retirement

---

[1] *Politique de la vieillesse : Rapport de la Commission d'Étude des Problèmes de la
Vieillesse*. La Documentation Française, 1962.

[2] Excluding miners and seamen, who have their own special schemes.

condition. Pensions may be awarded as from age sixty, but their value is doubled if they are not drawn until sixty-five, and is further increased for people retiring later. Thirty years' insurance entitles the individual to a pension equal to 20 per cent of pre-retirement earnings at sixty, 40 per cent at sixty-five or 60 per cent at seventy; i.e. an additional 1 per cent is awarded for every three months over the age of sixty. The same rules regarding age apply to men and to women. Although the General Scheme dates from 1945, contributions paid to the old social insurance scheme set up in 1930 are taken into account in calculating pensions. Consequently it was in the 1960s that people started to draw the full 40 per cent pension.

To qualify for a pension the insured must have contributed for at least fifteen years. The amount of the pension is directly proportional to the period of insurance, e.g. thirty years yields a 40 per cent pension at sixty-five, fifteen years a 20 per cent pension. Until 1971, however, periods of insurance in excess of thirty years conferred no additional pension rights, so that the maximum pension at sixty-five was 40 per cent. By 1975, however, up to thirty-seven-and-a-half years' insurance will be counted, thereby making the maximum pension at sixty-five equal to 50 per cent of pre-retirement earnings.

In France it is an accepted principle that pensions should be related to earnings, but how this is done raises interesting questions. In the General Scheme pensions are calculated as a percentage of average income during the ten years preceding retirement or during the ten years preceding the age of sixty, whichever is greater; before the averages are calculated each year's money income is revalued to take account of the general rise in earnings. Where a man's earnings over the ten years before retirement have risen in line with the national average, his personal average on which the pension is based is the same as his earnings in the final year. Having thus abstracted from the general rise in earnings we may now ask what are the advantages or disadvantages for the pensioner of basing the pension on earnings so late in life. Most white-collar workers will benefit since they continue to rise in the earnings 'hierarchy' until retirement. However, this is not the case for many manual workers whose earnings between the ages of twenty and forty (when revalued) would be greater than those between fifty and sixty. This problem of inequity is not encountered in the German scheme, for example, as its pensions are based on earnings (appropriately revalued) throughout the individual's working life, nor does the problem arise in the French complementary schemes which operate a system of pension points described on pp. 272–274.

It is understandable that French trade unions should recently have been voicing concern over the method employed by the General Scheme to calculate pensions. They have suggested that pensions be based not on the ten last years' but on the ten *best* years' earnings, revalued, of course, in line with the general rise in earnings. Although initially opposed to the idea on the grounds of administrative complexity, the Government declared itself in favour in the autumn of 1972 and the proposal may be implemented by 1974.

The earnings used to calculate the pension may not exceed the contributions ceiling, equivalent to about 135 per cent of average earnings of manual workers. This rule will also apply under the new system.

The General Scheme therefore provides pensions related to the individual's income (subject to a ceiling), to his length of insurance (subject to a maximum of 37·5 years and a minimum of 15) and to the age at which the pension is drawn, with the minimum age set at sixty. Table 6.3 shows pension as a percentage of pre-retirement earnings in various cases.

TABLE 6.3

General Scheme pensions as a percentage of pre-retirement earnings

	Period of insurance		
	15 years (per cent)	30 years (per cent)	37·5 years[1] (per cent)
Pension drawn at age			
60	10	20	25
65	20	40	50
70	30	60	75

[1] Not applicable until 1975. See p. 261.

Pensions are basically calculated in the way described above, but there are three cases in which the pension may be increased: where the insured has brought up three or more children; where the insured has a dependent wife or husband; where the insured is in need of constant help and attention. The pension is increased by 10 per cent when the insured has had three or more children. Also taken into account are children who have been dependent upon the insured for at least nine years before their sixteenth birthday. If both the husband and wife receive a contributory pension, each benefits from this 10 per cent increase.

An allowance may be paid in respect of a dependant spouse. This is a flat rate payment which has been fixed at the same value as the allowance known as the AVTS[1], i.e. 1,850F per annum in 1971. It is not paid if the *personal* income of the spouse exceeds a certain amount (3,050F per annum in 1971).

A pensioner who is an invalid and unable to look after himself may receive in addition to his pension an allowance towards the cost of constant attention. In October 1970 this amounted to 9357F per year: it is revalued annually in exactly the same way as pensions, as indeed it would have to be in order to fulfil its function. An applicant for such an allowance must satisfy the given medical requirements between the age of sixty and sixty-five. If the application is made after sixty-five, it is dealt with at the local level by social aid,[2] which involves a means test.

There are three cases where the basic pension is not determined in the usual way: where the pensioner has previously been in receipt of an invalidity pension; where the pensioner is classed as unfit to work, or has worked in a particularly arduous job for at least twenty years; where the pension of a recipient aged sixty-five or over calculated in the usual way is less than the AVTS. In these cases the pensions awarded are known as 'revised' pensions. At the age of sixty the invalidity pension is replaced by an old-age pension: the latter must be no less than the former, which for the seriously disabled is 50 per cent of previous earnings. At the very least it will be equal to the AVTS. As may be seen from Table 6.5, old-age pensions which replace invalidity pensions are on average the highest pensions paid by the General Scheme.

The 'full' pension of 40 per cent of previous earnings may be awarded to any individual between the ages of sixty and sixty-five

---

[1] *Allocation aux vieux travailleurs salariés*: see Section IV. *Note that the AVTS is adjusted in an arbitrary fashion.* While pensions were increased by 10·1 per cent and 11·5 per cent in 1971 and 1972, the AVTS was increased by 6 per cent and 5·6 per cent.

[2] The social aid allowance varies in size, being smaller where help is provided by a member of the invalid's family, and smaller still where several members of the family share the work.

K

who is classed as unfit to work or who has worked in a particularly arduous job for at least twenty years. This provision was extended in 1971 to take into account certain non-medical considerations, e.g. an individual might be awarded a full pension early if the economic situation and the state of the labour market made it impossible for him to find work. The notion of unfitness or *'in-aptitude'* has therefore become more flexible and each case is considered on its own merits. Since the 1971 reform it is no longer possible for persons certified as unfit to go back to work and earn unlimited amounts: payment of the pension from 1972 onwards is suspended if the recipient's earnings exceed 50 per cent of the minimum wage (SMIC), equal to 8,195F per annum in January 1972.

It is conceivable that an individual's pension when calculated in the usual way may turn out to be less than the AVTS (1,850F per annum in 1971) if he has been insured for little more than fifteen years. The pension is adjusted upwards to the level of the AVTS provided the recipient is aged sixty-five or over. Persons insured for less than fifteen years do not qualify. This minimum pension, being fixed to the AVTS, is less well dynamized than pensions as a whole, and in recent years has failed to keep pace with the rise in average earnings. It should be emphasized, however, that the minimum contributory pension is not really the safety net. As was mentioned in the introduction, there is a means-tested social minimum which is not only substantially higher than the 'minimum pension' but has recently been rising much faster.

Survivors' pensions. These may be paid to the widow or widower of an insured person. They are 50 per cent of the direct pension when this has already been drawn at the time of the insured person's death. If death occurs before the age of sixty-five and before any pension has been drawn, the survivor's pension is calculated as 50 per cent of the pension which would have been awarded at sixty-five. When the individual dies after sixty-five without having drawn his pension, the survivor's pension is calculated on the basis of the pension the insured person would have received at the time of his death.

Payment of a survivor's pension is subject to strict conditions. It may be noted, in particular that the survivor must be aged sixty-five or over, or else must be at least sixty and classed as unfit to work. (Another type of pension is payable to survivors under sixty who are invalids.)[1]

Finance. The General Scheme is financed solely by contributions from employers and employees. These contributions are a percentage of total earnings up to a certain ceiling which is approximately 135 per cent of average earnings. The percentage rate has varied according to the scheme's financial commitments: it was 9 per cent in 1946, 6·8 per cent in 1953, 5 per cent in 1958, 8·75 per cent in 1971, and it was to rise again to 9 per cent in 1973. Of the 8·75 per cent employers pay 5·75 per cent and employees 3 per cent. There are no state subsidies; in fact the scheme is obliged to use some of its contribution income to subsidize other schemes (10 per cent of its total expenditure in 1970), and to subsidize the supplementary allowance (representing a further 5 per cent of expenditure in 1970). The former obligation is partly justified as the General Scheme is favoured with a high ratio of contributors to pensioners, reflecting the movement of labour into industry. In 1970 two thirds of the scheme's revenue came from employers, and one third from employees' contributions.

Like virtually all French pension schemes, basic and complementary, the General Scheme is unfunded. One of the main advantages of pay-as-you-go is that when a new scheme is introduced or an existing one made more generous pensions may be paid in excess of what would be justified by contributions made in the

[1] The other conditions are: the survivor must be dependent upon the insured person at the time of the latter's death; in practice this means that the survivor's income at that time must not exceed the minimum wage (SMIC) which in January 1972 stood at 8,195F per annum. Prior to a reform in 1971 survivors were considered ineligible for a pension if their personal income was more than 3,050F per annum. Until 1971 a survivor's pension could not be paid to anyone in receipt of another social security benefit. Consequently 45 per cent of the widows whose husbands had been covered by the General Scheme did not qualify for a survivor's pension, as they already had pensions in their own right. They were however free to choose whichever benefit was more valuable, but it was unlikely that either would amount to much: the direct pension would usually be low because of a short period of insurance and low earnings, while the survivor's pension amounted at best to 20 per cent of the husband's earnings. A reform introduced in 1971 partially abolished this frustrating rule. The couple must have been married at least two years before the insured person drew his pension. If this is not so, no survivor's rights may exist until four years after the marriage. However, the regulations are lenient in one respect: remarriage does not affect a widow's pension.

past. However the General Scheme and the other new statutory schemes made only a limited use of this possibility of blanketing-in. Pensions in the General Scheme were related to the period over which contributions had actually been paid, but as contributions to the old social insurance scheme (1930–45) were also taken into account, some people were able to start drawing full pensions in the 1960s.

All this raises an interesting moral question. What in fact the General Scheme did was to commit future generations to paying the pensions of the post-war working generation while failing to impose on the latter the same obligation *vis-à-vis* their elders. For many years after the war the elderly received partial pensions and meagre allowances. The General Scheme therefore had the choice either of reducing contributions or building up a fund: as we have seen it opted for the former approach. Only two years later A G I R C, a private scheme, showed a greater sense of social fairness by awarding pensions to employees who had never contributed. The A R R C O schemes were to evolve a similar system of credited contributions. The General Schemes set up in Germany and Belgium in the 1950s also had blanketing-in. The 'morality of pay-as-you-go' seems therefore to have evolved since the French General Scheme was established in 1945, although in Britain the Crossman Plan in 1969 ascribed only limited importance to such considerations, preferring for other reasons to build up a large fund.

It might be objected that in a pay-as-you-go scheme one generation is bound to get something for nothing and that which-ever one it is has nothing to do with morality. This ignores the question of which generation is setting up the scheme. Further-more it is often argued that the present elderly generation is a specially deserving case for historical reasons, that having suffered hardship during two wars and the Depression they should be given a larger share in current prosperity. The debate will no doubt continue but what is most important is that a moral issue should be seen to exist and should be distinguished from other considerations, e.g. supply of capital, rate of growth, labour costs, competitiveness of exports, etc.

Dynamism. Pensions in the General Scheme are raised annually to reflect the rise in average earnings. Contributions are a percentage of earnings up to the social security ceiling (which also rises in line with earnings) so that when earnings rise there is a commensurate increase in the scheme's income from contributions. The scheme's resources are consequently sufficient to raise pensions in the same proportion, provided that the ratio of pensioners to contributors does not rise. When this ratio does rise the deficit may be covered by raising contribution rates, or by allowing pensions to rise less rapidly than average earnings.

The annual rise in pensions is determined by the annual rise in the amount of sickness benefit paid out daily to the average claimant. Sickness benefit is based on the individual's earnings so that it tends to reflect the growth in average earnings. (It is a convenient measure for the Ministry of Social Security to use.) The Government introduced this system in 1965, as the previous system had led to pension rises of 16 per cent, 12 per cent and 11 per cent in 1963, 1964, and 1965 respectively. During the first few years of the present system the annual increases dropped to 6·9 per cent, 5·8 per cent and 5·6 per cent (1966–68) but since then they have been about 10 per cent or 11 per cent. On the whole the rise in pensions has compared favourably with the rise in earnings, as may be seen from Chart 8.

The social security ceiling—i.e. the ceiling for income on which contributions may be levied and pensions based—is not dynamized according to the same criterion[1] and over the years has tended to rise slightly less than pensions.[2] Furthermore it is not adjusted at the same time of year. The effect this has on certain pensions may be seen in the following example:

In March 1971 A's pension was 7,600F per annum. As from 1 April pensions were raised by 10·10 per cent, which would have made A's pension equal to 8,367·60F. However, assuming that A retired at the age of 65, he could not receive a pension which exceeded 40 per cent of the social security ceiling which was 19,800F: thus 40 per cent of 19,800 = 7,920F. A's pension therefore rose a mere 4·2 per cent and it was not until 1 January 1972, when the social security ceiling was increased to 21,960, that A could get the rest of his rise.

---

[1] It is revalued in line with an average earnings index produced by the Ministry of Labour.

[2] Pension rises 1963–70 (per cent):   16 12 11 6·9 5·8 5·6 11·5   11·9
Rises in ceiling 1963–70 (per cent):   8   9   7 5   5   5   13   10·3.

Pensions in payment. On 1 July 1971 over 3 million persons were receiving a pension or allowance from the General Scheme, of whom ¾ million were also getting the assistance payment known as the supplementary allowance. The latter group is examined in Section IV. A frequency distribution of the values of pensions paid to the other 2½ million pensioners is given in Table 6.4.

TABLE 6.4

Frequency distribution of pension values in the General Scheme on 1 July 1971 (excluding recipients of the supplementary allowance)

Value of pensions: francs per annum	No. of pensions as per cent of total	Cumulative total
0–1,750	21·09	21·09
1,750–2,499	17·47	38·56
2,500–3,249	8·86	47·42
3,250–3,999	9·38	56·80
4,000–4,749	7·60	64·40
4,750–5,599	6·73	71·13
5,600–6,399	5·46	76·59
6,400–7,124	4·47	81·06
7,125–7,920	7·10	88·16
7,920 and over	11·84	100·00
Total	100·00	

Source: *Ministère de la Santé Publique et de la Sécurité Sociale.*

Many of the pensions in Table 6.4 are low as they are for people with short periods of insurance in the General Scheme who receive either a small pension, a very small annuity or an allowance. When interpreting Table 6.4 the existence of the means-tested social minimum and its level (3,250F in July 1971, 4,500F in October 1972) should of course be borne in mind. Clearly the 47 per cent of pensioners receiving less than 3,250F from the General Scheme either had another pension or some other non-pension income, *if we assume full uptake of means-tested benefits.* (The French seem much less concerned about people failing to apply for benefit than the British; little is known about the extent of the problem, if indeed there is one.) Table 6.4 also includes survivors' pensions, which, it will be recalled, are only 50 per cent of direct pensions.

Table 6.5 gives a more detailed picture by showing average pensions in various narrowly defined categories. These are expressed in money terms and also as a percentage of average gross earnings of manual workers, equal to 14,681F per annum in 1971.

TABLE 6.5

Average pensions in the General Scheme 1971 (estimates)
(including the supplementary allowance)

Category	Francs per annum	Percentage of average earnings (of manual workers)	Approximate number of beneficiaries (thousands)
Complete career pensions (i.e. 40 per cent of salary)	5,740	39	860
All direct pensions	4,800	33	1,200
Old age pensions replacing invalidity pensions	6,060	41	280
'Inaptitude' pensions	4,700	32	300
AVTS	3,040	21	160
All direct pensions and allowances	4,200	29	2,400
Normal direct pensions drawn in 1971 for the first time	6,000	41	n.a.

Source: *Ministère de la Santé Publique et de la Sécurité Sociale.*

It should be noted that Table 6.5, unlike Table 6.4, includes the supplementary allowance; however, in only one of the categories listed, AVTS recipients, is there a significant proportion of benefits (30 per cent) paid in the form of supplementary allowances. Complete career pensions are for people with at least thirty years' insurance. The second category ('all direct pensions') includes complete career pensions and also pensioners with fifteen to thirty years' insurance, but excludes $\frac{1}{2}$ million people whose pensions have been adjusted upwards to the level of the AVTS. These $\frac{1}{2}$ million people who receive minimum pensions are not listed separately but are included in the category 'all direct pensions and allowances'.

Pensions statistics must clearly be interpreted with care. They may include pensions paid by the General Scheme to individuals who have worked only a short time in private industry and have pension rights elsewhere. They give only a rough guide to income replacement levels, as was seen above. The figures are also inadequate when it is a question of adding the complementary pension to the basic, as the information available allows the combination to be expressed only as a single average, and not as a frequency distribution.

A second approach is to use the pension formulae to show what pensions would be as a percentage of earnings in various cases. This enables us to bypass many of the difficulties outlined above, and yields a detailed picture of whatever case we choose to examine. The weakness of this approach is clearly that it cannot tell us how many people fall into the various categories. This method is applied in Tables 6.6 and 6.7 when we consider the pensioner's combined income from the general and complementary schemes.

The complementary schemes

The French complementary schemes are of great importance to employees in the private sector and are unique in many respects. They may be distinguished from private schemes in other countries mainly by the fact that they are unfunded. It might even be argued that they are not private schemes at all since the initial agreements between the employers' association and the unions concerning coverage and minimum contribution rates were backed by Government decree. On the other hand the Government has no right to interfere with the running of the schemes. All decisions are taken by boards of management which consist of equal numbers of employers' and employees' representatives.

This formula of equal representation, known as *paritarisme*, is applied throughout the field of complementary social provision.[1] Since the social security reforms of 1967 it has also applied to the statutory schemes which were previously run by boards composed of three employees to one employer. Attitudes to *paritarisme* vary: employers are satisfied with it on the whole and some of the unions, e.g. *Force Ouvrière, Confédération Générale des Cadres,* regard it as a good framework for social progress. The largest trade union organizations, the *Confédération Générale du Travail* (CGT) and the *Confédération Française Démocratique des Travailleurs* (CFDT) dislike the formula, but co-operate in running the system.

Two pension associations cover the vast majority of employees in the private sector: the *Association des Régimes de Retraites Complémentaires* (ARRCO), and the *Association Générale des Institutions de Retraites des Cadres* (AGIRC). ARRCO covers manual and lower grades and had 8·8 million contributors and $3\frac{1}{4}$

---

[1] This principle is also applied in the Netherlands and Germany with, in some cases, an additional member to represent the Government.

million pensioners at the end of 1969, while AGIRC covers technical and managerial staff and had 1 million contributors and 326,000 pensioners on that date.[1]

Complementary pension schemes now cover all employees in the General Scheme aged twenty-one or over, except for domestic servants (500,000) and some employees in the retail trade (100,000). According to a Government policy statement in the autumn of 1972 the complementary schemes will be extended to cover those people in the near future. Until now the rule of the state with regard to complementary schemes has been to put its seal on collective bargains struck between unions and management. The domestic service sector, with almost as many employers as employees and with little organization on either side, may well pose problems in this respect. It seems likely that state intervention will have to be more positive than in the past.

Within the federal structure of the complementary schemes there are various administrative levels. At the bottom are the individual pension *institutions* which collect contributions and pay out pensions. These institutions belong to a *scheme* which consists only of a number of institutions which apply the same rules. Examples of such schemes are AGIRC and the *Union Nationale des Institutions de Retraites des Salariés* (UNIRS). They are to be distinguished from ARRCO which groups together schemes (including UNIRS) whose rules are not identical. ARRCO itself is not a scheme but a *federation* of schemes. Its task is primarily to ensure the financial co-ordination of the various member schemes.

The finances of a pay-as-you-go scheme are sensitive to changes in the ratio of pensioners to contributors and it is to minimize fluctuations in this ratio that the French schemes have joined together in large associations such as ARRCO, AGIRC or UNIRS. Individual institutions covering only one firm or industry would clearly face severe problems were that firm or industry to go into decline. Both ARRCO and AGIRC offer a very high degree of protection since they cover so many sectors of industry. However, the ratio of pensioners to contributors is affected by movements of labour not only between sectors but also between grades. The latter movements tend to be from manual to white collar grades and they benefit AGIRC at the expense of ARRCO. If, as seems likely, this trend continues, some sort of compensation

---

[1] Rapports des commissions du 6ᵉ plan, 'Personnes âgées'.

between AGIRC and ARRCO will be necessary to ensure ARRCO's solvency.[1] However, pensions in AGIRC differ widely from those paid by the ARRCO schemes, so that creating a financial link may pose certain problems.

The three pension associations mentioned above operate a system of transfers between member schemes or institutions, which we term interscheme compensation. These transfers correct for differences in the ratio of contributors to pensioners; a scheme or institution with a lower than average ratio receives compensation, while one with a higher than average ratio pays out compensation. UNIRS operates transfers between its own member institutions and at the same time participates in the ARRCO system of interscheme compensation, so that in this case the process takes place at two levels.

When a pension scheme is graduated there is the problem of how pensions should be related to earnings. In the complementary schemes the individual's pension depends on the number of points he has accumulated. As explained below, the effect of this system is to relate pensions to average career earnings, revalued in line with the general rise in earnings. Points may either have been purchased by contributions or credited for periods of employment prior to the scheme's creation. The value of the pension point in terms of francs per annum is fixed each year according to the total number of points the scheme will have to service. Every year projections are made of the scheme's commitments over the next ten years and the value of the point is decided in the light of these projections. The value of the point in UNIRS and in AGIRC has tended to rise almost as fast as earnings and substantially faster than retail prices.[2]

The amount of money required to purchase a point rises in line with earnings, the aim being to award the same number of points in every year to a person with average earnings. The points system is similar to that used by the general schemes in Germany, as it measures the individual's position in the earnings structure during each year of his working life. This is thought by some to be more

---

[1] It was suggested in *Le Monde* (15 April 1972) that discussions on this matter would soon take place between the CNPF and the trade unions.

[2] In UNIRS, the value of the point rose from 100 in 1958 to 220 in 1970. Average earnings had risen from 100 to 246 and prices from 100 to 164. For AGIRC, the value of the point rose from 100 in 1953 to 336 in 1970. The median salary had then risen to 385 and prices to 206.

equitable than basing the pension on the relative position of the individual at the end of his career, as the earnings of a manual worker as a percentage of average earnings tend to decline when he grows older, while those of the professional tend to rise or at least remain constant. The points system is more 'neutral' in this sense than the system used by the French General Scheme, or indeed any final-pay system.

In AGIRC contributions are paid only in respect of income between the General Scheme's ceiling and a maximum amount equal to about four times this ceiling. The minimum contribution rate laid down in the 1947 agreement is 8 per cent, of which 6 per cent is paid by the employer and 2 per cent by the employee. Under the ARRCO agreement a contribution equal to 4 per cent of all earnings.[1] must be made towards complementary pensions for manual grades. AGIRC consequently introduced a minimum contributions guarantee for its lower paid members: this ensures that the total contribution will amount to at least 8 per cent of earnings above the General Scheme ceiling plus 4 per cent of earnings below it, thereby eliminating the possibility of an employee being better off in ARRCO than in AGIRC. Various firms have recently also chosen to contribute 4 per cent on earnings below the General Scheme ceiling. This improves their employees' pensions significantly as is shown by the figures in brackets in Table 6.6.

Subject to agreement between employer and employees, any firm may opt for a higher contribution rate; above 8 per cent the contribution is shared equally by employer and employees. It has been thought desirable to have a maximum rate which is set at 16 per cent. Most firms opt to contribute at or near the maximum; in 1970 the average rate was 14 per cent.

The value of a person's pension depends on the number of points he has to his credit so that there is no direct link between final earnings and the pension. The level of income replacement provided by an AGIRC pension can only be calculated given certain information about the individual's earnings profile over his working life. Some examples are given in Table 6.6 where pension is expressed as a percentage of final salary. We assume a working life of thirty-nine years and a 16 per cent contribution to AGIRC. Table 6.6 also shows the basic pension which will be paid by the

---

[1] I.e. *all* earnings up to ARRCO ceiling—see page 275.

General Scheme from *1975* onwards when pensions will be based on up to thirty-seven-and-a-half years' insurance.

TABLE 6.6

Pensions in AGIRC: some examples

| Earnings profile | Pension as per cent of final salary | | |
	AGIRC	General scheme	Total
Always earns 150 per cent General Scheme ceiling	27 (39)[1]	34	61 (73)
Starts earning 150 per cent and finishes at 300 per cent G.S. ceiling	32 (38)	16	48 (54)
Starts earning 150 per cent and finishes at 500 per cent G.S. ceiling	31 (34)	10	41 (44)

Source: *ARRCO Bulletin*, June 1971, No. 20.

The average direct pension paid by AGIRC in 1971 was about 13,700F per year. (This figure does not include certain junior employees covered by AGIRC under special provisions contained in article 36 of the 1947 agreement.) In 1971 the General Scheme ceiling was 19,800F, which meant that the maximum pension at sixty-five was 7,920F. For the average member of AGIRC, therefore, the complementary pension greatly outweighs the basic pension.

Although it was set up in 1947 AGIRC awards pension points in respect of employment dating back to 1918, provided that the post was of the type covered by AGIRC.[2] In spite of these generous blanketing-in arrangements AGIRC accumulated a large surplus in its early years of operation. This may be partly explained by the absence of well developed actuarial techniques suited to the pay-as-you-go form of financing. In addition some people may have remained unaware of their pension rights or may

[1] Pension, when 4 per cent contribution is paid on earnings below General Scheme ceiling.

[2] For the period 1936–47 points are awarded on the basis of the individual's actual earnings at that time and the rate at which his firm *currently* contributes. Full allowance is made for any drop in earnings directly caused by the war. The average annual number of points awarded for the years 1936–47 is also awarded for each year of employment prior to 1936. The individual is obliged to furnish proof of his occupation. Where he worked with a firm that no longer exists, the assumed contribution rate is 8 per cent.

have been unable to produce evidence of employment. By 1952 the surplus was deemed excessive and AGIRC decided to collect only a proportion of the normal contributions. This proportion was drastically reduced in the last quarter of 1952 to 25 per cent. It was raised to 80 per cent in 1953 and gradually returned to 100 per cent by 1966. The contributions not collected during this period may be thought of as having been 'deferred', as AGIRC still has the right to require payment. The amounts involved are expressed not in money terms but as a percentage of the firm's annual contribution. The total amount not collected between 1952 and 1966 is almost two years' contributions. While member firms may be required to pay off this 'debt', the scheme may not demand more than 10 per cent extra contributions per year; repayment would therefore be spread over almost twenty years.

While pensions in AGIRC depend primarily on contributions, actual or credited, certain other factors may influence the amount of pension paid. If the individual has supported three or more children for at least nine years he receives a bonus of between 10 per cent and 30 per cent of his pension (depending upon the number of children). This is in recognition of the fact that men with large families are less able to save for their old age. If a person was born before 1895 he gets a small bonus for each year of employment after 1918. This is to help compensate for the effects of disallowing employment prior to 1918.

The normal pension age is sixty-five but reduced pensions may be paid as early as fifty-five. The pension paid at fifty-five is based on 43 per cent of the points which the individual has to his credit; the corresponding figure at age sixty is 78 per cent. The General Scheme makes early retirement less attractive, as a pension at sixty is only 50 per cent of that awarded at sixty-five.

The *ARRCO* schemes, which cover most of the other employees in industry and commerce, differ from AGIRC in that contributions are paid on earnings below as well as above the General Scheme ceiling. ARRCO's own ceiling is three times that of the General Scheme. The minimum contribution rate laid down in the national agreement is 4 per cent. This rate is rising to 4·4 per cent between 1971 and 1974 as ARRCO is faced with adverse demographic trends during the 1970s; the extra 0·4 per cent which has been agreed upon by employers and employees will confer no extra pension rights on those affected.

ARRCO itself resulted from the National Agreement of 1961 and its sphere of action is determined by that agreement and by subsequently agreed modifications. The agreement did not set up a pension scheme but allowed firms to join the scheme of their choice, on condition that the scheme in question then became affiliated to ARRCO and complied with the nationally agreed provisions. Membership of ARRCO does not mean that a scheme or institution must deal solely with ARRCO business.[1]

As in AGIRC, individual firms may opt to pay higher rates of contribution. In 1968 the average rate was 4·6 per cent. About three-quarters of the contributors paid the minimum 4 per cent, about a fifth paid 5·8 per cent and just under 1 per cent paid over 8 per cent.

The tendency shown by most firms belonging to ARRCO to remain at or near the minimum rate is in contrast with AGIRC where most firms choose the maximum rate. This difference may arise partly from the desire of the more highly paid employees who belong to AGIRC to minimize their life-time tax bill by deferring until old age as much income as possible.

Pensions in the ARRCO schemes are much smaller than in AGIRC as both earnings and contribution rates are lower. The average direct pension (excluding females) paid by UNIRS in 1971 was 1,510F per annum. (UNIRS accounts for just over half the total number of ARRCO pensioners.) What the pension represents as a percentage of final pay depends, as in AGIRC, on the individual's earnings profile. Table 6.7 illustrates this where working life is forty-four years and the contribution rate 4 per cent. The General Scheme pension is also shown (1975 onwards).

The average direct pension in UNIRS of 1,510F per annum is only 10 per cent of average earnings: this figure is not directly comparable with those given in Table 6.7 which give pensions in year $n + 1$ as a percentage of earnings in year n. However it is clear that even deflated for a year's rise in earnings the figures in the table are still well over 10 per cent. The smallness of this figure may be explained, at least partly, by the fact that many pensioners

---

[1] Many institutions deal with non-ARRCO business of three types: transactions with firms belonging to ARRCO which make supplementary contribution in excess of the ARRCO minimum, transactions concerning employees in grades not covered by the 1961 agreement, and transactions with firms belonging to sectors not covered by the CNPF. The interscheme compensation operated by ARRCO does not concern transactions in these three categories.

TABLE 6.7

Pensions in ARRCO: some examples

| Earnings profile | Pension as per cent of final pay | | |
	ARRCO	General Scheme	Total
Always earns 80 per cent General Scheme ceiling	24	50	74
Starts earning 60 per cent and finishes at 100 per cent G.S. ceiling	16	47	63
Starts earning 60 per cent and finishes at 150 per cent G.S. ceiling	14	34	48

Source: ARRCO.

will not have been employed in private industry for as long as forty-four years (the movement of labour away from agriculture and self-employment into private industry is clearly relevant in this context); furthermore an increasing number of people are retiring earlier on a reduced pension.

It will be noted that we have talked of a pensioner who has been *employed* for forty-four years rather than of one who has *contributed* over that period. Were complementary pensions to be based on contributions paid, then clearly most schemes would not be awarding full pensions until after the year 2000. However ARRCO schemes have generous blanketing-in for people who were in employment before ARRCO existed, and that even includes those already in retirement who have paid nothing at all in contributions.

UNIRS, like the other ARRCO schemes, has a system of credited contributions similar in principle to that in AGIRC. The number of points awarded for each year's employment in a member firm before the firm joined UNIRS is equal to a 'reference average' multiplied by the rate at which the firm contributes. 'The reference average is the annual average number of points for a 1 per cent contribution awarded to the individual between the time he joined UNIRS and his fifty-fifth birthday.'[1] Where this period is less than three years and where a person was fifty-five or over before joining UNIRS, a similar but hypothetical calculation is made to determine the average.

---

[1] Article 21 of the *Règlement* of UNIRS.

Pensioners born before 1 April 1886 benefit not only from credited contributions—few are likely to have contributed to UNIRS at all—but also from a 20 per cent bonus in view of their age. Statistics published in the UNIRS Bulletin in January 1972 show that the average pension being paid in 1971 to the over-eighty-fives was indeed higher than the average for all male pensioners.

Additional payments are made to pensioners who have dependent children under twenty; the pension is increased by 10 per cent for each child. Widows of men covered by UNIRS receive a pension equal to 60 per cent of their husband's pension or pension rights. To qualify a widow must either be aged fifty or over, or an invalid, or caring for two children. These conditions, which are similar in almost all the complementary schemes, are much less restrictive than in the General Scheme.

Many of the schemes which joined ARRCO were in existence before 1961 and operated under a variety of different rules. The amount of pension they provided for a given contribution also varied widely, sometimes because of demographic disparities, sometimes because of short-sighted financial management. *ARRCO's aim was not to abolish the variety of schemes but to ensure that for a given contribution each scheme gave benefits of an equivalent amount.* This standard amount is determined for ARRCO as a whole in the light of long-term financial and demographic projections. For the individual schemes it is expressed as a standard set of rules regarding benefits (*'règlement type'*). When interscheme transfers are being calculated it is not the actual benefits paid by a scheme which are taken into account, but the benefits which would have been paid had the standard rules been applied. For each scheme an amount x $(+)$ or $(-)$ is calculated such that:

$$\frac{p + x}{c} = \frac{P}{C}$$

where p is the pensions which the scheme would have paid under standard rules, c is the contributions received by the scheme, P is total pensions which all ARRCO schemes would have paid under standard rules, C is total contributions received by all ARRCO schemes.

When $p + x$ have been deducted from c, 90 per cent of the remainder must be paid into a reserve fund, called the *'réserve de solidarité'*. This leaves the scheme with only 10 per cent of $c - (p + x)$ at its disposal. If the scheme pays benefits in excess of those provided for under the standard rules, that excess cannot be greater than 10 per cent of $c - (p + x)$ without causing the scheme to dip into its own reserves or to run a deficit. Thus schemes are eventually forced into giving equivalent value for money, but they are still free to formulate their own rules and consequently to allocate benefits as they wish, e.g. regulations concerning direct pensions, special bonuses, widows' and widowers' pensions, and provisions for orphans are left to the discretion of the individual scheme.

The French complementary schemes boast certain refinements not normally found in private schemes. Thus they have an agreement with the unemployment insurance scheme U N E D I C under which UNEDIC pays the contributions of employees who are receiving unemployment insurance benefit. Moreover the probationary period for a new member is extremely short, e.g. a *month* is the maximum permitted by UNIRS; there is then full vesting of pension rights. These provisions facilitate labour mobility, as do the administrative arrangements for drawing a pension. The retiring employee need only fill up one application no matter how many firms he has worked for, provided that he has always worked in sectors and grades covered by ARRCO. The application is sent to the scheme to which he currently belongs and is then passed on to the other schemes concerned. Where the individual had been a member of different schemes he would receive separate payments from each scheme. If, however, he had been insured by various institutions all belonging to one scheme, e.g. UNIRS, he would receive his entire pension from the last institution.

Among the complementary pension schemes and associations which we have not mentioned is the scheme for employees in agriculture. In 1966 an agreement was signed which set up the *Association Nationale pour la Coordination et al Compensation des retraites complémentaires* (ANCORA). Prior to 1956 there had been two complementary schemes in the agricultural sectors, one covering the employees of the agricultural social security scheme, another—the agricultural counterpart of AGIRC—covering managerial staff. ANCORA opened up the opportunity of a complementary pension to ordinary farm labourers. The agreement did not impose a direct obligation on individual farmers. Instead it encouraged the farmers' unions to make agreements at the level of the '*département*', so that different provisions could be built in to take account of local conditions. Contributions are set at 4 per cent and may be based on real earnings, or on a flat rate amount, or on different flat rate amounts according to the employee's grade. It is recommended that real earnings should be used wherever practicable. Pensions are calculated as in ARRCO.

The development of social security provisions and in particular of complementary pensions has been rendered difficult by the declining proportion of the population working in agriculture. In 1920 40 per cent of the active population were in agriculture, while in 1970 the figure had dropped to 15 per cent. It is for this reason that the General Scheme has had to subsidize the scheme for agricultural employees: indeed the two schemes are now closely integrated. ANCORA wishes to join ARRCO, so that financial integration is also likely to take place at the complementary level. Such a development will be entirely in character with the principle of solidarity embodied in ARRCO's own system of interscheme compensation.

III—PENSION SCHEMES FOR OTHER
OCCUPATIONAL GROUPS

Various groups of employees and all self-employed persons are covered by schemes which remain separate from the General Scheme. These may all be called special schemes, but the French often reserve this term for the schemes covering employees, in order to distinguish them from the schemes for the self-employed which are classed as 'autonomous'. The distinction is useful as the two groups of schemes have very little in common.

There are more than 120 *special schemes* for employees. Many of them are extremely small: the eight largest schemes have 2,113,500 pensioners while the others have 25,000 in all, as compared with over 3 million in the General Scheme.[1] As regards finance, the

---

[1] We shall consider here only the eight largest schemes, covering Civil servants, Military staff, Local Authority staff, SNCF (Railways), EGF (Gas and Electricity industries), RATP (Paris transport), Merchant Seamen, and the Miners.

special schemes may be seen to differ significantly from the General
Scheme: contribution rates are much higher, ranging from one-
and-a-half to three times that of the General Scheme; contributions, except in the miners' scheme, are paid on the employees'
entire salary; many of the schemes are subsidized either directly or
indirectly. These special schemes provide a high percentage of
income replacement, and have favourable rules concerning the age
at which pensions may be drawn.

In France it is often felt to be unfair that the state should subsidize the very generous special schemes and give no aid to the
General Scheme. However, this situation is justified insofar as
many of the special schemes, covering sectors with a declining
labour force, have a low ratio of contributors to pensioners.

In calculating benefits the special schemes count up to 37·5
years' insurance, so that the maximum pension is normally 75 per
cent of final salary. However, in certain schemes, e.g. civil
servants, SNCF, additions are made if the pensioner has brought
up three or more children; the rules are the same as in the General
Scheme, i.e. plus 10 per cent for three children, and another 5 per
cent for each child thereafter. Furthermore civil servants may get a
basic pension of up to 80 per cent if they have served abroad or in
the army. In schemes with bonuses of this type it is explicitly
stated that the pensions must not exceed the individual's final
salary, unless as a result of post-awards dynamism (see below).
Few pensioners in the special schemes receive means-tested
assistance.

The pension age varies according to the category of employment,
the principle being that pensions should be awarded earlier to
people who have worked in more arduous jobs. This creates wide
disparities between the public and private sectors: railwaymen for
example may retire ten to fifteen years earlier than some private
sector employees working in equally tiring jobs. The best that a
member of the General Scheme can hope for is to be classed as
unfit and to receive a full pension at sixty.

While the special schemes all have slightly different conditions
and rules, their general features are similar. The only real exception
is the miners' scheme, which is unlike any other major scheme
in France. Pensions are related neither to individual's earnings,
nor to his contributions, but solely to his length of service.
On 1 October 1970 the pension for a miner after thirty years'

employment was 5974.20F per annum, approximately 45 per cent of the average gross earnings of manual workers in industry and commerce.

As the miners' scheme replaces a much lower percentage of income than the other special schemes, especially in the case of the more highly paid, complementary pensions have been introduced. Manual grades belong to UNIRS, while engineers are covered by AGIRC. White collar employees have been covered by a '*régime complémentaire réglementaire*' (a scheme set up by the public authorities, rather than by a collective agreement between the unions and the CNPF) but are being integrated into AGIRC and UNIRS, depending on their grade.

After the Liberation the aim of French legislators was to create a unified system of old age insurance, but this was never realized due to the opposition of various groups. Some of the most vehement opposition to the 1946 legislation on the extension of social insurance came from the *self-employed*. Consequently an Act was passed in January 1948 which departed from the original goal by creating autonomous pension schemes for the self-employed. According to the terms of the Act this arrangement was to have been purely provisional. Four organizations were set up for the different occupational groups: the artisans, the self-employed in industry and commerce (mainly shopkeepers and traders), the liberal professions (doctors, dentists, lawyers, architects, etc.) and the self-employed in agriculture (this scheme does not have the same autonomy as the others).

All these schemes provide a minimum pension or allowance which is equal to the AVTS. Generally speaking they also provide earnings-related benefits, but whether the individual receives such benefits depends on the amount he has paid in contributions. The schemes are financed on a pay-as-you-go basis.

The *artisans'* scheme is known as CANCAVA (*Caisse autonome nationale de compensation de l'assurance vieillesse artisanale*). Contributions are earnings related but instead of making the contributions a fixed percentage of income, CANCAVA has fifteen classes of contribution. Each class credits the contributor with a different number of points and it is possible to acquire from four to sixty points per annum. (One pension point is worth about 6F per annum.) The individual's income determines what class of contribution he must pay. He is at liberty to contribute more and thereby earn a greater number of points, but he is not allowed to contribute less. Artisans who continue to work after the age of sixty-five pay no further contributions. In addition individuals with a *very* low income need not pay contributions at all.

The artisans' scheme is run by forty-five local 'funds' and eight occupational 'funds' whose boards of management are elected by the artisans. These institutions are controlled and co-ordinated financially by CANCAVA.

The *self-employed in industry and commerce* are covered by the '*Organization Autonome Nationale de l'Industrie et du Commerce*' (ORGANIC). Within ORGANIC there are 100 'funds' of which seventy-six are local and twenty-four occupational. It is similar to CANCAVA in that it has different classes of contributions, although they number only eight. In 1970 it was decided that contributors in the top three classes should pay more if they are married than if they are single. In this connection it should be noted that a wife aged sixty-five qualifies for an additional allowance equal to 50 per cent of her husband's pension: there is no means test. Survivors' rights are also generous in comparison with some other schemes—75 per cent for a widow provided she is sixty-five or over. As in CANCAVA contributions may be paid in retrospect.

To qualify for a pension the individual must either have worked in industry or commerce for at least fifteen years or have acquired ninety points. In either case he must have paid all contributions due. The level of the pension will depend on the number of points purchased or credited and the current value of the point. In 1970 the point was worth 7·72F. In other respects the rules are similar to those of CANCAVA.

The *liberal professions*' scheme covers a great variety of occupations. Consequently when putting the provisions of the 1948 Act into effect, the professions set up fifteen occupational sections within their organization. Each section operates a scheme providing the minimum allowance compulsory under the Act: there is a co-ordinating body, the *Caisse Nationale des Professions Liberales*, but this does *not* operate any system of interscheme compensation. Earnings-related schemes also function within each section; however they are not described here as they differ widely from one profession to another.

Contributions towards the minimum allowance vary according

to the profession, as each section has a different ratio of contributors to pensioners and different rules for awarding the allowance. Contributions are fixed and periodically reviewed by Government decree and in 1970 they ranged from 460F per annum for medical auxiliaries to 1,450F for notaries.

The allowance itself may be drawn at sixty-five, or at sixty if the individual is unfit to work; it may be deferred, in which case entitlement increases by 5 per cent each year after the age of sixty-five. In order to qualify for the allowance the individual must provide evidence of at least fifteen years' activity in the profession concerned. Rules regarding the payment of the allowance vary, e.g. some professions have a retirement condition, others operate a means-test in the case of recipients who retired before 1949 and did not therefore contribute. The minimum allowance is equal in value to the AVTS and there is an allowance for a dependent spouse of the same amount.

The *farmers' scheme* is by far the largest of the schemes for the self-employed. The scheme is very heavily subsidized from a special budget known as the '*Budget Annexe des Prestations Sociales Agricoles*' (BAPSA). In 1969 the BAPSA subsidy accounted for 90·5 per cent of the scheme's revenue, while the nominal contributions paid by the farmers accounted for the other 9·5 per cent. BAPSA itself was financed in 1969 by general taxation (77·8 per cent), by taxes on farmers (19·1 per cent) and by taxes on agricultural produce (3·1 per cent).

The scheme covers farmers and the members of their families, including their wives, who work with them. Contributions consist of two elements:

(*a*) a contribution (45F in 1971) for each adult living and working on the farm.
(*b*) a contribution based on something akin to the rateable value of the farm ('*le revenu cadastral de l'exploitation*'). This expedient is used because of the difficulty involved in ascertaining the income of French farmers. Each year BAPSA decides what the total revenue must be from these graduated contributions: each *département* is then informed by the Ministry of Agriculture what it must provide, and this amount is then divided out between the farmers in the area, according to the rateable value of their farms.

Corresponding to these two types of contributions are two types of benefits, basic and complementary. The basic pension is the same for everyone, being equal to the AVTS. The level of the complementary pension varies with the amount paid in graduated contributions (in 1969 the average complementary pension amounted to 293F per annum). The qualifying conditions are similar to those of the other autonomous schemes, i.e. pension age is sixty-five, required period of time working in agriculture is fifteen years. If five years' contributions have been paid, the minimum allowance is awarded as of right. If this condition is not fulfilled then the allowance is awarded only on a means-tested basis.

It will be recalled that means-tested allowances ensure that elderly people may have an income at least equal to a so-called social minimum. The least adequate pension schemes tend very broadly to have the highest proportion of pensioners getting the *supplementary allowance*, as is shown in Table 6.8.

TABLE 6.8

Pensioners receiving the supplementary allowance, 1 July 1971

	As per cent of total
General Scheme	23·23
CANCAVA (artisans)	20·16
ORGANIC (industry and commerce)	12·08
Liberal professions	3·68
Farmers[1]	49·80

Source: *Ministère de la santé publique et de la sécurité sociale.*

IV—MEANS-TESTED ASSISTANCE FOR THE ELDERLY

Since the end of World War II, statutory pension insurance in France has been extended to cover the entire working population. Nevertheless many pensioners still rely on assistance-type benefits. This may be attributed partly to the fact that the statutory schemes

[1] It is thought that numerous retired farmers make false declarations in order to obtain the supplementary allowance.

did not credit contributions in respect of previous employment and partly to the inadequate level of income replacement which some of these schemes aimed at, e.g. the General Scheme in 1971 awarded widows' pensions which at best amounted to 20 per cent of the deceased husband's earnings.

Basic allowances are paid by individual pension schemes. The main allowance in this group is the '*allocation aux vieux travailleurs salariés*' (AVTS). Introduced by Vichy in 1941, this is the oldest of the allowances for the elderly and also the most well known. To qualify for the allowance, claimants must be sixty-five, or sixty and unfit to work, and must have been employed on French territory for at least twenty-five years. The AVTS is means-tested in the same way as the special and supplementary allowances; in July 1972 it amounted to 1,850F per annum. All the basic allowances as well as the minimum pension, and the supplement for a dependent spouse, are set at the same value as the AVTS. The supplementary allowance described below is determined independently.

Since virtually everyone retiring in the 1960s and 1970s after the twenty-five years required for the AVTS would be eligible for a substantial contributory pension, the AVTS has declined greatly in importance since the immediate post-war period. Recipients of the AVTS and the two associated allowances numbered just over a quarter of a million in 1970. All retired employees may be eligible for the AVTS subject to the conditions mentioned above, regardless of scheme. Since the special schemes for employees have almost all existed for a long time they rarely have pensioners receiving the AVTS. The allowance is in the main paid to pensioners in the General Scheme and in the scheme for agricultural employees. The schemes for the self-employed have allowances similar to the AVTS. Unlike the supplementary and special allowances, the AVTS group of allowances are not financed by a central fund, but by each scheme separately.[1]

---

[1] Recipients of the AVTS are treated like ordinary pensioners in several respects: if married they may receive the supplement for a dependent spouse; if they have brought up three or more children, they qualify for a 10 per cent bonus; widows (or widowers) who had been dependent on a recipient of the AVTS receive a survivor's allowance known as the '*secours viager*' (literally 'assistance for life'), which is the same value as the AVTS and means-tested in the same way.

A similar allowance is awarded to wives of employed persons who have reared five or more children ('*mère de cinq enfants*'). A mother who works as a self-employed person may become eligible for this allowance, but only if she works

Although basic allowances like the AVTS are set at the same level as the special allowance the former are in at least one respect more advantageous than the latter: like contributory pensions, the AVTS and other allowances *paid by individual schemes* automatically give sickness insurance coverage. Recipients of the special allowance must on the other hand depend on social aid for medical treatment. This is likely to be more closely controlled and the patient's choice of doctor or hospital may be restricted.

People over sixty-five may receive the *special allowance*, if they are not eligible for a pension from any of the statutory schemes. This allowance is paid by the Special Fund which was created by an Act of Parliament in 1952. The fund is financed by contributions from all the statutory pension schemes for employed and self-employed persons; each scheme's contribution is fixed every year according to its total number of pensioners.

In July 1972 the allowance amounted to 1,850F per annum, the same as the AVTS; the means-test is the same as for the AVTS and the supplementary allowances. Although the number of recipients has been declining gradually over the last decade (232,000 in 1971), the fact remains that over half of them are under seventy-five, which suggests that the problem of people without pension rights is not just a hangover from an earlier period. About three-quarters are, in fact, women who were single, widowed, divorced or separated.

A study[1] into the background of people receiving the special allowance revealed that the majority had either had no job, or had been mentally or physically handicapped, or had devoted their lives to religion.

The most important form of assistance for the elderly is the *supplementary allowance* paid by the National Solidarity Fund, an *ad hoc* body set up in 1956 by the Mollet Government. On 1 July 1971, 26 per cent of France's 8 million pensioners were receiving this allowance. These include pensioners from all the main schemes, but the proportion from each scheme varies widely. Only pensioners over sixty-five (or over sixty and unfit to work) are eligible. The allowance is means-tested.

In July 1972 the allowance was 1,800F per annum (about £150

---

long enough to qualify for an old age benefit under the legislation covering the self-employed.

[1] See *Rapports des Commissions du 6ᵉ Plan : Personnes Âgées.*

at the current exchange rate), or 12 per cent of the average earnings of manual workers. It is awarded to pensioners as long as their total income *including the allowance* does not exceed 5,150F per annum (July 1972). The allowance is reduced in cases where payment in full would bring the recipient's income above the limit. The corresponding limit for couples is one-and-a-half times the limit for a single person. These limits, rather than the allowances themselves, have often been regarded as the closest approximation in France to an official poverty line for the elderly.

As its title implies, the supplementary allowance may only be paid *in addition* to another cash benefit. In some cases the basic benefit is a contributory pension (equal in July 1972 to at least 1,850F per annum), in others it is one of several allowances, all of which amounted to 1,850F per annum in July 1972. Single pensioners over sixty-five therefore qualify for a minimum income of *3,650F per annum*, which is known as the *social minimum*[1]. The *social minimum for a couple is twice that for a single person*, i.e. husband and wife are *each* entitled to a basic allowance and a supplementary allowance, provided that their total income does not exceed *7,725F*.[2]

The National Solidarity Fund which pays the supplementary allowance is financed out of general taxation. Originally the finance was to have come from a tax on motor vehicles, the '*vignette*', but in practice the revenue from this tax was soon included in general state revenue and the Solidarity Fund received an annual allocation sufficient to cover its expenditure. It has long been thought in France that the revenue from the '*vignette*' was misappropriated by the Government, but the authorities insist that this revenue would now amount to less than the expenditure on supplementary allowances. Since 1959 the state has obliged the General Scheme to finance out of its own revenue the supplementary allowances which are paid to General Scheme pensioners.[3] This has caused great

---

[1] Thus a pensioner may receive 1,850F from the AVTS plus 1,800F supplementary allowance to make a total of 3,650F.

[2] It will be noted that the difference between the social minimum and the income limit is much smaller for a couple than for a single person. (7,725F minus 7,300 equals 425F for a couple; 5,150F minus 3,650 equals 1,500F for a single person.)

[3] In 1970 the General Scheme was in deficit but paid out supplementary allowances totalling 1,031 million francs (out of total revenue from contributions of 13,317 million francs). The state reimbursed 317 million francs in view of the scheme's weak financial position.

controversy in certain quarters and may help to explain some of the indignation felt over the *'vignette'* affair.

In 1956 the forecast uptake of the supplementary allowance was $4\frac{1}{2}$ million, but only about $2\frac{1}{2}$ *million have ever received it (i.e. in 1961) and in 1971, the figure was about 2 million*. The Laroque Report[1] suggests that this may be explained by the strictness of the rules, e.g. sons and daughters were expected to contribute to the upkeep of their parents, if their own income was above a certain minimum; expenditure on the allowance could be recovered from the estate of a deceased recipient; real property was taken into consideration in applying the means-test. The first of these rules is no longer adhered to, but the clauses relating to property and inheritances may still have some disincentive effect. It may be noted that the ability of old people in France to circumvent the rules of the means-test varies greatly according to their situation; a town-dweller living on his own is invariably less well placed in this respect than an old person living in a rural area, where local conditions seem to facilitate concealment from the authorities.

There has been a significant drop in the number of General Scheme pensioners receiving the supplementary allowances from 1·2 million in 1961 to under 800,000 in 1971. This fall reflects the maturing of pension rights in that scheme and also the development of complementary pensions. On the other hand the number of farmers has risen. Certainly one could hardly expect their numbers to fall as the average pension paid by the farmers' scheme remains very low.

Social Aid[2] or locally administered public assistance helps the elderly primarily by providing services such as home-helps, restaurants, clubs, old folks' homes, sheltered flatlets, and medical aid. In the past Social Aid has also played an important part in the provision of cash benefits for the elderly, but the introduction of various *national* allowances has in most cases eliminated the need for such benefits. Social Aid does still give financial assistance to a small group of foreigners.[3] Also in certain cities local offices make

---

[1] *Op. cit.* p. 69.

[2] This section owes much to Cindy Stevens, *Public Assistance in France,* Occasional Papers on Social Administration, No. 50, Bell, London, 1973.

[3] 'Those who have lived in France for at least fifteen years before the age of seventy and who are not covered by social security or a reciprocal agreement.' *Op. cit.*

discretionary cash payments to the aged to offset the higher cost of living.

Social Aid's main statutory benefits—statutory though locally administered—for the elderly are the home-help service and the provision of residential accommodation. Both are restricted to elderly people who fall below the income limit laid down for receiving the national allowances. The means-test for Social Aid benefits is more rigorous, particularly as regards family responsibility; 'the *"obligation alimentaire"* makes support of an individual legally binding on certain of his relatives, whether or not they live with him. Those bound by this law are grandparents, parents, children, grandchildren (indeed, great-grandchildren and parents where these are living), together with parents, sons and daughters-in-law'.

A home-help may be provided for thirty hours a month for a single person, or for forty-eight hours in the case of a couple. Where the local Social Aid office cannot provide the service itself it may pay an allowance covering 60 per cent of the cost of a private home-help.

Social Aid also used to pay a rent allowance which was superseded in 1972 by a housing allowance described below. The means-test was the same as for other Social Aid benefits. The allowance was inadequate for a variety of reasons: it covered only rented accommodation (it is estimated that only 2 million out of almost 8 million old people live in such accommodation); it could only be paid in respect of rents which did not exceed 190F per month for a couple in 1970 (in many French cities such low rents are rare); it could only cover three-quarters of the rent no matter how poor the recipient was; finally, tenants in furnished accommodation were ineligible.

Housing allowances in France have traditionally been reserved for families receiving family allowances. But an act passed on 16 July 1971[1] introduced a housing allowance for three other sections of the community: the elderly, the infirm (aged fifteen and over) and young employees (under twenty-five). The legislation came into force on 1 July 1972. This was the first time that most of the people mentioned above were able to receive direct assistance with the

---

[1] The act outlines only the general policy. For details, see Decrees Nos. 72–526 and 527 and the ministerial circular of 29 June 1972, published in the *Journal Officiel*, 30 June 1972.

cost of accommodation. Some admittedly have been receiving the rent allowance paid by Social Aid (130,000 elderly in 1972), but this is payable only to people whose incomes are below the ceiling for means-tested assistance, and whose children or relatives cannot afford to help them. Some 700,000 old people will be eligible for the new housing allowance. The old rent allowance provided under social aid meanwhile will not disappear completely but will no longer be of relevance to the groups covered by the new legislation.

The allowance is paid on condition that the recipient is paying rent or mortgage instalments and that the accommodation satisfies certain norms both in respect of its size and of its fitness for human habitation.[1] The actual rent, the recipient's income and, to a lesser extent, the size of his family all affect the allowance payable. Three examples may serve to illustrate what is provided.

(1) An old person living alone with an annual income of 4,000F (just above the social minimum) and a rent of 200F per month will receive in 1972 an allowance of 143F per month. He will therefore spend 17 per cent of his income on rent.

(2) An elderly couple with an annual income of 8,000F (just above the income limit for receiving social assistance) and a rent of 250F per month will receive an allowance of 125F per month. They will spend 19 per cent of their income on rent.

(3) An elderly couple with an annual income of 17,000F (approximately 109 per cent of the average earnings of manual workers in industry and commerce) will receive no allowance, as their 'minimum rent' (305F per month) exceeds the permitted maximum (300F per month).

The allowance is aimed only at households whose income is lower than average, although at the same time it is considerably less restrictive in this respect than the old rent allowance. All old people must still make a personal contribution towards their rent and this may amount to between 10 per cent and 20 per cent of

---

[1] These norms vary depending on whether the recipients are old, infirm or young employees. For the infirm there is no restriction regarding the number of rooms, while for the young not only the number of rooms is specified, but also the permitted surface area. Otherwise, conditions are the same as for the aged, namely: that the accommodation comprises a maximum of two main rooms (not counting the kitchen) in the case of a single person with one more main room (for each additional person); that it is self-contained; that it has drinking water, sanitation, and some form of heating; and that it is not partially sub-let.

total income for even the very poorest, i.e. those living on 10–14F per day in 1972.

The allowances are paid out by the family allowance funds in the form of cheques made out to the landlord or to the financial institution handling the mortgage. Allowances for the old, the infirm and the under-twenty-fives are not actually financed by the family allowance funds, but by an *ad hoc* National Housing Assistance Fund. The fund's resources come partly from general taxation and partly from a tax on employers equal to 0·1 per cent of salaries up to the social security ceiling. This has meant that the tax of 1 per cent previously paid by employers towards new housing construction has been correspondingly reduced to 0·9 per cent, so that social housing is being deprived of between 200 and 250 million francs per year. The irony of this is apparent: France suffers basically from a serious housing shortage which private enterprise has been unable or unwilling to remedy. New housing construction in France is widely recognized as being inadequate and year after year the number of houses completed has fallen far short of what the *Commission de l'Habitation* considers to be the essential minimum.

To conclude, the introduction of this housing allowance will improve the position of the elderly in the housing market relative to those sections of the population not eligible for the allowance. This improvement will be modest and partly at the expense of new housing construction. Furthermore, better housing for the aged can only be to the detriment of other poor sections of the population, as long as effective action is not taken to tackle the housing shortage.

V—CURRENT ISSUES AND CONCLUSIONS

In recent years there has been more activity in the pensions field than in any other area of French social policy. At the grass-roots level, dissatisfaction has been expressed by pensioners through their own organizations. The most important of these, the *Union Confédérale des Retraités*, is closely associated with France's largest trade union organization, the CGT. The pensioners have consequently had power to make their demands heard. A campaign in 1971 based on these demands attracted very widespread support from the working population, who showed their willingness even to take national strike action on this issue. Some of the views and feelings of pensioners and workers found expression in the Report by the Commission for the Elderly (*Intergroupe 'Personnes âgées'*) written in preparation for the VIth Plan (1971–75). However, the financial constraints imposed on the Commission were such that they could propose only modest improvements. The Government has acted on these recommendations and has indeed gone slightly beyond them in certain respects, in recognition perhaps of the increasing electoral power wielded by the elderly. Action often of a very direct nature has also been taken by certain sections of the self-employed, notably café-owners, small-traders and artisans. Pensions in France have therefore become a subject of considerable political controversy and may well remain so during the 1970s.

The social minimum

The AVTS (or other allowances and pensions of an equivalent amount) plus the supplementary allowance combine to form the *social minimum for old people in France (3,650F per annum in July 1972)*. This minimum is not fixed according to subsistence needs, but is more a matter of economic and political expediency. The maximum total income which a recipient of the allowances may have (5,150F per annum in July 1972) is loosely regarded as a subsistence income by pension scheme officials and others. The implicit assumption is that all old people have at least some resources of their own, but the validity of this seems doubtful.

Although still modest enough the social minimum has in recent years risen faster than either prices or earnings. However, it should be emphasized that by 1971 the social minimum was only 22 per cent of the average earnings of manual workers, compared with 19 per cent in 1963 (that is, for a *single* person).

This improvement owed much to the Laroque Commission, which was set up in 1960 to study the problems of the elderly in France. At the same time, however, it fell far short of the Commission's recommendation that the social minimum be raised by stages to 2,200F in 1965.[1] It stressed the need for a rise in the social

---

[1] *Op. cit.* p. 179.

minimum as a percentage of average earnings (in the period 1962–65); thereafter the minimum was to rise in line with earnings. In fact the minimum did not reach 2,200F until 1968 when it represented less in real terms, and much less as a proportion of average earnings than it would have in 1965.

An equally important recommendation made by Laroque was that the income limit for receiving the allowances comprising the social minimum should be set at twice the level of the minimum itself, and should also rise in line with it. Neither of these proposals was adopted and between 1964 and 1970 the income limit declined from 195 per cent to 152 per cent of the social minimum. In the same period the limit for a couple dropped from 147 per cent to 114 per cent of an amount equal to twice the social minimum.[1] In this way the range of people eligible for assistance was made much less wide than Laroque had desired.

Within the framework of the VIth Plan (1971–75) special priority is being given to the elderly, and most of the extra resources available for this group are being concentrated on raising the social minimum. It was initially intended that the social minimum should increase by 450F per annum, the objective being to make it approximately 50 per cent of the minimum wage (SMIC) in 1975. However, increasing the social minimum by 450F per annum would not be consistent with this objective unless price rises for the years 1971–75 averaged 3 per cent or less. Inflation has in fact been running at almost twice this level.

Even to raise the social minimum to 50 per cent of the minimum wage by 1975 is not an ambitious objective: this would have been achieved in 1965 if the authorities had followed the recommendations of the Laroque Report. The French minimum wage itself is about 50 per cent of average earnings.

Both 1971 and 1972 have seen considerable agitation about pensions in general and the social minimum in particular. No doubt conscious of the forthcoming general election (spring 1973), the Government announced an important package of social measures in the autumn of 1972. The most significant decision was to increase the social minimum on 1 October 1972 from 3,650F to 4,500F per annum, a rise of almost a quarter. As a result of the

---

[1] It will be recalled that for a couple the social minimum is simply doubled.

policy to raise the income limit by the same absolute amount as the rise in the social minimum the income limit for a couple rose to 9,000F, the same amount as twice the social minimum. In principle, therefore, any personal income will be deducted from benefit awarded to elderly couples.

The possible virtue of this policy in the eyes of the Government is that it raises the social minimum in the least expensive way. (Theoretically, an even cheaper method would have been to leave the income limit stationary, but this would have been unwise politically.) However to restrict state help only to the very poorest group of the population was deemed undesirable by Laroque and this view remains current in the 1970s. The policy will soon mean that any personal resources will have to be concealed if the allowance(s) is not to be reduced; as we know, such concealment is more difficult for some old people than for others.

As we have noted above, the social minimum consists of two allowances which are periodically adjusted by widely different amounts. In 1971 and 1972 the AVTS (and other basic allowances) has increased by about 6 per cent per annum, while the supplementary allowance has risen at an annual rate of 20 per cent. The reason for this is again one of economy: certain benefits which are tied to the AVTS are not means-tested, e.g. the minimum pensions in the General Scheme and elsewhere, the supplement for a dependent spouse. Rises in the AVTS are therefore held as low as possible, the policy being as before to restrict state help to the poorest group.

Reforms in the General Scheme

In recent years various issues have arisen in the General Scheme and we give a brief description of these issues together with the reforms which have come in response to them.

Pensions in the General Scheme have traditionally been based on a maximum of thirty years' contributions. As the first social insurance scheme dates from 1930, no one had a contribution record in excess of thirty years until the 1960s, so that it was only then that this became an issue. Not to take more than thirty years' contributions into account is regarded as unfair as the special schemes in the public sector base pensions on up to thirty-seven-and-a-half years, and as any restriction hits lower grades of workers hardest (since they tend to start work young and therefore have long working lives). The trade unions, with the latter point in mind, have stated their preference for no restriction whatsoever, or for a maximum of forty-four years as already exists in the ARRCO scheme.

If a 40 per cent pension was still to be awarded for thirty years' contributions, it is clear that taking forty-four years' contributions into account would mean General Scheme pensions approaching 60 per cent. This possibility was hardly considered by the Government, presumably because of the cost involved. However, it did appreciate the need to raise the maximum to thirty-seven-and-a-half years as in the public sector schemes and legislation was passed in 1971 ensuring that the new system would be fully operational by 1975. It is estimated that 1,170,000 pensioners will benefit from this reform in the period 1971–75, but for many the improvement will be slight, as only partial increases are awarded in the case of pensions drawn before 1975. From that date the full General Scheme pension drawn at sixty-five will be 50 per cent, with 75 per cent for retirement at seventy and 25 per cent at sixty.

The method of calculating pensions on the last ten years' earnings, or on earnings between fifty and sixty, has attracted criticism as it tends to favour those employees who continue to improve their position in the earnings hierarchy right up to retirement. Such employees are of course to be found in white-collar and managerial grades. Manual workers on the other hand are usually best off (relative to the average) earlier on in life. Here again the trade unions were able to demonstrate bias against manual workers in the General Scheme. The solution which they proposed was to base the pension on the ten best years' earnings (revalued in line with the general rise in earnings). This has been opposed for some time in certain official circles on the grounds of administrative complexity, but was finally adopted as government policy in the autumn of 1972. The change-over to the new formula should be implemented in 1974.

Perhaps the least satisfactory aspect of the General Scheme is the provision it makes for widows. Widows, it will be recalled, only qualify for a pension if they are sixty-five or over, and even then they get a mere 50 per cent of their husband's pension. However in the autumn of 1972 it was announced that from 1973 onwards widows aged fifty-five and over would qualify for a pension. It may be noted by way of comparison, that in the Netherlands and in Belgium the widow's pension is as much as the direct pension for a single person, while Germany and Italy both give widows 60 per cent of the deceased husband's pension. The minimum age is forty-five in Germany and Belgium and forty in the Netherlands; there is no minimum in Italy and most of the other countries, unlike France, pay pensions regardless of age, when the widow is caring for children.[1] The French complementary schemes are more generous than the General Scheme. Their widows' pensions are 60 per cent of direct pensions and the minimum age of fifty is disregarded if the widow is caring for two children.

Various minor improvements have been made recently on behalf of widows, in addition to the latest announcement regarding the age limit.[2] It seems reasonable to say that provisions for widows have improved more in 1970–72 than throughout the rest of the General Scheme's history. Nevertheless French widows, especially

---

[1] France's family allowance system compensates for this to some extent.

[2] To qualify for a pension a widow must have been dependent on her husband at the time of his death, the notion of dependence being interpreted in terms of the wife's personal income. Until 1971 a wife earning more than 3,050F per annum (about one-fifth of average earnings) at the time of her husband's death was ineligible for a widow's pension. Since then this amount has been raised to the level of the minimum wage (SMIC) which in January 1972 stood at 8,195F per annum.

Women who have worked may by the age of sixty-five have pension rights of their own, but until recently General Scheme rules have not permitted the payment to a widow of both a direct and a survivor's pension. Neither on its own could provide an adequate income: on the one hand the woman was unlikely to have a full contributions record if she had children, and she would probably have received low pay; on the other hand the survivor's pension would at best be only 20 per cent of her husband's final earnings. In view of this the Government decided in 1971 partly to abolish the rule preventing widows from receiving two pensions.

Another piece of legislation of some benefit to widows was the introduction of credited old age contributions paid by the Family Allowance Fund (CNAF) on behalf of women receiving the new *increased* '*salaire unique*'. (The '*salaire unique*' is an allowance paid by the CNAF to families supported by one salary; it has recently been increased for very poor families, and abolished for the rich.) This will make it easier for some women to build up decent pension rights of their own.

The increased '*salaire unique*' itself will help mothers widowed in earlier life, e.g. a family (or widow) with one income of less than 13,536F per annum and with one child to support will receive the allowance (worth 2,334F per annum in 1971). However, even at its new level the allowance cannot possibly constitute a replacement income.

298298298298298

those covered by the General Scheme, still seem to be very under-privileged, compared with their counterparts elsewhere in the EEC.

Unemployment and early retirement

According to an opinion poll carried out in May–June 1971 by *l'Institut Français de l'Opinion Publique*, 65 per cent of people interviewed on the subject of pensions gave as their main concern the lowering of the retirement age. At the same time a full pension at sixty was one of the principal demands of a campaign conducted by France's two largest trade union organizations.

The normal retirement age in most western societies is sixty-five, as in France. In some countries it is higher, e.g. in Canada, Ireland and Norway it is seventy, while in Denmark and Sweden sixty-seven is the official age. However, men retire at sixty in Italy, Japan, USSR, Czechoslovakia and Hungary, while in Yugoslavia retirement for men is at fifty-five and for women at fifty.

The campaign for an earlier retirement age is supported by unions which primarily represent manual workers and it is understandable that men who have worked since their 'teens in jobs which are often uninteresting or arduous should want to retire before sixty-five. The union demands may also be motivated by the very high levels of unemployment among older workers, a trend which seems to be equally prevalent in other advanced western countries.

A survey conducted at the end of 1970 by the unemployment insurance organization UNEDIC showed how serious the problem of unemployment among older workers has become. It was found that 61 per cent of men receiving insurance benefit were in the age group fifty to sixty-five while the corresponding figure for women was 43 per cent. The average period of male unemployment was 270 days (ages fifty to fifty-four), 320 days (fifty-five to fifty-nine), 608 days (sixty to sixty-five). The chance of finding another job grew worse with age: 51·9 per cent of the fifty to fifty-four age group ceased to receive benefit because they had found employment, for the fifty-five to fifty-nines the figure was 44·9 per cent, while for the sixty to sixty-fives it was only 20 per cent.

The campaign of the CGT and the CFDT demanded for all the right to retire on a full pension from sixty onwards. Complete opposition to this has been voiced by both Government and employers, as it would entail a significant rise in labour costs. It might also be argued that such a development would be unwise in the early 1970s when adverse demographic trends are already adding slightly to costs; by 1980 the age group sixty to sixty-five will be very small indeed (fewer babies born 1914–18, many of them killed 1939–45) and the total number over sixty may have dropped from 37·4 per cent of the twenty to fifty-nine age group in 1971 to 33 per cent by 1980.

While the demand for retirement for all at sixty has not been met, concessions have been made to the unions by Government and employers. These have been motivated partly by the Government's desire to bring 'unemployment' figures down from their post-war peak of 400,000 (at the end of 1971). Employers have also been anxious to get improved protection for the unemployed over sixty as they will then encounter less opposition from labour when old workers are made redundant.

Only workers classed as unfit may receive a full pension at sixty. By an Act of Parliament of December 1971 conditions were made less stringent for those wishing to be so classed; each case is to be treated on its own merits and economic as well as medical factors may be taken into account.

At the level of the individual firm numerous agreements have been signed by unions and management setting up *'pre-pension'* schemes for workers who are dismissed, or who wish to stop work between sixty and sixty-five. These schemes may assume various forms. Under some schemes employees remain attached to the firm but are given an extended holiday from age sixty-three or sixty-four on about 80 per cent of normal salary; only those employees who have served the firm over a long period qualify for this type of benefit. Under the terms of most other schemes the beneficiary ceases to belong to the firm. The firm may guarantee a certain proportion of previous salary, normally 75 per cent, by supplementing what the individual draws in unemployment benefit. Alternatively it may undertake to pay until the age of sixty-five an amount equivalent to what the beneficiary will receive as a pension (basic plus complementary). Under yet another type of scheme the individual draws his pensions before the age of sixty-five and the firm guarantees to compensate, wholly or in part, for the financial loss which this entails.

In the course of 1971 discussions began between the employers' federation (CNPF) and the unions, aiming at a national agreement on the question of pre-pensions. The *National Agreement on Guaranteed Incomes for the Unemployed over Sixty* was concluded between the CNPF and the smaller unions (FO, CGC, CFTC) on 28 February 1972. The CGT and the CFDT gave their approval some ten days later but expressed reservations about the agreement: the levels of income replacement provided for under the agreement were lower than the minimum which the unions had themselves agreed to accept, and of course the agreement did not give men the *right* to retire at sixty.

The new scheme is operated by UNEDIC, which was itself set up after a similar agreement in 1958 on unemployment insurance. In 1972 unemployed workers over sixty will receive 66 per cent of previous gross salary; this will rise to 68 per cent in 1973 and will be 70 per cent from 1974 onwards. These amounts may also be expressed as a percentage of previous salary minus social security contributions (which of course are not paid by the unemployed); income replacement would then be about 76 per cent in 1972, 78 per cent in 1973 and 80 per cent from 1974 onwards. (N.B. Pensions are normally expressed as a percentage of *gross* earnings, therefore care should be taken to use the *former* figures for purposes of comparison.)

To qualify for these provisions persons aged sixty must have been unemployed for nine months, those aged sixty-one for six months, those aged sixty-two and sixty-three for three months, while immediate payment is made to those aged sixty-four. The individual must have paid social security contributions for at least fifteen years, this being the minimum qualifying period for a General Scheme pension.

Committees composed of management and union representatives may consider cases where workers have been sacked between the ages of fifty-eight years four months and sixty. They may also examine cases where the employee has 'resigned' and may decide to proceed as if he had been made redundant.

Prior to the 1972 agreement unemployed persons over sixty were able to receive benefit both from the state and from UNEDIC until the age of sixty-five. For most people the new provisions will be an improvement on unemployment benefit, particularly for individuals without dependents and for the more highly paid, e.g.

an employee who had formerly earned 1,200F per month will be
15 per cent better off under the new system, while for an executive
who had been earning 5,000F per month the increase in benefit will
be about 50 per cent. The very low paid are unaffected by the new
provisions as they already receive between 70 per cent and 95 per
cent of previous earnings in normal unemployment benefit. Some
of the schemes run by individual firms give benefits superior to
those in the National Agreement, and these schemes will continue
to operate.

Other benefits under the agreement are free sickness insurance
and accredited contributions to basic and complementary pension
schemes (persons receiving ordinary unemployment benefit also
get these). Finally beneficiaries will not have to report to their
labour exchange.

The problems of the self-employed

Under the terms of an act passed in 1946 the General Scheme was
to be extended to the rest of the population, but this project,
inspired by notions of national solidarity, was abandoned in 1947
because of opposition from the self-employed. Instead autonomous
schemes were set up by an act of January 1948 to provide old-age
pensions for the self-employed. Under the terms of the act these
schemes were to be 'provisional' and it was not until the reforms of
1967 that reference to their provisional nature was removed from
the statute book. However less than five years later the status of two
of the schemes—ORGANIC and CANCAVA—has again come
into question with the publication of a Government plan to make
their benefits and contributions the same as those of the General
Scheme.

For many years the number of people contributing to
ORGANIC and CANCAVA has been declining while the
number of pensioners has been steadily rising. For autonomous
schemes run on pay-as-you-go lines such trends have very serious
financial implications. The liberal professions stand out as the only
group among the self-employed which is not in decline; in fact the
number of contributors to this scheme is expected to grow on
average by 4 per cent per annum between 1970 and 1975. Consequently its financial position does not give cause for concern. The
other schemes all have ratios which are much lower than that of the

General Scheme and are declining rapidly. The farmers have already been taken in hand, 90 per cent of their scheme's expenditure being financed by the state.

In both ORGANIC and CANCAVA contributions have been raised on successive occasions, so that these schemes have been giving increasingly poor value for money. In 1969 the board of management of CANCAVA appealed to the state for help. An Act was duly passed in January 1970 obliging firms with a turnover in excess of 500,000F per annum to pay a *'contribution de solidarité'* of 0·02 per cent of turnover to help pay the deficits of CANCAVA and ORGANIC. However this proved inadequate and supplementary assistance was provided in the form of state subsidies. In 1971 a study group was set up under M. Barjot, *Conseiller d'Etat*, to assess the feasibility of a national system of interscheme compensation for all the basic schemes. This would correct for differences in the contributor/pensioner ratios and would be similar to the arrangements already operating in the complementary schemes. According to government proposals published in March 1972, contributions and pensions in ORGANIC and CANCAVA are to be calculated as in the General Scheme from 1973 onwards. This will lead to massive deficits which will be covered partly by an increased *'contribution de solidarité'* and partly by larger state subsidies.

Various questions remain unresolved. The method used to finance the deficits of the two schemes will almost certainly be revised when the results of the Barjot study become available.

No change has yet been made in the status of ORGANIC and CANCAVA, which remain autonomous. The self-employed themselves are divided over this issue: the *Comité interconfédéral de l'artisanat* (CICA) led by Monsieur Lecoeur want integration with the General Scheme, while CID–UNATI led by the militant Gérard Nicoud want autonomy from the General Scheme and a merger of ORGANIC and CANCAVA. The new arrangements will also create at least one new problem: contributions and pensions will be based only on income up to the General Scheme ceiling whereas the present system in ORGANIC and CANCAVA caters for higher incomes. Many contributors will have incomes above the ceiling so that it will be necessary to set up complementary schemes.

Other legislation designed to help old artisans and shopkeepers was passed on 13 July 1972 (*Loi no.* 72–657). Under the terms of this Act a means-tested lump sum payment may be made to self-employed persons in these categories who sell off their businesses and undertake not to set up in business again. Recipients of this 'compensatory aid' remain free subsequently to take paid employment.

Conclusions

The French pension system is both complex and rapidly changing. In some ways it is clearly inadequate, for example, in its minimum provisions, and in its treatment of widows. Recent improvements in these spheres have been too minor to have any real effect in relieving poverty. For approximately a quarter of France's elderly population, therefore, the immediate future is gloomy.

On the other hand significant improvements have taken place in the field of contributory pensions. While it is not likely to disappear completely, the gap between the private sector and the public sector is narrowing: after a full career in the private sector workers may soon expect pensions between 60 per cent and 70 per cent of final pay. These will be paid by schemes to which all firms must contribute, so that workers do not suffer as a result of changing firms. Statutory control is contributing to the mobility of labour; however, the system remains flexible as firms can and do make provision in excess of the statutory minimum. Financed on a pay-as-you-go basis, pensions rise in line with earnings so that pensioners living into their seventies or eighties do not find themselves falling into relative poverty. This is particularly relevant as life expectancy is rising.

Prospects for certain sections of the self-employed have also improved since it was announced that ORGANIC and CANCAVA are to be brought into line with the General Scheme, giving their members 50 per cent pensions after 37·5 years' insurance. The artisans and shopkeepers need no longer fear the effects on pensions of demographic decline.

At the bottom of the line are the farmers whose pension scheme is very largely state-financed. The pensions it pays are so low that virtually all retired farmers must rely on private resources or on means-tested assistance. Large numbers of them almost certainly suffer hardship although fraudulent claims for assistance and the benefits of a closely knit community may to some extent alleviate this.

Moves to harmonize and unify the system have borne some fruit and will continue to do so in the 1970s and 1980s. It has been politically feasible only to harmonize in an upward direction and this factor perhaps more than any other explains the recent improvements in French pensions.

CHAPTER SEVEN

Belgium

I—INTRODUCTION

The system in outline

In Belgium, as in other European countries, the post-war period
has seen considerable improvements in pensions for the elderly.
Coverage has been extended to all sections of the working population and various schemes have been amalgamated with a view to
standardizing their provisions. Shortcomings still exist but the
Government is making an effort to eliminate them. It would be true
to say that at no time in the country's history has there been such a
high level of public awareness or of political commitment in this
field.

The main features of the pension arrangements in Belgium may
be briefly summarized. Employees in the private sector are
covered by the General Scheme, which has both graduated contributions and graduated pensions above an official minimum
(*minimum garanti*). In addition, most firms have complementary
schemes for white-collar and occasionally manual workers. Public
servants have their own special schemes providing substantial
benefits, mainly on a non-contributory basis. Unestablished
employees in the public sector are not covered by these special
schemes, and instead contribute to the General Scheme. The self-
employed also have their own special scheme which is financed by
graduated contributions but which provides low flat-rate pensions.
People who have no pension rights in any of these schemes or only
partial claims may receive a national minimum allowance on a
means-tested basis (*revenu garanti*). Assistance is also provided

subject to means-tests at the local level which really sets the effective minimum.

Table 7.1 shows the percentage of pensioners in each category: it does not include dependents of pensioners, nor those pensioners who have retired before the normal pension age (sixty-five for a man, sixty for a woman).

TABLE 7.1

Pension recipients in each scheme, 1969
(excluding pensioners under normal retirement age)

	As percentage of total
General Scheme	66·7
Public servants and railways	13·8
Self-employed	12·8
Recipients of national minimum allowance	6·7
Total	100·0

Historical survey

Pensions were first introduced in Belgium in 1844 by an Act of Parliament. Those who benefited from the Act were civil servants, magistrates and the clergy. Very soon afterwards, in 1845, merchant seamen also won the right to a pension.

The next important development was the 1850 Act setting up the General Pension Fund (to be renamed the General Savings and Pension Fund in 1865). The role of this institution was to enable people to save if they wished for annuities. In 1891 Parliament voted that the Government be allowed to provide subsidies to this fund. A further Act passed in 1900 made these subsidies statutory, although membership of the scheme was still voluntary.

In 1911 a compulsory scheme was set up for miners but it was not until 1924–25 that legislation was passed making pension provision compulsory for employees in general. There were two Acts, one covering manual workers, the other white-collar employees. Pensions were to be financed by contributions from employees, employers and the state, the contributions being paid to the General Savings and Pensions Fund which then invested them. The technique used was therefore essentially the same as that used in the private insurance business, so that full pensions could only be paid after a long waiting period. In the meantime the state paid out supplements to those who, being too old at the time the schemes were set up, had not contributed or had contributed for only part of their career. The pension schemes along with supplementation came into operation in 1926.

Currency depreciation made these funded pension schemes increasingly inadequate and a new system was applied in 1945.[1] Under this system only part of the contributions were invested while the rest was used to finance a pension supplement on a pay-as-you-go basis which was more substantial than the funded payments. It was, however, a flat-rate allowance and from time to time its level had to be reviewed.

As a result of these developments the earnings-related element assumed a very subsidiary role: the scheme was mainly providing minimum flat-rate pensions and the influence which Beveridge had at this time may easily be detected. The attractions of the subsistence approach to social security were, however, short-lived and the main preoccupation soon became one of income maintenance. In a way this development was a return to tradition rather than a departure from it, since pensions in Belgium both in the public sector and the private sector (e.g. the annuities managed by the General Pension Fund) had been related to the individual's earnings or contributions, from the very beginning.

In 1953 an Act was passed which renounced funding and proposed its replacement by a pay-as-you-go system of finance. Further Acts were passed in 1955 and 1957 for manual and white-collar workers respectively, setting out how the new principle would be applied. Under these arrangements pensions were to be related both to earnings and to the number of years in employment, so that a single pensioner would receive 60 per cent of his average earnings over his entire career, revalued in line with the cost of living, while a married man would receive 75 per cent. The provisions for white-collar employees and for manual workers were similar although *not* identical: the scheme for the former retained a certain element of funding, while that of the latter had no ceiling on contributions or benefits.

Before 1954 there were no compulsory arrangements for the self-employed, not so much from negligence on the part of the

---

[1] We have not been able to investigate the effects of the post-war currency conversion.

state, but rather because of the traditional opposition of the self-employed themselves to state interference. Facilities did, however, exist for voluntary contributions to a funded scheme. On retirement this scheme paid an annuity which could be supplemented by the state subject to a means-test. The system was very similar to the pre-war provisions for the employed population, the main difference being that it contained no element of compulsion. In 1954 an act was passed obliging the self-employed to contribute towards the cost of the state supplements. Further legislation in 1956 created a compulsory pension scheme for the self-employed.[1]

The next important reform came towards the end of 1967. Anxious to ensure the future stability of pensions for employees in the private sector, which was being jeopardized by demographic disparities between schemes, the Government decreed that the four schemes covering manual workers, white-collar employees, miners and seamen be merged into one General Scheme. At this point the last elements of funding disappeared. It should be noted that this amalgamation did not mean immediate standardization. Certain differences in pension age and formulae still existed where the miners and seamen were concerned. Harmonization of the two main groups, the manual workers and the white-collar employees, was to be spread out over a number of years. This process is to be completed by 1975.[2]

The last development which must be mentioned here is the creation of a national minimum for the elderly (*revenu garanti*). This allowance is aimed essentially at people who have hardly ever worked and who consequently reach retirement with little or nothing in the way of pension rights. Initially at a very low level, the allowance is being increased about twice as fast as real earnings. Most of its recipients are, however, still partly dependent upon local public assistance.

II—PENSIONS FOR EMPLOYEES IN THE PRIVATE SECTOR

Although the General Scheme was founded in 1968 uniformity has not yet been achieved between the four schemes concerned.

---

[1] The subsequent evolution of this scheme is examined on pp. 322–4.
[2] Some of the implications of this harmonization are examined on pp. 331–4, and also in the section which deals with occupational schemes.

Probably the most important question of principle is whether or not the scheme should have a ceiling for the earnings on which contributions are levied and to which benefits are related. At present the earnings of manual workers and miners are not subject to any ceiling while those of white-collar workers and the seamen are subject to a ceiling equal to approximately 130 per cent of average gross earnings (male and female). It would, indeed, be natural to suppose that a white-collar ceiling would be fairly high if applied to a manual scheme. Surprisingly this ceiling in Belgium is not only low for white-collar workers, but would be low even for manual workers. For in October 1971 this ceiling came to only 117 per cent of the average gross earnings of adult males in industry.

When the four schemes were amalgamated at the beginning of 1968 the decree stated that 'the King might, on 1 January 1974 at the earliest, introduce a ceiling on contributions and benefits of manual and mining workers'. Closely associated with the introduction of such a ceiling is the extension of private pensions to cover manual workers.

If it is assumed that standardization of white-collar and manual workers' pensions is necessary, it must still be asked why the model should be the former rather than the latter. There are certainly employees in Belgium who are far from convinced, and it is very significant that some of the white-collar workers, who already have complementary pension coverage, appear to have no great liking for private pension schemes.[1]

Since the General Scheme is not yet entirely integrated we may mention special rules applying to different groups. These will be treated briefly unless, like the question of the ceiling, they raise important matters of principle.

General Scheme benefits

For an employee with a full career record, the General Scheme pension is 75 per cent (married) or 60 per cent (single) of his average annual earnings revalued in line with the retail price index. This may be expressed in three formulae:

pension for a couple $= \dfrac{N}{45} \times \dfrac{75}{100} \times W$

[1] See p. 331.

pension for a single man $= \dfrac{N}{45} \times \dfrac{60}{100} \times W$

pension for a single woman $= \dfrac{N}{40} \times \dfrac{60}{100} \times W$

where $N =$ number of years in employment between the ages of twenty and sixty-five for a man or between twenty and sixty for a woman, and $W =$ the individual's average annual earnings revalued in line with retail prices, *not*, as for example in Germany, in line with earnings.

The formula for a widow's pension is $\dfrac{N}{P} \times \dfrac{60}{100} \times W$

where P stands for the period between the deceased husband's twentieth birthday and 31 December preceding his death. It should be stressed that the widow's pension in Belgium is higher as a percentage of the direct pension than in any other graduated scheme in Europe: it is 100 per cent of the direct pension for a single man (or insured person) and 80 per cent of the direct pension for a couple.

Three matters must be discussed, relating to age, to employment before 1946 and to periods of unemployment. If one had been twenty before the introduction of the statutory scheme in 1926, employment prior to this date would not count: consequently N could not equal 45 until 1971. Nevertheless individuals have not been penalized as a result of this, as a corresponding reduction has been made in the *denominator* for pensions drawn before 1971, i.e. the denominator was made equal to the number of years between 1926 and the individual's sixty-fifth birthday! The principle which operates here is similar to that already observed in the case of widows whose husbands die before pension age, i.e. the pension scheme should protect people from circumstances outside their control. This implies a departure from the 'insurance' principle primarily on the ground that it would be socially unjust to penalize a person virtually on account of his age. Some schemes in other countries have been less generous; for example, the General Scheme in France calculates the amount of the pension on the basis of years for which contributions have *actually* been paid and it was only in the 1960s that Frenchmen started to draw 'full'

pensions. A funded scheme, it may be noted, could not 'blanket-in'
as the Belgians did without ceasing to be fully funded. Nor is this
the only element of 'blanketing-in' because, regarding employment
before 1946, the law makes two assumptions[1] which may in some
cases be extremely generous. These assumptions were introduced
largely for technical reasons, since many people had little or no
documentary evidence to show whether they had been employed
before and during World War II. It should also be borne in mind
that the provisions we are now describing were introduced not
immediately after the war but in the mid-1950s so that pre-1946
papers were likely to have been discarded long before.

We must qualify the initial definition of N in a third way as N
includes other periods when the individual was not in employment
for any of the following reasons: involuntary unemployment;
incapacity for work caused by ill-health, industrial injury, or over
66 per cent disability; maternity; military service; official strikes
and lockouts; annual holidays as prescribed in the legislation. In
view of these factors it would seem that there are fairly good safe-
guards for the employee as far as length of service is concerned.

W has been described as the individual's annual average earnings
revalued in line with retail prices. For historical reasons, as with
N, the situation is somewhat less simple. When it was decided in
1955 that employees should have earnings-related pensions, there
were no comprehensive records of employees' past earnings.
Information has been collected since the war through the Social
Security contributions system but in numerous cases this was
deficient; and, of course, it would have been impossible to get
reliable details of earnings for the earlier period. Faced with this
lack of data, the authorities decided that everyone who had been in
employment before the introduction of an earnings-related scheme[2]
should be credited with the same annual earnings. This specified
amount was to apply to all employees in the private sector (except

---

[1] It is assumed:
(a) that anyone who was ever in full-time employment during the period 1938–
45 inclusive was continuously employed from then until the end of 1945; and
(b) that anyone in full-time employment from 1946 till retirement with not more
than two years of that period unaccounted for, was employed since his twentieth birthday (1926 at the earliest).
Consequently the term N in the formulae may be much greater than the actual
number of years spent in employment in the case of some individuals.
[2] 1955 for manual workers, 1956 for seamen, 1957 for white-collar workers and
1968 for miners.

for miners working underground) and, like earnings in general, was
to be revalued in line with the retail price index. In 1971 it stood
at 88,954FB per annum (106,745FB for miners working underground), just under £800 at the official exchange rate, and equal to
49 per cent of gross average earnings of adult males in manufacturing, or 54 per cent of gross average industrial earnings (male and
female).[1]

The individual's actual earnings are taken into account for the
years 1955 and after, but subject to a certain ceiling in the case of
white-collar workers and seamen. Consequently the change-over
to earnings-related pensions was a gradual process: there will in
fact be *some* flat-rate element in pensions until the year 2000 (i.e.
forty-five years after the introduction of graduated pensions in
1955). It may be noted that the system of dynamizing pension
rights (i.e. the earnings on which pensions are based) in line with
the retail price index makes recently earned pension rights more
valuable than those acquired some time ago, due to the rise in real
earnings. The relative weight of the pre-1955 flat rate element is
therefore being reduced all the faster.

Just as N includes periods of involuntary unemployment,
incapacity for health reasons, etc., so W includes earnings with
which people in such circumstances are credited. It may be
appropriate to mention that this sort of security is much less highly
developed in private schemes, credited contributions for periods of
unemployment being a case in point. It follows that greater
emphasis on private schemes will reduce the level of protection
afforded to employees who may find themselves in this sort of
situation. This consideration obviously has some bearing on the
question of the ceiling because this, in its turn, will be a crucial
factor for the future of private schemes.

There was formerly a *residence condition*, i.e. that pensioners
live in Belgium or in a country which had signed a mutual agreement with Belgium. Since 1 April 1970 this has been relaxed
somewhat: there is now no residence requirement for Belgian
nationals, refugees and expatriates (as defined in the 1952 Control

---

[1] The assumed earnings of white-collar workers had been higher than those of
manual workers, but the amounts were standardized with the launching of the
General Scheme in 1968. At the same time a compensatory change in the payment of annuities ensures that white-collar workers were at least as well off as
before.

of Aliens Act), nationals of EEC countries, of countries which have signed mutual agreements with Belgium and also countries which have only ratified the interim European agreement on social security schemes concerning old age, invalidity and survivors.[1]

The normal *pension age* is sixty-five for men[2] and sixty for women, but in either case pensions may be drawn up to five years earlier. For each year's anticipation there is a reduction in the pension of 5 per cent. Retirement may also be deferred and additional pension rights may thus be acquired, subject to certain limits and conditions. The flexibility in retirement age allowed by the Belgian system is not new, but it has been observed by pension schemes that there is a stronger tendency for people to retire early than there has been in the past. Furthermore, there have been demands in recent years that the age at which a full pension may be drawn should be lowered. It is interesting in this connection to examine the views of people involved in a survey carried out in 1968 by Professor Guy Spitaels and Danilo Klaric at the *Institut de Sociologie* in Brussels,[3] on behalf of the *Office Belge pour l'Accroissement de la Productivité*. Those interviewed were representatives of employers, on the one hand, and of employees on the other—only *seventy-five* in all. The criteria governing the choice of those to be interviewed was that they should be sufficiently informed on the subject of social security to give coherent answers to the questions, but sufficiently detached from administration or policy-making to ensure the independence of their views.

All the trade unionists voiced a clear preference for a general lowering of the retirement age. The proportion of employers in favour of this was very much smaller than that of the trade unionists. Similarly the proportion of employers opposed to any change was very much higher than that of employees, although

---

[1] It may be noted that there has never been a residence requirement in the miners' scheme. The 1970 reform may therefore be seen as significant not only in the international context, but also in the process of internal harmonization.

[2] Normal retirement age is sixty in the case of *seamen* and by 1 January 1973 the retirement age for *fishermen* will have been reduced from sixty-five to sixty. The *miners* are also an exceptional case: surface workers retire at sixty; those working underground retire either at fifty-five, or after thirty years' work in the mines, whichever is earlier. Miners and seamen may not draw their pensions any earlier.

[3] G. Spitaels and D. Klaric, *Sécurité sociale et opinions des groupes professionnelles*, Editions de l'Institut de Sociologie, Université Libre de Bruxelles, 1969.

most of the employers wanted *some* lowering. Manual workers were more favourable to a lowering than white-collar workers.

There is also an *age condition* for receiving a widow's pension. Unless the widow is caring for a child or is 66 per cent disabled, she must be forty-five years of age to qualify for a survivor's pension.

In Belgium, as in Britain, there is a *retirement condition*. An individual may receive a direct or survivor's pension only provided that he (*a*) does not work more than ninety hours a month, if he is paid on an hourly basis, or (*b*) does not have gross earnings from work in excess of about 33 per cent of average gross earnings (male and female) or 30 per cent (male only). The earnings limit in (*b*) does not apply to people earning an hourly wage, so that it is quite possible for a wage earner to earn considerably more than a third of average earnings, as long as he satisfies the ninety-hour condition. A pensioner who exceeds the specified limit, or rather one whom the authorities find out about, has his pension suspended. There is no mechanism for reducing the pension by an amount corresponding to the excess earnings, as there is in the UK.[1]

Broadly speaking there is *no retirement condition* attached to pensions in France, Germany, Italy, Sweden or the Netherlands. In this respect Belgium is clearly out of line, as is the UK. The imposition of a retirement condition has come to be widely regarded as a restriction of personal liberty.[2] In favour of restriction it has been held that a person should not receive a pension while still working and thereby have a greater income than he had before drawing his pension. This view has received more attention since the advent of pay-as-you-go: under such a system of financing pensions it is more clear that the working population is paying for the pensions of the elderly. There would seem to be something amiss if the benefactor ends up by being poorer than the beneficiary. Nevertheless we cannot ignore the possibility of pensioners being caught in a *poverty trap* situation, as the Belgian arrangements imply marginal tax rates far in excess of 100 per cent.

It now seems likely, however, that further relaxation will come

---

[1] It should be noted that the retirement condition does not necessarily apply to the pensioner's spouse. The spouse need not work within the specified limits as long as the pensioner only draws a single person's (60 per cent) pension. The same retirement condition applies in the case of a survivor's pension.

[2] For details of the debate carried on during the mid-1960s, see 'Second Report of the Pensions Study Group', in the *Revue Belge de Sécurité Sociale*, Aug. 1965, p. 1,099.

perhaps less in response to domestic pressure than to the need for international harmonization. (It would be most unjust if French pensioners were commuting across the border to work in jobs which were closed to Belgian pensioners). A step in this direction has indeed been taken. Although the basic pension in Belgium is subject to a retirement condition, people who do not wish to retire from full-time employment receive an unconditional pension. This is calculated like an annuity in a funded system, the assumed premium being 3 per cent of ranking earnings. Only income earned after 1 January 1968 is taken into account. These unconditional pensions are extremely small at present and although provision has been made for increasing them, they are never likely to become very significant. The drawing of an unconditional pension does not, however, affect the individual's pension rights proper.

A pensioner must renounce all claims to sickness, disability or unemployment benefits. However, annuities or allowances awarded in respect of industrial injury or occupational sickness may be paid in addition to pensions. The individual concerned may also ask for the length of time for which he has been disabled to be taken into account in calculating his pension. If this is done, however, it limits the extent to which the pension may be supplemented by industrial injury or occupational sickness benefits. The rules regarding other social benefits apply equally to direct pensions and survivor's pensions.

General Scheme pension statistics classify pensions in three categories: (*a*) complete careers; (*b*) partial careers; and (*c*) mixed careers.

Pensions in category (*a*) which were drawn before 1962 are not permitted to fall below certain minima[1] (*minima garantis*) which are given in Table 7.2.

The minimum levels are based on the assumed flat-rate earnings which apply to years before 1955 (manual workers) or 1957 (white-collar workers). In calculating pensions, all earnings, actual or assumed, are revalued in line with *prices*. Since there has been a

---

[1] By setting minimum pension levels for the few years following the introduction of earnings-related pensions, the authorities tried to ensure that lower paid workers retiring after 1955 were not worse off than people who had retired earlier. The measure was repealed in 1962 as the rise in real earnings since 1955 meant that most new pensioners were above the minimum anyway. However, it might well be asked why the minimum was not retained for pensions drawn after 1962, since by implication the cost would not have been very great.

TABLE 7.2

Minimum levels in July 1971 of 'complete career' pensions drawn before 1962

	Francs per annum	As per cent of average earnings[3]
Manual workers:[1]		
Couple	77,844	43
Single person	62,280	35
White-collar workers:		
Couple	100,632[2]	56
Single person	84,888	47

Source: *Aperçu de la Sécurité Sociale en Belgique, 1972.*

rise in *real earnings* the pension formula gives greater weight to average earnings in, say, 1972, than to average earnings in, say, 1956. Therefore in the years following 1955 individuals' actual earnings in most cases exerted a favourable influence on their pensions, i.e. caused them to be higher than the minimum level. At the end of 1969 beneficiaries of 'complete career' pensions numbered 524,000 (counting married couples as two), which represented 33 per cent of the elderly population (men over sixty-five, women over sixty).

As regards the other two categories of pension—partial and mixed careers—the situation is complicated and difficult to assess. One of the best analyses is contained in an article by J. Mertens.[4] He concludes that out of the 76,000 couples and 305,000 single persons drawing partial and mixed career pensions there were about 60,000 couples receiving less than 60,000FB per annum and about 180,000 single persons receiving less than 48,000FB per annum in 1969. Raised in line with subsequent increases in pensions, these amounts would have been 72,000FB and 58,000FB in July 1971 or rather less than the minima for full career pensions given in Table 7.2. The author further points, however, that some of these people may have other pension rights from periods

[1] Also surface workers in mining, and lower ranks in the merchant navy.

[2] The minimum levels for 'complete career' pensions drawn before 1962 are higher in the case of white collar workers, as the flat rate earnings assumed in computing their claims were at that time higher than those for manual workers. This ceased to be the case in 1968.

[3] Gross average earnings of adult males in manufacturing.

[4] *'Les ressources des personnes âgées en Belgique'*, J. Mertens. *Revue Belge de Securité Sociale*, No. 8, August 1971.

spent in military or public service, as the figures for mixed careers cover only pension rights in the General Scheme, a small voluntary scheme (*assurance libre*) and the scheme for the self-employed. There is no minimum insurance period required for a partial General Scheme pension.

The vast bulk of the General Scheme's benefit expenditure goes on retirement pensions and survivors' pensions. There are, however, various other types of benefit which, though of secondary importance, deserve to be mentioned.

Holiday allowance. An annual holiday allowance (*la pécule de vacances*) is paid in May to recipients of both direct and survivors' pensions. In 1971 the allowance amounted to 1170FB (£10) for a couple and 702FB (£6) for a single person;[1] it is tied to the retail price index. The holiday allowance is frequently criticized for being too low, considering that the working population must, by law, get at least three weeks' holiday with *double* pay!

Annuities. Although the state pension scheme is now wholly pay-as-you-go, annuities are still paid out to individuals who contributed to the *old* official funded scheme. Since 1968 these annuities have been tied to the retail price index. Their importance is, however, small for manual workers: in 1968 payments were equivalent to 3 per cent of the average pension of a married couple. For white-collar workers, however, the figure was just over 20 per cent.[2]

'Adaptation payment' for widows. Widows who do not satisfy the conditions laid down for receiving a survivor's pension, may claim an adaptation payment. This is a single lump sum payment equal to one year's instalment of the survivor's pension which the widow would otherwise have received.

Financing General Scheme pensions

The General Scheme has three main sources of finance: employers' contributions, employees' contributions and state subsidies.

---

[1] Where the monthly pension is less than the holiday allowance, the allowance is reduced to equal the pension. This only happens in the case of incomplete pensions awarded to individuals who have been covered by the employees' pension scheme for a relatively short time.

[2] Ministère de la Prévoyance Sociale.

Contributions, like benefits in some respects, have not yet been completely harmonized. The position on 1 October 1971 is summarized in Table 7.3.

TABLE 7.3

Contribution rates in the General Scheme: 1 October 1971

	Employees (per cent)	Employers (per cent)	Total (per cent)	Earnings ceiling FB per annum
Manual workers	6	8	14	—
White-collar workers	5	7·25	12·25	217,200 (£1,890)
Miners	6	8	14	—
Seamen	7·25	7·75	15	210,780 (£1,830)

Source: *Aperçu de la Sécurité Sociale en Belgique, 1972.*

The group which pays least in contributions is the white-collar workers. Their contribution rates are now being gradually raised and by 1975 they will be the same as those paid by manual workers.

Financial considerations were fundamental to the reorganization of official private sector pensions within a single General Scheme. As the structure of employment changed, so too did the ratio of employees to pensioners in the various schemes. Several schemes suffered from these trends, notably those for manual workers and miners, while the white-collar workers' scheme benefited. Government subsidies were used to compensate the losers, but the authorities naturally wanted a more permanent solution. This was plainly to be found in an integrated scheme: a scheme covering all groups of the population would not be affected financially by the movements taking place between the various groups. Of course the General Scheme does not in fact cover *all* groups but this need not concern it greatly as there is little chance of a mass movement of private sector employees into self-employment or the public sector. The General Scheme solution put pensions on a more stable financial basis and in so doing helped to relieve the financial pressure on the state itself. No particular group could now be identified as being at a particular disadvantage and for that reason deserving a subsidy. The figures show a clear drop in the relative size of state subsidies, as may be seen in Table 7.4.

Fluctuations in the ratio of employees to pensioners in a particular scheme may, as we have seen, be minimized by giving that scheme as broad a base in the population as possible. However the finances of the General Scheme will also be affected by demo-

TABLE 7.4

General Scheme revenue

Percentage	1966[1]	1969	1971[2]
Employers' contributions	40·4	41·7	45·0
Employees' contributions	30·5	31·8	33·4
State subsidy	17·0	16·2	13·6
Income from capital	12·1	10·3	8·0
Total revenue	100·0	100·0	100·0

Source: Ministère de la Prévoyance Sociale, *Rapport Général sur la Sécurité Sociale 1970.*

graphic changes which are altering the general ratio of pensioners to contributors. The population forecasts used in Table 7.5 assume: (*a*) a falling trend in fertility until 1974, and constancy thereafter at 1974 level; (*b*) a falling trend in mortality until 1974, and constancy thereafter at 1974 level; (*c*) net immigration of 10,000 per annum until 1974, thereafter zero net immigration. The population between the ages of twenty and sixty-five is not of course the same as the contributors to the General Scheme, but the two will move together if there is no dramatic shift in labour force participation rates.

TABLE 7.5

Over sixty-fives as a percentage of population aged twenty to sixty-five

1970	1975	1980	1985
24·0	25·5	25·9	22·7

Source: M. W. Cuveele, *Prévisions de la population de la Belgique,* 1972.

The ratio of the elderly to the active population will rise throughout the 1970s, although much faster in the first half of the decade; a very significant drop will then take place in the early 1980s. To meet the rise in the 1970s, contribution rates are being increased to 14 per cent in 1975 (in 1968 they were 12·5 per cent for manual workers and 10·25 per cent for white-collar workers) and the scheme is dipping into its reserves. The need for such action is reinforced by Belgium's desire not simply to maintain the level of pensions in terms of earnings but actually to improve the

[1] In 1966 there was of course no General Scheme but the figures cover the same groups of the population both before and after 1968.

[2] Figures for 1971 are forecasts.

position of the pensioner relative to that of the working population. There will of course be greater scope for carrying this on after 1980.

Private occupational schemes

Complementary pension schemes in Belgium are similar to British schemes in that they vary widely as regards the level of pension provision. This inequality derives mainly from the fact that the schemes are private and that it is left largely to the employer's discretion what pension provision he will make for his employees. Complementary schemes in Belgium have traditionally been restricted to salaried or white-collar staff. As we have seen, this is associated with the fact that there is a ceiling on contributions and benefits for white-collar workers in the General Scheme. However the authorities are encouraging employers to bring manual workers into their schemes and it has been indicated that a ceiling may be introduced in 1974 for manual workers in the General Scheme.

Existing complementary schemes tend in the main to provide insurance for that part of a person's salary which exceeds the ceiling of the General Scheme, but this salary offset method will be less appropriate if manual workers are to be brought into the schemes, as a full offset will prevent lower paid workers from effectively participating in the scheme. Consequently different methods based either on full integration with the General Scheme pension or on differential benefit scales on salary above and below the General Scheme ceiling are being adopted. Private schemes in Belgium are generally funded. As far as benefit levels are concerned, our knowledge is limited to the *best* schemes[1] which tend to aim at a total pension inclusive of General Scheme benefits equal to two-thirds of final pay. It will be recalled that the General Scheme targets are 75 per cent (couple) or 60 per cent (single person) of life-time earnings revalued in line with retail prices. Due to the rise in real earnings these targets represent less than two-thirds of final pay, and for white-collar workers they may be considerably less because they have also a low ceiling in their scheme.

---

[1] Especially that of the Bank of Brussels.

Information on private pension schemes is very deficient, as in the UK. The statisticians in the Belgian Ministry of Social Security have recently been making approaches to the Insurance Inspectorate, which is part of the Ministry of Economic Affairs, in an attempt to get more data on private schemes. One of the main difficulties seems to be that the reports issued in accordance with the legislation controlling life insurance companies (passed on 25 June 1930) supply plentiful information on ordinary life insurance business but little on group pension insurance (*assurance de groupe*). Furthermore this legislation does not apply to employers' funds[1] nor to some 400 group insurance funds which are constituted as ASBLs (*associations sans but lucratif* or non-profit-making organizations).[2]

As in the UK, the tax system has some influence on private schemes, certain conditions having to be fulfilled if full tax relief is to be granted on contributions. Two of these conditions are that the scheme must be compulsory for a well-defined group of employees. Moreover there must be *full vesting*, or *preservation of pension rights* after five years' membership, an important condition which means that, in this respect, the private arrangements in Belgium are superior to those in a number of other countries. If a scheme does not conform to these conditions, only ordinary life assurance relief may be claimed (tax relief is granted on life assurance premiums up to 15 per cent of the first 50,000FB of income and 6 per cent of income over that amount).

Company schemes must have a set of rules which form part of the contract of employment: these should specify the rights and the liabilities of members and the method of calculating benefits. The same procedure must be used in modifying these rules as is used in modifying the contract of employment.

The tax authorities require that both employers and employees be represented on the board of management of a pension scheme regardless of who pays the contributions. Under the terms of a national agreement signed in 1958 (later modified in 1962) the *conseil d'entreprise* in which employer and employee are *equally* represented should have control over pension funds when they

---

[1] These *caisses patronales* are tending to decline in importance.

[2] Six or seven of these funds are very large, e.g. Lever, where some 10,000 people belong to the scheme.

involve personal contributions from the employees and when they have the corporate identity of an ASBL (*association sans but lucratif* or non-profit-making organization).

III—PENSIONS FOR OTHER SECTIONS OF THE POPULATION

In Belgium two important groups of the working population are not covered by the General Scheme. These are the self-employed and public servants. Pensions for these two groups differ significantly from those provided by the General Scheme. On the one hand the self-employed receive low flat-rate pensions; until the summer of 1972 these were means-tested. On the other hand, public servants receive very good earnings-related pensions which replace up to 75 per cent of their *final earnings*. These pensions are markedly more generous than those provided by the General Scheme, under which a couple receive a '75 per cent pension', based, not on final earnings, but on average earnings during working life revalued in line with prices only.

A statutory scheme for the *self-employed* was set up by an Act of Parliament in 1956. Members contributed to a fund with the aim of providing annuities, equivalent to 31 per cent and 21 per cent[1] for a man and woman respectively of gross average industrial earnings (male and female). Contributions were dependent upon age and sex. If the target was not reached, the member concerned could apply for a supplement which was subject to a means test.[2] This was paid by a Solidarity Fund financed by income-related contributions. There were therefore two separate contributions, calculated in different ways. In 1960 these were replaced by a single contribution based on income, the system of annuities was abandoned and the scheme became wholly pay-as-you-go. Various increases in pensions took place. Their real value was thus raised but did not keep pace with earnings until, in 1970, new legislation improved the position. A five-year plan was then drawn up setting out projected increases in contribution rates and in benefits

---

[1] The annuities were fixed in cash terms. The rates quoted are therefore those applicable in that year.

[2] In 1968, the amount of income disregarded was equivalent to 18 per cent of average earnings for a married man and 12 per cent for a single man.

which in real terms, are to rise about a quarter between 1971 and 1975.[1]

In October 1971 pensions were in fact 52,877FB and 35,692FB, or 34 per cent and 23 per cent of gross average earnings, representing a substantial improvement on the situation in 1968 when the corresponding figures were 26 and 17 per cent.

In recent years various reforms have been introduced to reduce the disparities existing between the scheme for the self-employed and the General Scheme, e.g. flexibility in retirement (1968), abolition of the means test (1972), and the raising of the single person's pension from 67·5 per cent to 80 per cent of the pension for a couple (1971–75). Many of the rules and conditions regarding the payment of pensions are similar to those in the General Scheme. For instance, although the scheme pays flat-rate pensions, reductions are made if an individual is not deemed to have a 'complete career', i.e. has not been self-employed since 1946; about 20,000 pensioners consequently receive less than the basic pension, i.e. about a tenth of the 'self-employed' pensioners.

Table 7.6 shows the composition and growth of the scheme's annual revenue.

TABLE 7.6

Revenue of the scheme for the self-employed

	As percentage of total	
	1969	*1971*
Personal contributions	52·4	54·6
State subsidy	41·3	44·0
Income from capital	3·0	1·3
Other income	3·3	0·1
Total	100·0	100·0
Index (1969 = 100)	100	127

Source: Ministère de la Prévoyance Sociale, *Rapport Général sur la Sécurité Sociale, 1970.* (The figures for 1971 are forecasts.)

During the period 1970–75 personal contribution rates are to rise from 5·60 per cent to 6·65 per cent. This contribution is paid only on incomes up to a certain limit which in 1971 was equal to 107 per cent of average earnings of adult males in manufacturing industry. On earnings between this limit and another limit equal to 188 per

[1] Ministère de la Prévoyance Sociale, *Rapport Général sur la Sécurité Sociale, 1970.*

cent of average earnings there is a contribution of 2 per cent which is being raised to 2·25 per cent.

The increases are fairly modest and this fact bears witness to the political difficulties faced by a Government which wishes to tax the self-employed more heavily. It is certain that their pension scheme will continue to be subsidized out of general taxation and it is probable that the subsidy will become relatively more important given the decline of the self-employed as a proportion of the working population.

Sections of the self-employed in Belgium, as in other European countries, have suffered from poverty in old age. The scheme's pensions have in fact been well below public assistance levels and this is as true in 1972 as it was before the 1970 reforms. The recommended assistance rate in October 1971 for a couple was 62,280FB per annum compared with a pension of 52,877FB. However, there seems to be little doubt that Belgium has committed herself to change this situation in the next few years.

In Belgium *public servants* get better pensions relative to pre-retirement earnings than any other group of the working population. Their pensions tend to represent an aspiration level for employees in the private sector. It will be recalled that those covered by the 1844 Pension Act include civil servants, magistrates, the clergy, the military and the teaching profession (schools *and* universities).

Public servants : conditions and benefits

Public servants qualify for a pension at the age of sixty-five, assuming that they have completed twenty years' service. There is normally no flexibility in the age at which the pension may be drawn. School teachers, however, are a special case: if they have taught for thirty years they may retire at sixty.

In calculating the length of service, account is taken not only of employment by the Belgian state but also of time spent in the employment of the Congo and Ruanda-Urundi. In addition, years spent studying for a degree which constituted a condition either for admission to the service or for promotion are counted as years of service (minimum of three years' study required, permitted maximum usually four).

The amount of pension an individual receives is related both to his earnings and to his length of service. For each year of service he receives one sixtieth of his average salary over the last five years (or one fiftieth for 'active' (i.e. tiring or dangerous) service: one fiftieth for primary school teachers: one fifty-fifth for other teachers). 'Average salary over the last five years' does not mean the average amount of money actually received, but rather the *current* salary rates which correspond to the positions held by the individual over the last five years. This is therefore very nearly equivalent to a *final* salary scheme; the individual is protected from the effects of both rising prices and rising pay scales. It seems probable that the effect of other factors in raising the individual's earnings (e.g. promotion) would be fairly slight at this stage in his career.

A pension calculated in any of the ways outlined above is not allowed to exceed 75 per cent of the salary on which it is based. Therefore an ordinary civil servant has maximum pension rights after forty-five years' service, while a primary school teacher receives the maximum pension after thirty-seven-and-a-half years. Special bonuses may be awarded which are *not* subject to the 75 per cent maximum. Periods of military service in wartime and of colonial service may be counted twice, and military service for which one is decorated is counted three times. Under these arrangements the pension may not exceed 90 per cent of salary.

The state guarantees its employees a certain minimum pension, as shown in Table 7.7. It is to be noted that where the beneficiary has other pension income this is deducted from the specified minimum.

TABLE 7.7

Minimum public service pensions in 1969 as percentage of gross average earnings of adult males in manufacturing[1]

	White-collar	Manual
Married man	47	36
Single man	40	29
Woman	38	29

In fact about 12 per cent of direct pensions were less than 50,000 FB in 1969. It has been suggested[2] that the only plausible reasons

[1] Gross average earnings of adult males in manufacturing were equal to 151,840FB per annum.
[2] J. Mertens, *loc. cit.*

for such low pensions would be a relatively short career in public service. If this is so, then many of the people concerned will have worked elsewhere and will probably have pension rights in another scheme.

State employees may lose their pension rights if they are dismissed or resign or are found guilty of a criminal offence. In any of these circumstances the individual does not lose everything, however, as he may have his period of service to the state recognized as valid for the purposes of a General Scheme pension.

A public service pension combined with a salary or another public sector pension must not bring the pensioner's income above the highest total income (salary and pensions) he had ever been earning when he left any of his posts. The pension may thus be seen as a retirement rather than an old age pension.

Public service pensions are very well dynamized. As we have seen, they are based more or less on final income so that there is no question of pension *rights* being inadequately dynamized. In this respect, they are in clear contrast with General Scheme pensions. Pensions in payment, like salaries, are automatically tied to the retail price index and furthermore are automatically raised in line with public service salary scales.

Employees of the Belgian Railways (SNCFB) have their own special scheme which not only pays better pensions than the General Scheme but also has a lower retirement age. No figures on pensions in payment are available: the situation is reckoned[1] to be similar to that in the public servants' scheme, namely that *direct* pensions are substantial, but that a significant percentage of *widows* (30 per cent) were receiving less than 50,000FB per annum in 1969.

IV—MINIMUM PENSIONS AND POVERTY

There are three official minima to be taken into account. The first is the guaranteed minimum (*minimum garanti*) for full career pensions which has already been described and is not subject to a means-test. The second is the national minimum allowance (*revenu garanti*) for elderly people with low incomes who are not entitled to full career pensions. The third is the local assistance

[1] See J. Mertens, *loc. cit.*

which is operated in conjunction with the second minimum. The last two may now be briefly described.

The National Minimum Allowance (revenu garanti)

This payment is available to those people who have never belonged to any pension scheme or who have belonged to a scheme for such a short time that their pension rights are insignificant. In this category are people who have not been capable of working, people with a private income which by the age of sixty or sixty-five has become inadequate through inflation, and certain cases like that of a woman who had remained single in order to care for her parents and had been supported by relatives after the death of her parents. Those receiving the allowance at the beginning of 1972 numbered approximately 80,000 (5 per cent of the population over normal pension age).

The allowance was launched in 1969 as part of the Government's drive to ensure the rights of every citizen to a 'social minimum'.[1] For all that, the allowance can hardly be described as a social minimum (or even a subsistence minimum). Nevertheless its introduction was important since it put aid to the elderly on a national basis, thereby *reducing* the dependence of the elderly on local public assistance. This may be regarded as desirable for the following reason: the individual has no *rights vis-à-vis* the public assistance authority, since the latter has complete discretion as to the amount of any aid it may grant; on the other hand the 1969 legislation confers a right upon elderly persons to an allowance of a specified amount subject to specified conditions regarding any other income they might have.

The initial level of the allowance on 1 May 1969 was extremely low, equivalent to 24 per cent and 16 per cent for a couple and single person respectively of gross average earnings of adult males in industry. By October 1971 the allowance had risen by 33 per cent to 41,620FB for a couple and 27,746FB for a single person. In the same period (May 1969 to October 1971) average male

---

[1] To qualify for the allowance men must be aged sixty-five or over and women sixty. The individual must be a Belgian national, a refugee, or a national of a country with which Belgium has signed an agreement referring specifically to this allowance. Normally recipients must reside in Belgium, but dispensation may be granted in certain circumstances.

M

industrial earnings rose by 26 per cent so that the replacement factor for a couple was $25\frac{1}{2}$ per cent, for a single person 17 per cent.

It will be recalled that the minima in the General Scheme (*minimum garanti*) were equivalent, at mid-1971, to 43 per cent of average annual earnings for a married couple and 35 per cent for a single person (p. 315, above).

At the time the allowance was introduced, the authorities stressed their intention to raise the amount of the allowance rather than relax the means test, and they indicated that in addition to being tied to the retail price index the allowance would increase in *real* terms by 10 per cent per annum. However, due to the exceptionally rapid rise in earnings, the position of those receiving the allowance relative to the working population has improved rather less than might have been expected. Nonetheless there has been an improvement and we may expect this to continue, maybe at a slightly faster rate, in the next few years.

The most important qualifying condition is the means test. The *general* rule is that all the income and property of the individual (and his wife) are taken into account, regardless of type or source. However, certain income, whatever the amount, is disregarded: family allowances for children; certain old age annuities, including those awarded in respect of courageous action in the war and of captivity as a POW. The payments are also related to public assistance as explained in the next section.

It is possible that the recipient may have a partial pension (he will not, of course, have a complete career pension, as this would automatically make him ineligible for the allowance) and the first 6,960FB of pension income, in the case of a couple, or 4,640FB in the case of a single person, is disregarded. (These amounts are tied to the retail price index and refer to October 1971.) As for other income theoretically taken into consideration, the first 10,440FB or 6,960FB is disregarded.

An example might help to clarify these rules: let us take the case of a single person in October 1971 with a partial General Scheme pension amounting to 8,640FB per annum, and with other income totalling 12,960FB. He would qualify for an allowance of

$$27,746 - (8,640-4,640) - (12,960-6,960)$$
$$= 17,746\text{FB per annum, thereby bringing his total income up}$$
to 39,346FB per annum.

Clearly the allowance is low and taken alone could not satisfy an old person's needs. This point is in fact made quite clear in a pamphlet issued in 1969 by the Ministry of Social Security to explain the new allowance:

> 'Neither the Government, nor Parliament, considers that the level of benefits provided under this legislation constitute a subsistence income.'

Consequently, public assistance still has an important role to play in the provision of cash benefits for the elderly.

In Belgium the *public assistance offices* (CAPs) are controlled at the level of the town or commune. Traditionally the communes have had a large degree of autonomy *vis-à-vis* the central Government and they still cherish their freedom. One consequence of this is that there are no nationally enforceable rates for public assistance.

Recently, the Union of Belgian Towns and Communes has taken an increasing interest in public assistance and in 1969 it published a guide to benefit levels.[1] The introduction to the booklet stresses that the Union is not attempting to *impose* norms, but simply suggesting some figures as *guidance* for those public assistance offices which are less well equipped to assess individual cases of need. The importance of individual treatment is amply recognized but, of course, this requires skilled social workers who may be scarce or non-existent in the smaller communes.

The guide to benefit levels mentioned above bases its recommendations on the guaranteed minima for complete career pensions awarded by the manual workers' scheme before 1962: ordinary cash benefits (designed to cover food and rent) should be 80 per cent of these minima in the case of a single person and 85 per cent of these minima in the case of a couple. In October 1971 the recommended assistance rates would therefore be 4,152FB and 5,514FB, 28 per cent and 38 per cent of average gross earnings of adult males in industry. As we have noted assistance is operated in conjunction with the national minimum allowance. That is to say, the local payments are made in order to bring incomes up to these percentages after the national minimum allowances have been taken into account.

---

[1] Union des Villes et des Communes Belges, *L'octroi des secours par les commissions d'assistance publique*, 1969.

Finally, the guide stresses that its recommendations should be regarded as *minima* and that CAPs should be ready to grant more in cases of particular hardship, e.g. when the individual does not enjoy good health.

In general Belgium has tried to get away from the practice of giving *benefits in kind*, as these are so much associated in the public mind with charity and paternalism.[1] Medical care, however, may be thought of as assistance in kind, and the elderly in Belgium do benefit significantly in this respect.

All pensioners are automatically covered by the health insurance scheme without paying any contributions. In addition to free insurance, pensioners have a higher proportion of medical costs covered than other people in the scheme, as long as their income does not exceed a certain limit, fixed and periodically altered by Royal Decree. The majority of pensioners seem to qualify for this preferential treatment. While the costs of treatment for minor ailments is normally reimbursed at the rate of 75 per cent of the fixed tariffs (*tarifs conventionnels*), pensioners qualify for reimbursement at the rate of 100 per cent. The costs of other treatment are reimbursed 100 per cent in all cases. The normal prescription charge of 25FB (22p) is waived in the case of pensioners, and the charge made for special drugs is 25FB instead of the normal 50 FB.

The role of the CAPs[2] in the field of health care is predominantly to help people who for one reason or another are not covered by health insurance. However, they should also grant assistance to anyone with an income not in excess of the recommended scale rates, and to other people who cannot afford to pay small medical expenses not covered by insurance. It is interesting to note that the means test applied by the CAPs in the case of medical aid is usually much less restrictive than for general cash benefits. Public assistance therefore provides supplementary medical protection from which pensioners and other sections of the population may benefit.

---

[1] According to the guide published by the Union of Belgian Towns and Communes.

[2] I.e. the public assistance offices.

V—THE FUTURE OF OCCUPATIONAL SCHEMES

The future of private schemes is closely bound up with the way in which the General Scheme itself is going to develop. The question of the ceiling on contributions and benefits in the General Scheme is particularly relevant in this connection. The existing ceiling in the white-collar workers scheme (130 per cent of average earnings) makes the statutory pension quite inadequate for most white-collar workers and would have the same effect on the more highly paid manual worker. The more inadequate statutory pensions are, the more necessary private schemes become, and the more likely they are to flourish. The correlation is logical and furthermore may be observed in various countries in Europe.

If the Belgian authorities do introduce a ceiling for all employees in the General Scheme this will tend to confirm the position of private pension schemes, unless the ceiling is quite a high one. Are employees likely to regard such a development favourably?

A statement made by the union of the white-collar workers, the *Centre National des Employés* (CNE), suggests that they may not.[1] It expressed the following views, which had been those of the union's last conference: the General Scheme pension should be equal to 75 per cent of average earnings over the last five years or during the ten best years of the insured person's career (this is the same policy as formulated by the *Confédération des Syndicats Chrétiens* (CSC) at their 1968 conference); statutory pensions should be sufficiently high, so that *all* white-collar workers might benefit more fully from them, and private schemes would thereby become superfluous; in the meantime all private schemes should be placed under the jurisdiction of the Ministry of Social Security and this Ministry should implement a programme of standardization.

Another familiar weakness of private occupational schemes is the problem of dynamizing pension rights and pensions in payment. Admittedly the return on capital invested in pension funds is likely to rise over time, unless the choice of assets is unduly restricted. But as long as the rate at which prices and earnings rise tend to vary over time, it is unlikely that funded schemes will be able to guarantee pensioners either a stable standard of living or a standard which rises in line with that of the working generation.

---

[1] Professor Spitaels' admittedly limited survey conveys, on the whole, the same impression.

Uncertainty therefore is the main problem for private schemes which wish to dynamize. A different but also an intractable problem may arise if funds have been badly invested or if the return to capital has declined compared with the return to labour. The pension scheme run by the Bank of Brussels has some provision for dynamizing pension rights and pensions in payment: in this case uncertainty is dealt with by special subsidies provided by the bank on a pay-as-you-go basis. However, private firms can make only limited use of pay-as-you-go, although clearly a large bank is better placed than most. To use pay-as-you-go on a large scale requires an almost watertight guarantee of solvency and normally only schemes with statutory backing can provide this.

VI—DYNAMISM IN THE OFFICIAL SCHEMES

In one respect dynamism is no longer a burning issue in Belgium since there now seems general agreement on the principle which should govern the periodic revaluation of official pensions, namely that pensions should rise in line with earnings, so that the elderly may share in the country's growing prosperity. However there is not yet any automatic mechanism to ensure that this will always happen and until one is introduced dynamism is likely to remain a topical issue. According to Professor Spitaels' study[1] employees' representatives were unanimously in favour of the principle mentioned above and almost 90 per cent of employers felt likewise. Between 1962 and 1967 the gap between pensions and earnings had grown wider and wider (see Chart 9, p. 413); experience during this period made Belgians conscious of the inadequacy of tying pensions to the retail price index. Nor is it simply coincidence that over the same period Belgium fell badly behind her European partners in what she provided for her elderly.[2]

In the autumn of 1967 it was decided to raise the level of pensions significantly: as from 1.1.68 the *real* value of the guaranteed minimum for couples was increased by just over 13 per cent in the manual workers scheme and by more than 10 per cent in the

---

[1] *Op. cit.*
[2] See EEC Social Accounts 1970, published by the Office Statistique des Communautés Européennes. The measure used is social benefits for the elderly per head divided by per capita GNP.

white-collar scheme. Since 1968 there have been annual increases in the *real* value of General Scheme pensions: these were awarded in June of 1969, 1970 and 1971 when the rises were 4 per cent, 5 per cent and 5 per cent respectively. In 1972 there was also a 5 per cent increase and the newly installed Government made the generous gesture of bringing the increase forward from June to January. Meanwhile increases have continued to be granted automatically after a 2 per cent rise in the retail price index.

As may be seen from Chart 9, the 1968 rise in pensions did help to close the gap between pensions and earnings. But if it was intended that the pensions curve should meet up again with the earnings curve the increase was not sufficient. Subsequent rises in the real value of pensions have kept pensions and earnings moving in a roughly parallel direction. It now seems unlikely that Belgian pensioners will recover all the ground they lost in the 1960s, although this *was* the explicit aim of the government's *rattrapement* ('catching up') policy.

If, as seems certain, pensions in payment continue to rise broadly in line with earnings, then a similar system of dynamizing pension *rights* will have to be introduced. Between 1968 and 1972 four increments in the value of pensions were awarded totalling 20·4 per cent and in calculating *new* pensions in 1972 this percentage has been added to the amount derived by the traditional formula. If the system continues to function in this manner increments in the early 1980s will total about 100 per cent, at which point pensions may be about 75 to 80 per cent of *final* earnings. However it seems likely that in the medium term the Government will introduce a system whereby the earnings on which the pension is based will be revalued in line with average earnings. Basically this would be the same as in France and Germany. If the pension targets of 75 per cent for a couple and 60 per cent for a single person remain the same in such a system, then clearly the level of income replacement will be far higher than at present.

CONCLUSION

Introduced in 1968, Belgium's General Scheme is still in its infancy and even the oldest of its component parts, the scheme for manual workers dates back only to 1955. Initially the scheme appeared to aim high by making its pensions target 75 per cent of earnings for a married man. It might almost have seemed that workers in industry had won parity with civil servants. However, this was not the case as dynamizing pension rights, based on life-time earnings, only with respect to prices resulted in pensions which were far less than 75 per cent of *final* earnings. It was this incomplete dynamizing that led to a deterioration of Belgian pensions relative to others in the EEC during most of the 1960s. The defect is now very widely recognized and since 1968 the Government has been taking *ad hoc* measures to redress the situation, An automatic mechanism has yet to be installed but there seems no doubt that it will embody the present policy of raising pensions in line with average earnings.

If General Scheme pensions ever approach 75 per cent of final earnings, private pensions will be almost superfluous for manual workers even if a ceiling is introduced. However, the more highly paid would continue to depend largely on private pensions. As the General Scheme improves the defects of the private funded schemes tend to become more apparent: they cannot normally ensure that pensions in payment maintain their real value, still less can they guarantee a rise in line with average earnings; they do not credit the individual with contributions during periods of unemployment. Moreover, since they are unco-ordinated and extremely diverse in their rules and provisions, they are peculiarly ill-shaped to meet the needs of a society which is aiming at greater mobility of labour combined with greater economic security for the individual.

PART III

CHAPTER EIGHT

Comparative Analysis

I—INTRODUCTION

The purpose of this final section is to summarize the main features
of the European policies described in Part II, to compare these
policies with those followed in the UK and the USA and to assess
the merits of the different approaches to common problems. These
approaches differ greatly from country to country. This is so even
if attention is confined to the original members of the EEC, as the
preceding chapters have clearly shown, and variety in these
arrangements has been still more increased by the admission of
new members to the Community. Western Europe may have its
common market, but it is very far from having a common welfare
state. These differences are not necessarily something that should
be deplored. If, however, fiscal policies are to be harmonized
within the Community and if it is further assumed that harmonization means uniformity, then some very large changes will be
needed and very great difficulties are bound to be encountered.
Harmonization, in this sense, must lie far in the future. What is by
no means clear, however, is that harmonization in this sense is an
objective that is likely to be adopted by the Community.[1] The
Community must indeed be concerned to ensure as far as possible
that differences in benefits and in the taxes used to finance them are
not such as to hamper the achievement of other objectives; but
uniformity is a very different matter. Indeed one can go further
and assert that uniformity would not be desirable and ought not to
become an objective. If the same benefits were paid subject to the

[1] See *Guidelines for a Social Programme*. Supplement 4/73 to the Bulletin of
the European Communities, Brussels, 1973, especially paragraphs 8 and 11.

TABLE 8.1

Rates of payroll tax

Country	Schemes	Benefits covered	Employer	Employee	Total	Approximate range of income on which tax is levied (as percentage of average earnings)
			%	%	%	
Germany 1973	Manual workers + white collar	Old age, disability + survivors	9·0	9·0	18·0	0–150
Netherlands 1973	General old age insurance (AOW)	Old age	—	10·4	10·4	0–150
	General widows' insurance (AWW)	Survivors	—	1·6	1·6	0–150
France 1972	General scheme	Old age + survivors	5·75	3·0	8·75	0–135
	ARRCO	Old age + survivors (average rate)	2·52	1·68	4·2	0–400
	AGIRC	Old age + survivors (average rate)	9·0	5·0	14·0	135–550

Belgium 1972					
Manual workers + miners	Old age + survivors	8.0	6.0	14.0	No ceiling
White collar	Old age + survivors	7.25	5.0	12.25	0–130
Italy 1970					
General obligatory scheme	Old age, survivors + disability	13.9	6.9	20.8	No ceiling (see [1] below)
Sweden 1971					
Basic scheme	Old age, disability + survivors	—	5.0	5.0	
Graduated (ATP)		10.25	—	10.25	25–200
USA 1971					
OASD	Old age, invalidity + survivors	5.0	5.0	10.0	0–120
UK[2]	National insurance All social insurance				
1) Oct. 1972		6.3	6.0	12.3	No limits for basic flat rate
2) New scheme		7.3	5.25	12.5	(see [2] below)

[1] The contribution is levied on taxable income up to a maximum contribution of 150 Kr.

[2] The UK tax covers all social insurance and industrial injury together with a contribution of about 0.6 per cent of payroll tax revenue for the National Health Service. About four-fifths of expenditure is on pensions for the old, for survivors and for the disabled. The figures for 1972 consist of two parts: (a) the flat charge as a percentage of average male earnings, and (b) the graduated charge for the graduated pension for someone not contracted out. The limits under both the old graduated and the new scheme are fixed periodically in money terms which vary as percentages of earnings as the latter change.

same conditions and financed by the same taxes in different countries without regard to differences in productivity and other conditions, serious problems would arise. Not only would huge transfers
have to be made through Brussels but economic development could
be seriously affected and the maintenance of full employment
would almost certainly become more difficult. Moreover it would
seem desirable for the individual members of the Community to be
able to express in their social legislation the valuations they would
wish to place on different social objectives. Harmonization need
not mean uniformity; it may be interpreted in ways that are more
limited and in some respects more indirect.

One of the indirect aspects of social security arrangements is
their possible effect on migration. Apart from any differences that
may persist in the benefits provided by different countries, the
restriction of important benefits to citizens could impede the free
movement of labour which is one of the objectives of the EEC.
The importance of this issue—and its relevance to a wider area
than Western Europe—had, of course, been recognized before the
EEC was founded and the ILO together with national governments has sought to establish satisfactory arrangements. It is the
problems posed by migrants that have received much of the
attention of the EEC itself. On the broader issues of differences in
national social policies little appears to have been done apart from
the collection and analysis of information and, more recently, the
preparation of forecasts of future expenditure.[1] As Barbara Rodgers
has observed: 'If the more specifically social sections of the Treaty
of Rome have so far contributed little to the actual policies of the
Six, this is largely because they are as ambitious as they are
abstract.'[2]

Another indirect aspect of different social security arrangements
is the possible effect on foreign trade of having payroll taxes levied
at various rates in different countries. (The main purpose of these
payroll taxes is, of course, to finance social security.) The committee which investigated this matter on behalf of the International
Labour Office,[3] pointed out that payroll taxes had to be considered

---

[1] See *L'évolution financière de la sécurité sociale dans les États membres de la
Communauté*.

[2] See 'Implications of Britain's Entry into the Common Market', *Journal of
Social Policy*, Cambridge University Press, Jan. 1973.

[3] See *Social Aspects of European Economic Co-operation*, Report by a Group of
Experts, I.L.O., Geneva, 1956. See also 'Problems of Harmonisation of Social

along with wages and salaries and both had to be related to differing levels of productivity and to exchange rates. A high payroll tax should not cause balance of payments problems any more than high money wages provided relative productivity levels and exchange rates were appropriate. In short it was no more necessary to aim at equal rates of payroll tax than it was to aim at equal money wages. Three further points must, however, be made. First, if exchange rates are fixed—as would be the case with European Monetary Union—then the scope for accommodating changes in the rates of payroll tax in the member countries of the Community will be limited. This, of course, is similar to the limitations imposed on differences in rates of change of money wages relative to changing productivity. The point is not that there is a difference in principle but rather that, in assessing the case for new or enhanced benefits to be financed by altering payroll taxes, the balance-of-payments effects may be more inhibiting with fixed exchange rates. With mobile capital one consequence might be that the location of new plants would be affected. The second point relates to those countries where welfare provisions and corresponding payroll charges are not uniform for all industries. (The special schemes in Italy are an example.) When this occurs the pattern of trade may be distorted at least in principle, although it may be doubted whether the quantitative importance of this distortion is particularly serious. Third, changes in the methods of financing social security may affect the prices of imports and exports. Naturally this consequence may also follow from changes in the structure of the general system used to finance general public expenditure. Some attention has, however, been given to the possible consequences of reducing payroll taxes and raising a corresponding sum from a value-added tax.[1] Finally, variations in the payroll tax have been used deliberately as an instrument of economic policy, including regional policy.[2] We cannot pursue these matters further in the present context but their relevance must be kept in mind. The different

Security Policies in a Common Market', by Norbert Aadel in *Fiscal Harmonisation in Common Markets,* ed. Carl S. Shoup, Columbia University Press, 1967; and *The Theory of Economic Integration* by Bela Balassa, Irwin, 1961.

[1] A reduction in the payroll tax with a corresponding rise in VAT would make exports cheaper (because a payroll tax falls on exports but VAT does not) and would also make imports dearer (because a payroll tax does not fall on imports but VAT does).

[2] See the discussion of Italian practice by Kevin Allen in Chapter 5 above.

levels of payroll tax for the financing of benefits are shown above in Table 8.1. The extent to which these payroll taxes contribute to total cost is shown in Table 8.2 together with any contributions from general exchequer revenue and from interest.

II—DIFFERENCES IN BENEFITS

The possibility of harmonization receives a reference in Article 117 of the Treaty of Rome, but this is related to a general upward harmonization of general economic conditions and the reference is too vague to have much immediate significance. The fact remains that statistics are presented in the EEC publications which include comparisons of expenditure on welfare in different countries expressed in Belgian francs.[1] The meaning of such comparisons is, to say the least of it, doubtful. The conversion from different national currencies into Belgian francs raises the whole question of the extent to which exchange rates adequately reflect purchasing power and still more difficult questions are begged if inferences are drawn about welfare. Unfortunately such statistics come to be regarded as a 'league table' and a country does not like to find itself at the bottom of a table. Political pressures may then be stimulated which, on a broader view, may not always be beneficial.

If meaningful comparisons are to be made, these comparisons should be ordinal. That is to say, the bill for welfare may be expressed in each case as a fraction of gross national product, total personal consumption and the like. Even these comparisons must be interpreted with caution for needs may differ. For example, the demographic structure may differ between countries. Moreover, as we have already conceded, social valuations may differ from country to country and it should not be taken for granted that such differences should be erased. In economists' jargon, the social welfare functions need not be the same in each country. It is also necessary to bear in mind, however, that these social valuations are not static and unwarranted complacency may be shaken by international comparisons. The complacency with which the British welfare state was regarded, until recent years, in Britain is a case in

---

[1] See *L'évolution financière de la sécurité sociale dans les États membres de la Communauté.* EEC, 1971, p. 45.

TABLE 8.2

Methods of financing the main official schemes; percentages of total revenue in 1970

Country	Scheme	Benefits provided	Employers	Employees	Total payroll tax	General exchequer	Interest
Germany	Manual + white collar schemes	Old age, disability, survivors	40.0	42.0	82.0	14.0[1]	4
Netherlands	General old age insurance (AOW)	Old age	—	95.0	95.0	5.0	—
	General widows insurance (AWW)	Survivors	—	99.0	99.0	0.5	0.5
France	General scheme	Old age, survivors	66.0	34.0	100.0	—	—
Belgium	General scheme	Old age, survivors	44.0	33.0	77.0	13.0	10.0
Italy	General obligatory scheme	Old age, survivors disability	58.0	30.0	88.0	12.0	—
UK	National insurance scheme	All social insurance	43.0	40.0	83.0	15.0	2.0
Sweden	Basic pension scheme	Old age, disability, survivors	—	31.0	31.0	69.0	—
	Graduated pension scheme		100.0	—	—	—	—
	Weighted average basic + graduated		42.0	20.0	62.0	38.0	—
USA	OASDI	Old age, survivors, disability	47.0	47.0	94.0	1.0	5.0

[1] Although there is an exchequer contribution to the scheme, it is not to be used for old age pensions. That is, it is available for survivors' and disability pensions.

point. Sweden may be another example. The USA, for its part, might benefit if more Americans were aware of what is done in Europe and, indeed, in Canada.

Our first statistical exercise, therefore, is to express social expenditure as a fraction of gross national product at market prices. This is done for the old Six by the EEC statisticians and calculations for Britain, Sweden and the USA have been added below on a basis as nearly comparable as the statistics permit.[1] The percentages for 1970 are as follows: Germany, 19·8; France, 18·1; Italy, 18·9; Netherlands, 20·4; Belgium, 17·1; Sweden, 20·2; UK, 15·5; USA, 14·3 (federal, state and local).

The Six and Sweden spend between a sixth and a fifth of their gross national products on those welfare services; Britain spends over a seventh; the USA about a seventh.

As might be expected, there are variations in the ways in which this expenditure is distributed over various categories. The two largest items are health on the one hand and old age and survivors on the other. Family allowances come next and are particularly important in France and Belgium. Our main concern is, however, with old age and survivors. These items absorbed the following

---

[1] Defined as expenditure on: sickness, old age, death and survivors, invalidity, disability, industrial accidents, unemployment, family expenditure and some miscellaneous items (EEC classification, including administrative costs.)

Expenditure on education is excluded and so is assistance with housing except in so far as it is part of other cash transfer schemes. (Thus in the British case, assistance with housing from the Supplementary Benefit Commission is included but not general rent subsidies on local authority housing.) Occupational pensions are included in order to keep in line with the EEC. The following is the explanation given in *L'évolution financière de la sécurité sociale dans les États membres de la Communauté*: 'L'étude a inclus dans plusiers pays (Belgique, France, Luxembourg, Pays-Bas) certains régimes complémentaires qui, bien que d'initiative privée, créent des obligations et des droit permanents et ont atteint un développement qui les situent au niveau des régimes établis par des dispositions législatives ou réglementaires.' (Para. 17.)

The main sources of the figures are: *Comptes Sociaux 1962–70*, Brussels, 1972, and supplement; *Social Trends* and *Occupational Pension Schemes 1971*, both HMSO, 1972; *Social Security Bulletin, Annual Statistical Supplement*, 1971 and subsequent issues of *Bulletin*, US Department of Health, Education and Welfare; Swedish Statistisk Arsbok 1972. It will be appreciated that many questions of detail arise in preparing comparative estimates of this kind. The figures above for Germany, France, Belgium, Holland and Italy are from *Comptes Sociaux* and may differ slightly from some estimates from other sources. As far as possible, the estimates for the UK and Sweden have been made on the same lines. In the case of the USA, it seemed appropriate to include expenditure on health by the various private organizations.

percentages of total social benefit expenditure in 1970:[1] Germany, 45·4; France, 38·7; Italy, 36·3; the Netherlands, 41·3; Belgium, 38·8; Sweden, 28·9; UK, 45·5; USA, 35·4.[2]

Expressed in terms of GNP the percentages were: Germany, 8·5; France, 6·0; Italy, 6·2; the Netherlands, 8·2; Belgium, 6·3; Sweden, 5·5 (if expenditure on residential homes is included); UK, 6·1; USA, 5·1.

The variations in expenditure, expressed as a percentage of gross national product above, are not to be taken as adequate indications in themselves of the generosity of the provisions made for the elderly in each country as compared with the incomes received by other members of the respective populations. Apart from the obvious fact that there are demographic differences, allowance must be made for the fact that national expenditure is distributed in different ways between personal consumption, Government consumption of goods and services, domestic capital formation and foreign investment. It is, therefore, of interest to go on to compare pensions and other forms of assistance with total

TABLE 8.3

	Expenditure on old and survivors as percentage of current consumption at market prices in 1970	*Population sixty-five and over as percentage of total*
Germany	15·7	13·0
Netherlands	14·4	10·2
France	10·2	12·9
Belgium	10·6	13·4
Italy	9·7	10·6
Sweden	10·2	13·4
UK	11·5	12·8
USA	8·0	9·9

Sources: Consumption: OECD, Main Economic Indicators. Population: UN Demographic Yearbook.

---

[1] Social benefit expenditure does not include administrative costs.
[2] 40·7 per cent if total social benefit expenditure is taken to exclude expenditure on health by private organizations.

personal consumption. It is all the more appropriate to do so because the old cannot be expected to be net savers. This comparison is made in Table 8.3 above and the figures can be allowed to speak for themselves. This table also includes a column for the population over sixty-five as a percentage of the total in each case. It must be recalled, of course, that these groups do not correspond exactly to pensioners in view of the differences between different countries in pensionable age.

Tables of the kind just presented are always liable to be regarded as league tables and conclusions may then be drawn which the statistics themselves cannot support. After all, there is nothing wrong about being at the bottom of a particular league table if this corresponds to a nation's preferences! It will not do to beg questions about the value judgements and we must return, at the beginning of the next section, to the discussion of social objectives.

III—INCOME REPLACEMENT

In the first chapter, it was observed that official pensions policies may have two main objectives. The first is to protect the elderly from 'poverty', in some acceptable sense of the term; the second is to replace, in retirement, some satisfactory proportion of the income received in active life. Before we attempt to analyse the policies of the countries with which we are concerned, it may be helpful to recall some of the main points raised in the preliminary chapter. The pursuit of these two main objectives may sometimes lead in the same direction but, sometimes, the paths may diverge. Thus a high level of income replacement will be needed in order to provide a tolerable minimum to elderly people whose wages had previously been close to the poverty level. For those who were rather better off, this will not be so, even if they are entirely dependent upon an official pension. The case for graduated pensions is based on the argument that too sharp a fall in income below the level to which a person has been accustomed will entail hardship, even if he is still well above the general poverty line. The argument, as we saw in Chapter 1, raises difficult issues. Is it the responsibility of the state to protect the individual in this way? Or should he be expected to provide for his own retirement on a scale which will reflect his own preferences among the alternatives available to him? If the state accepts some degree of responsibility, will it wish to limit this responsibility to incomes below some specified maximum? The poverty level is not something that can be unequivocally defined and the difficulties are even greater when pensions are considered from the point of view of income replacement. Clearly there is no 'right' level of income replacement, nor even a 'right' scale of income replacement. Value judgements are necessarily involved, and these value judgements are by no means straightforward. It is not just a question of saying that it would be 'nice' if the elderly received so much by way of income replacement! For resources are limited and hard choices have to be made. There are other claims on the social budget which must not be forgotten and it will not do to treat pensions in isolation. Even if attention is confined to the needs of the elderly, it will be seen that a conflict can arise between income replacement higher up the income scale on the one hand and, on the other, the use of resources to lift the poverty level. Is such a conflict probable? What is the scope for diverting funds from income replacement at the higher levels to more help for the poor if the funds are derived from hypothecated taxes? And so on.

Questions such as these must be kept in mind in attempting to review the policies of the various countries with which we are concerned, and this is by no means the end of the difficulties. For supplementary pensions, whether official or private, differ in importance between countries and, within countries, their importance differs between income classes, between occupations and, still more, between individuals. Moreover occupational pensions may be backed by varying degrees of legal compulsion and regulation. Then there is the further complication that, in many countries, what the state itself provides is not a retirement pension but an old age pension which will be paid whether or not an old person continues to work and earn.

Faced with these difficulties, we may at least attempt to establish some further factual benchmarks. This can be no more than a first step and will not, in itself, resolve the problems indicated above and discussed more fully in the first chapter; but the setting of various benchmarks as we proceed may at least reduce a little the range of debate.

One such benchmark is the proportion of gross income before

retirement which the average wage-earner will receive as an official pension in each of our countries. A similar calculation can be made for those with, say, half average earnings and those with say, twice average earnings. The answer is usually different for a single man and a married man, except in Germany where there is no additional allowance for the wives of pensioners. More formidable is the complication that some of the European schemes are not mature. That is to say, the targets for the replacement of income which are often quoted have not yet been realized. Thus two sets of benchmarks will be needed: first, the fractions of income replaced in some recent year and, second, the fractions likely to be replaced if some stated objectives of policy are ultimately achieved. The number of benchmarks required will be increased if account is taken of the fact that, even within countries, there is often a lack of uniformity in basic official pensions, apart from the still greater diversity in supplementary occupational pensions. The differences between the treatment of the employed and the self-employed is an obvious example. There may also be a number of special schemes even for the employed. State employees are perhaps the most important groups, as we have seen, but there are special private schemes in some countries, notably in Italy (pp. 201 *et seq.*). Unfortunately the complexity of these arrangements will not yield to the summary treatment required in a final chapter. For the most part we have no alternative but to stay in the main stream but we must not forget that there are various other channels which have been charted in the preceding chapters.

As might be expected, we are beset not only by differing value judgements but by statistical complications. Thus the figures for earnings are far from satisfactory and it would be foolish to suppose that any exact comparability can be achieved with the result that the comparisons set out below should be regarded as only approximate. Then there is a special problem created by the under-reporting of income for tax evasion. This is not confined to the self-employed. In some countries the wages recorded for tax are below the wages actually paid which may affect not only the statistics for wages but also claims to social security benefits.[1] In view of the time-span involved we cannot simply assume that both wages and pensions are affected in the same proportion.

---

[1] This practice, which implies collusion between employer and employee, is referred to in Italy as 'fuori busta'—'outside the envelope'.

With these qualifications and warnings in mind, we shall now attempt to summarize at least the main features of the various pension schemes from the point of view of income replacement. We shall begin by comparing *pensions in 1971 with gross income before tax in 1970*. As prices will have risen meanwhile it is necessary to scale up the previous year's earnings to allow for these higher prices in order to obtain estimates of the effect of retirement on the pensioner's previous standard of living. This revalorization has been made throughout. That is to say, we shall be attempting to assess the effect of retirement on the standard of living on the assumption that the pensioner has no source of income other than the pension that is specified. Naturally this assumption will often be unrealistic. A retired person may have some earned income or some property income or, for that matter, an additional pension from some other source. Indeed the British pension can only be explained on the assumption that there is in fact some other source of income, for this pension stands below the official poverty level and the elderly person has a right to have his standard of living lifted to this level if his application is supported by a test of means. Although our immediate objective is the more limited one of assessing what the pensions themselves will do, it must be kept in mind that these pensions do not set the official minima in Britain nor, indeed, in the Netherlands.

The proportion of income replaced by the official pension in *Britain* is low by international standards. The year chosen for our comparisons is 1971 and, before the rise in pensions in September of that year, the pension received by an elderly couple would have replaced only about 26 per cent of average male earnings recorded for October 1970. The September increase was a substantial one but the new replacement rate of 32 per cent was still below that reached in a number of other countries.[1] For a single pensioner the replacement fraction was about a fifth. To this some addition should be made for occupational pensions but this is not easy. About 3 million former employees, widows and other dependents were receiving occupational pensions at the end of 1971 or about a third of the population of pensionable age. There was a wide scatter in the size of pension received, with 10 per cent amounting to £1 or less a week, 30 per cent to £2 or less and almost a fifth to

---

[1] Pensioner couples where both are over eighty got a supplement of 50p.

£10 or over. The median was £4 and the mean £6½. There is no
very illuminating way of combining these figures with the state
pension in assessing the scale of income replacement. But it may be
observed that any married couple who happened to receive the
median occupational pension would have had about 40 per cent
more than the state pension and would therefore have received the
equivalent of almost 45 per cent of average gross earnings. This is
not to suggest that the former average *wage earner* was usually in
this position![1]

Of the countries we have considered, the *Netherlands* is the only
other one with a flat-rate scheme, and it is therefore the one that
can be compared most easily with Britain. In both countries, the
complications caused by immature claims to official pensions
do not affect the basic scheme significantly. The Dutch pension
was substantially above the British and replaced about 48 per cent
of the average male earnings in the case of a married couple and 34
per cent in the case of a single pensioner. Here too occupational pensions should be taken into account but we have not been able to
obtain statistics which would allow this to be done in a fully illuminating way. It has been estimated, however, that in 1970 the
average pension paid by an industry-wide occupational pension
scheme might have added some 15 per cent to the state pension for
a single person and some 10 per cent for a married couple. The
average pension paid by an enterprise scheme would have added
substantially more, possibly 50 per cent to the pension for a single
person and just under 40 per cent for a married couple. Pension
rights accruing to those still in the labour force were considerably
higher.

Flat-rate pensions imply more vertical redistribution than
graduated pensions. Thus, obviously enough, a person who had
earned half average earnings in Britain would have received a
pension for himself and his wife which would have replaced about

---

[1] For the statistics, see *Occupational Pension Schemes*, 1971, Fourth Survey
by the Government Actuary, HMSO 1972. Official graduated pensions have
been ignored as being of trivial importance. The omission may not be appropriate in all cases. Thus someone who retired in 1973 with a full record of graduated contributions from the introduction of the scheme would receive about
£1·50 which would have been much the same as perhaps a fifth of the occupational pensions in 1971. But not many people would have had a graduated
pension of this amount. Over a longer period, the size of the graduated pensions
in nominal money value will grow and their number increase; but it is crucially
important to observe that these pensions are not protected against inflation.

two-thirds of his previous earnings; in the Netherlands his previous income would have been roughly maintained. On the other hand someone with one-and-a-half times average earnings would have received less than a quarter in Britain and about a third in Holland.

The *USA* stands between countries with fully graduated benefits like West Germany and those with flat-rate benefits like the UK and the Netherlands. The basis of the pension is an average of previous earnings. The pension in 1971 was designed to replace about four-fifths of the first $100 of monthly earnings, and about 30 per cent of the next $290, about 28 per cent of the next $150 and about a third of the next $100. Although the US pensions are graduated, the graduation is so arranged that the replacement of income is greater for smaller incomes than for higher. Moreover the range of pensions is limited by a maximum (about $295 a month in 1971) and a very low minimum ($70 in 1971). Thus the pension replaced about 48 per cent of the gross income of the average married wage-earner in private industry in 1971, or about 32 per cent for a single person. These figures would apply to persons newly retired at the normal retirement age and with a full entitlement to benefit. The average pension in payment, which reflects deductions for various reasons and different earnings histories, was lower, as might be expected, i.e. about a third for a couple. About two-fifths of those retiring in the two years 1969 and 1970 had occupational pensions. A sample investigation suggested that in 1970 the median private pension replaced about a quarter of previous earnings in the case of men. Two-thirds of these pensions replaced between a tenth and two-fifths of previous earnings.[1]

Sweden has a flat-rate basic pension like the basic British and the Dutch pensions but there is also an official supplementary pension scheme, which is still immature (see p. 165). The flat-rate pension for a couple would have provided about 37·5 per cent of the income received by the average wage-earner. If he belonged to the supplementary graduated scheme he might get the equivalent of an extra 10 per cent of pre-retirement earnings.

---

[1] 'Private Retirement Benefits and Relationship to Earnings Survey of New Beneficiaries', by Walter W. Kolodrubetz, *Social Security Bulletin*, May 1973. See also 'Second Pensions Among Newly Entitled Workers: Survey of New Beneficiaries', by Lenore E. Bixby and Virginia Reno, *Social Security Bulletin*, November 1971.

About half the Swedish pensioners also claimed a means-tested housing allowance which is provided by the pension scheme in addition to the pension. This assistance with housing might come to another 10 per cent of average earnings. Thus over 55 per cent of previous income might be replaced. If the pensioner received no (or only very little) income from the supplementary graduated scheme he would, in addition to the housing allowance, receive a pension supplement. In this case some 52 per cent of pre-retirement earnings would be replaced. Occupational pensions would add a further amount for some pensioners but no figures are available.

Germany has a fully graduated scheme which links pensions to earnings with no minimum but only up to a maximum. Up to this maximum which corresponds to twice the individual's earnings, the German pension was replacing about 47 per cent of previous earnings at all levels of previous gross income (see p. 83, above). There was therefore none of the vertical redistribution present in the Dutch and British schemes and, in a modified way, in the US scheme. A married pensioner who had earned average wages would have had a higher proportion of his gross income replaced in Germany than in the UK, notwithstanding the lack of any supplement for his wife, and much the same proportion as in the Netherlands. A single man who had had average earnings would be substantially better off in Germany than in Britain, but the comparison becomes less favourable to Germany when we move down the income scale. *At half average earnings* the replacement rate would still be 47 per cent in Germany but would have risen to 66 per cent for a couple in the UK, about 100 per cent in the Netherlands and two-thirds in the USA. As we have observed above (p. 69), occupational pensions are of some importance in West Germany though less so in the private sector than in Britain or the Netherlands. Whereas in Britain, the Netherlands, and the USA these pensions are equivalent to about 1 per cent of gross national product, in Germany they are equivalent to less than one third of 1 per cent.

In *Belgium* also the official pension for a married couple was equivalent to about 45 per cent of average earnings in 1971. This percentage remains unchanged as one moves up the income scale for there is no maximum to pensionable earnings for manual workers, although there is one for white-collar workers (at 130 per cent of average earnings). For incomes below the average, the percentage also holds until the minimum pension level is reached. Naturally the percentage of income replaced increases as one moves further down the income scale. The white-collar workers would normally receive occupational pensions on top of the official pension (see pp. 320–2, above).

The general basic pension for a married couple in *France* replaced roughly 47 per cent of average earnings in 1971. But the calculation of income replacement is complicated by the fact that the wife's allowance[1] was a flat sum. Thus, at half average wages, about 60 per cent of income was replaced and slightly more when the minimum wage level was reached just a little lower down. In the upward direction, the flat allowance pulled down the percentage to about 44 per cent of income replaced at the upper ceiling which stood at 135 per cent of average earnings. A further substantial addition would often be derived from the complementary schemes, probably about 15 per cent. The married pensioner who had been an average wage-earner might therefore have about three-fifths of his income replaced.

Whereas Germany has an upper limit but no lower limit in the graduated scheme, *Italy* has lower limits but no upper ones. Thus, in principle, the Italians have the most ambitious of graduated schemes in coverage of income levels above the minimum and have also a very high target for income replacement. Targets are one thing and current achievement another. As is recorded in Chapter 5 above, the bulk of Italian pensioners in 1971 were receiving only minimum pensions, almost as though the pension scheme were flat-rate! Moreover the minimum levels were low. In the general obligatory scheme these pensions were equivalent for a married couple in 1971 to only about 26 per cent of the pre-retirement earnings of the average worker. As a fraction of previous earnings Italian pensions were thus well below even the British level. Those elderly people who had no claims at all under the contributory pension schemes and thus had to fall back on the 'social pension' were getting the equivalent of about 21 per cent of average earnings. Although, as we have mentioned, the accuracy of Italian wage statistics may be dubious, these calculations may be accorded enough validity to support the view that the Italian

---

[1] The wife's allowance is payable only if she is largely financially dependent on her husband.

pensioner was far worse off than might be supposed from the Italian target figures for income replacement which are sometimes quoted out of context.

At this stage it may be convenient to summarize the statistics about allowances made for *dependent spouses*. In the table below these allowances are expressed as percentages of the pensions available in 1971 to single pensioners.[1]

UK	62	France	38
USA	50	Belgium	20
Sweden	55	Netherlands	42
West Germany	nil	Italy	15

The comparisons we have made above relate pensions to gross earnings. This is the normal procedure but a somewhat different picture emerges when the comparison is with incomes less income tax and the employee's social security tax. Once more we have taken the pensions (excluding complementary pensions) which would have been received by an average wage-earner who retired at the beginning of 1971 and compared these with net average earnings for the previous year, adjusted for changes in retail prices. The pension levels used are those applicable for the wage-earner and his wife, assuming that she has no rights to a pension of her own.[2] The results may be briefly summarized:

TABLE 8.4

Netherlands	64·3
Germany	60·0
Belgium	56·8
France	51·5
Italy	33·3
UK	35·1
USA	56·0
Sweden	52·5

[1] In some cases there are conditions relating to the age of the dependent spouse. In others she must have been financially dependent on the insured.

[2] In principle pensions are taxable in all countries except Italy but in most cases pensioners with no additional income other than the basic pension would be below the tax threshold. In Belgium and the Netherlands tax of about 3 per cent of the pension would have been payable in the examples cited. (Since 1973 the tax threshold in the Netherlands has been adjusted so that all pensioners with only the basic pension will in future be entirely exempt from payment of income tax.) We are indebted to the Inland Revenue for assistance with the calculations although any remaining errors are our own responsibility.

Summary tables of this kind are convenient but may be misleading unless the complications mentioned in the preceding paragraphs and elaborated in the preceding chapters are kept in mind. The difficulty of allowing for complementary pensions in some countries or for such items as the Swedish housing allowance and expenditure on residential homes are examples.

It is clear, however, from these estimates above that some basic pensions are replacing quite high proportions of net income before retirement. There is a further consideration to be taken into account. This is the fact that work entails costs (for travel, etc.) and a lower net income is needed in retirement in order to maintain the same standard of living. This is brought out in a calculation made for the USA and summarized thus. This calculation takes account not only of direct taxation but also of the expenses saved by not having to go to work.[1] The broad conclusion was that these savings would come to 11–12 per cent of gross earnings before tax. The average US couple needed about 73 per cent of their *gross* pre-retirement income to have the same income in retirement after allowing for savings in taxes and expenses.[2] In fact the equivalent of about 48 per cent in the case of a newly retired married man, where both husband and wife are 65, was being provided by the official federal pension.

Of course, this is still only part of the story for account should be taken of all indirect taxes and subsidies and of benefits in kind, in particular free health services. A comprehensive comparative assessment of this kind lies beyond our scope. It is, however, worth while to remind ourselves of the complication caused by one particular indirect tax: the employers' social security contribution. If higher benefits are financed by a rise in these contributions, part of the cost, possibly a tenth in Britain, will fall on the beneficiaries themselves because of the effect on prices.

In discussing the replacement of income, whether before or after tax, we have hitherto been confining our attention to employees. The special position of the *self-employed* has been discussed in the chapters on the various countries and it must suffice

[1] 'Recent Trends in Retirement Benefits Related to Earnings' by Peter Henle. *Monthly Labour Review*, June 1972. The basis of the calculation of the savings from retirement is discussed in the *Bureau of Labour Statistics Bulletin*, 1970–72, 1973.
[2] Cf. the calculation made by Dr Pekka Kuusi for Finland in his *Social Policy for the Sixties*, Finnish Social Policy Association, Helsinki, 1964.

at this stage to record, first, that contributions and pensions are often flat-rate, usually for administrative reasons; second, that these flat-rate pensions are often less than the pension received by someone who was formerly an average wage-earner. Perhaps it is often assumed that the self-employed will have been better able to make personal provision for retirement, but this is by no means always the case. In Germany there has indeed been some official concern about the position of the self-employed and provision was made in 1973 for those not previously covered at all to join the official scheme on a voluntary basis (see pp. 90–2, above).

We must, moreover, say a little more about *the position of women*. Let us look first at pension provision for the woman who tries to earn a pension in her own right; this would include both single women and wives. In all the countries with fully earnings-related pensions schemes, earnings and the length of the insurance period are directly reflected in the pension earned. The position of women is therefore adversely affected, first, because their earnings are usually lower and, second, because their earnings records are likely to be intermittent. For example, in Sweden, only about 20 per cent of all recipients of supplementary pensions in 1969 were women and their average pension was only some 60 per cent of the male average.

In Germany, where there is no minimum pension, the position of women is liable to be particularly difficult. The importance of this problem has been recognized and the reforms implemented in 1973 have been designed to ease the position (p. 92, above). The problem is alleviated to some extent in France, Belgium and Italy by the existence of minimum pensions, although these are low, especially in Italy. In these countries some modest provision is also made for those elderly persons who have had employment records that are too short to qualify at all for an old age pension. In Germany anyone in this position would have to rely on social aid. In Sweden there is, of course, the basic citizen's pension and if the working woman has accumulated few or no rights to supplementary pension there is the smaller pension supplement mentioned earlier. In some countries there would also seem to be some discrimination against women in occupational schemes. One example which came to light in the Netherlands was that in many cases the minimum age of entry to an occupational scheme was higher for a woman than for a man, thus reducing the pension which she could hope to earn. In countries where such obstacles exist women are unlikely to have second-tier pensions of a level sufficient to raise their first-tier pensions significantly. Discrimination of this kind is not, of course, confined to the Netherlands.

The practice regarding payment of supplements to an insured man in respect of his wife varies greatly between countries, as we have seen. There may be no such supplements, as in Germany, or means-tested ones as in France,[1] Italy[1] and Sweden (if the wife is over sixty but below the pension age of sixty-seven), or supplements embodied in the basic pension and payable almost invariably only when the man reaches pension age, as in the UK, the Netherlands and Belgium. In Sweden both must be of pensionable age. A married woman may, however, be in an inferior position to the single or widowed woman.

The addition to a man's pension for his pensioner wife does not equal a single person's pension for which an unmarried or widowed woman is eligible. This is not necessarily wrong for it should be cheaper to run a household of two than two separate households. The US investigations show clearly that, at the bottom of the range, single persons are more likely to be in poverty than couples.

The problem of an inadequate level of income replacement is, however, most acute in the case of widows. This is a group which forms a large part of the recipients of means-tested assistance not only in Britain but in various other European countries. There seems to be a general awareness of the difficulties facing widows and a great deal of concern has been voiced on the subject. In the Netherlands, a national insurance scheme specifically for widows' and orphans' benefits has been established separately from the old age pension scheme (see p. 120, above). A widow, if she is aged between forty and sixty-four, receives an amount which is equivalent to the old age pension for a single person (about 34 per cent of average earnings in 1971), or if the widow has a child under eighteen, she receives a pension from the age of thirty-five equivalent to the old age pension for a married couple (about 48 per cent of average earnings). The position is similar in Sweden where a widow, if she is over fifty, or has dependent children, receives a pension equal to the old age pension for a single person (see p. 175,

---

[1] In France and Italy it is the income of the pensioner's wife which is subject to examination before she is granted a pension. She must be financially dependent on her husband.

above). In other countries, where earnings-related pensions are the rule, a widow often receives only a percentage of the old age pension which her husband had been receiving or to which he would have been entitled.[1] The percentages vary from 50 per cent in France to 60 per cent in Germany and Italy and 80 per cent in Belgium. (In Sweden it is lower (40 per cent) but then the Swedish widow has her citizen's pension too.) If the husband's pension is low for some reason it follows that the widow's benefits will be still lower and thus often totally inadequate. The position may be further aggravated by the often extremely stringent qualifying conditions attached to receipt of the pension relating to her age, length of marriage or to the amount which she can earn. It should be noted that widows with children would, in most countries studied, also receive children's allowances in addition to any widow's pension. In some cases, for example in France, this might serve to offset the low level of the basic pension. It would not, however, prevent hardship arising when the widow is older; it might serve indeed to make the financial position of an elderly widow more difficult as she will suffer a substantial fall in income when her children become independent.

Where the younger widow is concerned practices vary widely again. The UK (like the Netherlands) is relatively generous in allowing even the youngest of widows a period in which to adjust to her change of status and there are relatively generous allowances for the first twenty-six weeks of widowhood. For the widow with a dependent family there are almost invariably pensions of some kind for herself and her children although we have already seen that these may often be less than adequate. The UK and Sweden allow a widow to keep what she can earn without reducing her pension. A young childless widow, however, is almost invariably expected to provide for herself. Some countries, however, pay some pension to a woman widowed in middle life who may find difficulty in taking up work.

There are two final issues of some importance on which no more than brief comments are possible here. First we must draw attention to differences between different countries in the scope for supplementing pensions by means of earnings. In Britain, the USA and Belgium the pension is a retirement pension and limi-

---

[1] The provision, if any, for widows in private occupational schemes may often be still less generous.

tations are placed on permissible earnings. In our other European countries, it is an old age pension. This latter approach would indeed appear to be logical if it is thought desirable to regard pensions as 'social insurance'. For the pensions should then be received as of right whether or not the pensioner continues to work. If he postpones the date on which he starts to draw his pension he should naturally receive a higher pension; if he retires early the pension should be less. That, however, is a different point. If he chooses to claim the pension due to him at, say, sixty-five then no restriction should be placed on how he uses his time and energy merely because he is drawing his insurance pension. This is the 'insurance' argument, so explicitly recognized in Germany. But there are other reasons for imposing no limitation on subsequent earnings which do not depend upon the retention of the 'insurance' analogy. By earning he can supplement his income by his own efforts and it is hard to see why the freedom to do so should be denied him. From a wider national point of view, the contribution to output should be welcomed. This is all the more important in view of the growing importance of early retirement. If more people retire completely at an earlier age, the contribution to output of those pensioners who do not choose to stop working is all the more desirable. This is true both of the production of those who go on working after the age when a full pension can be claimed and of those who do so while drawing a reduced pension at an earlier age.

Whereas on the one hand there are those pensioners who are capable of continuing to work and would like to do so, there are on the other hand some other people whose circumstances are such that, although not yet entitled even to a reduced old-age pension, they are unemployed. This is the second point. In those cases where the likelihood of their obtaining employment is small, it may be possible to place them in a special category entitled either to a disability pension or to an abnormally early old-age pension. Sweden is experimenting along these lines (see p. 186, above). The administrative difficulties may, of course, be formidable unless one is dealing—as is largely the case in Sweden—with those who live in remote areas. A quite different approach is to make a special effort to reinstate the middle-aged who are unemployed. Germany is making some attempt to tackle this problem by simple retraining arrangements and by special subsidies to employers although it is necessary to add that success so far has been limited (see page 99, above). Japan is, of course, the country where this problem is presumably most acute. For retirement in the many important industries normally occurs well before pensionable age. Other countries might benefit from a study of Japanese experience and a consideration of the degree of success achieved.

IV—DEALING WITH POVERTY

Since World War II there have been large increases in the real income reached during active life in all of our countries and welfare benefits have also been greatly raised, both in cash and in kind. What has been the effect on poverty among the elderly? If the question is a natural one, it is also extremely difficult to answer. As we have had occasion to observe, there is no measure of 'poverty' that is unambiguous and likely to be unanimously accepted even in any one country at any one time. Conventional yard-sticks have, it is true, been adopted but these have been stretched over the years with expanding affluence. Moreover with any given poverty level, the numbers in 'poverty' will depend partly upon the extent to which assistance is selective. With a policy based on selectivity, benefits paid as of right may stand below the official poverty level, or levels, used for means-tested assistance. Suppose then that the number receiving means-tested assistance were to be taken as a measure of the extent of poverty. In this sense 'poverty' might persist indefinitely. Presumably this meaning of poverty does not fully correspond to what people have in mind when reference is made to the hardship which many people still face even in a country as rich as the USA. An index of selectivity can scarcely be regarded as an adequate index of poverty.

These points must be kept in mind as we attempt to review the experience of our six European countries and to relate this experience to that of the USA and Britain. How have official poverty levels been fixed and how have these levels been altered over the years? What basis, if any, exists for international comparisons? In all countries there is still some reliance on means tests for providing assistance for the elderly, but the extent of this reliance varies. Moreover means tests are used in different ways for providing different kinds of assistance. What lessons can be learned from these diverse administrative practices? Then we shall wish to go on and ask whether there are reasons to expect that means tests for the elderly will decline in importance in future.

Or in so far as some tests of means are still thought to be appropriate, perhaps a more acceptable and more effective arrangement would be a negative income tax rather than a variety of different tests for a variety of purposes.

Although there is no fully objective test of poverty, it should be possible at least to reduce the scope for possible disagreement by estimating the cost of various 'baskets' of commodities designed to achieve certain objectives, such as some specified nutritional standard, 'reasonable' housing conditions and so on. Such calculations have been made in a number of countries though less generally and less frequently than one might perhaps have anticipated. *Germany* has estimates of this kind which have been used to guide the Länder in providing means-tested assistance without their being applied in any rigid way. The German 'basket' was augmented in the early sixties to include more additional items above the base necessaries, and for an elderly couple this assistance, including an allowance for rent, was equivalent to about two-fifths of average earnings in 1971.

In *Britain*, early post-war policy was much influenced by Beveridge's idea of a social minimum but, in fact, the official poverty level in the autumn of 1972 was nearly twice as high (at constant prices) as in 1948 (see Chart 3). In the event, the poverty line has risen roughly in line with average gross earnings, although there had been no official acceptance of this relationship as the objective of policy. In real terms the British poverty line now rises every year.

In *France* the minimum level of pension income is discussed in relation explicitly to the minimum wage level; but both this relationship and the minimum wage itself have been altered from time to time with regard to estimates, or opinions, about 'adequacy'. Much concern has been expressed about the lowness of the poverty level and the recommendations made by M. Pierre Laroque led to some improvement, though less than he had wished for (see p. 293, above). Thus the social minimum was raised rather more than the wage level for a number of years but remained at about 46 per cent of the average wage in the case of a married couple in 1971, and at about 23 per cent in the case of a single person.

The poverty level in the *Netherlands* is linked to the minimum wage and, together with this minimum wage, is linked automatically to an index of wage-rates. Thus the Dutch poverty line is now adjusted twice a year! In Germany, France and Belgium changes in the social minimum are taken at the discretion of the authorities, as in the UK; but in practice, the minima have risen at least as fast as wages. In *Sweden*, the minimum levels of income used by both the central Government and some of the local authorities have been adjusted only for rising prices; some local authorities, however, have adjusted for rising real wages as well. *Italy* has been more conservative: the social pension was not adjusted automatically even for rising prices until the beginning of 1973 (see p. 249, above) although there were substantial changes on a discretionary basis.

In *Germany*, where there is no minimum level of statutory pension, elderly people with inadequate pensions must turn to the Länder for means-tested assistance. Social aid is thus a regional responsibility and very different poverty lines could be applied as in the USA. In practice these differences are small in Germany and have grown smaller over the years. In the *UK, the Netherlands and Sweden*, there are flat-rate pensions which can be regarded as the bedrock minima below which no one is likely to subside unless the circumstances are rather exceptional (for example an elderly person who has spent most of his life abroad). But in all three countries, more is available subject to means test. If the level to which one can be raised by means-tested assistance is identified with the official poverty line, then the flat-rate pensions in these three countries are below the poverty level. But in Sweden no one need be living at the basic pension level itself; the housing allowance and pension supplement (see p. 169, above) will be paid to anyone without, and to many people with, other sources of private or pension income. Strictly speaking one should speak of poverty levels in the plural when referring either to the Netherlands or Sweden. For, in both cases, this assistance is provided by local authorities and there are differences between localities. These differences, however, have tended to grow less, as in Germany, and in the Netherlands such differences are now considered to have virtually disappeared as regards basic assistance. There are of course still differences reflecting variations in rent levels.

In *Britain*, the official minimum levels of income are set by supplementary benefit. This assistance is provided in different packages. First, there is the scale rate which was £9.45 in September 1971 for a couple or £5.80 for a single person. Second, there is the long-term addition to which retired people (and some other categories) are entitled. This came to 50p for pensioners under eighty and to 75p for those over eighty. Third, housing costs are met up to a 'reasonable' standard of housing which was equivalent on average to £2.42 (or £2.16 for a single person). Thus a couple received the equivalent of 40 per cent of average gross male earnings of the previous year or 54 per cent of earnings net of tax.[1] A single person received 28 per cent of gross earnings or 40 per cent of net earnings in September 1971.

In view of these differences of approach in different countries it is interesting that the various poverty levels, measured as a fraction of gross average wages in each case, are not even more divergent than is, in fact, the case. Let us attempt to sum up some of the points made above. Thus in the case of married couples, the Netherlands has the high figure for social aid (including rent) of about 56 per cent of the previous year's earnings. In Britain it is about 40 per cent; in France about 46 per cent; in Germany about 40 per cent; in Belgium about 38 per cent; and in Italy about 21 per cent. All these percentages are only approximate, but it can be said that there is some clustering of our European countries with a replacement rate in the region of two-fifths to one-half gross average earnings.[2] In the *USA* public assistance is not a federal responsibility and there are wide differences in the aid extended in different parts of the federation, as is shown clearly in chart 11 which depicts assistance to the elderly in May 1972. The chart also shows that there was a fairly clearly defined mode of about $65 a month. This $780 or so a year may be compared with the poverty lines suggested by the Social Security Administration of $1,940 for a single person over 65 at 1971 prices and of $2,448 for a couple (i.e. 30 per cent and 38 per cent respectively of average earnings in 1970, adjusted for prices). It is also worth observing that, in 1971, the minimum federal pension for a retired worker was $845 a year. It must be borne in mind, however, that the chart relates to

---

[1] Again the previous earnings have been adjusted in order to allow for the rise in prices over the year. This has been done throughout.

[2] Cf. ILO Convention No. 128, 1952.

assistance provided and does not show the poverty scales that were in fact applied in different parts of the Union. Most of the elderly would have had other sources of income. Thus the federal pension itself provided a minimum of $845 for a sole survivor. We can fairly conclude, however, that large numbers must have been left badly off in some states, such as Mississippi, where assistance was significantly less than the mode. These regional differences largely reflect differences in prosperity and public revenue in different parts of the federation which are not as much offset by transfers between governments as is done in some other federations, e.g. Canada, Germany and Australia. Under the new Supplemented Security Income Program, however, the federal government has become responsible for providing basic assistance to the aged (and some other categories) since the beginning of 1974.

In the preceding paragraphs, means-tested assistance has been compared with average earnings. Various bench-marks are, of course, possible. Account should also be taken of differences between countries in the amount of personal capital that is disregarded in the assessment of means and the amount extra of income that can be earned. Reference to such 'disregards' has been made in some of the preceding studies of some of the European countries; but these details defy summary treatment.

The effectiveness of any given volume of expenditure ought in principle to be increased if the expenditure is made with some regard to need. Thus it has been estimated that an extra £700 million would have been required in 1972 to raise the flat-rate British pension to the level of supplementary benefits.[1] This would have required higher taxation, probably including higher social security contributions. Moreover, the case for incurring such additional expenditure for this purpose would have to be weighed against other claims for increased public expenditure. Alternatively, the gap between the basic benefits and the poverty level could be closed, either immediately or gradually, by raising the former relative to the latter without increasing total expenditure under both headings above what it would otherwise have been. The number in 'poverty' could thus be dramatically reduced, but the poor would be worse off. For out of the given volume of expendi-

---

[1] *Strategy for Pensions*, Cmnd. 4755, p. 5. The additional cost for all benefits would have been £1000 million. See also the section below on the Tax Credit scheme (p. 383).

ture on pensions, more would go to those with other means and less would be available for those genuinely in want. This is the case for selectivity and the case for at least some selectivity has been accepted in other countries as well as Britain. The point was put as follows in *Strategy for Pensions*: 'Maintaining the value of supplementary benefits must always be the first priority and this means that the gap could only be closed by increasing the value of contributory benefits by about one-third.' It is interesting to ask how much of this extra expenditure would have gone to those with incomes appreciably above supplementary benefit level. At a rough guess about a quarter are 40 per cent or more above.

There is also a case against selectivity and it is one that has been strongly advanced in the UK. Means tests are said to be resented and, whether for this reason or from ignorance or inertia, a substantial proportion of those entitled to such assistance do not submit their claims. It does not follow, of course, that there is no safety net for the elderly. This is provided, as we have seen, by the basic statutory pension. The point is rather that some people who should receive the difference between supplementary benefit and the basic pension fail to do so. The extra amount available subject to means test was equivalent to about a quarter of the basic flat-rate pension in September 1971.[1]

We must record at this point that we have encountered surprisingly little criticism of means tests in the European countries we have studied, although there has been some strong criticism in the USA.[2] This, of course, is no more than an impression and, no doubt, a superficial one. Without placing too much stress upon it, we may nevertheless ask whether there are any reasons for expecting means tests to be more unpopular in Britain than in these European countries. Means tests were indeed severely applied in the 1930s in Britain and much natural resentment was aroused. But the procedure has subsequently been greatly reformed and humanized and recent experience ought to be more relevant than

---

[1] Supplementary benefit has here been taken to mean the scale rate, the long-term addition and the average housing allowance. The figures relate to a married couple.

[2] Cf. e.g. J. A. Pechman, H. J. Aaron and M. K. Taussig, *Social Security: Perspectives for Reform*, Brookings Institution, Washington D.C., 1968, pp. 59–60. The authors record that: 'Experience with the means test under public assistance has resulted in an unfortunate tendency in the community to reject indiscriminately any eligibility test . . .'

distant memories. Certainly we have found no positive evidence which would suggest that means tests in general are applied more harshly in Britain today than is the case elsewhere. The opposite may sometimes be the case. For example, the locally administered social aid in France appears to be handled with greater severity than is supplementary benefit in Britain. Are there, however, other differences in procedure which may help a little to explain differences in attitudes?

First, means tests are embodied in the regular statutory arrangements for pensions in some countries. This is true of the social minimum in France, the minimum allowance[1] in Belgium (*revenu garanti*) and the minimum pension in Italy. That is to say, instead of having an unconditional minimum in these graduated schemes (corresponding to flat-rate pensions in Britain, the Netherlands or Sweden) which might then lie below the poverty lines, there are minima in the pension schemes themselves, granted subject to means tests. It may be that means tests operated inside the pension structure in this way are more acceptable than means tests applied by some different authority for a different benefit. This certainly seems to be the case with the housing allowance in Sweden. Possibly a further important factor is that the need to claim the housing allowance in Sweden or public assistance in the Netherlands is related to the high cost of housing and of residential accommodation respectively for which the individual can in no way be held responsible. It is true that this is not the end of the matter in these countries. In France, some of the elderly have to seek assistance for particular purposes from the local authorities. (This is the social aid referred to above.)[2] In Belgium, the pensioner may also be able to supplement his guaranteed minimum by turning to the local authorities for their means-tested assistance (see p. 329, above). In Italy, he may expect little further help from local sources but charities may assist. (See p. 230 above.)

Second, the old who turn to the local authorities for assistance in Germany and the Netherlands (see pp. 75, and 139, above) are placed in a category separate from any other claimants for such assistance. In Germany, specially augmented allowances are given; in the Netherlands, a special status is accorded to the elderly poor.

---

[1] Not to be confused with the minimum pension. (See p. 237, above.)
[2] Social aid does not include general cash grants on any significant scale. See p. 289, above.

Thus the stigma attached to means-tested assistance may seem less and there may be correspondingly less reluctance to claim benefits. Of course it is possible that by treating the old with special favour in this way, the stigma of poverty may be made to seem all the greater to the poor of working age, but the psychology of those concerned may be still more complex. For it may be that there will be no residuary legatee when assistance is divided by category in this way for the division itself may dispel the image attaching to general assistance. If this reasoning is valid, it would constitute a case for reducing the scope of general assistance but there is then the problem of a diversity of forms of assistance which can cause confusion. This consideration lies behind proposals for a negative income tax.

A third explanation may be that means tests are more readily accepted when the assistance is for some specific purpose. Housing is clearly the most important example. In Sweden roughly half the pensioners receive means-tested assistance with housing; in Britain about a fifth.[1]

In order to receive this assistance in Britain, it has been necessary to apply for supplementary benefit. The new Housing Finance Act will ease the position. For more elderly people will have their costs met, subject to means tests, in this way without resort to supplementary benefit, although the fair rents policy was not designed to remove all need for assistance with housing from the Supplementary Benefits Commission.[2] This reform, together with the tax credit scheme and proposed increases in the basic pension, should reduce the numbers 'in poverty' in Britain in the future, as determined by the old conventional definition. This, however, is to anticipate the next section.

European practice and experience in these matters should be

---

[1] This refers of course to assistance from the Supplementary Benefits Authorities. In addition many old people have received the benefit of local authority housing subsidies in the past, or will be assisted through the Fair Rents policy. That is to say a substantial number of elderly people who are not receiving supplementary benefits could receive assistance with housing in that form.

[2] Many elderly people in Britain have, of course, benefited in the past from the subsidization of local authority housing and from rate rebates. Some have also benefited from rent control although the long-run effects of excessively rigid rent control were clearly bad for the supply, renovation, and proper maintenance of houses, which must be counted as a debit on the other side of the account. The decision in 1972 to go for fair rents with subsidies for people rather than bricks and mortar was clearly a sensible one in principle.

studied but it should not be forgotten that large changes have
already been made in Britain over the years. The local officers
responsible for the payment of supplementary benefit clearly try to
treat the elderly as a separate group. This treatment does not
appear to be less generous in the case of disregards and capital than
elsewhere. The same book serves for the payment of the statutory
pension and of supplementary benefit and payments can be sent
through the post so that the earlier and much disliked associations
of the public assistance office can be avoided. That is to say, in
terms of administration if not in other respects, Britain has moved
some way towards building the minimum into the pension scheme.

The Supplementary Benefits Commission may be one of the
most unfairly maligned public institutions in modern Britain.[1] The
fact remains that means-tested assistance is unpopular and severe
hardship has been caused by incomplete take-up.

V—RISING PENSIONS

Pensions will rise in the future for a number of reasons. First, it
will be recalled that some of the schemes described in the last two
sections were still immature in 1971. This immaturity may take
two forms: (*a*) some schemes had not been in existence long
enough to permit even those who had been in a scheme from the
outset to acquire full rights by 1971; (*b*) some people in the main
schemes had come into them rather late in life as a result of a
change in occupation (e.g. move from agriculture to industry) and,
once more, records were incomplete. In both cases, of course, the
extent of any arrangements for 'blanketing-in' were crucial.

Second, pensions may rise because some decisions may be
taken—in some cases have already been taken—to lift pensions
relative to incomes from work. These are what have been
described as 'structural' changes.

Third, pensions will naturally be affected by whatever arrangements are employed to adjust their value to rises in prices and thus
to protect their real value. The links with other incomes may,
however, do more than this. For pensions may be made to rise in
some relationship to wages, and pensioners will thus be given a

---

[1] The disputes that arise often relate to cases of cohabitation and the like.
For a general review see *The Penguin Guide to Supplementary Benefits* by Tony
Lynes, Penguin Books. 1972.

share in growth. The nature of these linkages and their effects in the past have already received some attention but further reference is necessary in assessing future prospects.

In some of our countries the targets for mature pensions are above, even substantially above, the levels reached in 1971, as measured in terms of income replacement. It must be recalled that these targets themselves often refer to earnings averaged over a period of years in order to allow for any decline in earnings in the last years of working life. The objective is greater fairness although some fairness may in the event be lost in those cases where these averages are not fully adjusted for rises in the general wage level or even for rises in prices. This is one of the difficulties in interpretation. As usual international comparisons must therefore be made with caution.

In the Netherlands, the target for a retired couple is a pension equal to the net minimum wage and it has been almost attained (see p. 120, above). This is equivalent to about three-fifths of gross average earnings. Supplementary occupational pensions play an important role in official policy in the Netherlands, as in Britain. It is hoped that the official pension together with occupational pensions will together replace about 70 per cent of the previous gross income of the average wage-earners, or 85 per cent of net income. Naturally this implies a larger role for occupational pensions as one moves up the wage scale, for the official pension is flat rate. These occupational pensions are now compulsory over a wide range of occupations, and when there is compulsion there is a ceiling. There is, of course, no ceiling to further voluntary topping-up. If, however, attention is confined to the average wage-earner, the target of 85 per cent of previous net income would provide the pensioner with a real income roughly equal to what he received before retirement if some allowance is made for lower costs (see p. 355, above). Moreover, the basic pension would be raised twice a year in line with wages. What is implied is clearly provision for the old on a generous scale.

The statutory pension schemes for manual and white-collar workers in *Germany* aim to replace 60 per cent of the individual's average pre-retirement earnings (revalorized in line with general earnings level) after 40 years insurance, up to a ceiling of twice the average earnings. The replacement level is increased by $1\frac{1}{2}$ per cent for each further year of insurance above the 'standard' period. As we have seen, however, the target replacement level is reduced in practice to some extent by the fact that a lagged measurement of general average earnings is used in calculating the pension level. Some pensioners may supplement their statutory pension by either occupational or private provision. The target replacement rate adopted, inclusive of these additions, was 75 per cent of gross pre-retirement earnings. It is, however, unlikely that the majority of pensioners will have attained this level of replacement.

The French general scheme (*régime géneral*), aims at replacing 40 per cent of earnings up to a ceiling for earnings of 135 per cent of average earnings (see pp. 261-2 above). This percentage relates, as in Germany, to a weighted average of previous earnings, but the period is ten years,[1] not three. The effect could be to pull down the proportion of final income replaced to an even greater extent than in Germany were it not for the fact that the French, unlike the Germans, scale up the figures in proportion to rises in money earnings, whereas in Germany the three-year average mentioned above is calculated in current marks unadjusted for changes in prices or wages over these years. Nevertheless, if a worker's position in the earnings *hierarchy* had declined a little in the years just before retirement, the use, as in France, of a revalorized ten-year average as a base would leave him with more than 40 per cent of his *final* year's earnings. The French scheme was set up in 1945 with a thirty-year maturity period which will be complete in 1975. Although the arrangements for blanketing-in were less generous than in Germany, there was little or no gap between the target and the actual for new pensioners in the early 1970s. By 1975 a modified formula will allow a period of thirty-seven and a half years to count towards a pension and this gives a replacement figure of 50 per cent. We must also take account of the French complementary schemes which, in view of the blanketing-in arrangements, provided mature benefits quickly. ARCCO provides a varying supplement equivalent to about 15-20 per cent of wages. A French pensioner may therefore expect about two-thirds of his gross income to be replaced, if his position is somewhere between the minimum and the maximum.

The Belgian scheme has targets for income replacement which,

---

[1] These may be the ten years before retirement or the ten years before the age of sixty, whichever is better. The figures above refer to a *single* person in view of the complex nature of the addition for wives.

at first sight, appear quite high: 75 per cent for a married couple, 60 per cent for a single person. But the percentages here are deceptive. They relate in this case to life-time earnings which means earnings over an insurance period of forty-five years. But this earnings base is adjusted only for changes in prices, not for changes in real earnings. Moreover, there is a flat-rate element in the calculation inherited from the past which is diminishing in importance but will not disappear until the year 2000 (see p. 312, above).

There is no ceiling in the Belgian scheme for the wage-earner but there is for the salary-earner at a level corresponding to about 130 per cent of the average earnings of a wage-earner in manufacturing. The salary-earner thus depends upon private occupational arrangements for his supplementation. One of the topics of current debate is whether there should also be an upper limit in the workers' scheme. The respective merits of funding and pay-as-you-go are thus under debate in Belgium, as elsewhere.

The Italians have a very ambitious pension plan which, as we have observed, is in sharp contrast to current actuality (see p. 231, above). The aim of the general obligatory scheme is to replace 74 per cent of gross earnings after forty years insurance—with no ceiling. In this case the earnings base is the average of the best three out of the last five years before retirement. There is no provision for revalorizing and this would pull down the percentage of final income replaced to 68 per cent if money wages were rising at, say, 8 per cent a year—as did industrial wages in the 1960s. In 1969 the Italian Government declared itself anxious to do still more by aiming at 80 per cent of the best three out of the last ten years before retirement. The extension of the period of choice was designed to help the worker but the opposite may sometimes happen in view of the inadequate arrangements for revalorizing. In practice, Italian pensions replace only a modest proportion of previous income but the targets are high, especially when account is taken of the fact that there is no upper income limit.

Sweden has an even more complex scheme than some of those mentioned above. The flat-rate pension represented about 37·5 per cent of average earnings in 1971 for a couple; but this percentage will decline in the future if Sweden retains the practice, described on pp. 167–8 above, of adjusting pensions in payment for changes in prices but not for changes in money wages. Thus as real wages rise, a decreasing proportion will be replaced by the basic pension. The supplementary graduated pension, on the other hand, will grow in importance with the approach to maturity in 1980.[1] The official aim for this second-tier pension is the replacement of 60 per cent of 'pensionable earnings' averaged over the insured person's fifteen best earnings years. This suggests a high target but the catch lies in the meaning of 'pensionable earnings'. This is a band of income lying roughly betweeen 25 per cent and 200 per cent of average manufacturing earnings which, again, is revalorized only with regard to prices, not to wages. Thus the Swedish practice of linking pensions to prices, not to wages, will pull down the replacement value of both pensions, and the objective of the two pensions is to replace two-thirds of previous peak earnings may not be reached.

The calculations presented above of the percentage of average earnings replaced by the British pension related to 1971 for the sake of comparability with the figures for other countries. Pensions were raised in 1972 and in 1973. The rise from the level prevailing just before the 1971 increase to that reached in the autumn of 1973 was substantial: about $32\frac{1}{2}$ per cent after correcting for prices by using the retail price index. It is true that the retail price index may not seem wholly appropriate in estimating real pensions, but the use of the special pension index makes less difference over the years than might be expected. The rise in the general index including housing (as used above) was 72·2 per cent between the first quarter of 1964 and the third quarter of 1971; the special pensioner index for a couple rose by 73·8. The latter index does not, however, include housing. The retail price index, excluding housing, rose over this period by 69·6 per cent. The gap between the indices in the early seventies must, however, be noted. The rise in real pensions between the level reached before the rise in the autumn of 1971 to that reached after the increase in the autumn of 1973 was 32·6 per cent as measured by the general price index including housing, 33·8 per cent by that index excluding housing and 31·6 per cent by the pensioner index. The corresponding comparison between 1972 and 1973 was 5 per cent, 5·5 per cent and 4·4 per cent. The omission of housing from the pensioner index presents a problem. Fortunately the poorer pensioners will

---

[1] That is to say, the end of the twenty-year period beginning in 1960. Thereafter the required period is to be gradually extended to thirty years.

have their housing costs met from supplementary benefit—apart from those who fail to claim their rights.

Account should also be taken of future growth of occupational pensions in Britain. Some estimates have been given for the official Reserve Scheme on the assumption that real wages grow at 3 per cent a year on average. (The assumption about the rate of return on the fund is not made explicitly.) The estimates given can be translated as follows. A man retiring in 1990 could expect a pension equivalent to 6 per cent of his earnings at retirement (up to a maximum of £48 a week in terms of 1972 earnings). Someone who retired in 2000 would get 10 per cent; in 2010, 15 per cent; in 2015, 17 per cent; in 2019, 19 per cent. These forecases are scarcely intoxicating. It is clear enough that in the early years of the next century the proportion of income replaced in Britain would still be low on these assumptions unless the basic pension were to be raised relatively to earnings. Of course the funded Official Reserve Scheme may perform substantially better than the Government Actuary has felt able to forecast. It is also quite likely that privately run occupational schemes will be more generous than the strictly funded official scheme. With uncertainty about the basic pension and uncertainty about the complementary pensions, it is more difficult to talk about targets in Britain than in some other member countries of the EEC, but it is a reasonable forecast that Britain will still occupy a low position on the league table unless the basic pension rises a lot.

We must now recapitulate briefly the arrangements for adjusting pensions in payment. Traditionally, pensioners are regarded as the victims of inflation but in all our countries protection is now provided, at least with regard to official pensions. In Britain there was no commitment to this effect until recent years but in fact, over the trend, the increases in pensions have done substantially more than offset rising prices. Thus, between 1948 and 1972, real pensions in Britain rose by over four-fifths. New pensions rose roughly in line with gross weekly earnings and rather more than net earnings which are affected by fiscal drag to a greater extent than are pensions. There is no official commitment to keep pension increases in line with average earnings. It seems highly probable, however, that this will in fact be achieved in the future as it has been in the past. Under the Act of 1973, contributions are to be graduated and revenue will therefore rise in line with total earnings.

This would not in itself keep the pension in line with average earnings a head if demographic changes raised the proportion of retired people relative to the active population;[1] but in fact demographic changes are likely to become gradually favourable after 1980. A trend towards earlier retirement could, it is true, have an offsetting effect and this has become important.[2] But there are also indications which we have noted above of a desire on the part of the main political parties to make structural changes in favour of the aged. It is a fair presumption that pensions in Britain will rise at least as fast as gross average earnings in the future. This is not, of course, to make any conclusive statement about the *adequacy* of pensions. That is a different matter which, as we have seen, involves an important value judgement. In the Netherlands pensions are reviewed twice a year and adjusted automatically in line with the index of negotiated wages (see pp. 117-8 above). Structural changes in pensions may also be made and this has been done in practice, as can be seen on Chart 5. In France, pensions are automatically linked to changes in wages (see Chart 8, and pp. 266-7, above) and in Germany there is also an automatic link to a lagged average of wages (see Chart 4 and pp. 84-5, above). In Belgium the automatic link is to prices but, as in Britain, the link in practice has been usually with wages (see Chart 9 and pp. 332-3, above). Perhaps surprisingly, Sweden now follows a different course and since 1968 pensions have been adjusted, both in principle and in practice, only in line with rising prices. Before 1968, sporadic adjustments had lifted pensions by more than prices (see Chart 6 and pp. 161-2, above). In Italy a link with prices, but not with wages, was initiated in 1969 (except for the social and some non-INPS pensions). In the USA there has hitherto been no official link at all between pensions and prices although the increases in pensions made from time to time have offset inflation over the trend (Chart 10). From 1975 onwards, however, US pensions will also be adjusted each year in line with prices.

Although pensioners have been protected against inflation over the trend, their standard of living has fallen between reviews. This is shown clearly in Chart 2, where the course of real pensions in Britain is traced quarter by quarter. The Conservative Government

---

[1] See Ch. 1, page 34, and see also the Mathematical Appendix.
[2] See *Social Security: Another British Failure* by Sir John Walley, Charles Knight, 1972.

introduced annual reviews in 1971 which means that pensions are now adjusted as frequently as most incomes from work. This is clearly an improvement but it may be doubted whether even annual changes would be frequent enough for people with low incomes if inflation were to continue at the rate experienced in the early seventies. The position is made more difficult in Britain by the fact that changes in pensions are determined by the budget in March or April but do not come into force until September or October. Pensions then remain unaltered for a further twelve months. This means that forecasts of future changes in prices have to be made for a long period ahead. Thus a Government may underestimate an acceleration in the rise in prices and real benefits will, as a result, be less than was originally envisaged.

The Dutch have been more skilful in reducing the lags and their experience should be studied. A more radical change would be to introduce a threshold arrangement as in Belgium where pensions are changed when prices rise by 2 per cent; or as in Sweden, when a 3 per cent rise leads to a change in pensions. Threshold agreements, however, can pose administrative problems as the Dutch discovered when they operated such a system and had to raise pensions four times in 1971! In the Netherlands, pensions are now reviewed twice a year.

The speed and nature of the adjustment become particularly important when the pace of inflation begins to accelerate. Consider, first, a situation in which prices are rising at a steady rate and suppose that adjustments are brought into force every October as in Britain. Suppose, furthermore, that the purpose of these adjustments is simply to restore the purchasing power of the pensioner to the level reached a year ago. In November and subsequent months the real value of the pension will begin to fall once more and the average over the year will be below the point reached at the time of adjustment. This average value will, however, be steady. It will be a different matter if inflation begins to accelerate for the average in real terms will then drop. The pensioners will, so to speak, be pulled to the surface once a year but will be allowed to sink deeper and deeper between the reviews. Adjustments made simply by linking pensions (or other indexed incomes) to a price index may therefore fail to protect such incomes from inflation, unless there is provision for retrospective compensation. When pensions are linked in practice to money wages—whether or not a formula is applied—then there will be an additional margin for the protection of the pensioner. If, however, the link is with *average* wages at the time of the reviews, then pensions will not be allowed to leap-frog as wages do in particular occupations. In the British case this effect can be seen by taking the annual average of quarterly figures for real pensions. With 1964 equal to 100, the index for 1968 was 115; for 1969, 112; for 1970, 114; for 1971, 108; for 1972, 119; for 1973, 122. A real advance had been made by 1973, but presumably a smaller one than was intended by Government.

Frequent adjustments in pensions will add to the inflationary pressure on demand and costs. One may suppose, however, that there could be a good deal of support for the value judgement that the standard of living of pensioners should not be used any more than can reasonably be avoided as an anti-inflationary stabilizer. If, then, inflation were to continue at a high level, Britain might well have to adjust pensions (and many other welfare payments) even more frequently than once a year. The only satisfactory solution is, of course, to control inflation.

The view that pensions should rise in real terms roughly in line with real incomes from work is more controversial when it is the case that the number of old people is rising relative to those at work. If pensions are then linked to an index of average earnings, total expenditure on pensions will rise more than total income from work, and the pensions tax will have to go up. This is a problem which confronts a number of European countries.

VI—TAX REFORM AND SOCIAL SECURITY

Can the tax authorities be made to undergo a sea-change and themselves become the providers of benefits? A good many proposals to this effect have been put forward and discussed especially in Britain and the USA over the past thirty years or so. As far as we have been able to ascertain, schemes of this kind have attracted less attention in the countries of continental Europe with which we are concerned in this volume.[1]

---

[1] One of the objectives of the negative income tax proposals is to bring together the different ways of providing assistance with the cost of children: allowances

In Britain these suggestions have been taken up officially and a possible scheme was presented to Parliament in October 1972 in the form of a Green Paper.[1] This plan was still in tentative form and the various figures it contained were described as illustrative. This is one difficulty and there is the still more formidable difficulty that a balanced assessment would involve a long and complex discussion of the British system of personal taxation which would be out of place in the present volume. It is, however, clearly necessary for us to say a little about what is entailed in proposals of this kind and, in particular, to consider how the elderly might be affected.

The usual allowances which tax-payers can set against their liabilities are of no benefit to those with incomes that are too low to allow them to derive any advantage—or, at best, no more than partial advantage—from these allowances. With arrangements of the kind we are considering, tax-allowances would be replaced with credits which would be available to everyone within the scheme and would, of course, vary with size of family. One would then both receive a credit and be liable for tax on all other income. If one's income were low, the credit would exceed the liability to tax and the tax authorities would pay out a net sum in such cases. At a break-even point the credit would just offset the tax-liability. Above this point there would be a positive payment to the tax collector.

A number of advantages can be claimed for a scheme of this kind. Thus under existing arrangements in Britain parents receive a cash allowance for each of their children except the first and are

---

against tax and cash payments. This has long since been done in Sweden. In Italy the whole system of personal taxation has not been such as to encourage more refined developments.

[1] See 'Poverty in the Welfare State', by J. E. Meade, *Oxford Economic Papers*, November 1972; *Negative Taxes and the Poverty Problem*, by Christopher Green (The Brookings Institution, Washington, DC, 1967); *Poverty in Britain and the Reform of Social Security*, by A. B. Atkinson (Cambridge University Press, 1969). These authors analyse the issues that arise and also give biographical references to earlier literature on the subject which need not be repeated here. On the British proposals of 1972, see: *Proposals for a Tax-Credit System* (Green Paper), Cmnd. 5116, HMSO, October 1972; *Report and Proceedings of the Select Committee on Tax Credit*, HMSO, June 1973 together with the *Minutes of Evidence* submitted to the Select Committee; *Conference on Proposals for a Tax-Credit System*. Institute for Fiscal Studies, London, 1973; 'The Tax-Credit Proposals', by G. C. Fiegelen and P. S. Lansely, *National Institute Economic Review*, May, 1973.

also given tax allowances for all dependent children.[1] These two ways of assisting families can be brought together in the form of a single tax credit which reduces the amount of paying out and paying in. Another advantage is that certain problems of selectivity can be handled in a way that gets round at least some of the difficulties of the existing arrangements in Britain. As we have observed on many occasions in the book, there are families, both working families and retired families, that fail to claim as much as they would be entitled to receive subject to means-tests. If the reason is the stigma associated with an approach to the body responsible for such aid—in Britain, the Supplementary Benefits Commission —this difficulty would be removed. Presumably most people would feel a sense of triumph rather than shame in extracting money from the tax authorities! In any case neither a sense of shame nor ignorance of their rights would affect the issue because the payments would be automatic. The worker would receive the benefit to which he was entitled as part of his pay packet[2] and thus the incomplete rate of take-up which has been one of the weaknesses of existing arrangements, notably with regard to the British Family Income Supplement, would be avoided. It is believed that the rate of take-up has improved but, as we have observed in discussing the elderly, hard statistical information is lacking. What we can say is that, if inadequate take-up is still thought to be a serious problem, then the tax-credit scheme deserves to be awarded some marks under this heading. The retired pensioner, for his part, would receive his credit automatically.

Let us now turn to some of the problems raised by a scheme of this kind. If the credits were to be set at the official subsistence level in order to guarantee a minimum income for all who came

---

[1] Since 1968 this has been done in a way that reduces the gain to families that are better off by means of a tax adjustment. This is usually referred to as 'the claw-back'.

[2] It has been questioned whether the tax authorities could react with sufficient speed to changing family circumstances. Cf., e.g., 'Universal and Selective Social Security' in *Commitment to Welfare*, by Richard M. Titmuss, Union University Books, 1968, pp. 119/20. The introduction of the non-cumulative principle should largely get round this difficulty. As Prest has observed: 'We can now see that cumulative annual witholding was the albatross round the neck of many of the other schemes for negative income tax and the like which have been put forward in recent years.' *Conference Proposals for a Tax-Credit System*, p. 2. This is not to deny that a non-cumulative scheme may encounter objections on other grounds.

within the scheme, the total sum required for these benefits would be very large. For fixed credits would be given to everyone irrespective of income. For those with positive tax liabilities, large tax credits would be equivalent to a rise in allowances under the present arrangements together with a higher proportionate rate of tax on other income and this high marginal rate of tax could be damaging to the economy. The British proposals are so designed as to lessen the difficulty by setting the credits at levels well below the subsistence level. The illustrative figures are £4 for a single person, £6 for a married couple and £2 for each child. Thus the income corresponding to the credits would be well below the official 'poverty levels', i.e. the Supplementary Benefit levels for families of different sizes. It follows that this tax credit scheme could not replace existing social insurance payments but would have to be combined with them. The latter payments are selective, not on an individual basis, but by category, i.e. the elderly, the disabled, the unemployed, etc. If such payments are to continue and these groups of beneficiaries are also to receive tax-credits, this naturally raises the question whether these categories could not be helped just as effectively by a rise in their basic social security benefits. This is what is implied by the plea for a 'New Beveridge'. Thus Professor Atkinson proposes[1] that the increased benefits would be combined with tax changes in order to reduce the benefit to the better-off. This extension of the 'claw-back' should, he suggests, include the treatment of National Insurance retirement pensions as unearned income and therefore eligible for smaller allowances. The Tax Credit Study Group of the Inland Revenue has replied that 'claw-back' arrangements are unpopular and difficult for tax payers to understand. Moreover 'the claw-back of any significant amounts in additional taxes poses the unavoidably difficult choice between, on the one hand, trying to confine additional benefits to a fairly narrow group, involving high marginal rates of withdrawal and 'poverty trap' problems, and, on the other hand, permitting a more gradual rate of withdrawal and allowing benefits to extend to much higher income groups.' In defence of the tax-credit scheme, it can be pointed out that some of those who would benefit under it do not fall within any of the social insurance categories. Although the head of a family may be

---

[1] See 'Conflict in Social Security Policy', by A. B. Atkinson, in *Conflicts in Policy Objectives*, ed. by N. Kaldor (Basil Blackwell, Oxford, 1971).

at work, his income may be lower without the tax-credit scheme than is thought to be tolerable. He could be helped by higher allowances for children, including an allowance for the first child; but single workers and childless couples with one, or both, at work would not be assisted by the 'Beveridge' style of assistance and, although usually less in need of help, would sometimes be so and would in fact be helped by the tax-credit scheme. The question then is whether it would not be possible to devise some more selective form of assistance by which all families, including those with working heads, could be brought up to some official poverty line. This would clearly require means-tests. Thus the British Family Income Supplement, which provides means-tested assistance to families with children, could be extended to all families. Or the 'Stockholm social wage' might serve as an example for study.[1] One would also have to decide upon the weighting to be placed upon two opposing dangers: inadequate take-up on the one hand, and, on the other, the abuse and exploitation of the scheme by the unscrupulous.

If the scheme had been in force in the autumn of 1972, a single pensioner with no other source of income would have had his income raised by 29 per cent; a married couple would have had a rise of 25 per cent; a widow with two children a rise of 24 per cent. From a social point of view, this would obviously have been a marked improvement. With the official 'poverty level' unchanged, 'something like a million national insurance beneficiaries, most of them retirement pensioners, might have had their incomes raised above supplementary benefit levels'. (Green Paper, para. 110.) Thus the numbers 'in poverty' of those receiving means-tested benefits would have fallen by about a third and many of those who, although entitled to such benefits, failed to claim their rights, would have gained. Moreover there would have been about a third of the total, in the case of pensioners, who neither pay tax nor are eligible for supplementary benefit. The proportion of previous

---

[1] The 'social wage' was introduced in Stockholm in 1970 and later by some other towns. The incomes can be raised by means-tested payments from local assistance funds. The social wage is at the same level as the basic pension. An allowance for the cost of housing is included (as it is with the pension). The social wage is regarded as a simpler device than the provision of assistance for a variety of different purposes (food, clothing, rent, etc.). It is presumably attended with much the same advantages and disadvantages as would attend an extension of the coverage of supplementary benefit.

incomes replaced by pensions plus tax credits would thus have been significantly above that actually replaced by pensions alone. This might have been admirable—if the scheme had been in force in 1972! But it is not to come into operation until 1978. Meanwhile wages and salaries will have gone up. It is true that the credits are to be adjusted yearly in order to take account of inflation. (It may be noted in passing that the extension of the practice of annual adjustment to children's allowances marks an important change. In Britain, as in many other countries, children's allowances have been eroded by inflation to a greater extent than pensions.) Real incomes should also have gone up by 1978. Unless the *real* value of the tax credits were to be raised as well, then the proportion of income replaced would obviously be less in 1978 than is implied by a hypothetical estimate of the effect the tax credits might have had in 1972. Moreover in view both of past experience and of the strong political pressure for higher pensions, we can reasonably suppose that real pensions will also be substantially higher in 1978 than in 1972. Tax credits would therefore represent a smaller addition as a percentage of pensions than the figures above suggest unless the *real* value of the tax credits were also to be increased, i.e. their value after correcting for changes in prices.

We can put the matter in another way. Given the rate of tax, it follows that tax credits of any given monetary amount are redistributive because they represent a larger proportion of low incomes than of high incomes. If, however, this redistributive effect is to be preserved with the passage of time, the real value of the tax credits must also increase with rising real incomes.[1] An increase in the real value of the tax credits would, however, raise the cost of the scheme. Here is the rub.

If the scheme had been in force in 1972, it would have added £1,300 million (net) to government expenditure. This would have been so for three reasons: first, the credits would have raised the threshold over which people start to pay tax; secondly, those

---

[1] The proposed arrangements can be shown by the following formula:

$$y_d = y_g (1 - r) + c$$

where y_d represents disposable income; y_g gross income before tax; r the percentage rate of tax; c the tax credit. If we consider a range of incomes over which the proportional rate of tax is unchanged, then the ratio of disposable income to gross income will obviously fall as one moves up the income scale. But this effect will be retained over time only if c rises in real terms as well as y_g.

below the tax-threshold would have received net credits; thirdly, the net assistance provided for children would have been raised. To have financed such additional expenditure in 1972 would have posed a pretty problem! In fact, as we have noted, the year 1978 is the one suggested for bringing the scheme into operation, and it is hoped that 'with the growth of the national income, more resources will become available for eliminating poverty: the Government consider that, taking all factors into account, and given the right order of priorities, the cost of the scheme would be a manageable one.' (Green Paper, para. 117). It is a reasonable assumption that the growth of output should indeed make it much easier to find an extra £1,300 million (at constant prices) in 1978 than in 1972. But the trouble is that, for the reasons given above, £1,300 million would not be enough to do the same job in 1978 as it would have done in 1972. If more will be needed in real terms, how is the scheme to be financed? One cannot simply rely upon growth if—broadly speaking—the cost of the scheme itself is to rise with growth. If taxes have to be raised, whether direct or indirect, then the whole pattern of the proposal will have to be modified and its merits will need to be assessed afresh. Where, then, would the extra burden fall? Of course it is always possible, in principle, that a fall in other items of government expenditure would release resources sufficient to finance the scheme in whole or in part. This is what may occur, but we are clearly involved at this point in some very difficult speculation. It is also clear that with this crucially important question of finance so uncertain at this stage in the official proposals, it is impossible to make an adequate assessment of the scheme. It is also fair to add that it would have been impossible for any official document to remove all these uncertainties. Time is required both for public discussion of proposals of this kind and for the preparation of the administrative arrangements; thus some uncertainty in forecasts has to be expected. (It should be recalled that the figures in the Green Paper are intended to be only illustrative.) The real question is whether the *general* case for a scheme of this kind is sufficiently strong to justify preparations for its ultimate adoption with the figures to be inserted later.

In part this general case has already been discussed above and some of the objections have also been considered. It is, however, necessary to say a little more about the effect of introducing such a scheme on the probable need for means-tested assistance provided from other sources outside the negative tax system itself. Any belief that a negative income tax would almost completely remove the need for such assistance must clearly be rejected. The situations in which poor families find themselves vary too much to be dealt with adequately by means of the tax machinery.[1] The cost of housing is, of course, the outstanding case and assistance will still have to be provided whether through a body such as the Supplementary Benefits Commission or through a scheme for fair rents combined with subsidies. There are also bound to be other cases of need. Thus, in Britain, those with incomes of less than about a quarter of average earnings would be outside both the compulsory social security arrangements and the tax-credit scheme. The self-employed will also be outside the latter scheme as proposed in the Green Paper and some of them may be far from affluent. Some of these people, and no doubt some others, will clearly require general means-tested assistance apart from means-tested assistance for the various specific benefits (housing, university education, etc.). The fact remains that the tax-credit scheme, together with a policy of subsidizing families with housing costs rather than subsidizing 'bricks and mortar', should greatly reduce the number of families in Britain in need of such general cash assistance.

About £545 million or two-fifths of the net cost of the £1,300 million would go to families below the break-even points in the tax-credit scheme.[2] The break-even level would have come at about £14.70 a week for a single person, about £19.60 for a couple and about £28.80 for a family with two children. Average male earnings of manual workers were £35.8 in October 1972. (The £545 million and the £1,300 million would, of course, be additional to social security benefits but allow for a saving of means-tested assistance.) It is, however, proper to ask whether it would not be still better to use whatever additional funds may be available in order to raise social security benefits to the official poverty level. As we have observed above (p. 364), about £1000 million would have been needed to do so in 1971; or £700 million for the elderly

---

[1] On this point, Titmuss was clearly right. *Op. cit.*, p. 119. It is also the case that, for the same reason, a New Beveridge could not remove completely the need for some means-tested assistance.

[2] *Select Committee on Tax Credit. Minutes of Evidence.* 29th March 1973, p. 242.

alone. If this approach is thought to be too costly, can one contemplate with consistency the expenditure of £1,300 million in the form of tax credits in order to provide the same credits to all members of the employed population who have more than a quarter of average earnings? If a New Beveridge would be insufficiently selective, what is one to say about the tax-credit proposals? The latter would indeed be a way of helping the working poor in addition to help with the cost of children. But this may not appear to be a decisive consideration. Although it is scarcely possible to believe that this would be the best way of spending an extra £1,300 million if the verdict were to depend solely upon the effect of the scheme on the nation's social security arrangements, it would be wrong to rest the verdict on these considerations alone. For this is a programme for tax reform which is to embrace the bulk of the working population and the verdict must rest upon a wider assessment and allow for additional considerations, whether favourable or hostile. As usual there will be conflicting views about social values and, as usual, there will also be conflicting empirical assessments of the economic effects of one course rather than another. To carry the discussion further would take us far beyond our scope.[1]

There is, however, one point which can reasonably be made without straying beyond the context of the present book. The employee's social security tax starts at anything above zero income for those inside the social security scheme and remains at $5\frac{1}{4}$ per cent to the point of $1\frac{1}{2}$ times average earnings. Over this range, the rate of direct taxation—income tax plus social security tax—is therefore $35\frac{1}{4}$ per cent. The tax rate on income above this upper limit then falls to 30 per cent (income tax alone) until the higher tax rate becomes operative for a single person at £5,000 a year—about $2\frac{1}{2}$ times average earnings in the autumn of 1973. This odd feature of the tax system would not be removed by the tax-credit proposals which, in this sense, fail to weld the social security and the tax proposals together although it is true that the anomaly is rather less than it appears when account is taken of tax allowances. If the upper limit of $1\frac{1}{2}$ times average earnings were

---

[1] On this controversy, see in particular the evidence submitted by N. Kaldor and A. B. Atkinson to the Select Committee on Tax-Credit on 23 March and 12 April 1973, respectively. See also the reply by the Tax-Credit Study Group in the Minutes of Evidence of 29 March 1973.

removed and the social security tax levied at $5\frac{1}{4}$ per cent on all income, this would meet an obvious criticism of the tax system and would also provide about £200 million for additional expenditure on social security. This net addition to receipts would naturally be less if there were some offsetting reduction in the higher rate of tax on incomes above £5,000. This surtax threshold level is, of course, being swiftly lowered in real terms by inflation. It would always be possible to confine any adjustment of the higher tax rate to the lower ranges of income. Obviously various possibilities would be open and views would differ sharply on their desirability. The objection that any such removal of the upper income limit in levying the employee's social security tax would imply a departure from the principle of social insurance is not, in my opinion, decisive, in view both of the fact that graduated contributions for flat-rate pensions have already been accepted and of the other points made in our first chapter about 'social insurance'. The change need not, of course, imply the abandonment of the principle that the social security contributions are earmarked and need not lead to the further step (which would be undesirable) of financing all benefits from general taxation.

This reform would be more simple and easier to administer than complex schemes for different rates of personal taxation below £5,000. It is true that the earnings on which contributions for the basic scheme were levied would not then be the same as the tranche of income on which contributions for the second-tier Official Reserve Scheme were levied and this would make administration a little more complicated in the case of those employees who were in the official Reserve Scheme. This can scarcely be regarded, however, as a fatal objection.

Finally, there is the case discussed in the first chapter for a much more radical reform: the abolition of the employers' payroll tax with a corresponding rise in the employee's rate of tax and a corresponding reduction in prices. The obvious difficulty would be to ensure that all prices were reduced in practice by the appropriate amount. In this case it is the American critics who, as we have observed, have been most forthright in their demand for reform and their case deserves more attention both in Britain and in other countries of the EEC. That this is a very difficult as well as an important issue goes without saying.

VII—THE FUTURE OF PRIVATE SCHEMES

Can private occupational schemes compete with modern public schemes based on the pay-as-you-go principle with benefits raised at least in line with the cost of living and often in line with wages? It is possible to reply with another question. Why should private schemes have to compete in this way if they serve a different purpose? If the state has established whatever public arrangements are thought to be appropriate, there must still be freedom for private concerns to offer something more. This topping-up will depend upon the arrangements made between these concerns and their employees with the trade unions playing an important part in the negotiations in some countries. The private schemes, it may be held, are supplements rather than substitutes and comparisons of respective performance are of academic interest. Are private schemes not a private matter in which Government need not be involved? It must be conceded that there may be some validity in this line of reasoning but it will not quite do.

First, apart altogether from the competitiveness of private schemes, there are certain matters which the Government may regard as being quite properly its business. The security of the pensions is one. If a firm undertakes to provide certain pensions, is there any reasonable assurance that it will be able to fulfil its undertaking? When deductions have been made from wages, the employees will feel that to this extent they have paid already and should not lose what they have paid. The employer's own contributions will often have entitled him to a tax remission. Apart from any deliberate cheating,[1] there is the much more important danger that the firm may not be in a financial position to pay up unless appropriate protection has been built into the scheme. The backing may be the firm's own assets and it has been recorded that this is often the case in Germany (see p. 70, above). In Sweden, this balance-sheet reserve has not been thought to offer sufficient protection and arrangements have been made to provide insurance against this risk of default. In Britain, pension funds have to be established with their own trustees who invest in a range of assets, or appropriate pension schemes have to be negotiated with an insurance company. In these ways one of the possible disadvantages

---

[1] In Britain this would not be permitted by the Inland Revenue.

of private pensions can be removed, i.e. the risk of loss. In public schemes the future of the pension depends upon the decisions of Government and here, too, there is risk. The risk in this case can be reduced when the social insurance principle—dubious though it is in some respects—is so applied as to provide at least some autonomy for the official pension 'fund' and thus some safeguard.

Another weakness of the private occupational scheme—and, indeed, of public occupational schemes for civil servants and the like—may be the loss of pension rights on change of job. The state may feel that it has a right to intervene partly because mobility of labour may then be discouraged.[1] The private employer, for his part, can object that he should be free to offer a reward for loyalty. This objection has some force but only when the employee leaves voluntarily, not because he has been dismissed.

There are various forms of protection for the worker who moves. His pension may be 'preserved', i.e. held for him until he retires when he will be entitled to draw pensions from his various employers. This is administratively cumbersome and may well result in some rights not being claimed. Moreover the rights preserved are often preserved in the money value ruling at the time when the employee changed his job and this is unsatisfactory. Another solution is to have his rights transferred to the new employer with some corresponding transfer of assets from one pension plan to another. The German balance-sheet reserve system is not very suitable from this point of view, but the difficulties should not be insuperable when there is a fund invested in a portfolio of assets outside the firm. In Britain, the proposed Occupational Pensions Board will be charged with the task of reviewing the situation. It will not be enough to ensure simply that rights are protected. The conditions for protection (in particular length of service) should not be unduly restrictive. Moreover, the future pensioner should be able to expect that the sum with which he is credited when he leaves one job for another will not only be protected against inflation but will earn a real rate of return, if the returns achieved by pension funds are generally enough to do more than offset rising prices.

Complementary occupational pensions may, of course, be unfunded, as in France. The pension is then protected against loss

---

[1] There is little evidence of this happening in Britain.

because firms belong to pension federations (see p. 271, above). There is also no problem when an employee moves from one firm to another within a federation. If he moves from a firm in one federation to one in another, then he will be entitled to draw two pensions. For example he might have a pension from UNIRS (as a salaried employee) and one from AGIRC (as a manager). But this will occur much less often than movement between firms in the same federation.

Enough has been said to indicate that there is bound to be some degree of state supervision, and control is needed even when private schemes are funded. It may be argued, however, that this is the end of the matter. It might, perhaps, be the end of the matter if there were not still a choice to be made between pay-as-you-go and funded schemes. If Britain wishes to have *compulsory* graduated pensions up to certain minima, then this could be achieved by an official pay-as-you-go graduated scheme or by semi-private arrangements backed by some compulsion and control as in France. Instead, the new pension strategy in Britain involves reliance on private occupational schemes together with a funded official Reserve Scheme. The Dutch, of course, are following a similar policy, without anything corresponding to the British official Reserve Scheme. There are two questions which must then be faced. First, do the funded schemes provide as good value for money?[1] Second, how quickly can funded schemes extend the scope of graduated pensions over the population?

In considering the question of value for money, we must postulate that contributions are levied at the same percentage rate under the pay-as-you-go and the funded schemes that are being considered. With a cash-purchase scheme these contributions will be made over the future pensioner's working life and, given the contribution rate, his accumulated pension rights will depend upon the pay he has received and the rate of return on the pensions fund. His pension claim can then be expressed as a capital sum on the date of his retirement. If commutation is permitted this sum can be put at his disposal and used to purchase an annuity. He will then

---

[1] This matter has been much discussed in the USA and strikingly different answers obtained, mainly because there have been wide differences in assumptions—quite unnecessarily wide differences, in my view. For a review of this debate and for a new attempt to assess the various issues and reach a reasonable conclusion, see Brittain, *op. cit.*, Ch. 4.

have a choice between a fixed annuity and a variable one. The fixed
annuity will depend upon actuarial assumptions about expectation
of life and upon the fixed rate of discount used. If inflation continues, the value of his annuity will decline in real terms over his
period of retirement. Alternatively he can buy a variable annuity
which will rise over his retirement but will begin at a lower level.
The value of his first year's pension will reflect something more
akin to the return on equities than to the return on fixed-interest
securities. He will thus have some protection against inflation but
it will not necessarily be to his advantage to take the variable
annuity. This will depend (*a*) upon how long he lives, (*b*) upon the
initial gap between the fixed rate of interest and the initial
dividend yield, and (*c*) upon subsequent increases in this dividend
yield.

A variable annuity may not necessarily be expected to grow fast
enough to promise as much as a fixed annuity to someone with a
fairly short expectation of life. The gap between fixed-interest yield
and dividend yield at any point in time—usually termed 'the
reverse yield gap'—reflects all the forces operating in the market
and is presumably larger than it would be if the gap were determined solely by the preferences of elderly people.

This point is important in assessing the performance of pension
funds. It is true that a pensioner may not be given a lump sum
with which to buy annuities on his retirement, but the managers
of a fund may have similar considerations in mind. The Government Actuary reports that the increases in pensions in payment
in Britain have averaged about $2\frac{1}{2}$ per cent a year between 1961 and
1971, insufficient to offset rises in prices of about $4\frac{1}{2}$ per cent a year.
But pensioners may start off with higher initial pensions than would
be the case if the pensions were determined as though they were
variable annuities purchased at the time of retirement and invested
in a portfolio consisting largely of equities. We must therefore be
careful in interpreting the evidence. This is not, of course, to say
that the policies of pension funds have in general been fully
appropriate for a period of inflation. That is a different matter
which cannot be resolved without further evidence.[1]

---

[1] To secure recognition private schemes in Britain which do not provide for
increases of pensions in payment will have to start at a more generous level. See
Explanatory Memorandum on the Social Security Bill, 1972, Cmnd. 5142.
HMSO, Nov. 1972, pp. 11–12.

A pay-as-you-go official pension for someone who has earned an average income depends in its first year upon the total income from work in that year multiplied by the given contribution rate and upon the number of retired people relative to the number of people at work. In subsequent years, it will depend upon increases in income from work and upon any subsequent changes in the demographic structure. It is therefore a variable annuity of a different kind from that described above. This, too, can be expressed formally as a capital sum which represents the value of his pension claims at the point of his retirement (see the Mathematical Appendix, p. 397, below). There it is shown that the respective values of a funded pension and a pay-as-you-go pension will turn upon a number of issues, in particular the rate of growth of wages, the rate of return on a pensions fund and demographic changes.

An important qualification must be noted at this stage. Although it is possible to examine along these lines the position of an individual pensioner and to ask whether he is doing well or badly under an official scheme, it is a very different matter to assess the effects of a general switch from funding to pay-as-you-go, or vice versa. *For such a change would not be marginal.* The flow of savings and consumers' expenditure would be affected and the rate of interest appropriate for discounting. In short one may easily be guilty of the fallacy of composition. Thus the question of transfers between the generations, referred to on p. 15, above, raises difficult questions of interpretation and assessment.

Under pay-as-you-go, there is uncertainty about the course of taxable earnings after retirement from which the scheme is financed and this must be considered in the light of probable changes in the ratio of the active population to the retired population. The adjustment of a pension may also depend entirely upon the discretion of the government of the day or may be determined by a formula linking his pension to prices or to wages. This formula, in turn, may be altered and so may the rates of pension tax. In fact, as has been recorded, pay-as-you-go pensions have kept well in step with rising wages, often at the cost of a rising pension tax.

Under a cash-purchase scheme there will be uncertainty about the rate of return on the pension fund up to the date of retirement. Thereafter a pensioner with a fixed annuity will have certainty with

regard to pension payments in current money values but grave
uncertainty about their real value. If the pension is variable, then
there is uncertainty about the future return on the pension fund
and this may vary a good deal from one fund to another.

Uncertainty up to the point of retirement has been reduced by
the general abandonment of the cash-purchase principle by which
the pension depends upon the accumulated value of contributions.
According to the Government Actuary's Report for 1971, almost
half the pension schemes reported were on the 'salary service' basis,
by which the pension is a fraction of salary in the final year, or
years, of working life, multiplied by the number of years in pensionable employment. Just over a quarter were 'salary range'
schemes in which the pension is linked to salary over the whole
career. In this last case, of course, it is crucially important to know
whether salary payments have been revalorized for changes in
prices or, better, for changes in average earnings. If there is
uncertainty on this score the pensioner is left all the more at risk.
About 12 per cent were on a flat-accrual basis for each year of
service. If this flat-accrual is adjusted regularly with changes in the
price-index or the wage-index, then to that extent risk will be
reduced. But this may not be done, or may not be as generally done,
as it should be. Information is scanty. So much for numbers of
schemes. The figures for numbers of members are still more striking: 72 per cent in salary service schemes, 7 per cent in salary
range and 14 per cent on a flat accrual basis.

When the pension is not on the cash-purchase basis, then its
value may be greater or less than what strict funding would provide.
The pension may sometimes exceed a cash-purchase pension and,
when this is so, some element of pay-as-you-go may enter in, or
some supplement may be provided from the firm's general
revenue. Alternatively the fund may safeguard against risk to itself
in its actuarial calculations by assessing its pension commitments—
say on a salary service basis—on very cautious assumptions. It may
turn out that the fund may then be sufficient to provide a better
pension. Any surpluses thus accumulated may be used to supplement pensions in payment.

Enough has now been said to show how difficult it is to try to
answer questions about 'value-for-money' from pension funds.
There are, however, some statistics worth quoting in order to
throw at least a little more light on these matters. In the first

o

place it must not be assumed too readily that such funds cannot cope with inflation. As we have seen, it is important to distinguish between the earning of pension rights and what happens to pensions already in payment. As we have seen above a large majority are in salary service schemes and their pensions will therefore be related to final (or near final) earnings. Thus their pension rights will rise with their earnings and this will afford reasonable protection against inflation. The scale on which an employer feels replacement can be offered will, however, be influenced by the return on his pension fund although individual pensions will not usually be determined in this way, for any given rate of contributions, as with cash-purchase. Pensions in payment are a different matter. The latter have gone up by only about $2\frac{1}{2}$ per cent over the years 1961–71, as the Government actuary reports; but, for the reasons given above, this evidence must be interpreted with caution. It is also of interest to note that the real rate of return on insurance funds has been above 3 per cent in Britain in recent years.[1] The calculations made by Messrs. Phillips and Drew[2] on the basis of a large sample, show a return on the average fund of 9·1 per cent over the years 1963–72. (The return would have been 13·2 per cent on a hypothetical model fund fully invested in equities and 2·5 per cent on a model fund invested entirely in gilts.) This rate of return reflects both capital gains and reinvested income. The

---

[1] See D. D. McKinnon in *The Investors' Chronicle*, May 1973. It is also interesting to look at the performance of the 'Cambridge college' portfolio as reported regularly in the same journal. (This is rumoured to be a real college, not a hypothetical one.) Thus in the issue for 10 August 1972, there is an article on page 556 which gives the following results.

Percentage increase at end-July in the value of a sum invested in 1953 in:
        (i) shares contained in *Financial Times* index: 262
        (ii) college portfolio: 681
          Annual percentage income in 1973 on sum invested in 1953 in:
        (iii) *Financial Times* index: 11·0
        (iv) college portfolio: 39·7
These figures may be compared with the rise of 109 per cent over these years in retail prices and the rise of 278 per cent in average weekly earnings in manufacturing (October to October). Of course much depends upon the run of years considered. The early seventies tell a very different story! Those who wish to forecast on the basis of extrapolation have, as usual, a fine range of alternatives.

[2] *Pension Fund Indicators*, 1973. I am grateful for permission to quote some of the figures from this report which was prepared for private circulation. The calculations above exclude property. By 1972 about 70 per cent of assets, excluding property, were in equities.

capital gains will, for the most part, have been unrealized—and would, of course, shrink dramatically if funds holding assets valued in £11,000 million at 1972 were to attempt to realize these gains on any significant scale. Naturally any assessment of the position of individual pensioners involves a different kind of investigation which would take full account of the inflow of contributions as well as the outflow of pensions and of various other considerations.

The main purpose of the calculations made by Phillips and Drew was to provide a standard against which the performance of individual funds may be judged. It is a noteworthy feature of these calculations that there have been very wide differences in the performance of different funds. The range for annual percentage rates of return is from $-8·3$ to $+38·4$ with a mean deviation of $10·7$. This dispersion shows that those whose pensions are based on a strict cash-purchase formula are clearly faced with a good deal of uncertainty. It is true that only a minority of pensions are on a cash-purchase basis and it must be emphasized once more that, in most funds, there is no simple link between invested contributions and payments. As we have seen, occupational pensions are usually based on some formula such as a fraction of final salary, and this may give a different answer from cash-purchase. What is also relevant, however, is that the new official reserve scheme is essentially a cash-purchase scheme.

It is clearly not at all easy to answer the question whether pay-as-you-go schemes provide the pensioner with 'better value for money'. In an age of inflation the answer might well be in the affirmative if the growth of gross national product could be taken as given. From a national point of view, there *may* be an offsetting advantage in favour of funded schemes in the form of larger net savings and more investment. As a consequence it is *possible* that the gross national product itself may be larger and the pensioners themselves may ultimately benefit. This, however, raises complex issues. We have sought in this volume to say a little about the effect of growth on pension schemes but we shall not venture to assess the effect of pension schemes on growth. It may, however, be useful to record some orders of magnitude. The net growth of private funds in 1971 was equivalent to 23 per cent of personal saving; or to 19 per cent of corporate saving. The net addition in the public sector was equivalent to 26 per cent of the saving of central government as defined in the *Blue Book on National Income and Expenditure*. These were far from negligible quantities. We must recognize, of course, that if compulsory contributions had been lower and if, furthermore, the fiscal system had not been biased against personal thrift, people might have saved more on their own account.

The next big question is that of blanketing-in. One of the merits claimed for private schemes is that they permit variety.[1] If, however, these schemes are to be used to provide graduated pensions at least on a minimum scale for all, then variety is less of a virtue. In countries such as Britain, the USA, Sweden and the Netherlands, the variety which has developed over the years may then become a cause of embarrassment. In particular, large numbers of manual workers may have no private pension rights, or very small ones. It is true that if the official pension scheme is a reasonably generous one, they will to that extent be less dependent upon such supplementation from occupational pensions in order to bring them up to some target figure for income replacement. But this answer clearly carries more force in, say, the Netherlands than in Britain.

In Britain the proposed official Reserve Scheme will not pay full pensions until the year 2019 and, even at maturity, the pensions will be modest enough. New entrants to private schemes, some of whom may be middle aged, will also get only modest pensions if these are not supplemented by the employers in one way or another. No doubt such supplementation will often be provided and the large private schemes will probably offer substantially better prospects than the more strictly cash-purchase Reserve Scheme. It is also the case that the latter is likely to be popular with small firms because it offers a saving in costs of administration.

A funded arrangement of this kind requires, in the nature of the case, a long period for its working. We must therefore ask whether any official funded plan is likely to survive unaltered into the next century with the various changes in Government that will take place. Its chances of survival for at least a reasonable period will depend in part upon raising the basic flat-rate pension to a higher level relative to average earnings.

---

[1] See Ch. 1, p. 37.

VIII.—FINAL COMMENTS

The purpose of this chapter has been to review the main features of policy and achievement in the countries with which we are concerned, including the UK and the USA. To attempt at this stage a further summary of what has already, in the nature of the case, been something of a summary would be a wearisome exercise as well as an unnecessary one. Some concluding comments may, however, be in place.

The first general point to be made is that, although the means employed have been varied, there has been a large and general improvement in the provision made for the aged since the early post-war period when the welfare state was reconstructed in many countries. The cash incomes and other benefits available to them from public or private sources have grown on a scale that is undeniably substantial. Over the trend pensioners have been more than protected against rising prices and have shared in growth. This is, indeed, so clearly the case that it would be unnecessary to make the point at all were it not for the complaint that neither the welfare state nor the general growth in output have had much effect in reducing poverty or in easing the lot of those who, if not classified as poor, are nevertheless worse off than need be the case in humane and affluent societies. As we have seen in the first chapter much genuine improvement may be obscured by the current habit, apparent at least in Britain, of using a measurement of selectivity as an unequivocal measurement of poverty.

Although the real incomes of the elderly have been raised substantially, it is not to be inferred that their share of gross national product in each country is now satisfactory. That is a different matter and one on which different views are likely to be held. It is still necessary to consider whether the various minimum benefits are set at levels generally felt to be appropriate. It is still necessary to consider the question of income replacement above these minima and to determine the proper responsibility of the state. It is still necessary to reach conclusions about the use of means tests as opposed to benefits not conditional on any test of means. The effects of inflation have been offset over the trend but rising prices can still bear hardly on the elderly in the short run. Even apart from inflation, we must continue to express concern about those groups of elderly people in a number of countries who, by any reasonable standard, must be deemed to be in distress.

To analyse the variety of policies adopted in dealing with the old, to assess these policies and to consider the various recommendations requires skills additional to those with which an economist is equipped. (This, indeed, is something we had very much in mind in assembling a research group consisting of both economists and specialists in social administration.) The economist, for his part, has the particular responsibility of stressing the dreary facts of scarcity and choice. In Britain, pensions are relatively low and are felt to be so. It may not be easy for Britishers to appreciate that in some countries the provision made for pensioners, especially through graduated schemes, might reasonably be regarded as unduly ambitious. Concern for the aged is admirable but there must also be concern for the young and, indeed, for the working population. More expenditure on pensions may compete with the expenditure on health, and the forecasts for health expenditure in Europe suggest a sharply rising burden. We need not list the other obvious competing claims on what is likely to be available, but it is important to remember that all recommendations must be regarded as provisional until set in a wider context. Then there are bound to be differences in social valuation and conflicting views are only to be expected, even if the force of self-interest and the strength of pressure groups are set aside. Even those who are themselves disinterested may reach different conclusions. Such differences may reflect differences in basic value judgements: that is to say, differences that would persist even if the same views were held about the facts and about the factual consequences of particular changes in policy. It may often be the case, however, that conflicts between different recommendations reflect varying opinions about what are essentially empirical matters. If a comparative study, such as this one, has made it at least a little easier to lay hands on some of the factual building-blocks it may, perhaps, have served its purpose.

Mathematical Appendix[1]

(1) The purpose of this appendix is to set out rather more precisely some of the propositions about various types of pension scheme discussed in the text.

It is convenient to begin with an equation designed to show the accumulated value of the contributions made by a pensioner or made on his behalf by his employer. Admittedly this suggests a funded scheme of the old-fashioned cash-purchase type. It will be seen, however, that the formulation can also be used to illustrate other kinds of arrangement by changing the identity of the dependent variable, and can be used in making a comparison between funded and pay-as-you-go arrangements.

It will also be convenient if we consider initially the position of a pensioner who has received the national average of earnings throughout his working life. He starts work, helpfully, on 1 January and retires, say, n years later on 31 December. No one dies before retirement.

Let

C = the accumulated value of his contributions on the date of his retirement which is assumed to be 31 December of a given year.

$\bar{e}_i$ = national average earnings in year, i ($i = 1, \ldots n, n + 1, \ldots . t$).

g = the annual rate of growth of average earnings.

k = the percentage contribution rate (by employer and employee combined).

m = the annual rate of return achieved by the pension fund.

The parameters $\bar{e}_i$, g, k and m are assumed, initially, to be given. Then the accumulation of his pension rights to the date of retirement can be expressed thus:

---

[1] I am much indebted to Mr C. J. Cornwall, manager of the Courtaulds pension fund, and to Mrs Margaret Cuthbert of the Department of Political Economy at the University of Glasgow for assistance in preparing this appendix. Neither is responsible for any errors of which I may be guilty.

$$C = k\bar{e}_1(1+m)^{n-1} + k\bar{e}_2(1+m)^{n-2} + \ldots + k\bar{e}_n \tag{1}$$

$$= k\bar{e}_1(1+m)^{n-1} + k\bar{e}_1(1+g)(1+m)^{n-2} + \ldots + k\bar{e}_1(1+g)^{n-1}$$

$$= k\bar{e}_1(1+m)^{n-1}\left[1 + \frac{1+g}{1+m} + \frac{(1+g)^2}{(1+m)^2} + \ldots + \frac{(1+g)^{n-1}}{(1+m)^{n-1}}\right]$$

$$C = k\bar{e}_1(1+m)^{n-1}\left[\frac{1 - \left(\frac{1+g}{1+m}\right)^n}{1 - \frac{1+g}{1+m}}\right] = k\bar{e}_1\left[\frac{(1+m)^n(1+g)^n}{m-g}\right]$$

(2) Let us now derive an expression for the present value of his future pension which begins after n years of working life. The pension may be paid weekly, monthly or at other intervals within each year and strictly speaking each instalment should be described. For simplicity we shall ignore discounting within the year as though the pension were paid annually.

Let

V = the present value of the pension on the date of retirement.

$\bar{p}_j$ = pension of the average wage earner in year j $(j = n+1, \ldots, t)$ (It is assumed for simplicity that this corresponds to the average national pension, although it need not do so.)

s_j = the rate at which the pension is increased in year j.

r = the rate of discount.

q_b = the probability at the time of retirement of surviving at least b years after retirement.

t = the largest number of years deemed to be worth including (according to the mortality tables used).

The pension, even under funding arrangements, may be fixed or variable. It is assumed that, if the annuity is variable, its rate of growth will be s. In the case of a fixed annuity

$$s_j = 0 \quad (j = n+2, \ldots, t).$$

$$\therefore \quad \bar{p}_{n+1} = \bar{p}_{n+2} = \ldots = \bar{p}_t$$

$$V = q_1\bar{p}_{n+1}(1+r)^{-1} + q_2\bar{p}_{n+1}(1+r)^{-2} + \ldots + q_t\bar{p}_{n+1}(1+r)^{-t*}$$
where $t* = t - n$.

If this were a certain annuity, i.e. no allowance had to be made for probable mortality over the years, then the series could be summed. Suppose the period of years over which this certainty held was t^*, at the end of which no further sum would be paid. Then we have an annuity certain.

Then

$$V = \frac{\bar{p}_{n+1}}{(1+r)} \left[\frac{1 - \left(\frac{1}{1+r}\right)^{t^*}}{1 - \left(\frac{1}{1+r}\right)} \right]$$

$$= p_{n+1} \left[\frac{1 - (1+r)^{-t^*}}{r} \right]$$

Summation would also be possible if q_1, q_2, q_3, etc. could be shown to follow a simple mathematical pattern; but this cannot be done.[1]

If the annuity is variable but expected to rise at a constant rate:

$s_{n+2} = s_{n+3} = \ldots = s_t = s$, then

$$V = q_1 \bar{p}_{n+1} (1+r)^{-1} + q_2 \bar{p}_{n+2} (1+r)^{-2} + \ldots + q_{t^*} p_t (1+r)^{-t^*}$$
$$= q_1 \bar{p}_{n+1} (1+r)^{-1} + q_2 \bar{p}_{n+1} (1+r)^{-2} (1+s) + \ldots$$
$$+ q_{t^*} \bar{p}_{n+1} /1+r)^{-t^*} (1+s)^{t^*-1}$$

If the annuity were certain for t^* years then this in turn would be reduced to

$$V = \bar{p}_{n+1} (1+r)^{-1} \left[1 + \frac{1+s}{1+r} + \ldots + \left(\frac{1+s}{1+r}\right)^{t^*-1} \right]$$

$$= \frac{\bar{p}_{n+1}}{1+r} \left[\frac{1 - \left(\frac{1+s}{1+r}\right)^{t^*}}{1 - \frac{1+s}{1+r}} \right]$$

$$= \bar{p}_{n+1} \left[\frac{1 - \left(\frac{1+s}{1+r}\right)^{t^*}}{r-s} \right]$$

---

[1] I am indebted for this point to Mr C. J. Cornwall, manager of the Courtaulds pensions fund.

(3) Under the cash-purchase arrangements, V is determined by C which, in turn, is determined in the manner shown in equation (1). We have assumed above that m is fixed. If in fact it were known that this would be so from the outset, then the uncertainty attaching to C would be restricted to future changes in $\bar{e}_i$ and in k. In fact, m will depend upon what is happening on the capital market and upon the skill with which the pension fund selects its assets. That is to say, m will in practice be variable and hard to predict. A future pensioner, when he is considering what he is likely to receive on his retirement some years ahead, thus faces uncertainty. What he gets will depend upon m, the return on his accumulated contributions, and upon g and k.

Most private pension funds reduce uncertainty by adopting some other formula for the value of the pension. The most common is to express the initial pension as a fraction (f) of final earnings multiplied by the number of years of employment. Thus his initial pension will be:

$$\bar{p} = nf\bar{e}_n$$

Naturally there will still be uncertainty about his final salary. There may also be some possibility that his pension will be increased in later years, although the pension fund may accept no definite commitment to this effect.

Clearly C, the accumulated value of invested contribution, may no longer be equal to V when the cash-purchase principle has been replaced by another formula. If $C < V$, then the pension will have to be augmented from some other source. Suppose that V is given and assume that (in the formulation of C) k, $\bar{e}_i$, and g are also given. Then we can find i such that $C = V$; i is thus the internal or implicit rate of return. If m, the actual rate of return on the pension fund, is less than this internal rate of return, then pensions have to be augmented. Naturally i can be calculated for a fully pay-as-you-go official scheme as well as for different variants of private schemes. When i is greater than m, a transfer between generations is sometimes said to have taken place.

(4) Under pay-as-you-go arrangements, with no additions to or withdrawals from a pension fund, the total amount available for pensions in any one year will depend upon k and the total income from work upon which the pensions tax is levied. This statement will need to be modified if there is an exchequer contribution but it will be assumed here that there is none. Then:

Let

R_i = the number of pensioners in year i $(i = 1, 2 \ldots t)$

Q_i = the number at work in year i

then for any i

$$R_i \, \bar{p}_i = k \bar{e}_i \, Q_i$$

$$p_i = k \left(\frac{\bar{e}Q}{R} \right)_i$$

To revert to our initial assumptions, consider the position of an average pensioner who retired after n years at work, and assume that pensions which are paid at the end of each year are adjusted to earnings in that year, then his initial pension will be

$$\bar{p}_{n+1} = k \left(\frac{\bar{e}Q}{R} \right)_{n+1}$$

It should be noted:

$$V = q_1 \, k \left(\frac{\bar{e}Q}{R} \right)_{n+1} (1 + r)^{-1} + q_2 \, k \left(\frac{\bar{e}Q}{R} \right)_{n+2} (1 + r)^{-2} + \cdots$$

$$+ q_{t^*} \, k \left(\frac{\bar{e}Q}{R} \right)_{t} (1 + r)^{-t^*}$$

$$= k \bar{e}_n \left[q_1 \left(\frac{Q}{R} \right)_{n+1} \left(\frac{1+g}{1+r} \right) + q_2 \left(\frac{Q}{R} \right)_{n+2} \left(\frac{1+g}{1+r} \right)^2 + \cdots \right.$$

$$\left. + q_{t^*} \left(\frac{Q}{R} \right)_{t} \left(\frac{1+g}{1+r} \right)^{t^*} \right]$$

(5) We can now begin to compare a strictly funded scheme with a pay-as-you-go scheme. If k and $\bar{e}_i$ are given, then the comparison will depend upon (i) the relative values of m, s, and g; (ii) changes in the ratio $Q_i : R_i$; (iii) the effect of correcting for q_1, q_2, q_3, etc., which will be different according to any differences in the time-stream of receipts after retirement.

It follows that a funded scheme will not necessarily yield a smaller pension than a pay-as-you-go scheme if $m < g$. For this deficiency—which favours the pay-as-you-go scheme—may be offset by adverse demographic changes, i.e. a decline in the ratio $Q_i : R_i$. This, of course, is only one of several possibilities. The offset, if any, may be incomplete. Or $Q_i : R_i$ may be increasing. Or g may be less than m. And so on.

Moreover we have assumed in the equations above that g is constant. This may not be so. An acceleration in the growth of earnings may occur and the growth of pensions will also be faster than it would otherwise have been. Naturally r or m or both may also vary. If the pension is already in payment, then it is only changes in m that will matter, and this only when the annuity is a variable one. It is possible that any economic forces which raise g might raise m as well, i.e. a rising state of growth of both wages and dividends (in current money). But m is applied to a pensions base which reflects earlier values of g and the funded pension may fail to keep pace with the pay-as-you-go pension as a consequence.

In pay-as-you-go schemes, a new pension is often determined by some formula such as y per cent of final earnings or y per cent of average earnings over the final three years at work. Pensions in payment may then be increased in line with average wages. As we have observed above[1] difficulties will then arise if $Q_i : R_i$ declines. For the payroll tax relates the total sum available for pensions to the total income from employment $(\bar{e}Q)_i$ and the scope for raising the average pension also depends upon $Q_i : R_i$. In such circumstances, either the pensions formula must be changed so that the average pension rises less than average earnings; or k must be increased at the expense, of course, of the working population.

We must also note in passing that Q_i is not determined simply by age-structure but also by the activity rate, the level of unemployment and the retirement age.

With funding, the pensioner will not be affected by subsequent adverse demographic changes, unless these react indirectly on m if the annuity is variable. With a fixed annuity he may not be affected at all in terms of receipts in current money values.

---

[1] P.401, above.

CHARTS

U.K.

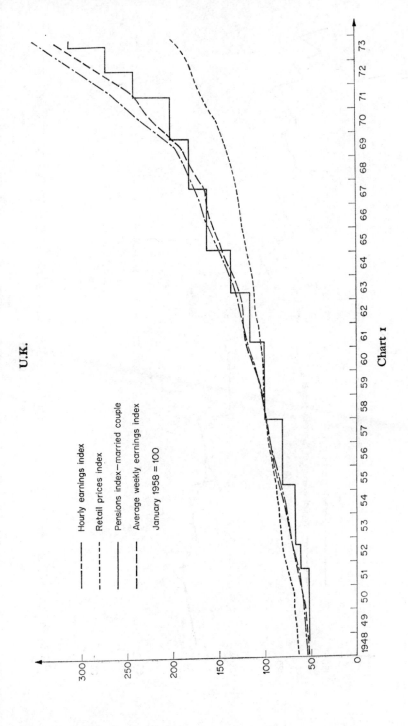

- — · — Hourly earnings index
- - - - - Retail prices index
- ——— Pensions index—married couple
- - — - Average weekly earnings index

January 1958 = 100

Chart I

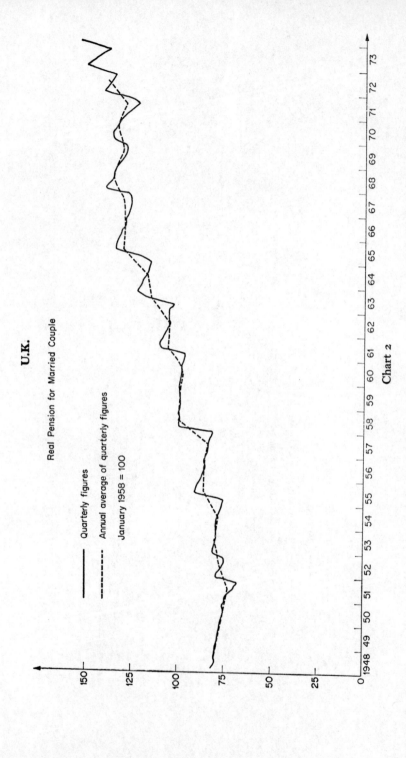

U.K.

Real Pension for Married Couple

——— Quarterly figures

– – – Annual average of quarterly figures

January 1958 = 100

Chart 2

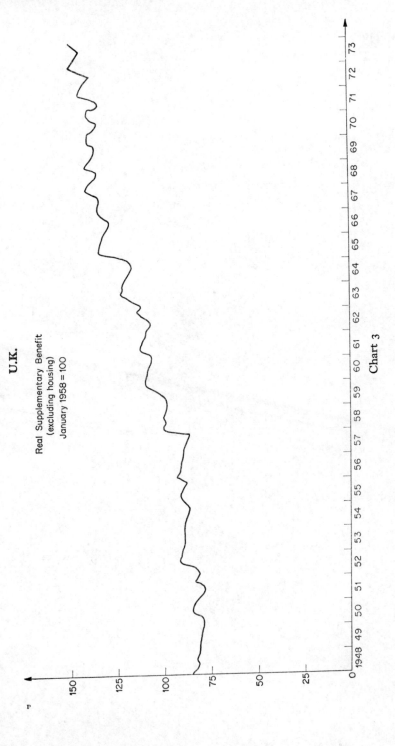

U.K.

Real Supplementary Benefit
(excluding housing)
January 1958 = 100

Chart 3

408

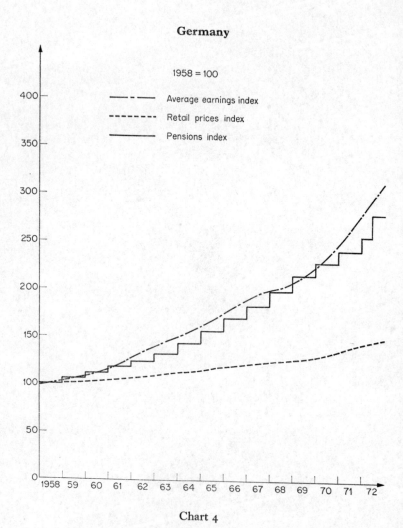

Germany

1958 = 100

— · — Average earnings index

- - - - Retail prices index

——— Pensions index

Chart 4

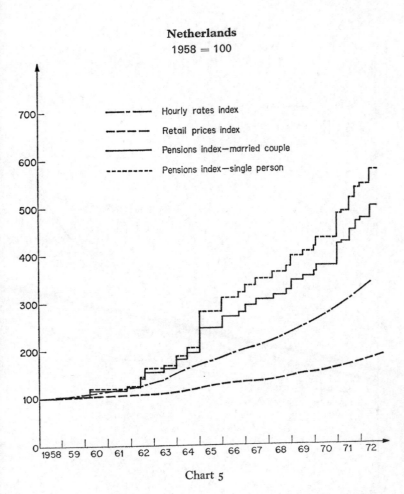

Netherlands
1958 = 100

Hourly rates index
Retail prices index
Pensions index—married couple
Pensions index—single person

700
600
500
400
300
200
100
0

1958 59 60 61 62 63 64 65 66 67 68 69 70 71 72

Chart 5

Sweden
1958 = 100

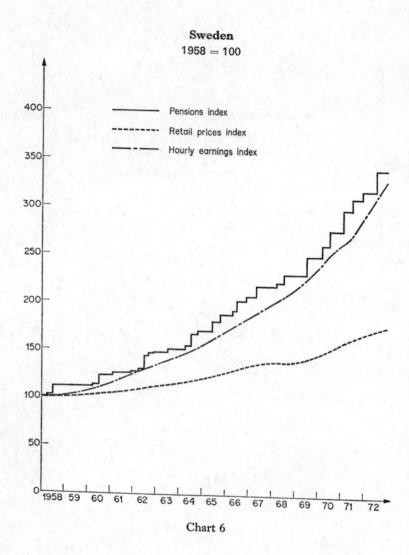

Chart 6

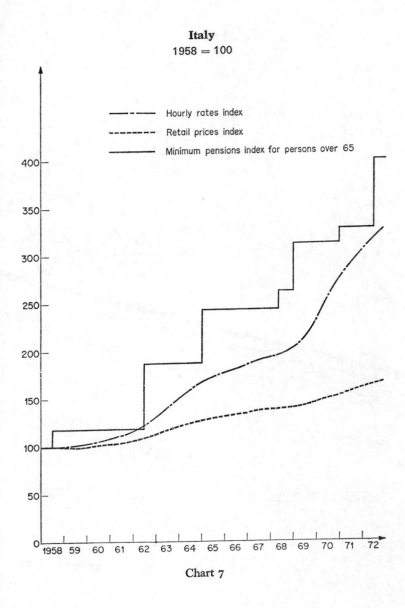

Italy
1958 = 100

- — · — Hourly rates index
- - - - - - Retail prices index
- ——— Minimum pensions index for persons over 65

Chart 7

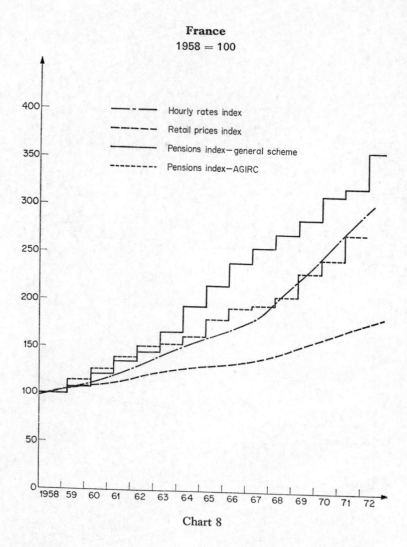

France
1958 = 100

— · — · Hourly rates index

— — — Retail prices index

———— Pensions index—general scheme

- - - - - Pensions index—AGIRC

Chart 8

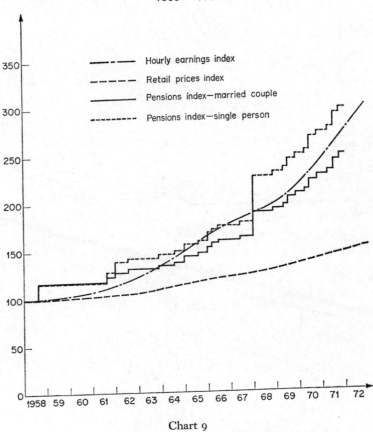

Chart 9

USA (OASDI)
1958 = 100

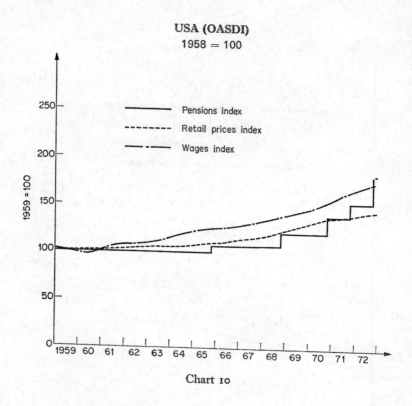

Chart 10

USA
Old age assistance, May 1972

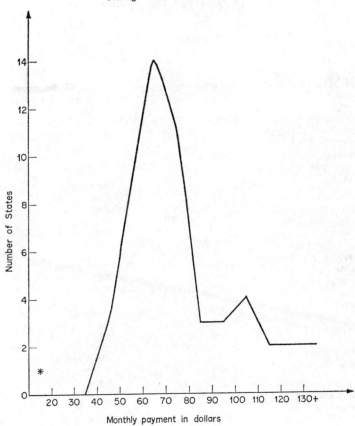

* Puerto Rico

Chart 11

Name Index

Subject Index

(Detailed references to the arrangements in UK, USA, Germany, Netherlands, Sweden, Italy, France and Belgium are given under the headings for each country respectively and are not repeated elsewhere in the index.)

Australia, 5, 15, 364

Belgium:
  Expenditure on the elderly relative to GNP, total social benefit expenditure and consumption 344–5
  Pensions:
    Historical evolution 306–8; targets 334, 370–71; types of scheme 305–6 General schemes (manual and white collar): allowances and annuities 317; blanketing-in 311; coverage and residence condition 311–3; dynamizing 332–4, 374; financing 317–20, 343; formula for benefits 309–12; minimum pension (*minimum garanti*) 305, 315; national minimum allowance (*revenu garanti*) 326–9; payroll tax 305, 339; population changes 318–20: replacement of earnings 316, 328, 352–4; retirement age 313–4; retirement condition 314, 358; revalorisation of earnings 311–2, 315–7; size of pensions 315–6; spouses 354, 357; survivors 310, 317, 358; women's pensions 310, 356
    Special schemes: public servants 324–6; railway workers 326; self-employed 322–4
    Private occupational: 36; dynamizing 331–2, 334; funding 321–2, 334; protection, preservation and transferability 321–2
  Poverty and means tests: means tests 328–9; national minimum allowance (*revenu garanti*) 326–9, 363, 366; poverty level 324; public assistance (CAP) 327–30, 362, 366
  Centre National des Employés (CNE) 331; Confederation des Syndicats Cretiens (CSC) 331; health services 330; Ministry of Social Security 331; Spitael's survey 332; Union of Belgian Towns and Communes

Canada, 364
Czechoslavakia, 298

Denmark, 16n
Deprivation, 9–10
Destitution, 6
Difference principle (Rawls), 10n
Dynamizing, 'linking benefits to prices or wages) – see under Pensions and under Means Tests

Elderly: expenditure in different countries relative to GNP, total social benefit expenditure and consumption 334–5